SOCIETY AND HISTORY

SOCIETY AND HISTORY

Essays by Sylvia L. Thrupp

Edited by

Raymond Grew

and

Nicholas H. Steneck

Ann Arbor   The University of Michigan Press

*Published with the assistance of a grant from the
Horace H. Rackham School of Graduate Studies of
The University of Michigan.*

Grateful acknowledgment is made to the following for permission to reprint copyrighted material:

The Provincial Archives of British Columbia, for "The Pedigree and Prospects of Local History." Reprinted by permission from the *British Columbia Historical Quarterly* (1940).

The Broadwater Press, for "The Problem of Replacement Rates in Late-Medieval English Population." Reprinted by permission from the *Economic History Review*, 2nd Ser., XVIII (1965).

Cambridge University Press, for the following: "Editorial" (Vol. 1, 1958); "Hierarchy, Illusion, and Social Mobility" (Vol. II, 1959–60); "Tradition and Development: A Choice of Views" (Vol. VI, 1963–64); "The Creativity of Cities" (Vol. IV, 1961–62); "Plague Effects in Medieval Europe" (Vol. VIII, 1965–66); and "Some Historians on Generalization" (Vol. VIII, 1965–66). Reprinted by permission from *Comparative Studies in Society and History*.

The University of Chicago Press, for "History and Sociology: New Opportunities for Co-operation." Reprinted by permission from *The American Journal of Sociology* (Vol. 63, 1957–58). Copyright © 1958 by The University of Chicago.

The Conference on British Studies, for "The Economy and Society in Medieval England." Reprinted by permission from the *Journal of British Studies* (Vol. II, 1962).

Congress of Historical Science, for "Dynamics and Equilibrium in Medieval Society." Paper delivered at the XIIIth International Congress of Historical Sciences 1970.

Economic History Association, for "Social Change in the Medieval Town" (Vol. 1, 1941); "Medieval Guilds Reconsidered" (Vol. 2, 1942); and "The Role of Comparison in the Development of Economic History" (Vol. 17, 1957). Reprinted by permission from the *Journal of Economic History*.

The Free Press (Division of Macmillan Publishing Co. Inc.), for "Diachronic Methods in Comparative Politics." Reprinted by permission from *The Methodology of Comparative Research,* edited by Robert T. Holt and John E. Turner. Copyright © 1970 by The Free Press.

Hodder and Stoughton Ltd., for "Aliens in and Around London in the Fifteenth Century." Reprinted by permission from *Studies in London History.*

Massachusetts Institute of Technology Press, for "The City as the Idea of Social Order." Reprinted by permission from *The Historian and the City,* edited by G. Handlin and J. Burchard (1963).

The Mediaeval Academy of America, for "The Problem of Conservatism in Fifteenth Century England," XVIII, 1943; and "A Survey of the Alien Population in England in 1440," XXXII, 1957. Reprinted by permission from *Speculum.*

Prentice-Hall, Inc., for the Preface to *Change in Medieval Society: Europe North of the Alps—1050–1500,* © 1964. Reprinted by permission of Prentice-Hall, Inc., Englewood Cliffs, New Jersey.

University of Southern California, for "What History and Sociology Can Learn From Each Other." Reprinted by permission from *Sociology and Social Research,* University of Southern California, University Park, Los Angeles, CA 90007.

The Unesco Press, for "Comparative Studies in Society and History." Reprinted by permission from the *International Social Science Journal,* Vol. XVII: 4, © Unesco 1965.

Acknowledgments

For the encouragement and help in meeting the costs of preparing the manuscript, we wish to thank the Department of History, Dean Alfred S. Sussman of the Horace H. Rackham School of Graduate Studies, and Vice-President Frank H. T. Rhodes, former dean of the College of Literature, Science, and the Arts at the University of Michigan. Robert Gottfried and Elinor G. K. Melville worked with diligent enthusiasm to track down these essays and prepare correct copies.

Contents

IV. Social Change

V. On Historical Method

Introduction

RAYMOND GREW AND NICHOLAS H. STENECK

A distinguished medievalist, Professor Thrupp is most widely known and has had her greatest influence as the founding editor of *Comparative Studies in Society and History*. For a generation she has prodded social scientists to think more broadly by generalizing the particular more clearly; and she has propagandized indefatigably with wit, diplomacy, and solid example. If the vision is grand, the approach is modest and practical. Concerned from the first that we not simply put "a fresh label on the old bottle" but make a "better brew," she advocated better comparison as the best defense against the errors that would follow if scholars "snatched at systems based on cursory leaping at apparent similarities." Comparison was simply the best way to be sure that one was not mistaking the atypical for the typical, and the things to compare were "problems capable of isolation in contexts that are being studied intensively."

There was in this historical program something of an archival historian's impatience with easy theorizing and a medievalist's perspective on the pretentions of modern scholarship. "Any medieval peasant who ever sold a cow could have told the historian as much or more about the forces of supply and demand as was tó be learned from nineteenth-century theory."[1] The fault, she insisted, was structural, the result of separating the theoretical from the empirical and of isolating academic disciplines. Together, the essays reprinted in Part V of this volume constitute the careful, restrained case for comparative study. They include a historian's history of comparative studies itself that underscores past errors and probes for the lessons they teach. These essays also tackle the economic historians, the sociologists, and the political scientists (anthropology is treated more gently), beginning—in the earliest essay here—with a salute to that most prosaic field of historical research, local history, which leads her to a kind of manifesto: "The writing of history is therefore now essentially a co-operative enterprise . . . a working partnership. . . ." In 1957 she founded *Comparative Studies in Society and History* (*CSSH*), and in its seventh year she surveyed that "working alliance" and found it good, noting that "nothing human is alien to comparative study." Happily, she has not rested.

If her contributions to comparative studies stand as a kind of capstone to her scholarship, Professor Thrupp's own research is the kind of analysis out of which fruitful comparisons can be made. She uses her knowledge of medieval Europe to test common assumptions about modernization, progress, and changes in social practice from marriage to medical care. Most of her studies deal with medieval England; but the Middle Ages are shown again and again to contain many cultures as much like our own as they are different, and England is always placed in the larger context of European civilization. Throughout these studies topics such as cities, ideology, aliens, or economics recur, but the essays are conceived in broader terms. We have chosen, therefore, to organize this volume in categories that represent something of Professor Thrupp's own analysis. Trained as an economic historian, she looks first at those social structures that shape human behavior in a particular context, then at the values and attitudes that guide (and are reflected in) that behavior. And always, her generalizations rest on the firm ground of primary research. Society, however, is never static. She insists on that point and is therefore drawn to the process of change, emphasizing those specific, concrete, and structural changes that—like demography—can be the subject of precise and meticulous research. It is analysis so framed that defines the problems on which scholars need to compare their results.

For this volume we have chosen essays that essentially stand alone yet gain by being viewed together. Thus we have omitted all but one of the introductions she has written to volumes of articles and collected sources even though they are as provocative as the essays included here, triumphs of the able scholar's ability to wring significance and interest from a dull text,[2] or models of meticulous scholarship.[3] We have, on the other hand, included some of her review articles, for they tend to be examples of that discussion across disciplines, historical periods, and societies she consistantly urges. Her careful skepticism is illumined by faith in the accruing worth of careful scholarship as when she calls for ever more work on the family, Asian agriculture, Puritans in business, professional associations, or notes in passing that "no one has ever collected the terms of abuse signifying what was considered anti-social in medieval villages."[4] Always stimulating, these suggestions are sometimes a prescient program, like her call nearly twenty-five years ago for comparative work on social stratification, demography, the family, inheritance, social control, urban and rural popular culture, and for more attention to the lower classes and to quantitative data.[5] Even as she criticizes the books she reviewed, she confidently concludes that "we are learning not more about less, but more about man."[6]

These essays of research and review are written with style, for Professor Thrupp has taken pains to remain distinct from those scholars who "seem to regard the act of writing down their ideas as though it were an act of interment, to be completed by a repellant title as gloomy as a gravestone."[7] At the same time there runs throughout them a strong appreciation of predecessors and contemporary scholars—the frequent tributes to Marc Bloch as both scholar and founder of the *Annales* particularly stand out—and that appreciation has been reciprocated by students, followers, and other scholars. It is thus essentially appropriate that four famous scholars from different countries and disciplines should provide introductions to the sections of this book. Part V, On Historical Method, which stands as a conclusion to this book, is introduced by Thomas Cochrane, who has been both president of the American Historical Association and editor of the *American Historical Review*. Part IV, Social Change, is introduced by Eric R. Wolf, the noted anthropologist who for more than a decade was Professor Thrupp's colleague at the University of Chicago and the University of Michigan and who is now coeditor of *CSSH*. Most of the essays in this section are indeed a kind of historical field research, and the proposal that economists might calculate the capital overhead devoted to ritual suggests that the lessons of anthropology have been well learned even if there is little reaching for grand theory, "the demand . . . [for which] is perhaps largely motivated by the desire to give our work more aesthetic elegance and ourselves the prestige of philosophers, always an aid in the classroom."[8] Similarly skeptical about the quantitative use of aggregate data, Professor Thrupp was nevertheless drawn to demography as a factor in change, drawn to it perhaps for much the same reason that she noted of a historian a century earlier that "his passion for statistical information helped to keep him on a sound course."[9] Part III, Historical Demography, is introduced by M. M. Postan, formerly Regius Professor at Cambridge, whose comments on sociological generalization and historical minutiae cut to the heart of Sylvia Thrupp's approach. Social attitudes and demographic patterns both relate social structure to social change. Attention to attitudes makes the topic of social change richly human; and as Philippe Wolff, the dean of French medieval historians, shows in his introduction to Part II, Social Attitudes, the essays in this group reflect the range of weapons Professor Thrupp employs in her search for insight as even the study of aliens becomes "a question not of law but of the opinion of rather obscure citizens."

Social Structure, the topic of Part I, logically comes first, although the essays here include one of the earliest and one of the latest in this book. The treatment of social control, well before the term was faddish, looks not just at external controls but inner values as well and thus moves from public institutions to the family and to general culture. It treats the medieval town as a microcosm of medieval society and as a type for comparative study, striking sparks of generalization off the flintstone of historical data from primary and secondary sources. The remaining articles are framed as reviews and comments, but they range from England to China to Russia and back. An introduction to medieval studies, a warning against facile assumptions about social mobility or traditional society, they also constitute a discourse on the study of social structures, calling on scholars to look to groups outside the state, to study status in terms of gilds and villages and demography, to use parish registers and quantitative data in order better to define the real structures within which real people lived and more effectively to measure the changes that occurred. They are models of how the world of scholarship can stimulate a determined scholar to new efforts and to new questions, and they serve therefore as the solid point of entry into a collection that ranges as wide as a good conversation and cuts as deep as a carefully conducted laboratory experiment. This volume is Sylvia L. Thrupp's, assembled by some who have enjoyed her conversation and benefitted from her experiments in order that the circle of those who have shared these experiences may continue to widen.

NOTES

1. See the essay, "The Role of Comparison in the Development of Economic History," p. 286 of this volume.

2. She makes of William Scott's rather priggish discourse a source for insight into business practice, a reflection of important economic and social change, and a document of intellectual history (*An Essay of Drapery by William Scott*, ed. Sylvia L. Thrupp [Cambridge, 1953]). Study of the Medieval London Company of Grocers becomes the occasion for comments on the medicines Londoners used and on the variety of their commerce as well as rates of profit, weights and measures, and efforts at preventing the adulteration of food stuffs ("The Grocers of London, A Study of Distributive Trade," in *Studies in English Trade in the Fifteenth Century*, ed. Eileen Power and M. M. Postan [London, 1933]).

3. See, for example, the technical skill employed in, "The Earliest Canterbury Freeman's Rolls, 1298–1363," *Kent Records* 18 (1964): 173–213.

4. See "The Dynamics of Medieval Society," p. 47 of this volume.

5. See "History and Sociology: New Opportunities for Cooperation," p. 297 of this volume.

6. "The Writing of West European History: A Bird's-Eye View of Trends between 1960–1964," *The Annals of the American Academy of Political and Social Science* 359 (May 1965): 157–64.

7. See "Comparative Studies in Society and History: A Working Alliance among Specialists," p. 344 of this volume.

8. Characteristically, that comment on the lack of a theory of growth was followed by the suggestion of one: the larger markets of the fifteenth century were necessary to provide the capital to sustain innovations, capital otherwise consumed for more pressing demands, "The Role of Comparison in the Development of Economic History," pp. 287–88 of this volume.

9. The comments to political scientists about the use of aggregate data are in "Diachronic Methods in Comparative Politics," p. 313, and the comment on Roscher's passion in "The Role of Comparison in the Development of Economic History," p. 284, both in this volume.

I

Social Structure

Social Control in the Medieval Town

I

The power of the church in the medieval town was ever-present and all-pervasive. It operated through the ritual of the sacraments, the jurisdiction of the ecclesiastical courts, the charitable foundations of the orders, through the pictorial teaching on church walls and windows, open-air sermons, public inflictions of penance, the celebration of saints' festivals, and in many other ways. There can be no reasonable doubt that the social teachings of the church, along with its other doctrines, were by one means or another impressed upon every townsman, in so far as he was capable of understanding them.

The central note of these teachings, echoing steadily down the centuries from St. Augustine to St. Antonino, was the subordination of individual interest to the common good. Out of this fact there rises the question how the medieval man in the street, as ends of action took shape in his mind, may have interpreted the idea. In academic discussion the principle was axiomatic, but it was also severely abstract. To St. Thomas Aquinas, for example, whose mind marched in the realm of pure normative theory, the common good meant the good of "society." In regard to questions of price, property, and usury, he did, it is true, attend to specific problems and lay down some specific rules for conduct. These applied in the

Reprinted from *The Journal of Economic History* I, supplement (December 1941):39–52.

market-place, the shop and the counting-house, in the individual's relations with his neighbors, and in other chance contacts during his lifetime. But what was wanting, in medieval teaching, was particularized definition of the common good, as the citizen should have conceived it. Was it sufficient to consider the good of one's neighbors and peers, the "commonalty" of the merchant gild or lesser craft? Was it necessary always to consider the good of those poorer inhabitants of the town who were unable to help pay for its chartered privileges? What should have been the citizens' relations with the people of the surrounding countryside with whom they bought and sold? How should they have dealt with other cities with which they were linked in a common system of trade? What were their duties in the nations of which they formed a part?

Where the record of any medieval city government is one of failure, the failure came about through confusion on one or other of these questions. There was little or no guidance from ecclesiastical thinkers, who for the most part failed to apprehend the complex nature of the bonds of the community in an age of economic expansion.[1] The preachers and the humbler clergy with whom ordinary citizens had personal contact had no more practical imagination than the abstract thinkers. In dealing with the question of social duties, they habitually fell back upon stereotyped allegories in which society was likened to a human body, or to a vineyard.[2]

It would be an error to conclude that the social teaching of the church was without effect. It fed reservoirs of high ethical aspiration. In the matter of usury it was reinforced by detailed counsel and formidable legal sanctions. But in many other matters the citizen was left with no specific aim beyond a sense that he ought to sink his personal interest in that of a group. His religious faith helped to predispose him to cooperate with others. But the further definition of his motives was left wide open to influence by extraneous guides.

II

Were other nuclei of authority within the towns, then, apart from the church, inspired by the canonist ethics? The chief power, in the early phases of town history, was everywhere that of outside governmental authority, represented by the king or some intermediate

feudal lord. Although in Italy and Germany this power later re-
ceded, in England it was always present in the background, and in
France its pressure increased. However self-seeking the representa-
tives of the public authority may have been in the exercise of powers
of taxation and in the supervision of justice, there was at least one
direction in which their policy may be considered as in full harmony
with canonist doctrines. This was in regard to the practice of regulat-
ing the price of bread, and, in case of need, of other victuals and of
drink, and of supplying weights and measures by which to facilitate
honesty in trade. The administration of these policies in towns
usually came to be entrusted to the municipal authorities.[3]

Pirenne has paid generous tribute to the creative abilities and
high public spirit of the great merchants who everywhere took the
initiative in evolving the institutions of municipal government.[4]
Their devotion to civic duty was the more remarkable in that, except in cases where the public authorities had been hostile or
obstinate in their attitude to demands for self-government, there is
little evidence of any strong sentiment of solidarity among the different elements of city population. Again, the essentially creative
part of their work was completed, in many places, before the end of
the thirteenth century. It thus coincided with that phase in the
development of long-distance trade during which there was a wide
measure of cooperation between cities, when trade was in general
free from the restrictions of local protectionism, when merchant associations, as Pirenne has described them, had "rather the appearance of regional than of urban organisms."[5] Nevertheless the social
policies of the city magistrates were not framed, as might have been
expected, solely in the interests of the dominant merchant classes,
but took account of the whole of the urban population. It was only
at a later period, when there was less stimulus to constructive energy, that the merchant patriciate began to lost sight of the common
good. It is only fair to add, however, that even in decadence they
were capable of fierce local patriotism in the face of external danger.[6]

Additional agencies of control existed in the shape of the gilds.
It is evident, after any examination of gild records, that here the
common good only too often meant no more than the good of the
narrow "commonalty": the gild might be a community, a world in
itself. It may be recalled that in France the ecclesiastical authorities

originally opposed the organization of gilds on the grounds that their rites involved non-Christian elements, and that the exaction of an oath to support the special interests of the group might conceivably force members into the sin of perjury.[7] In England Wycliffe was vehemently of the opinion that if the purposes of a gild were truly Christian, it would be unnecessary to bind members by an oath. But the clergy, pleased by the devotion of the gilds to the altars of their patron saints, were not ordinarily opposed or in any way critical.[8] Nor did the general public share the misgivings of the early French ecclesiastics. It was common knowledge that the gilds were essentially privileged bodies, and were naturally anxious to extract as much advantage from their privileges as possible. But, as Levasseur pointed out, in an age when nearly every right was a matter of special privilege, such an attitude was taken for granted and shocked nobody.[9]

The authorities and organizations that were vested with legal powers were not the only agencies for formulating ends of action and controlling behavior. One must take account also of custom, and of that strongest of all institutions, probably more powerful than any other in setting the bounds of custom, the family. Within the urban community the family enjoyed a virtual *imperium in imperio*. It could, at the will of its members, provide an ideal pattern of social stability, or it could, as occurred over and over again in the cities of Italy and of the Low Countries, rend and tear government and order in pieces.[10] It could dignify its traditions by a pure devotion to the public interest, yet the current of family ambition could turn and flow in diametrical opposition to all doctrines of the common good.

Finally one must remember the influence of public opinion. One of the most important of all the means of social control, it is at the same time one of the most difficult to analyze. Its sources and its effects were best developed and revealed in scenes and corners where the historian is least able to penetrate. The gossip of the tavern and the parish gild meeting, for example, gave voice to neighborhood opinion. This may often have run along channels of class prejudice. The more conventional prejudices of the upper classes are stamped upon the literature of the age. But who knows the views of the poorer and less literate groups? The ideals of a community as a whole were expressed, on their highest plane, by the reformers and the satirists, but one needs to know more of the plane on which ideals were embodied in criteria of prestige and in actual judgments upon leaders and upon groups. It is seldom that chroniclers or moralists discuss such matters frankly. One has to read between the lines to find their inarticulate assumptions; but much also might be gleaned among the stray scraps of genuine reporting of the language of rumors and of quarrels that occur sometimes in the pages of the chroniclers and not infrequently in the records of legal proceedings.

In so far as all were attuned to similar ends the influence of these various agencies of control was so interwoven that one can scarcely distinguish the part that any one or other may have played in the general processes of urban development. Yet in the study of particular items of social and economic policy it is helpful to consider them separately, for shades of difference then appear between them in the aims expressed or upheld.

III

One salient item of social and economic policy is the matter of wages. It is remarkable that no medieval writer ever made any very explicit statement of the rules that would best conduce to the common good in the payment of wages. St. Thomas merely observed that the question came under the principle of justice;[11] St. Antonino recommended the payment of "good" wages;[12] sermon-writers spoke of "true" wages;[13] and there are the abundant and familiar references in legislation and elsewhere to "excessive" wages. Mr. George O'Brien hazarded the somewhat vague explanation that

> ". . . the proper remuneration of labor was so universally recognized as a duty, and so satisfactorily enforced, that it seems to have been taken for granted, and therefore passed over, by the writers of the period."[14]

More skeptical students are often inclined towards an opposite interpretation. Perhaps both are apt to overlook the devastating effects of recurring famine and epidemic disease, which go far to explain both the incidence of medieval poverty and the fatalistic attitude that people assumed towards it.

Meanwhile so little is known of the actual rates of medieval wages, that it is still impossible to draw any comparisons between them in terms of real wages. All that can be discussed here, therefore, is the spirit in which regulation of wages was undertaken. It must be admitted in the first place that we do not know when official regulation of wages by urban authorities was initiated, nor what proportion of the trades or workers in any city it came to affect, nor what factors were taken into consideration in setting the figures. In all probability regulation merely had the effect of freezing customary flat rates for different types of work, although in some trades it may have allowed for the differing capacities of individual workmen.[15] In any case the latter were supposed to be content with what they received. In London the men who unloaded and carted wine casks were made to swear upon the Bible that they would give faithful service for the wages officially set.[16] When associations among workmen for the purpose of improving their position became of common occurrence, that is, from the thirteenth century onward, city magistrates were invariably opposed to raising the rates, whether they had been set by custom or fixed by authority, and whether the men were under employers who were organized or not. It is therefore likely that wages were extremely slow to respond to any rise in the cost of living.[17] Yet the hardship of such a lag was in many trades mitigated by allowing the men all or part of their food and drink, and was still further reduced when it was customary to allow them full board and lodging.

In England it is difficult to find record of any appeal to principle in the regulation of wages in unorganized trades. In the case of organized trades, regulation by the employers was reenforced by the authority of city magistrates, and records are in consequence fuller and more illuminating. They indicate, as one would expect, that wages were ordinarily pegged for long periods.[18] They also indicate that throughout the later middle ages masters sought to associate in the public mind the customary wage levels with concepts of justice and reason and the common good.[19] Evidently they considered this a good card to play.[20] Certainly the city magistrates paid homage to these ideas. They felt it their duty to see that justice was observed. And they did not, it may be noticed, trust the gild masters. In a dispute between the London saddlers and their men, in 1396,

the mayor and aldermen, while forbidding the latter to hold fraternity meetings, warned the masters sharply that they were to treat
their men properly, and held out the promise of "due and speedy
meed of justice" to any worker who should complain of undue
grievance.[21]

It would therefore be a mistake to assume that it was through
the gilds that the principle of justice was brought to bear upon the
question of wages. In trades in which prices were rigidly fixed, their
stubborn opposition to the raising of wages may have been justifi-
able, but it is plain from the case of the London saddlery trade just
cited that masters could be under suspicion, from their own contemporaries, of taking unfair advantage of this situation. Moreover, they
were very generally guilty of exploiting the labor of apprentices by
prolonging their terms unreasonably, and, by the exaction of high
premiums, of exploiting the resources of the boys' families.[22] Nevertheless, wage-workers were probably better off within well-organized
gilds than without, simply on account of the advantage of monopoly.
When limitation of the number of apprentices and journeymen that
each master might employ was in force, a scarcity of skill was induced, and the pecuniary results of this scarcity may to some extent
have been shared between masters and men. It is in the highest
degree unlikely that any industrial gild ever enjoyed any complete
monopoly, yet the responsibility that their officials undertook in
maintaining the quality of goods no doubt always helped to give
members a preferential advantage in bidding for the goodwill of
new customers.

IV

The force of public opinion, therefore, combined with the monopolistic tendencies of the gilds to ameliorate urban labor conditions.
But, as Pirenne showed long ago, this could have occurred only in
those sectors of trade and industry that catered to the local market
and to the custom of the immediate hinterland of the town. It was
only here, where demand was relatively stable, that efforts to build
craft monopolies could have met with any degree of success. And
it was in these sectors, where the relations of economic life were
for the most part directly personal, that public opinion could respond most wholeheartedly to the moral teachings of the church.

Here personal reputation, family reputation, and the satisfying consciousness of supporting the good name of the city might all hang, for the worker, upon the obligation of doing faithful work contentedly, and, for the master, might depend at least in part upon having his apprentices and journeymen appear well-fed and well-clothed.

But, as every economic historian is aware, in the sectors of trade and industry that were organized in relation to inter-regional and international markets, the situation was vastly different. The domination of trading capital and enterprise, and the occurrence of inevitable fluctuations in trade, made it impossible for industrial gilds to obtain any monopoly advantages in which their subordinate workers might share. The same circumstances, cutting off the master craftsman from any contact with, or even knowledge of, the consumer, and rendering his relations with his workmen less happy, created an atmosphere in which it was obviously much more difficult for people to think of economic conduct in terms of moral values. For the most part the church's doctrines of justice, as they applied to social affairs, were presented as they affected close personal relations. But the great merchant who "put out" work, through his factors, among scores of poor competitors in an overflooded labor market, or the lesser merchant who collected the wares of unenterprising, plodding craftsmen and distributed them for sale in different localities, could easily fail to conceive of his business contacts as actual personal relations. The doctrines of justice could penetrate the widening sphere of impersonal dealings only when, as in the matter of usury, detailed rules were worked out, or when there was flagrant personal responsibility for individual sufferings. Community opinion, when it awoke to the fact of discontent among workers in the capitalistically organized cloth industry, sought for tangible proof of personal fraud, compelled the passage of laws forbidding the abuse of truck, and subsided with conscience appeased.

No one has discovered whether any genuine effort was ever made to enforce medieval legislation against truck. Even if they were a mere gesture, the laws may have helped to prolong the confidence that urban communities reposed in their governing merchant classes. In time, however, in the more flourishing centers of capitalist industry, the latter wore out this confidence. Gradually relaxing their hold on their earlier traditions of public service, they induced among the masses a more and more dangerous temper of despair. The circumstances in which actual revolution broke out were always a tangle of complexity and differed from one city to another, yet the core of the situation was always the decay of public spirit among the patrician merchants.

To those who take a linear view of economic history this situation may present no problem. It is obvious that the lure of the material rewards offered by long-distance trade had more and more emancipated the greater merchants from the moral sanctions of the more restricted and personal sphere of local economic activity. In a word, they came to be economic individualists, and as such were no longer able to conform to the old communal traditions. In Douai, for example, where revolution broke out in 1280, the victims of popular vengeance were men like Jehan Boine-Broke, to whom business meant only the single-minded, unscrupulous pursuit of profit, and to whom public office meant only the opportunity to convert justice into a mockery and a fraud serving their own ends.[23] But to dismiss these men as individualists is to neglect one half of the situation in which they found themselves. It has been said of the city of Douai at this date that it was composed less of individuals than of family groupings.[24] The individual merchant was moved not only by passionate desire for gain, but also by so deep-rooted a loyalty to his family that he could engage in vendettas, and by a fervor for the accumulation of lands as a means of endowing his children with aristocratic leisure. None of these sentiments were altogether new in the late thirteenth century, but they became intensified then, at the same time as public spirit was declining. To give a complete account, therefore, of the waning of patrician allegiance to the ideal of the common good, one would have to take note of the individual as a member of a family, and explore more fully the history of the patrician families. Clues to the growing pride and insularity of the family might be found in the nature of their contacts and relations with the feudal aristocracy.

v

Another cornerstone in the ethical system by which the medieval church sought to maintain order in the economic life of the age was the doctrine of the stewardship of the rich. This was more fully and more simply expressed than the teaching on justice in regard to wages. Although it cannot be properly understood except as an integral part of a system of hierarchical social theory and philosophical thought, all that is needful here is to notice the way in which it impinged upon urban policies and the behavior of the wealthy merchant classes. Its deeper philosophical implications were probably at all times lost upon the ordinary layman. In its directly practical aspect the first point that stands out is a firm belief in the necessity of the institution of private property.[25] Aquinas, however, laid equal stress upon the precept that ownership of property involves the duty of using it for the good of others.[26] But he attached several significant qualifications to the definition of this duty. It is a duty, he explained, only according to natural law;[27] again, one need give alms only to those who would otherwise be without any succour;[28] and finally, none need give alms except out of the surplus that is left after providing all that is necessary "to live in keeping with one's station."[29]

If one could assume that medieval standards of living were fixed, then there would be no grounds for criticism of these precepts as a logical system. Aquinas, presumably, made this assumption. He conceived of a hierarchy of "stations" in life, each demanding certain material standards, not fixed rigidly, but fixed within certain limits.[30] He realized that excessive desire of, or reverence for, wealth might disturb the fixity of the scheme, but these were to be regarded as sins which could be avoided.[31]

Medieval sumptuary legislation may have been in part the outcome of acquiescence in these doctrines. If standards of living were allowed to rise, obviously the surplus available for alms would dwindle, and talk of the stewardship of the rich might become mere pretense. Therefore all forms of conspicuous consumption must be pegged within sharply defined limits on a graduated scale. When municipal authorities undertook this task, they did so with puritanical thoroughness and zest, prescribing limits, not only to luxury in dress and jewelry, but, with an admirable logic, to the forms of display that appealed more strongly to family and class pride— expenditure on wedding presents and wedding feasts and funeral processions and ceremonies.

But it is well known that the sumptuary legislation was as ineffective as it was general. There is no record of any consistent campaign to enforce any code anywhere as a whole. This gap between theory and practice is one of the more familiar aspects of late-medieval society, and has been various and vaguely interpreted in terms of hypocrisy, inefficiency, the after-effects of the Black Death, and the decadence of an age of prosperity and transition. Certainly the permeation of habits of life and habits of thought by the desire for ostentatious display became increasingly characteristic from the thirteenth century onward. Even leaders of moral and religious thought who sought to keep alive the spirit of traditional precepts checking excessive desire for wealth found it impossible to be too austere. St. Antonino, for example, indulgently allowed that women might wear false hair "if their station demands it or if thereby they are more pleasing to their husbands."[32]

Psychological analysis might single out a number of factors that would help to explain late medieval habits of extravagance in terms of desire for prestige. But very prominent among the ends of which luxury-pursuing and acquisitive persons were themselves conscious was the honor and prestige of the family from which they were descended or which they hoped to found. Margery Kempe, fifteenth-century merchant's wife and mystic of Lynn, recalling her days of pride, when she had worn "gold pypis on hir hevyd," and hoods and tippets and cloaks "daggyd and leyd wyth dyuers coloures," and when she had attempted to run a brewing business in order to make more money to spend, explained that she had done all this not only "for to be worshepd of the pepul," but for the sake of "the worschyp of hir kynred."[33] And another English writer of the same period, speaking of men who bought land and built fine houses, added, "And all is for her childre such goodis to wynne."[34]

While the cult of the family thus vitiated in practice much of the public willingness to condemn acquisitiveness in the abstract, it did not seriously detract from the sincerity with which individuals could believe in the doctrine of the stewardship of the rich. Wealthy merchants sometimes referred to their fortunes in their wills as "the goods that our lord hath lent us," and left sums of money to charities as a matter of course. These legacies were spread widely among the poor of both town and countryside and went to support and found

hospitals and other institutions conducted by religious orders. To
earn the real gratitude and acclaim of his fellow-townsmen, however, a medieval merchant had also to be generous during his lifetime. The ideal character of an urban magnate seems to have been
that sketched in the Dialogues that Caxton brought from Bruges:[35]

> Fraunseys the drapier
> Is a riche man;
> It is well bestowed;
> He gyveth gladly for goddes sake;
> He visiteth them that be not hole,
> The prisoners,
> Also counseilleth the wedowes
> And the orphans.

V I

Whatever aspect of their life be examined from the point of view of
the ends of which medieval townsmen were conscious, the same or
similar problems will emerge. It is easy enough to grasp and expound the theoretical system of ethical ends which the schoolmen
upheld, but it is less easy to follow the way in which public opinion
assimilated the various points of the system, and extremely difficult
to discover how successfully they were translated into practical
aims in circumstances of flux and change. Moreover, ends that
would ideally have harmonized the conflicting interests of different
sections of the community could, when embraced by exclusive
groups such as gild or family, lead to clash and discord.

There are three main reasons for the confusion into which
popular discussion of the subject usually falls. One is the profundity
of our ignorance as to the formation and working of public opinion,
especially in regard to economic policy, in the middle ages, or, for
that matter, in any other period. Another is the persistent exaggeration, in the older elementary text-books, of the rôle played by the
gilds. Sufficient detailed studies have been made to show that gilds
were far from being inspired solely by sentiments of brotherhood,
that in some places they were not well organized until very late in
the middle ages, and that they did not in any case cover the whole
of urban industry. To speak of a "gild economy," or to try to explain
the absence of ideal fraternal harmony in the sixteenth century by

the rise of "the economic motive" within the gilds, is to over-simplify and even to falsify the facts. To identify the gilds with the idealized pattern of control which sixteenth-century reformers persuaded themselves had once been dominant but had in their time decayed, is doubly fallacious. Yet such views are still appearing in popular surveys.[36] It may not be the business of the scholar to pounce upon every minor abuse or misunderstanding of his findings in journalistic or reformist circles. But when uncertain history is adduced as evidence in the discussion of important social and political issues, the scholar surely ought to make his voice heard. Why could not the professional academic associations make it a part of their business to see that sound but readable corrections and discussions are produced in such cases?

Finally, knowledge of medieval social control will remain fragmentary and unsatisfactory until more is known of the history of the family in medieval urban environments. Local researches have made a great deal of significant material available, but much more remains to be done before any very substantial conclusions can be drawn as to the circumstances in which bourgeois ambitions were canalized into the building up of the urban community, or were drawn off into the aping of aristocratic culture.[37]

The detail of these researches will not interest the specialist in modern economic history, nor will their general conclusions, when reached, be of any startling value outside the medieval field. Yet theoretical problems that the student of this side of medieval history encounters, also make their appearance in modern dress. Professor F. H. Knight once observed that what we have styled individualism might better be termed "familism."[38] If this clue could be grasped and put to use it might prove to be of far-reaching service to both medievalist and modernist.

Notes

1. Some practical advice on civic affairs is to be found in manuals on government written for princes, but it is not ordinarily sympathetic with the democratic or oligarchic or republican régimes common in the towns.

2. The best account of this type of preaching in England is in G. R. Owst, *Literature and Pulpit in Medieval England* (Cambridge, 1933), chapter 9. There are some suggestive comments on this level of thought in Karl Mannheim, *Man and Society* (1940), 276–77.

3. In 1254 Henry III took over the government of the city of London on the pretext that the assize of bread and ale had not been observed. H. T. Riley, *Chronicles of the Mayors and Sheriffs of London* (1863), 22. The management of weighing machines was in London actually entrusted in part to merchant companies. See S. L. Thrupp, "The Grocers of London, A Study of Distributive Trade," in *Studies in English Trade in the Fifteenth Century*, ed. Eileen Power and M. M. Postan (1933), 257–58.

4. *Medieval Cities* (translation, 1925), 214–19; *Belgian Democracy* (translation, 1915), 119, 123.

5. "The Stages in the Social History of Capitalism," *American Historical Review*, XIX (1913–14), 505.

6. M. Bloch, reviewing G. Espinas, *Une guerre sociale interurbaine dans la Flandre wallonne au XIIIᵉ siècle: Douai et Lille 1284–85*, notes how even at a time of social revolution, factions in Douai, when there was danger of attack from Lille, immediately reunited, . . . "se sentent une même âme." *Annales d'histoire économique et sociale*, t. 3 (1931), 293.

7. Levasseur, *Histoire des classes ouvrières et de l'industrie en France avant 1789*, I, 298–9.

8. *Ibid.*, 42.

9. *Ibid.*, I, 272–73, 275, 281, 283, 468.

10. For some details see *Documents nouveaux sur les moeurs populaires et le droit de vengeances dans les pays-bas au XVe siècle*, ed. Ch. Petit-Dutaillis (1908), 39–224.

11. Citations given in G. O'Brien, *An Essay on Medieval Economic Teaching* (1920), 120–121.

12. *Ibid.*, 122.

13. Owst, 363, n. 3.

14. O'Brien, 122.

15. Ordinances of the year 1467 in Worcester demanded only that employers hire laborers standing in the market-place for "reasonable summes," Toulmin Smith (ed.) *English Gilds* (Early English Text Society, Original Series No. 40), 395.

16. *Calendar of Letter Books of the City of London* (ed. R. Sharpe) C, 111 (date 1301).

17. See Levasseur's conjecture for the thirteenth century in France, *Histoire des classes ouvrières et le l'industrie en France avant 1789* (1900), I, 458, and H. Sée, *Histoire économique de la France* (1939), 43.

18. ". . . no one shall take for working in the said trade more than they were wont heretofore . . . ," ordinances of the whittawyers of London, 1346, H. T. Riley (ed.), *Memorials of London and London Life* (1868), 234; ". . . thei taken now noon other wise thanne hath ben usid amonge

theym of tyme oute of mynde . . . ," statement of bakers' men in 1441, proceedings in the court of aldermen, *Letter Book K* (ms. archives, city of London), ff. 198b–199; ". . . that the said servants and workmen should not take more wages than of old time is accustomed and ordained," ordinances of the fullers of Bristol, 1406, *English Gilds*, 284. There are also instances of provision for setting the wages of unenfranchised workmen at figures varying with their skill, Lipson, *The Economic History of England*, I, 301, case of London shearmen, 1352; also among London carpenters, 1487, ordinances in *Journals of the proceedings of the court of common council* (ms. archives, city of London), 9, ff. 136b–141.

19. The shearmen in 1350 appealed to the mayor and aldermen to order their men to work for customary rates as a matter of charity and for the profit of the people, Riley, *Memorials of London and London Life*, 251; the fullers in 1363 asked that servants combining "to obtain more than their proper wage, to the hurt of the people," be imprisoned for a year, *Calendar of Letter Books of the City of London*, G, 160.

20. Mr. Postan's remarks on the preambles of acts of Parliament are pertinent: ". . . the object of a preamble was to justify the act by relating it to those moral and political principles which could command a general acceptance; the more hypocritical they were the more conclusive they are as evidence of the spirit of the times." M. M. Postan, "The Economic and Political Relations of the Hanse (1400–1477)," in *Studies in English Trade in the Fifteenth Century* (1933), 103.

21. Riley, *Memorials*, 542–44.

22. Levasseur, 303–09; Thrupp, 255–56.

23. G. Espinas, *La vie urbaine de Douai au moyen âge* (1913), I, 223–24, 241; II, 1019, 1105–08, 1120–40.

24. M. Bloch, in *Annales d'histoire éonomique et sociale*, t. 3 (1931), 293. See above, n. 6.

25. *Summa Theologica* (literal translation by the Fathers of the English Dominican Province, 1929), Pt. II, ii, Q. 66, Art. 2, reply, objection 1.

26. "The temporal goods which God grants us are ours as to the ownership but as to the use of them, they belong not to us alone but also to such others as we are able to succour over and above our needs . . . ," *ibid.*, Pt. II, ii, Q. 32, Art. 5, reply, objection 2.

27. Pt. II, ii, Q. 66, Art. 7, reply, objection 3.

28. *Ibid.*, Q. 32, Art. 5, reply, objection 4.

29. *Ibid.*, Q. 32, Art. 6, reply to objections.

30. *Ibid.*, Pt. II, ii, Q. 32, Art. 6, reply to objections.

31. *Ibid.*, Pt. II, ii, Q. 63, Art. 3, reply, objection 3: ". . . The rich ought to be honoured by reason of their occupying a higher position in the community; but if they be honoured merely for their wealth, it will be the sin of respect of persons."

32. Cited in Bede Jarrett, *Saint Antonino and Medieval Economics* (1914), 74.

33. *The Book of Margery Kempe* (Early English Text Society, Original Series No. 212), 9.

34. *Peter Idley's Instructions to His Son*, lib. 2, 11. 1112 ff.

35. *Dialogues in French and English* (Early English Text Society, Extra Series No. 79), 35.

36. Bernard L. Dempsey, S. J., "Medieval Society," in *Planned Society* (ed. Findlay Mackenzie, 1937), 65; Lewis Mumford, *The Culture of Cities* (1938), 31.

37. The following is a sample of some of the more useful studies: E. M. Lambert, *Das Hallische Patriciat* (Halle, 1866); Sigmund Keller, *Patriziat und Geschlecterherrschaft in der Reichsstadt Lindau (Deutschrechtliche Beiträge. Forschungen und Quellen zur Geschichte des deutschen Rechts*, Herausgegeben von Dr. Konrad Bayerle, Band 1, Heft 5, 1908); Aloys Schulte, *Geschichte der grossen Ravensburger Handelsgesellschaft* (1923); id., *Der hohe Adel im Leben des mittelalterlichen Köln* (Bayerischen Akademie der Wissenschaften, 1919); R. Aubenas, "La famille dans l'ancienne Provence," *Annales d'histoire économique et sociale*, t. 8, 523–41; A-E. Sayous, "Aristocratie et noblesse à Gênes," *ibid.*, t. 9, 366–81; Roberto Lopez, *Aux origines du capitalisme génois*, t. 9, 429–54; Margarete Merores, *Der Venezianische Adel, Vierteljahrschrift für Sozial-und Wirtschaftsgeschichte* (1926), 193–237; Heinrich Kramm, *Landschaftlicher Aufbau und Verschiebungen des deutschen Grosshandles am Beginn der Neuzeit gemessen an den Familienverbindung des Grossburgertums, ibid.* (1936), 1–34.

38. *The Ethics of Competition* (1935), 49.

Hierarchy, Illusion, and Social Mobility

Historic China and pre-industrial Europe were both once typed as rigid societies with their population more or less frozen into fixed social groupings. Since in both cases the trend of research has altered this view, one cannot help wondering why it ever prevailed. The present revision in Chinese studies is the more dramatic in being a return to the view of Quesnay, namely, that Confucian ideals guaranteed a constant social circulation: men of merit could rise in the world, but their sons, if they were inept, would sink. In medieval and early modern European studies there has been a steady shift away from emphasis on hereditary fixity to recognition that very considerable currents of social mobility may exist within a stable social structure.

In both fields writers had begun by relying on ideals of order, rather incautiously, as a clue to actual custom. Confucian philosophy and ethical doctrine, it is true, gave rise to Quesnay's happy guess, but when this was discarded as doubtful, scholars fell back on legal texts. Here they found ideals of order expressed in an array of distinctions of juridical status. Instead of still postulating that these were mere lines of demarcation between groups, lines that a man could cross, they chose to regard them as effective barriers to mobility. The same kind of over-interpretation and misinterpretation of

Reprinted from *Comparative Studies in Society and History* 2, no. 1 (1959): 126–28. A comment on the article of Ping-ti Ho, "Aspects of Social Mobility in China, 1368–1911," *Comparative Studies in Society and History* 1, no. 4 (1959): 330–59.

juridical distinctions occurred in European studies. In the use of medieval philosophical and ethical writing, too, references to ranked orders and estates were taken as implying that the lines of demarcation between these hemmed people in for life.

How did this presumption against social mobility arise? In European studies one might say that it came through a too liberal extension of the principle of heredity which was present at the top of the scale, in the nobility, and at the bottom, in medieval serfdom; but for China, where the hereditary nobility were known to be insignificant in number, this is hardly a reasonable explanation. It is more likely that Western writers in both fields developed the presumption by drifting into a certain mechanical way of using the concept of class. In historical work on a remote scene over a broad sweep of time, without attention to the tedious detail of family histories, it is particularly easy to assume that the members of any group were in it for life. As Schumpeter remarked, the circumstance of a class being fairly stable in character, changing only slowly, may create a false impression that the membership is equally stable. He likened this to the illusion of supposing that the people in a hotel were always the same people.

The inferences that were drawn from Western traditions of hierarchical thought about the nature of medieval society certainly require some such explanation. Even the cult of ancestry among the nobles themselves, put together from legends and the lore of stable and mews, had to recognize the ennoblement of new men and the rise of their families. The emphasis of social philosophy on the structural order of medieval society, on its ranked estates, gives no ground for inferring disapproval of the existing institutional means to social mobility, in the towns, in the service of nobles and monarchs, and within the hierarchy of the Church. Although organic social theory, stressing the value of every function in society, from the humblest to the highest, carried overtones of the lesson of contentment with a given task or lot in life, it never implied that a man should not avail himself of legitimate means of improving his lot or of securing a better lot than his father's.

In the second main form of Western hierarchical tradition, derived from the fifth century writings of the pseudo-Dionysius, the scheme of the downward diffusion of power through the nine grades of celestial beings and through the government of the Church is clearly theological, juridical, and political. Yet the scheme is so extraordinarily impressive, it dwells so on the splendor of the celestial hierarchy, as to create an emotional presumption that its intent went further, that it was designed to inculcate a spirit of respect, not only for government but for all social superiors, and would thus militate against social mobility.

Essayists could the more readily pass on this impression because medieval commentators rarely said anything about the application of the scheme to society except in the government of the Church and in the duty of civil obedience. William of Auvergne turned it into a theoretical model of monarchy, with a rather flatfooted comparison of the work of royal officials to the functions of the angels in the service of God. In his effort to glorify the officials in this way he did not stop to note that they were likely to be men risen through education and looking for promotion in the royal service. Bonaventura saw the principle of hierarchy as upholding the separation of the three estates of Church, nobles and commoners but there it is simply a matter of juridical separation. One of Berthold of Regensburg's popular sermons draws an arbitrary grouping of the non-noble lay population by occupations into the scheme; he censures upward movement into the knights and nobles, but not at lower levels. A fifteenth century English writer who drew out nine distinctions of rank among gentlemen, by analogy with the celestial orders, allowed upward movement both into the lower ranks from outside, and for the descendants of the new men, into the higher ranks.

It is not only for emotional reasons that the scheme lent itself to over-interpretation, but through the principle of functional separation of grades. This held throughout the celestial hierarchy. Celestial beings were fixed in one or other of the nine grades because they were incapable by nature of performing any other functions but those attached to the grade to which they belonged. They could rise a little within that grade by striving to shine more brightly, but they could not be promoted. They were like aristocrats serving at court by virtue of ancient titles. In a slightly different form, to the effect that a lower function could not be combined with a higher, the principle is applied again in the ecclesiastical

hierarchy, to drive home the lesson that monks are not to interfere
with the work of the secular clergy. The eighth appendix to the
pseudo-Dionysian treatise on the ecclesiastical hierarchy is a scath-
ing letter to the monk Demophilos, who had turned a priest out of
his church and taken over his function of preaching to the people.
He is told that he is a wolf in sheep's clothing, too ignorant to
preach, that he should not have leapt out of his proper grade, he
should have been content with his station. The same principle is applied again to the laity but only as they attain a measurable status
in the hierarchy, that is, as they strive to draw nearer to God, by
devotion to holiness. Fixity in such status was however not so much
a fact as an ideal, to be achieved only by steadfast devotion, in the
higher grades, to virginity. Jonas of Orleans points out that one
cannot leap in and out of such a state. Thus the principle of functional separation within the hierarchy carried no clear opposition
to social mobility in the ordinary sense of the term. Medieval towns
were applying the principle in their ruling that a citizen should
belong to only one gild.

Nor did the ideal of the individual's fixity in one function run
throughout the whole scheme of hierarchy. Pseudo-Dionysius makes
a point of the fact that priests can be promoted and become bishops.
He mentions also that the higher officials of the Church have more
knowledge. One might infer that study would help in obtaining
promotion, but there is no suggestion of urging study in the spirit
of Confucius. The picture of the secular clergy as they form the
upper part of the ecclesiastical hierarchy is more like that of a
bureaucracy in which knowledge comes with seniority and promotion by mysterious favor.

The presumption against social mobility in Chinese and European studies thus came in both cases by misinterpretation of the
historic emphasis on juridical order through too mechanical a concept of class. In the first case this encouraged doubts as to the
influence of philosophy, and in the second it ascribed a kind of conservatism to philosophy which is now hard to conceive as part of its
intent. Meanwhile it is to be hoped that the advance of quantitative
research will serve the end of more than incidental qualification of
the old generalizations about rigidity, the end of better theoretical
understanding of the so-called traditional civilizations.

Economy and Society in Medieval England

In British historiography, economic and social history were first thrown together when both were young and backward offshoots of the study of institutions. Economic history, by exploring records in which no one else was interested and making some use of the elements of economic theory, rapidly outgrew that status. But social history lags and its future is uncertain. It has no special records to call its own, for its materials, though rich, are embedded in all classes of documentation. It has no generally recognized set of questions to call its own, for although historians have always drawn on political science for questions relating to the state and to constitutions, and are respectful of economics, they have been distrustful of sociology because this has not yet done much with long-run problems of change. Is social history then to become another specialty, working out its questions as it goes along? This course would not rule out the need of defining better its relation to other specialties. Is social history to remain a mere footnote to politics and law, literature and art, science and technology, describing the ways in which these impinge on social custom? If these points are numerous and puzzling, can it fulfil the promise of the school of Marc Bloch and Lucien Febvre, becoming the nucleus of a new kind of historical synthesis? Or has it only some peculiar affiliation with economic history?

These questions can be answered only through new work and discussion of it. They give point to commentary on some recent

Reprinted from *The Journal of British Studies* 2 (1962): 1–13.

English work on the medieval period. In this period the affiliation between the social and the economic aspects of institutional history has been a particularly strong tradition and, despite G. C. Homans' resolute attempt to set medieval English social history on its own feet, the greater interest over the last few decades in administrative history has tended to keep its status ambiguous. The discussion that follows is of the degrees of success of genuine efforts respectively to make the social more than a footnote to general history, to make it an equal partner with economic history, to give it depth in the history of a minority group, and to show the uses of one of its special tools, the science of genealogy.

The publication of E. F. Jacob's *The Fifteenth Century*[1] brings to completion the first great scholarly effort to write general English history in one period after another. The enterprise has not radically departed from the model set by the earlier Methuen series on the political history of England, but its authors have tried much harder than their predecessors to write a history of English society in other aspects besides the political. In this aim Sir Frank Stenton's volume on Anglo-Saxon England, having to deal with three conquests and three processes of thorough-going change—Christianization, the growth of ecclesiastical organization, and Norman feudalization—has been the most successful of the medieval contributions, its story of political leadership having at every step to be related to one or other of these processes. Owing to the elusiveness of information on the Anglo-Saxon economy, the economic context of social relations remained vague. But this was admitted: the book was a guide to future research as well as a masterly summary of existing knowledge.

E. F. Jacob's book is of necessity weighted by the emphases of the research of the past few decades. For this reason it is strong on government finance, foreign policy, the magnates' organization of regional influence, and on the role of the commons in Parliament. At a number of points fresh detail is added, as for example on the exploitation of Normandy in the 1420's, on the financial breakdown of the Lancastrian government, and on changes in the method of handling revenue from Crown lands under Edward IV. So far as is possible the book is lightened by dramatic arrangement of its parts. After the Congress of Arras, the story of war finance and foreign policy is broken by three chapters on the Church, the machinery of government, the households of the magnates, and the economy. There is relief, too, in turning from the field of Bosworth to survey the arts of peace. The last few pages are given not to Henry Tudor nor to any attempt at summary, but to Margery Kempe and the cult of women saints as exemplifying the vitality of popular religion.

Endorsing Kingsford's judgment of the fifteenth century as an age of ferment, Jacob tries to dispel the atmosphere of gloom that recent studies of the long years of agricultural depression, which lasted into the 1470's, have wrapped around it. He would like to view these years as engendering a new kind of recovery by forcing people out of ancient ruts. The retreat of the lords to rentiership is seen as the first act, as it were, in a social and economic revolution that opened the way to innovation through larger-scale tenant operation and some degree of enclosure, the latter in turn helping to displace population that could provide a labor supply for new textile entrepreneurs serving foreign markets. This view allows for great regional variation and is on the whole advanced with the caution that our present dearth of quantitative information demands.

The dictum that "The Fifteenth century is not a time of stagnation but of mobility in the population of town and country alike"[2] is, however, more dramatic than logical, for the two conditions coexisted, and much of the mobility that is illustrated had no bearing on the process of economic revival. Many of the villagers who left home merely settled nearby in other villages of similar type. As for upward social mobility in the towns, if it was possible for trading artisans to move upward into merchant gilds quite rapidly, and for workers to move into artisan gilds, this was in part because of the high death rates that depleted gild ranks. There is no discussion of the population problem beyond the offer of "about 2.1 million" (J. C. Russell's tentative estimate for 1400) as the figure for the first half of the century, and the statement that it began to rise "towards the end of the depressive years." Nor is there any discussion of the extent of the internal market as distinct from production for export. Like the population question, this is of course still a research frontier, but it would have been helpful to refer readers to the debate on it that is printed in the proceedings of the historical congress held in Rome in 1955. Austerely, England's first important industry catering to mass consumption—the brewhouses of Netherlands and Ger-

man   immigrants, which did cheerful business through the age of
stagnation—is overlooked. The sole drink referred to is the rich man's
imported wine.

There is lacking any explicit reflection on the negative economic
consequences of the magnates' activities. To be sure, the reader can
reflect on this for himself. The negative contributions of the magnates lay not only in their fostering of local disorder where this was
to their political advantage and in their financial exploitation of the
feeble Lancastrian state. It lay also in their swelling of the administrative "overhead" of society to no purpose but to serve the private
ends of their rentiership. In staffing the administration of their huge
estate complexes they drained off ability that might conceivably
have helped in the diversification of production that the age needed.
True, Jacob notes that their bailiffs and sergeants were often among
those who farmed manorial demesne. But he does not note Raftis'
observation, from analysis of Ramsey Abbey accounts of the period,
of the heavy indebtedness on the part of the farmer to which these
arrangements could lead.[3] The small working capital of a succession
of men may have been wiped out. Faithful servants of a magnate
might of course expect pensions and other handouts. But redistribution of a portion of the great rentier's income in this way promoted
a spirit of obsequious parasitism rather than risk-taking enterprise.
A predatory and parasitic spirit, as well as yeoman thrift and constructive merchant enterprise, was a large element of the legacy
that the fifteenth century passed on to the Tudor world.

In his few pages on the countryside, Jacob leans to the widely
favored but still not very well documented judgment that the general trend throughout the fourteenth and fifteenth centuries was
towards a more competitive village society in which a land market
was leading to increased differentiation. He tries to believe[4] that
competition for land was particularly strong, due to a supposed
increase in sheepkeeping, in the early fifteenth century, although on
the next page citing samples of the evidence that exists as to a
shortage of tenants at this time. It is true that competition persisted, in the sense that more takers were available for better land
than for poor, and for land on which improvements in the shape of
buildings, garden, and pasture enclosures, and small industrial
facilities, had been kept up. It is hard to conceive of a peasant

society in which this would not be so. That kind of competition could hardly have been new. As to differentiation among the peasantry, so far as one can tell there had always been a scale, with freeholders who were on the way to becoming petty landlords at the top and cottagers at the bottom. The evidence from the depression years is so far of change only in the sense of a slight and variable upgrading in the amounts of land held all down the scale. It is not necessary to invoke a more competitive man to account for this. One of the circumstances that helps to account for it is the long spell of stagnation in population growth, which caused a high rate of dying out of village families. Some men added to their holdings those of neighbors who had died without heirs. Such holdings could be acquired for no payment but a small entry fine and a money rent to the lord on which in the worse years the tenant could at least partially default.

The notion that the peasant was becoming a more competitive man has rested on the fact that the new wave of demesne leasing was for competitive rents, rents set by supply and demand instead of by custom. But can it be said with confidence that apart from these particular transactions with the lord, or before they developed, the peasant was familiar with nothing but fixed custom? The answer calls for more comparison with earlier periods than the piecemeal type of English historical synthesis, period by period, to which the Oxford volumes are directed, permits. The piecemeal procedure is a necessary stage in the synthesis of research in political and administrative history. But questions of economic development and of its relation to changes in the character of rural society require, at least for the medieval centuries, a longer-term setting. In casting back as he does into the fourteenth century Jacob concedes this point. It was simply not possible for him to go back far enough.

The pre-fourteenth-century history of the village land market has in fact been rather neglected. Information has accumulated since Maitland first noticed it, in the 1880's, but because interest has tended to concentrate on the manor rather than on the village and hence on the peasants only in their relations with the lord, no one but the late E. A. Kosminsky and G. C. Homans has given it much weight as an institution. Both these writers interpreted its activity in the late thirteenth century as due to growing economic pressures.

Homans believed that until then its activity had been traditionally restrained both by the lord's interest in preventing alienation of tenements owing labor service and by peasant reluctance to permit permanent alienation of any part of a tenement that was subject to the custom of partible inheritance.

M. M. Postan, in an essay forming part of the introduction to a Peterborough Abbey cartulary of tenant sales by charter between the 1250's and the 1330's, sales largely by unfree men, has now brought new evidence and new questions to bear on the problem.[5] The new evidence is drawn from inquests recorded in the Peterborough cartulary and in court rolls from other estates, which trace the descent of property from buyers of unfree status through several generations. Coming from manorial sources, this evidence substantially reinforces the conclusion to which a number of cases in the earliest royal court records and in Bracton point, namely, that a village land market was well institutionalized by 1200. Postan's main contribution is to draw an analytical distinction between two opposite characteristics that this market could assume. On the one hand, it could bring about a redistribution of land, tending to level out abnormal inequalities and to preserve a given social structure. Especially in the form of inter-peasant leasing it may be regarded as one of the prime economic devices by which peasant society was able to maintain itself with so little change over long periods of time. In this form it may have been very ancient, perhaps even "as old as the village itself." On the other hand, a land market could have the opposite effect of increasing inequalities. It is this second and later form, associated with growing commercialization, that has been the subject of Marxist interpretation.

The essay argues that the levelling type of market prevailed in English villages through much of the twelfth and all of the thirteenth century. The argument starts from the practical problems of a peasant family: how to meet needs that vary throughout its life cycle. The variation in needs dictates some resort to the labor market but could lead also, in the absence of any effective legal ban, to a land market. Could the modest chronic needs of the peasantry bypass manorial controls? Historians have not really considered this as a serious possibility. But they have not been much interested in peasant needs. By and large they have adopted the point of view of a lord resting on his legal right to forbid the alienation of unfree land. Although our earliest manor court rolls reveal quite widespread evasion of the rule, it has been assumed that manorial controls were breaking down under abnormal pressures in the period from which these come, the late thirteenth century, and that they continued to break down progressively while still on many manors remaining firm into the fifteenth century. It is true that there were manors where the record notes only the traditional standard units of unfree land, the virgates, half-virgates, and other smaller units, with none of the irregularities in the size of holdings that a market might be expected to produce. On these the lord supposedly kept to a conservative policy partly in order to facilitate the enforcement of labor services, which were assessed on the standard units. There has however long been some doubt about this whole interpretation, for a careful reading of court rolls shows clearly that alienation could occur without affecting the method of listing tenements in manorial surveys or of entering in the accounts the rents and services collected. For example, subtenants of a tenant, who had become collectively responsible for performing his services or paying some of his rent, may be mentioned only on the occasion of a default. Notice of that tenant as holding a standard unit in a stable tenemental system is a mere fiction of the accounting record. If it be admitted that there may be a good deal of this kind of formal fiction in the records, then it is time to consider Postan's proposal that the picture of a stable tenemental system is a delusion, and that a village land market may have existed not only where the record reveals it but where the record does not reveal it. This proposal does not imply that manorial records are valueless; it means only that historians need to ask new questions of them. It opens up the general question whether peasants may not have been reacting to similar economic circumstances in much the same way all over medieval England, regardless of their status at law and regardless of the degree of manorialization in a region.

From this standpoint one would think of the emergence of a village land market as determined by the character and extent of local land supply. Access to suitable land that could be brought under cultivation easily would have delayed its emergence. Availability of demesne land for leasing could also have acted as a damper. This

supply reached a peak in the twelfth century and again in the fifteenth. Inter-peasant dealing was preferably in land that, whether
free or customary, was held from the lord wholly or mainly for
money rent. Postan estimates that the amount even of customary
land that was so held in the thirteenth century would have been
"more than sufficient to sustain an active land market." The criterion
of "activity" in a market of the levelling type is not high. Two or
three transactions a year, between peasants who found their holdings too large to manage and others who had too little land, might
be the normal expectation in a small village.

The role of manorial controls over unfree land and tenantry was
to legalize, in the late thirteenth century, what had formerly been
an illegal market. Far from beginning to weaken in the late thirteenth century they began to stiffen then after a century of laxity.
The motive for stiffening, Postan demonstrates, had nothing to do
with labor services but was fiscal. In a time of rising land values
the illegal practice of alienating land outside the manor court, which
deprived the lord of the opportunity to levy fines or raise rents at
the time of transfer, could no longer be tolerated. The policy adopted
was therefore to bring transactions into court for the payment of
license fees or fines and increasingly after 1300 to go through the
procedure of surrender of the land to the lord for regrant to the
buyer. There is a clear analogy with the banning of subinfeudation
by *Quia Emptores* in favor of substitution, the new tenant replacing
the old, a policy which was also adopted in defence of the lord's
fiscal rights. But the peasant still sought to evade the rules, and
the fifteenth-century record, especially in manorial surveys, may still
conceal subtenants. The historian has still to be a detective in search
of supplementary information.

The analytical distinction between the levelling type of market
and the type that would cumulatively increase inequality is an ingenious device for exploring at the same time the economy and the
social arrangements of peasant England, but it will not so serve if
it is oversimplified. To look for a sharp transition from one to the
other would be an error of this kind. Postan would agree with
Reginald Lennard that more study is needed of the free peasantry.
As the latter has emphasized, these appear already in the late
eleventh and early twelfth centuries as less trammelled in any drive

for accumulation than the unfree; Lennard discovered more differentiation and more use of money in the rural economy of that age than he had expected.[6] Again, other agencies besides the land market had diverse effects on differentiation, notably inheritance customs and the dying out of families. In the late fifteenth century the levelling type of market probably persisted not only in areas isolated from trade but fighting a rearguard action, as it were, in the small-holding sectors of regions in which graziers or industrial villagers were thriving commercially.

In a concise, graceful and well-documented study of the English Jewry, H. G. Richardson has wrestled with another twelfth- and thirteenth-century market, the money market.[7] As with the village land market, the problem is to recognize the different forms of demand and supply that were in play. Perfect knowledge of these factors would cover all forms of credit operation, both lending for productive purposes and consumption loans. Research is still so far from this ideal that Richardson is content to draw only a few distinctions, mainly between international financiers and those whose business, like that of the English Jews of this period, lay in England alone, and between the different forms of security that the latter accepted. He sufficiently indicates that deeper study of their roles in the economy should lead to more objective assessment of their social position, but rather than raise questions to which he has no answer he goes on to apply his skill in administrative history to trace the evolution of the procedures by which the Crown exercised protection and control. He makes clear that this protection was adequate to prevent the hostile ecclesiastical legislation of the thirteenth century from taking effect. But the cost of protection rose.

Whether they can be answered or not, some of the questions that Richardson does not raise are worth raising. For example, were Jews helping to mobilize hoarded English wealth as some Italians were in the thirteenth century by inducing people to make deposits with them for loan? Another question is whether the common assumption is valid that the smaller Jewish loans were all of the pawnbroking variety and not for productive purposes. Although a customer or merchant might provide him with raw materials, a medieval craftsman had always to find his own tools and equipment. Especially in the early thirteenth century, when little new towns

were still developing, many small men must have been in need of
credit for productive purposes. A minority of the debtors of Abraham
of Berkhamstead and of Oxford Jews were craftsmen and retailers
whose borrowing may well have been of this nature. The chief
stimulus to native activities that Richardson notes resulted from the
legal incapacity of Jews to acquire a freehold interest in land, and it
could have affected only people who were already wealthy landowners or merchants. The practice grew up in the thirteenth century of transferring debts of Jewish creditors that were secured on
land to a third party, either an individual Christian or a religious
house. This third party obtained a permanent title to the land from
the debtor and paid off the Jew, at a discount. Other types of
Jewish bonds were also discounted by high officials.

Social relations between these wealthy investors and the Jews
with whom they dealt were friendly. But otherwise Richardson has
little positive evidence as to the nature of Jewish-Christian social
encounters. It is apparent that most of the Jews were craftsmen or
victuallers of humble status, and he wonders whether gilds, which
would necessarily have excluded them from religious fraternities,
made it difficult for these men to earn a living. This is quite unlikely, since artisan gilds were still rare, and craftsmanship and
trading skill were welcome in towns. The reasoning by which
Richardson decides that, although by the late twelfth century the
taking of interest on loans was so general among Christians as not
to carry opprobrium, the profession of moneylending was "never
fully respectable" is perhaps stated a little too broadly. The conclusion would hold true of pawnbroking. However, it is unclear
whether the greater members of the English Jewry engaged in this
more than peripherally.

A supplementary note ascribes the Expulsion to a personal decision by Edward I, turning at the end on a sudden urgent need for
cash to be realized through confiscation of Jewish houses and outstanding bonds. Edward was caught in a crossfire of opinion from
his mother and anti-Semitic clerics and from his wife and high
officials who had profited from business association with Jews and
were friendly to them. The attempt to reconstruct the stages by
which decision was reached, whether or not it is wholly correct, is
an interesting piece of investigation. If the Jews had still been

doing enough business to remain useful to the King as a continuing source of revenue his action would have been extraordinarily stupid. The interpretation is less convincing than Elman's,[8] which turns on the fact that the tallages on Jews had in effect been taxation of the small landowners who were their most substantial debtors. A tallage necessarily brought severe pressure on such debtors, often direct pressure from the Crown, to pay up their debts quickly. It was the mounting resentment of this group that supported anti-Semitic legislation. Ultimately the Jews became dispensable both as private moneylenders and as a source of revenue to the Crown because of the activities of the Italians. Provided that one recognizes the differences between Italian and Jewish operations and does not simply regard the Italians as replacing the Jews, Richardson does not specifically reject this interpretation. He is perhaps merely tired of insular hero-worship of kings. His criticism of Edward is further backed by comparison with Gascony, where the effectiveness of Expulsion orders was hampered by friendliness.

A very different kind of book comes from Sir Anthony Wagner, Richmond Herald. His *English Genealogy*[9] was written to reveal some of the broader implications of genealogy to the growing number of people who are curious about their ancestry and who wonder, with a character of George Gissing's, what a funeral would be like if all of the deceased's blood relatives were to attend. Much of the book is given to the techniques by which blood relationship can be established through records, and to the history of genealogical literature. Much also is given to findings that might be of popular interest, for example, to the downward diffusion of aristocratic and royal blood. But the discussion goes beyond this level. It draws on Sorokin's valuable work on *Social Mobility* to show how history will reveal patterns in downward as well as upward mobility, even though the latter are for individual families better documented. Families that endure in the male line for any length of time have often seesawed up and down in the social scale, as Jane Austen's did. The frequency of this seesaw pattern, Sir Anthony points out, is due to the fact that waves of population growth may tend to increase the proportionate numbers of the poor.

The backbone of the book is the chapter on the Social Framework, against which mobility has to be measured. In the absence

of any general history of social status in England Wagner has had
to construct one for himself from the scattering of books and articles
that are most relevant. Although more could have been gleaned
from some articles in *Speculum* and in *The Economic History
Review*, he has read practically everything that deals directly with
questions of status. Any criticism of this chapter reflects therefore
on the current state of social history rather than on the author.
Both for reasons of space and because his sources are studies of
groups definable by differing criteria, he has chosen to sketch the
main changes in the fortunes of each of these groups separately
through history instead of attacking the more difficult problem of
how the groups discernible in any one period were articulated and
how the articulation altered as a whole through time. This might
indeed require several books. Inevitably, perhaps because the word
"framework" suggests solid carpentry, there is some bias towards
the idea of a continuing structure in which the difference between
high place and low place had always much the same meaning. In
an earlier chapter on mobility Wagner envisages the framework as
"a lofty structure with many shallow steps by which the skilful and
persistent may climb, while some others slipped down and many
more kept the framework solid by standing still." This is an admirable statement of the English concept of a reliably solid tradition,
which is not however always the most reliable guide to the past. It
may not be usual for English historians to regard German historians
as more imaginative, yet a recent article on the question of how the
concepts of freedom and of unfreedom and of gradations in these
varied from one region to another in early medieval Germany and
altered through time is by contrast quite disturbingly imaginative.[10]
This problem becomes particularly important in Germany with the
rise of the *ministeriales*, but the approach is applicable also to all
aspects of social status in England. Wagner is indeed well aware
that the notion of an immovable structure may be deceptive, for he
adds to his picture of it the story of a small farmer who did not
know that his ancestor living on the same land something over two
hundred years earlier had been a gentleman of coat armour. The
phasing of the kinds of change that have succeeded each other will
not be easy, but a Lewis Carroll picture of the status game through
time as a game of croquet in which not only the players and the

hoops and the mallets move but also the goalposts might be in order as a fresh start.

Sir Anthony Wagner is too modest about the contributions that genealogy can make to history, but he has many suggestions that would be worth drawing together and expanding into specific research proposals. His broadest suggestion occurs in his discussion of the dragging down of families by rising waves of population growth. The correlation of such waves with war or emigration, or with social, political, or technical revolution "ought to be among the meeting-points of historians and genealogists." At the end he makes highly practical proposals for cooperation between record offices in making the results of local research more widely available.

Along the same lines it might be a further help to reflection on the problems of social history if the essays and documents that local record societies continue to publish were periodically reviewed together. Specialists of course follow them, but there is often some lag before they come to more general notice. Festschrift literature notoriously suffers from the same disadvantage, the contents of any one volume being ordinarily so mixed that a reviewer not primarily interested in social history cannot be expected to comment on isolated contributions that may yet be significant. One of the essays recently presented to Bruce Dickins, for example, summarizes a colloquy on life in a late tenth-century rural monastery which gives an engagingly plausible view of a little town of that period as a centre of social life, a town elder having invited the entire monastery to a banquet.[11] It refers also to pilgrims buying provisions from the priest of a church where they have stopped to pray. Another of these essays maps the fortresses built in preparation for the campaigns of 917–18 against the Danes.

Among the dedicated groups publishing sources none sets a higher standard of scholarship than the Canterbury and York Society in its editions of medieval episcopal registers. Of prime importance to church historians, they are a most valuable source also for social history in revealing the workings of ecclesiastical patronage. The registers of Roger Martival, Bishop of Salisbury, impeccably edited by Kathleen Edwards so as to show the full procedures followed, cover the years 1315–30.[12] Martival, who had been Chancellor of Oxford University, was an unusually conscientious administrator.

His chief problem was the insufficient supply of educated clergy. He dealt with this by requiring underqualified men to report to him for periodic personal examination until they could show adequate progress in study. In the early years of his administration a considerable number of the vicars and rectors could be ordained only as acolytes, being presumably young, but the proportion of those who were priests rose. Among his disciplinary problems were two rectors who after being excommunicated hopefully presented men to be their vicars, one of whom was unfit from lack of learning and the other as being himself under sentence of excommunication. Another problem was the constant use men made of influence in competition for preferment. At least three exchanges were preceded by incidents of persecution or intimidation. To have kinsmen or "powerful friends" in a diocese was helpful. Episcopal registers are obviously an important source for studies of the parish clergy as a social group. Their names often indicate their origins, their movements can be traced, and in many cases careers can be followed to the end, the exact date of death being often a part of the record.

Notes

1. E. F. Jacob, *The Fifteenth Century (1399–1485)*, *The Oxford History of England* (Oxford, 1961).

2. Jacob, *Fifteenth Century*, p. 370.

3. J. A. Raftis, *The Estates of Ramsey Abbey* [Pontifical Institute of Mediaeval Studies] (Toronto, 1957), p. 293.

4. Jacob, *Fifteenth Century*, p. 375.

5. C. N. L. Brooke and M. M. Postan (eds.), *Cartae Nativorum* [Publications of the Northampton Record Society, XX] (Oxford, 1960).

6. Reginald Lennard, *Rural England: 1086–1135* (Oxford, 1959), pp. v, 179–80.

7. H. G. Richardson, *The English Jewry under Angevin Kings* (London, 1960).

8. P. Elman, "The Economic Causes of the Expulsion of the Jews in 1290," *Econ. Hist. Rev.*, VII (1937), 145–54.

9. Anthony Richard Wagner, *English Genealogy*. Corrected edition (Oxford, 1960).

10. Karl Bosl, "Uber soziale Mobilitat in der mittelalterliche Gesellschaft." *Vierteljahrschrift für Sozial und Wirtschaftsgeschichte,* XLVII (1960), 306–32.

11. G. N. Garmonsway, "The Development of the Colloquy," in Peter Clemoes (ed.), *The Anglo-Saxons, Studies in some Aspects of their History and Culture presented to Bruce Dickins* (London, 1959), pp. 248–61.

12. Roger Martival, *Diocesis Sarisbiriensis: Registrum Rogeri Martival,* pars prima and Index, ed. Kathleen Edwards [Canterbury and York Society, LV, LVI] (Oxford, 1959–60).

The Dynamics of
Medieval Society

European medievalists command the best-stocked laboratory in the
world for the study of pre-industrial civilization in a gamut of
forms running from tribal society to pioneers in state sovereignty
and international finance. Evolutionary bias, and the quantities of
records that these more advanced areas have left, have combined to
give their achievements pride of place, general histories often leaving laggard or deviant areas out in limbo. Yet the main interest of
the medieval world lies in the scale of variability at any time, and
in the degree to which different areas were in communication with
each other. A true social history would be concerned with all areas,
perhaps especially with frontiers of settlement and with backward
corners of prosperous regions, and would try to trace every current
of travel and migration. Its central enquiry would be into the ways
in which people's energies were controlled, stimulated, and mobil-
ized, not only through formal structures of power but through
kinship and households, informal structures and access to meeting-
places, and it would pay as much attention to persistent patterns
as to changing ones.

No single person could undertake such a work, but it begins to
seem possible that a group of scholars interested in these matters
could devise a feasible plan and carry it out. The possibility depends, however, on the extent to which people are really working

Reprinted from *"The Dynamics of Medieval Society,"* *Proceedings
of the XIII International Congress of Historical Science,* vol. 1 (Moscow,
1973), pp. 93–112.

on similar problems. It would save a great deal of time if there were enough international communication to have comparative study built into the process of basic research. The object of this paper is simply to stir discussion, through a selective review of recent work, of how such intellectual cooperation might be speeded.

Research on medieval social relationships made good headway in the third quarter of the last century, but came to be overshadowed by the need to know more about the development of formal institutions. Social history in general was for a long time regarded as a mere appendage to economic history or as a frivolous sideline best left to popular writers, while institutional historians tended to lose sight of the people behind the records. The necessity of ordering the mounds of fact on record about institutions, however, obliged them to think in terms of structure and function. It is still possible to write about formal institutions solely in these terms, as though they were pieces of machinery. But the professional bent against mechanistic theory, and awareness of the human frailties that weakened governmental machinery and ecclesiastical organization, now turn attention, once the character of a structure is clear, to the men who operated it.

At that point institutional history turns into social history. Karl Bosl's work on the rise of the imperial ministeriales is still the most comprehensive study of an administrative class, but career patterns among the lawyers of Capetien France have been followed,[1] and the English passion for administrative history has led to numerous skirmishing attacks on the problem of low standards of probity and efficiency. Urban history, where interest in the local articulation of social groups began, now seems on the point of dissolving towns into webs of social relationships reaching far beyond town walls, and it will be logical to examine all settlements from this same point of view.[2] Population research is no longer just a matter of trying to estimate changes in total numbers, but is going into age-grouping and the sex ratio.[3] The growth of the celestial population raises questions about the protective and the socially integrative functions of the saints,[4] and also about their healing role at popular shrines, questions which can be answered only piecemeal. They merge into the problem that Marc Bloch considered central, that of the nature of medieval modes of perception and how they altered.

Jacques Le Goff's documentation of the invasion of monasteries and
castles by the folkloric culture of the countrysides is a welcome
revival of vigorous attack on it.[5]

With research advancing on these and many other fronts, we
shall soon be much better informed. Yet, so far, knowing more about
medieval society has not produced any radically new way of thinking about it. The processes of state formation and of market expansion, along with urbanization and population growth movements,
remain the salient dynamic elements. Reflection revolves largely
around the antinomies of power and freedom, as it must, but continues to pose them in terms of nineteenth-century political and
economic philosophies and as though the later middle ages existed
only to prepare the way for the Leviathan-state and the capital-
intensive production of the future. This constricts the view of freedom, at the end, to rights and privileges guaranteed by custom, fiat,
or law, in the past.[6] Paradoxically, the theme of freedom as a dynamic element is the mainstay of both the liberal and the Marxist
models of the course of medieval development.

If we are to look at Europe as a whole, generalization as to the
forces at work will have to take a new tack. Kiev, Moscow and
Prague, Genoa, Venice and all of the other great cities whose hinterlands and spheres of economic and cultural influence had no fixed
bounds, may be regarded as centers of a kind of pre-industrial imperialism collecting the lion's share, for a time, of their world's
moveable wealth, promoting but using the state system as best they
could, and to some extent disturbing the balance of social relations
in every region where their trade reached.

It is significant that biological analogy, which could hardly
grasp so dynamic a scene, is being replaced by physical analogy.
The physical analogy, which can no longer permit anything to be at
rest but presents us always with a system of forces either locked
into some form of equilibrium or interacting to produce ongoing
change in a given direction, has its uses. Historians of international
relations have based much of their work on the concept of balances
of power. But when the image of a balance tending to restore itself
after swings of disturbance is combined with a functionalist type of
systematic sociology, one that sees every part of a social system

locked into the whole, and every social relationship a matter of reciprocity, the result is a purely abstract model. Ongoing change will always come to a halt. G. C. Homans explicitly kept such a model in view in describing open-field villages in thirteenth-century England as though each was a social system.[7] He was in consequence able to describe better than anyone else the interdependence of village customs as to work, family arrangements, inheritance and transfers of land, settlement of disputes, ritual and ceremony. By assuming the virtual fixity of practices, and the acceptance, if only as a fiction, of a sense of reciprocity in relations with the lord, he was able to stress the harmony of village life. In a sense, the evidence of disharmony of conflict over the lords' efforts at this period to increase services and dues, of their uneven incidence, that has been accumulating, proves his main point, that the complexity of the interlocking of different aspects of the villagers' activities and habits served to keep tension within tolerable limits. Most of the time, it did, with the result that most of the time we know very little about the villagers' conscious reflections on their lot. The occasions when tension mounted, occasions of violent quarrelling within a community or between communities, or of protest against a lord's officers, or revolt, give us almost our only direct evidence of the people's ideas of justice. Much has been written on the literature of social protest, from later centuries, and medieval sermons sympathetic to the poor are often quoted, but no one has ever collected the terms of abuse signifying what was considered anti-social in medieval villages, nor has anyone ever brought together what fragments survive of the wording of demands presented in movements of popular resistance or revolt, nor of the wording of discussions of innovation in towns. Evidence of this kind might suggest several different models of dynamic situations and of equilibrium in medieval society.

Periodization and Developmental Typology

The conventional threefold sub-periodization of the middle ages is not very satisfactory, but the sketches it stimulates bring out the ideas that are guiding research and emerging from it. Edith Ennen's presentation of the functional analysis she used to such good effect in tracing the fate of Roman cities in the west comes close to being a typology of a unique kind, a typology of regression and fresh starts.[8]

Peter Munz, in lighter but philosophical vein, has essayed the same thing on a broad canvas.[9] He proposes that the middle ages be equated with the sociological category of disequilibrium and be regarded as terminating when fresh starts in civilization begin to diverge along national lines. Munz's argument ingeniously converts the philosophy of Thomas Hobbes into a political allegory of the destructive effects of imperialism in eroding traditional kinship bonds among tribal peoples beyond the borders of the empire. Roman pressures atomized the Germanic world, making it inevitable that militarization and invasion would follow. The empire dug its own grave. The same reasoning accounts for the despotic character of barbarian rule, the failure to solve succession problems, and the ensuing anarchy. Hobbes' war of each against all, which Hobbes himself mistakenly placed in a primitive state of nature, is on the contrary the result of destroying the social controls of tribal society without providing an opportunity for new ones to form. The appearance of the classic feudal ties between lord and vassal is to Munz a sign that the rule of force and fear was passing, that genuinely civilizing processes were under way.

Munz admits to some purposeful rhetorical exaggeration in this picture. Nobody bothers to look for new evidence to refute an idea that is put forward with cautious timidity and qualified by numerous exceptions. Atomization is a strong word to use of Germanic society when we know so little of the history of the loosening of its tribal controls. Despotic conquest-regimes have occurred in African history in circumstances not attributable to detribalization and where traditional religious sanctions for orderly conduct had not been weakened, as Munz assumes to have been the effect of Christian missionary work among the Germans.[10] Munz's sketch makes no reference to the peasant unrest that was one of Rome's legacies to the Roman world, nor to peasant capacity for organization for constructive ends as well as for revolt. St. Isidore of Seville, who knew about both, in his terse outline of what he considered basic sociology goes out of his way to mention rustic *conciliabula* in which the inhabitants of scattered hamlets came together to make common decisions, presumably to regulate land use. Although the hamlets themselves were not in his opinion true societies, the rustics of a district, in expressing a common will, acquired the moral dignity of a society. He also mentions the holding of rustic festivals (*compita*) at crossroads.[11] Since in his time these were almost certainly still predominantly pagan, the good bishop seems to be indirectly recognizing that they had a social function. The family, defined as inhabiting a *domus*, was also, to St. Isidore, a society. He describes artisans as a low sort of men who do not know their fathers, but makes no criticism of peasant family arrangements. It surely is also relevant that towns were symbols of social order, that in many regions of the early medieval West they were able to exercise some integrative role through trade,[12] and that the coincidence of fairs with religious festivals is an aspect of this role.

Munz has nevertheless done a service in bringing the philosophy of Hobbes into the open in a form that reaffirms the social basis of political order. Early medieval historiography has suffered from the tendency to idealize the Roman and the Carolingian empires. Edouard Perroy's Sorbonne lectures have sufficiently exposed the weakness of the latter,[13] and J. M. Kelly's analysis of Roman litigation has shown how greatly the courts were influenced by *gratia, potentia* and *pecunia*,[14] but the lack of a comparative study of the various provinces in the late empire is a handicap. If it were possible to show how the local populations were reacting to abuses of official power, and which groups were able to protect or to insulate themselves by other kinds of power, we would have a better starting-point for observing these phenomena over the next few centuries, within the former bounds of the Roman empire. Concentrating on matters in which government was ineffective or worked badly, we would find common problems right across the map, if we are to move towards comparative study of the ex-Roman areas and the other cultural areas that made up the medieval world.

The idea of segmentary polities may help in framing the broader developmental typologies that are obviously needed even within the early medieval west. Coming into use among political anthropologists who are trying to reconstruct the history of political organization in Africa, and who were familiar beforehand with medieval Europe, the term refers to polities so weak that they can fall apart

without really disrupting the local units composing them.[15] The
headship of the state has not integrated the life of the whole body,
it has important ritual functions, but has so largely parcelled out
authority for mobilizing defence and for presiding over adjudication
of disputes that the unity of the whole is very much of a facade.
The delegation of authority may not even be fixed; at the extreme
there may be continuous segmentation. Being weak, unable to offer
security to all groups or to articulate their interests satisfactorily,
such a state is beset by internal competition for the influence that
protective power can bring; the weak therefore find security only by
playing off one would-be master against another, turning from one
to another as the balance of influence shifts, and thus reducing the
incidence of violence. The conqueror of such a state may be able
to strengthen the headship but will find it extremely difficult to alter
the rules of the game; besides, the very strength he gains invites the
challenge of rebellion aiming to replace him.

Derived from Durkheim's distinction between different systems
of social organization, the idea of segmentation would serve us
much better, when the Carolingian empire breaks up, than the idea
of fragmentation. The ultimate splitting of the count's authority,
and progressive subinfeudation of jurisdictional rights, exemplify
continuous segmentation. But this could proceed in other ways, and
though it is important to know the precise part that feudalization
played, especially as an index of the influence of northern France,
it is desirable to bring the northern French world into a common
perspective with the Mediterranean and the Celtic, the Scandinavian and the Slavic worlds. For example, in France south of the
Loire continuous segmentation occurred through transformation of
public office into a family possession divisible according to the
prevailing custom of partible inheritance, in Lombard Italy through
feudalization of jurisdictional rights; the Celtic world presents
parallels more directly comparable with African history. The process
of continuous segmentation was reversible and for some centuries
repetitive. Archibald R. Lewis stresses the peaceable working of the
southern French system, with its resemblance to re-aggregation of
family estates when only one of several heirs survived, the whole to
be divided again if need be in the next generation.[16] Elsewhere we
see a mixture of lineage custom, rebellion and conquest.

The idea that balancing devices keep down violence in a weak segmentary state comes from observation on the fringes of today's modernized world rather than from African history, where sources are thin. The notion implies that most groups will not be much disturbed by contenders for power. Liudprand of Cremona put his finger on one of the principles involved when he remarked that "The Italians always prefer to serve two masters."

Ignorance of the actual incidence of violence and extortion in the early middle ages, in areas and years unaffected by raids and invasions, has not prevented lurid generalization about it. So soon as there is evidence of free men turning to patrons it tends, at least in respect of France, to be interpreted in a monolithic perspective presaging classic feudalization. The chances of playing ecclesiastical against lay patrons are rarely considered, and lower echelons of influence helping people to keep out of trouble, to sell and buy land, arrange marriages and get loans are assumed to have left no record. Yet Pierre Bonassie has been able to reconstruct, from a set of deeds relating to the fortunes of a Catalan family of peasant origin, much of the angling for cathedral patronage through the intermediary of scribes and priests that set this family on the rise at the turn of the tenth century.[17] Many features of the scene are peculiar to Catalan society at this time, but similar kinds of people—market-gardening peasants in the environs of a city—might well have been approaching patrons through intermediaries in any city in any part of Europe at any time.

Sketches of the central and late middle ages all now have to note change in population numbers as a major factor in the disturbances of social equilibrium that are the bases of the sub-periodization, but often handle it awkwardly. It can be handled with more confidence only as regional studies advance in depth. George Duby's detail from the Maconnais was especially welcome in showing so clearly how generational increase in population, building up competitive pressure among the landed proprietors for power to extract more from the tenantry, precipitated segmentation of the count's authority, the shaping of the more severe' regime of the seigneurial banalite under military coercion, and continuing segmentation into the classic feudal pattern.[18] His detail shows, too, how cannily the lesser nobles protected themselves from the heightened power of the greater by systematically contracting fidelity to two or several of them. As regards the parallel segmentation where communal associations won a measure of autonomy, it is obvious enough that gravitation of a growing population to town centers was the initial force making old administrative arrangements unsatisfactory. The impetus to church reform, which achieved a kind of lateral segmentation of power, though springing from long-standing moral dissatisfaction, gathered real force in the larger monasteries and in the more thickly populated regions. Unlike the early medieval types of segmentation, all of these eleventh-century resumptions of the process entailed new ways of mobilizing people's energies, and it is the interest of these that so long obscured the seemingly mechanical question of population growth on which they all depended at the start.

Social reasons for this growth, and its actual dimensions, still elude us.[19] Indeed, one can eliminate all social reasons save irregular depression of growth by war casualties and army camp diseases and by abnormalities in the sex ratio due to slave trading, and still, simply because availability of mates would have been reduced by extreme dispersal of small settlements, find differential increase in numbers inevitable and tied to the degree of dispersal of the early medieval population. Extended families may have counteracted this factor to some degree by the practices that missionaries despairingly denounced as incestuous. Again, concentrations of population on better soil speeded the slow drift of technological innovation, even though the sword checked agricultural improvement by competing with the plough for scarce supplies of iron. The interplay of all these circumstances can never be pinned down precisely; rates of growth may have been uniform and infinitesimal. The critical point at which numbers could disturb a social balance was nevertheless bound to be reached first in regions where settlement was more concentrated. North Italy and northern France were bound to reach this point first, regardless of cultural antecedents. In so doing they set up a regional differentiation that enormously widened cultural variations around the medieval map.

Generalization drawn from these particular regions provokes a pointing up of contrasts which are, however, explicable. Thus Karl Bosl admits an archaic aspect to the long German retention of differ-

ent types of law for different social groups, archaic because it preserved a vertical stratification in contrast to the horizontal stratification emerging in twelfth-century France, and is seemingly still close
to the origins of social differentiation through service in the households and retinues of chieftains in pre-Germanic Celtic society.[20]
Is this not at least partially explicable by the fact that feudalization
did not arise in Germany out of the bitter competition for resources
found in northern France, but was imported at a time when population was still sufficiently dispersed to leave at least some groups of
free peasantry some military functions? Competition for power was
competition for patrimonial authority akin to the king's power in
England over the royal demesne. Again, looking back from the
vantage point of the seventeenth century, Dietrich Gerhard sees
Germany as ultimately following the same path as other western
countries in that the end result of the medieval centuries was an
estate society embodying the principle of corporatism first introduced through town privileges, and since the Russian hold on this
principle was weak, he wonders whether Russia had a middle
ages.[21] For explanation he falls back on differences in legal and
religious culture but also on the pull of the frontier in dispersing
the lesser nobles. Both this last factor and the strong hold that the
Kiev princes had on the town through direct interest in trade could
be adduced in explanation of the dominance of patrimonial authority over feudal segmentation in the French mode.[22]

Georges Duby's study of the northern French nobility has now
deepened to a point that suggests a new way of viewing medieval
Europe as a whole, one that can take full account of the spectrum
of national differences but would look more to the processes of cultural differentiation among classes. His method cannot be extended
by facile generalization about principles but demands a focus on the
meeting-places where people's notions of what was admirable took
shape in imagery related to ethical concepts that were general
enough to be communicable. His own focus is on the castle as a
meeting-place of peers and their servitors. It was here, if I understand him correctly, that the nobles, content earlier with sharing in
the aura of the sacred and the heroic that anciently surrounded the
figure of the king, forged in the eleventh and twelfth centuries
around the figures of their own young men the more specific and

accessible ideal of the knight as an embodiment of perfection, finally even foisting this onto the king himself. The new ideal also, as he points out, greatly influenced the self-image of the cleric who was not a contemplative, but was turning to intellectual life in a combative spirit.[23]

One may ask, if the nobility and the clergy prolonged their ascendancy by arrogating to themselves and reshaping symbols of perfection that included, as is manifest in noble heraldry, the predatory ideal that Stone Age man must have formed for himself as a hunter, what was left in the culture to dignify other groups in the productive and organizing roles that were so badly needed and were in fact advancing in the twelfth century? The sheer bulk of chivalrous French literature, and its superior popularity in translation into other vernaculars, would at first sight seem to indicate that in class struggle for symbols of dignity, the nobles were victors over all other lay groups. Yet even in so biased a sample of cultural expression, which naturally makes noble characters the subject of the psychological analysis towards which it moves, one cannot fail to note the rising dignity of bourgeoisie in its background. Except at the start, when they are vehicles of crusading propaganda, the *chansons de geste* never derogate the power of money; their heroes cry out for gold, glory in it, swear by it, hire themselves out as mercenaries; they are indifferent only as to how production gives rise to wealth; they are indifferent to technology except as it produces engines of destruction.

Medieval society could never have achieved even the modest levels of French economic development had the noble's been the only model of life afloat. Warfare and demand for the trappings of elegance would have been the only springs of economic effort, and though these were important even to Italians, Italian merchants were creating symbols of superior power through measurement of time, risk and profit. Jacques Le Goff has fittingly fused these into the leading theme that an all-European view of the later middle ages must take.[24] What remains to be shown is how far the peasantry and artisanry shared in or obstructed a mentality that could turn them into instruments. This problem can best be attacked not by the usual method of treating these groups separately, but by looking more closely into their symbiotic relationships.

The earlier social context of non-peasant lines of work has first to be recalled. For art industries it had been service to the great, still glorified after they had slid into the urban market, in the goldsmith's veneration of Saint Eloi, perfect workman, perfect royal servant and servant of God, paragon of charity and above cheating. Mining and base metallurgy also, to some degree, retained their prehistoric isolation in their own settlements. Masons retained their original migrancy through the thirteenth century. The service villages of central Europe heard of in the tenth century seem arrested half way between market freedom and the condition of the little groups of manorial craftsmen in the West who under weaker authority and more active demand were permitted to redistribute themselves in the best market sites.

In contrast to the growing towns with their specialized craftsmen, the peasant world stands out as one of relatively unspecialized activity. As regards traditional crafts it was a reservoir of rough skills differentiated only by age and sex and under family authority whose main end had always to be the assurance of food supply. Evidence of the spread of water-mills in the West, and instances of peasant ownership of them and of initiative in constructing them, testify to technical intelligence and to an interest in cutting time spent on laborious grinding; but the earliest type adopted, the small horizontally-wheeled mill, did not require the attendance of a miller.[25] However, Kosminsky long ago drew attention to the frequency of occupational surnames in thirteenth-century English villages, and they are not confined to England. His suggestion that rural social position need not have rested on quantities of arable land worked has still not been fully exploited, because interest has focussed on merchant-organized industries.

A simple question that may carry us further is how the peasantry, in different forms of family, spent their time. Comparison with other peasant economies sharpens the question. Chayanov's analyses of the allocation of peasant time not spent in sleep, under the still primitive conditions of arable farming in several regions of early twentieth-century Russia, show barely fifty per cent of waking time going into farm work and the odd jobs of making and repairing equipment.[26] Putting such estimates on an annual basis distorts the problem: harvest occupied almost all of the men's time and put pressure also on the women. Another investigation, in a mountain district of Greek Macedonia, recently estimated household chores as taking only thirty-eight per cent of women's time.[27] Neither Chayanov's nor the Greek figures are correlated with the extent to which clothing and equipment was bought rather than home-made, and in any event, owing to differences in tools and in the strength of work animals no figures from this century can be transferred bodily to a medieval scene. Chayanov's proof of an inverse correlation between the size of family holdings and the importance of craft production for the market is, however, demonstrably relevant. To the extent that the last point has been recognized, it has been associated with the effects of partible inheritance carried to disastrous extremes, merchant-organized industry being seen as gravitating naturally to the cheap labor of miserable cottagers. The social historian should rather ask whether craft production for local markets had not something to do with the origins of differentiation of inheritance customs, making for separation, enlargement or narrowing of households through differing work rhythms and equipment needs and different patterns of family authority. The refashioning of family custom was as complex a matter among peasants as Duby has shown it to be among nobles.[28] Among both it was caught up in the bouncing back and forth between popular and canonical thought that accompanied redirection of the tight but tension-ridden fraternity of the ancient family into narrower forms. Ernest Champeaux in the 1930's traced this theme in French history, and its corollary, the spilling over of the sense of fraternity into wider associations,[29] but its treatment in depth and in an all-European social perspective lags.

Towards More Systematic Organization of Findings

The planning of a social history of medieval Europe would entail some better preliminary organization, through mapping and coding techniques, of what is already known that would be relevant to it. Anything that can be mapped is known better after it is mapped by modern techniques. Would plotting the areas of iron-working and arms manufacture and horse-breeding in the eleventh century turn out to have covered the areas initiating feudal segmentation or being the first to borrow and implement its ideas?

Would a map of peasant family forms in Germanic areas show any correlations with the conclusions reached in the essays on *Adel und Bauern im deutschen Staat des Mittelalters* edited lately by Theodor Mayer?

Coding techniques would serve better in bringing the massive information in hand on administrative and professional groups and their powers into perspective in regard to the formation of state power, and for selected areas a comparable reduction of information on ecclesiastical organization would be essential. The object here would be to catch the process of bureaucratization, in terms of definitely structured roles, types of training and promotion and rewards, and of contacts with subjects or parishioners. Some indices of the character of complaints about corruption, and of the norms of venality that were accepted, would be useful in order to see how far the more old-fashioned types of administration were moving in the general direction of the more rational ones or were frozen. If economic and political historians would add up their information on taxation as a way of redistributing wealth, and on loans as a means of anticipating revenue, and chart the chronology of public and private taxation, it would be an enormous help. The chronology of changes in the forms of military service, and the size of the floating body of mercenaries could be roughly charted; hopefully the numbers of people taking arms in rebellions could sometimes be pinned down. How smaller incidents of violence arose, and how they subsided, are vital pieces of information.

To cover the map would be neither possible, even for the later medieval centuries, nor necessary on these and other matters. To study a few types among the hundreds of little towns that flourished for a time would be sufficient, though they need to be examined from many angles, from the point of view of the social bases of credit structure in the countrysides,[30] of proto-legal services available to help people keep out of trouble, of degrees of differentiation between peasant and artisan consciousness.

In the end perhaps the question that would loom among the larger puzzles, is that of the use people made of their time. Chayanov's peasantry were calculated to spend roughly a quarter of their waking time at festivals, including presumably, weddings and funerals. Late medieval studies show saints day observance dimin-

ishing, but give us little evidence on the intensity of work.[31] The
ceremonial "overhead" of the society seems to have remained very
high in proportion to its resources.

NOTES

1. Franklin J. Pegues, *The Lawyers of the Last Capetians*, Princeton
University Press, 1962.

2. F. Vercauteren, "Conceptions et méthodes de l'histoire des villes
medievales au cours du dernier demi-siècle," *XIIe Congrès International
des Sciences historiques*, vol. V, Actes, Vienna, 1965, pp. 649–66 at
p. 663. Ira M. Lapidus has developed the same idea in regard to medieval
Islamic cities, with more emphasis on religious solidarities, in conference
papers edited under his name, *Middle Eastern Cities*, Berkeley, 1969,
pp. 47–79.

3. David Herlihy, *Medieval and Renaissance Pistoia*, Yale University
Press, 1967, chapter 4.

4. Gabriel Le Bras' phrase, in "Sociologie de l'église dans le haut
moyen age," in *Le Chiesi, Settimane di studio del centro italiano di
studi sull'alto medioevo*, 1960, translated in my *Early Medieval Society*,
New York, 1967. On social study of local popularity of saints' names, see
Ch. Higounet, *Bordeaux pendant le haut moyen age*, Bordeaux, 1963,
pp. 214–20.

5. "Culture cléricale et traditions folkloriques dans la civilisation
mérovingienne," *Annales ESC*, 1967, pp. 780–91.

6. Harry A. Miskimin's *The Economy of Early Renaissance Europe*,
1969, like many other recent essays, turns on a pessimistic view of late
medieval state power as a threat to freedom.

7. G. C. Homans, *English Villagers of the Thirteenth Century*, Harvard University Press, 1942. Homans' ideas on social equilibrium have
been developed further in sociological writings: *The Human Group*,
New York, 1950 and *Social Behavior: Its Elementary Forms*, New York,
1961.

8. Edith Ennen, "Les differents types de formation des villes euro-
péannes," *Le Moyen Age*, t. LXII, 1956, translated in my *Early Medieval Society*, 1967.

9. Peter Munz, "The Concept of the Middle Ages as a Sociological
Category," An Inaugural Address: The Victoria University of Wellington,
1969.

10. Max Gluckman, *Politics, Law and Ritual in Tribal Society,* Aldine Publishing Company, Chicago, 1965, chapter 4.

11. *Etymologiarum,* Lib. XV, cap 11, 14, 15.

12. David M. Nicholas has drawn together the results of a great deal of recent research on this point in his "Medieval Urban Origins in Northern Continental Europe: State of Research and Some Tentative Conclusions," *Studies in Medieval and Renaissance History,* VI, University of Nebraska Press, 1969, pp. 55–114.

13. Edouard Perroy, "Les Carolingiens" (mimeographed, "Les cours de Sorbonne." Centre de Documentation Universitaire, 1961), chapter 8 translated in my *Early Medieval Society,* 1967.

14. J. M. Kelly, *Roman Litigation,* Oxford, 1966.

15. See Aidan W. Southall, *Alur Society,* 1956, and Max Gluckman, *op. cit.*

16. Archibald R. Lewis, *The Development of Southern French and Catalan Society 718–1050,* University of Texas Press, 1965.

17. Pierre Bonassie, "Une famille de la campagne barcelonalse et ses activités économiques aux alentours de l'an Mil," *Annales du Midi,* t. 76, 1964.

18. Georges Duby, *La société aux XIe et XIIe siècles dans la région mâconnaise,* 1953.

19. For a critique of Lamprecht's work on the Mosel valley see Goran Ohlin, "No Safety in Numbers," in Henry Rosovsky, ed., *Industrialization in Two Systems: Essays in Honor of Alexander Gerschenkron,* 1966, at pp. 81–84.

20. Karl Bosl, "Ueber sociale Mobilitat in der mittelalterlichen Gesellschaft," in his *Frühformen der Gessellschaft im mittelalterlichen Europa,* 1964.

21. Dietrich Gerhard, "Regionalismus und ständisches Wesen als ein Grundthema europäischer Geschichte," *Historische Zeitschrift,* 1952, Bd. 174, pp. 301–37.

22. For discussion and applications of the concept of patrimonial authority see Serif Mardin, "Power, Civil Society and Culture in the Ottoman Empire," *Comparative Studies in Society and History,* II, 1969.

23. Georges Duby, "The Diffusion of Cultural Patterns in Feudal Society," *Past and Present,* April 1968.

24. Jacques LeGoff, "Le temps du travail," *Le Moyen Age,* t. LXIX, 1963, pp. 597–613.

25. Abbott Payson Usher, *A History of Mechanical Inventions,* 1929, pp. 177–81.

26. A. V. Chayanov, *The Theory of Peasant Economy,* ed. Daniel Thorner et al., Richard D. Irwin, Inc., Homewood, Illinois, 1966.

27. Cited from work of G. J. Kitsopanides published in 1965, in Colin Clark and Margaret Haswell, *The Economics of Subsistence Agriculture,* 2nd ed., 1966, pp. 135–64.

28. Georges Duby, "Structures de parenté et noblesse. France du nord IXᵉ–XIIᵉ siècles," in *Miscellanea Medievalla in memoriam Jan Frederik Niermeyer*, Groningen, 1967, pp. 149–66.

29. See his two articles in *Revue historique de droit français et étrangers*, in 1933 and 1937.

30. An article by Ellen Wedemeyer to appear in *Mediaeval Studies*, Toronto, 1970, "Social Groupings at the Fair of St. Ives 1275–1302" goes very thoroughly into the kinds of men who stood pledge for others.

31. See J. A. Raftis, "The Structure of Commutation in a Fourteenth-Century Village," in *Essays in Medieval History Presented to Bertie Wilkinson*, ed. T. A. Sandquist and M. R. Powicke, Toronto 1969 and Bronislaw Geremek, *Le salariat dans l'artisanat parisien aux XIIIᵉ–XVᵉ siècles*, The Hague, 1968. International migrations of labor may have stepped up work intensity, as the Flemish did in England: see my "Aliens in and around London in the Fifteenth Century," in *Studies in London History Presented to Philip Edmund Jones*, London, 1969, and also p. 101 in this volume.

II

Social Attitutes

Introduction

PHILIPPE WOLFF

I am very pleased to write an introduction to this series of articles from the work of Sylvia Thrupp since they deal so much with London. For in London we met, Sylvia Thrupp and I, in 1939. I was then in search of a field for my research, under the guidance of Marc Bloch. As I had received a grant for this work in London, he sent me to Eileen Power and suggested that some study of the economy and society of later medieval London might be attempted. As soon as I met Eileen Power, she exclaimed: "But someone is doing the job and quite well!" That person was Sylvia Thrupp; and the result of her work, as everybody knows, was to be *The Merchant Class of Medieval London, 1300–1500*. From this clash developed a strong and lasting friendship.

This series of articles is extremely varied and shows her extraordinary range both of knowledge and of methods. The first one is unpublished—and incomplete, though well elaborated. Much has been written about the progress of Western medieval civilization and a good deal about the zenith of the Islamic world. But what about the attitudes of the Westerners confronting—as much as they could—this Islamic world? The survey of the early Middle Ages has perforce to be restricted to ecclesiastical authors and to lay leaders. Already the ideal of the city is coming to the fore: only peoples which possess cities can be praised. In common with Edith Ennen, Jean Lestocquoy, and other scholars, Sylvia Thrupp makes the remark of a true historian: ". . . to smile at early medieval pride in these towns is ahistorical. To insist that by the standards of times of denser population and more vigorous economic life they were not really urban may in many instances be true but is irrelevant." Then, with the eleventh and twelfth centuries comes the treasure of the French chansons de geste and romances—full of legends, of course, but also reflecting the experience that Western warriors and pilgrims had of Muslims. Curiously enough, the stress is not so much on the religious as on the social attitudes: the "French" nobles admire the Muslim way of life, as well as their enemies' skill in war, their ability to build as well as to organize, their knowledge of the secrets of Nature (which at the same time is exemplified by the quest of Western scholars for Arabic science), and they boast only of being as shrewd as their opponents. By the thirteenth century, as economic advances in the West confront a decline in the Muslim economy, the impact of the rising bourgeoisie is to be felt in the changed depictions of the Muslim world. Thus, though incomplete, this essay is no less interesting for its original research than for the conclusion to which it leads: that social attitudes count first.

No essay is more illustrative of what Sylvia Thrupp meant by "comparative studies" than the second one. The perception of a modern traveler may be at its origin: "We are as conscious as any people of the visual esthetic order, or lack of it, in our cities; indeed, air travel, especially when night blots out the countryside and leaves only the patterns of street lighting, makes us conscious in a new way of the beauty or defects of their ground plan. Yet few are aware of the part that the esthetic character of the city has played in developing and maintaining the sense of order out of which civilization grew and on which it depends." The initial, cosmic sense of order that she describes and the endeavor of any significant settlement to conform to it are at the root of the city's importance in antiquity, even if it came with the passage of time to be supported by the machinery of government and social order. The "idea of the city as standing for social order" survived the age of barbarism and was inherited by the modern and contemporary periods, in which the city more and more becomes the source of economic progress, which will develop so as to make "any urban-rural dichotomy patently unrealistic." But through the centuries, this ideal has its counterpart: the criticisms proferred by moralists in the Judaic and Greek traditions, much later by economic pessimism, and more recently by sociologists who approach "the city" as something pathological. Thus we come to questions with which we are today urgently confronted. Sylvia's conclusions are both pessimistic and an incentive: "There are vast gaps in our knowledge of city history. . . . Today's planner cannot wait for the long labor that historians have before them on such questions. History can tell him only what he knows already, that his problem is a philosophical one." These lines happily emphasize that our labor—I mean, that of historians—is more than a scholarly game with more or less sophisticated rules. It answers fundamental questions, and I agree that, between the historian and those entrusted with present responsibilities, there is no unbridgeable gap, that they belong to the same world of thought—an idea, of course, which has to be taken with care.

For the reader, who may be astounded by such winds off the high sea, nothing can be more reassuring than the third essay: "Aliens in and around London in the Fifteenth Century." For the method used in it is a very classical one, and it is used with much caution. The main piece of evidence is the collection of the Exchequer records of the alien subsidy introduced in England in 1440. Six full pages are devoted to the description of the documents, to the discussion of the problems associated with their use by the historian, to the consideration of possible misinterpretations, before Sylvia Thrupp comes to the happy conclusion that "even in plague years, the City [of London] returns inspire confidence." Then she proceeds with her own statement and displays a great range of interest and a fine sense of the questions that really matter. With the supplementary help of a number of wills, she is able, not only to assert—as much as can be done—how many of these aliens there were and what their nationality, their business, and their wealth were, but also to form some idea of the mutual attitudes of aliens and Londoners. The conclusions are rather optimistic: "Evidence that fifteenth-century Londoners were at all bothered by cultural differences between themselves and the aliens is hard to come by." Of course there was commercial rivalry, and there were outbursts of wrath against Italians or Lowlanders. But it never lasted long. And the "pragmatic temper" of the Londoners, "judging a person not by his origins but by his practical intelligence, gave aliens a meeting ground with Englishmen on terms of mutual respect as individuals." The history of "mentalities" is much in favor today. Cannot this essay, published in 1969 but after many years of elaboration, be considered in its way as a pioneering work?

Altogether—and these lines should already have shown it— among the many historians that I know, Sylvia Thrupp's originality is, in my opinion, to combine to an unequaled degree qualities which usually belong to two different types of scholars, who for that reason are rather unsympathetic to each other: the cautious, matter-of-fact scholar, who analyzes his documents with the utmost scrutiny, who answers only the questions to which they obviously

point, who does not like to swerve very far from his evidence, and
for whom some narrowness of view may be the price for this solid
soundness; and the more ambitious thinker, who considers evidence
as material at his disposal and treats it in the way that his reading,
his personal reflections, his sense of historical problems suggest to
him, who likes comparisons between comparable situations in different peoples and times, but who pays for that wide horizon by
some adventurous or even debatable assertions. To avoid the defects
of both types is not so easy a task, and very few people indeed are
able to manage it as does Sylvia Thrupp.

Comparison of Cultures in the Middle Ages: Western Standards as Applied to Muslim Civilization in the Twelfth and Thirteenth Centuries

The more is known of relations between West Europeans and the Muslim peoples in the Middle Ages, the less satisfactory the older generalizations seem. Rationalist historians, assuming that religious prejudice was a major barrier, took the "commonsense" view that personal contact in interludes and areas of peace naturally reduced this, enabling Christians to assess Muslim culture objectively.[1] Sir Hamilton Gibb took us much further, in the light of general principles that appear to govern all borrowing by one culture from another.[2] The West borrowed from Islam, he shows, only what it could absorb into its own pre-existing activities and ideas, and it could absorb nothing that conflicted in any way with its own fundamental values. As he implies, a sense of conflict of values narrows the field of perception. The question is raised here, whether one's perception of another culture is not also affected by a predisposition to classify it as inferior, equal, or superior, to one's own. How, outside the sensitive sphere of theology, did Westerners compare Muslim peoples with themselves? It will be shown that long before they encountered Islam they had secular standards for making such judgments.

The evidence has to be mainly evidence of opinion. Whenever possible, it is desirable to distinguish between opinions that were correct and those that were exaggerated or false, though not for the purpose of rejecting the latter. It is patterns of bias that best reveal emotionally charged attitudes. Between the sixth century and the eleventh the evidence sampled here is of three kinds: ecclesiastical opinion about European pagans, contemporary expression of the values associated with town life, and efforts to take stock of Western advances along the road of civilization. For the twelfth and thirteenth centuries the choice is from the reworking of experience of contact with Muslims in the body of French chansons de geste and romances which so delighted northern Europe. These reveal the emotional response of those who were excited by the world of Islam but who stayed at home.

The earliest medieval Western thinking about people and customs held to be inferior is to be found in ecclesiastical judgments of European pagans. These are monotonously biased. The pagan, as in Bede's picture of the Britons,[3] is perpetually drunk, disorderly, and immoral. The stereotype is the inverse of the ideal of the rational man. Caesarius of Arles's abhorrence of the diabolical (i.e., pagan) New Year's festival which peasants celebrated is illuminating.[4] The peasants, he says, eat and drink all night as though to persuade themselves they will have abundance throughout the coming year. Whether he was consciously condemning the element of sympathetic magic apparent here, or only the drinking, gluttony, and wastefulness, is not clear. He is even more disgusted because men at these festivities degrade themselves by putting on animal skins and heads, *ut homines non esse videantur;* some also basely dress up as women. The whole condemnation is on grounds of irrationality. It has much in common with the attitude of a modern who is contemptuous of primitives as childish, improvident, and lazy. The charges of immorality against pagans and backslipping converts are of course known to refer mostly to the yardstick of Christian rules, novel to pagans, demanding strict exogamy outside any commonly recognized degrees of kinship. Clergy sought to uphold these rules by intimating that the head of a pagan household would sleep with any woman living there: such a man was bestial, no better than a pig.[5]

Attacks on pagan religion for its falsity carried overtones of secular values that were dear to Christian clerics. Missionaries were proud of their superior cleverness in religious debate, of being able to trap pagans in illogical absurdities. There was pride also in Christian liturgy as being more orderly and impressive, especially musically, than pagan ceremony.

Scandinavian pagans were looked down on for an additional reason: they lived in the frozen north. Geographical lore made the

northern zone fade into a grim waste. The missionaries who ultimately went north would have known beforehand of the existence of
seaports, but they might reasonably have expected inland settlements to be scanty and poor, rustic rather than urban.

The laity of early Western Christendom can hardly have seen
eye to eye with their ecclesiastical teachers on all these criteria of
inferiority. But their royal leaders undeniably concurred with the
bishops on one crucial matter, that of the necessity of having urban
headquarters. E. Ewig has fully documented the point, showing
that all of the Visigothic, Ostrogothic, Burgundian, and Frankish
kings, from the start, had their seat in a capital city or town, some
using auxiliary capitals as well.[6] This was not so much to keep up
with the bishops, as to prove themselves worthy successors of Roman
governors in the West. The royal counts followed suit, basing themselves on provincial urban headquarters.[7]

Through the work of Edith Ennen, Jean Lestocquoy, and other
scholars it is coming to be realized that to smile at early medieval
pride in these towns is ahistorical.[8] To insist that by the standards of
times of denser population and more vigorous economic life they
were not really urban may in many instances be true but is irrelevant. Pirenne's narrow economic definition of a town, like Max
Weber's emphasis on differing degrees of civic integration, was
designed for the purpose of drawing particular historical contrasts.
Early medieval urbanism is best understood through Edith Ennen's
method of inventorying the functions of different types of towns as
they declined or grew, and through Lewis Mumford's perception of
the psychological stimulus that may arise from the close physical
proximity of different social groups. To Mumford, one of the prin-
cipal functions of a town is to serve as a meeting place for heterogeneous elements permanently settled there and for strangers.[9] By
choosing towns as headquarters, the early medieval kings and counts
ensured the superior dignity of these places as centers of political
and military ceremonial as well as of religious ceremonial. Although
governmental administration soon dwindled into the work of a
palace staff, the choice ensured also that life in these places would
be more exciting, socially and culturally more complex, with more
economic activity, than if they had been reduced simply to cult
centers and centers of ecclesiastical administration.

It is simpler, however, to start from the psychological fact of early medieval pride in the places where the political and ecclesiastical elites had their main residences. This pride created and sustained, in the minds of the time, a very sharp status gradient between these places and others thought to be humble and dreary. The more austerely otherworldly monks embraced an opposite scale of values, but as a protest against secular values their withdrawal from the world was not very effective. The most concise expression of the accepted status gradient and of the secular values it embodied comes from Bishop Isidore of Seville.[10] St. Isidore ranks the different types of settlement known to him by four parallel standards: the nature and relative size of the population, and jurisdictional and protective functions. At the very bottom are the hamlets (*loca*), tiny communities huddled among the fields in the open country (*pagus*). The village (*vicus*) is a more considerable nucleus, laid out around roads; but like isolated forts in the hills or in the plains (*castella, castra*) and like the *pagus* with its hamlets, it is inhabited only by the vulgar sort of men and is jurisdictionally dependent on places higher in the scale. To be a larger center with better buildings, surrounded by a protective wall, gives a place the higher status of a little town (*oppidum*). If a town is the seat of minor jurisdiction, St. Isidore calls it a *municipium*; if it is the seat of higher jurisdiction, exercised under the prince's immediate supervision, it has the dignity of a city (*civitas*). From the *oppidum* up, these higher-level communities are all urban, *urbs* being a generic term for the tangible characteristics that distinguish them from villages and forts. Satellite suburbs built around a city have a half-way status. *Civitas*, too, is for St. Isidore a generic term for an intangible characteristic which should be manifest in all forms of human society—the ideal norm of harmony. One may fairly infer that the places actually called cities had a distinctive symbolic aura; they were the supreme symbols of social order. Like Gregory of Tours, St. Isidore departs from common opinion in not deriving the right to be called a city from the establishment of a bishopric. Except on this last point, and despite the use of variant terminology at the middle of the scale, the nomenclature that chroniclers and poets apply to particular places in Gaul over the next few centuries confirms Isidore's picture of a sharp status gradient.

It is therefore easy to see how a degree of urbanization that was in reality absurdly slight could affect Western attitudes to other cultures in which there was less or none at all. A people with no permanent settlements but poor villages and a few fishing ports, as in the frozen north and along the southeastern shores of the Baltic, would be looked down on because their conditions of life were so much on a dead level. Small ports made not much difference. The fortified garrison towns in which Slav princes lived could command more respect because of the presence of those dignitaries, but their open market settlements, though periodically swollen by traffic, were physically no better than the numerous Western villages that were equipped with a church and a tavern.[11] The German colonists who in the twelfth century infiltrated these market centers and multiplied small towns of the Western type would have had reason to feel that they were introducing a superior culture.

Urbanism, then, gave a tangible measure of comparison between cultures which took account also of intangible qualities. It follows that early medieval Westerners were vulnerable, by their own standards, to knowledge or rumor of people whose cities were grander than theirs, with citizens more renowned for enterprise and brains. As the heirs of what remained of Roman urbanism in the fifth-century West, early medieval men had always lived with the consciousness of their inferiority to the ancient Romans in their great days. Only the educated gratefully realized the immensity of their cultural debt to Rome, but everyone, in areas of Roman construction, was reminded by ruins that Roman cities had been more splendid. For nonintellectuals the notion of Roman superiority at some point began to carry a sting. There were several kinds of balm for the sting. Pilgrims' reports of the magnificence of the churches in Rome were gratifying: the transformation of Rome into a great religious capital was a more or less contemporary achievement. Imitation of the Romans in adopting the Trojans as ancestors was a move that went beyond imitation; it was a symbolic assertion of kinship, of the inheritance of common potentialities, a way of removing the stigma of "barbarian" origins. Like the claim of kings to divine descent, it may have been open to skepticism. The legend of Trojan origins was sanctioned only by the imaginative appeal of the stories with which it could be embroidered. These were far richer than any that could be woven around the alternative notion that more biblically minded writers offered, of descent from Japhet. Father Noah was beguiling, but Japhet was only a name; he could not stand beside Aeneas or Antenor as a hero. Nor did he bear the glory of a city whose citizens were famed for the very things the Franks most admired—wealth, beauty, valor, endurance, skill in building, and success in love. Historians have taken the Frankish legend of Trojan origins seriously only as a possible clue to the later Frankish migrations. In its seventh-century form, its interest is in the fact that the migration was from one city or town to another.[12] Numerous towns, as is known, sooner or later appropriated the legend. Outside the Scandinavian world its connection with urbanism may be obvious, but this gives the legend a symbolic significance which warrants emphasis.

A third source of balm to Westerners bored with talk of Roman superiority lay in reflection about change and civilizational progress. The Romans and the Trojans had fallen, but the Trojans who migrated had shown the capacity to rise again. This idea is written into the seventh-century Frankish version of the legend. To avoid trouble with the Romans, the Trojans abandoned the city they had founded in Pannonia, where they had flourished under a king, and moved to the right bank of the Rhine. Here they regressed; they did not found a city but lived first in little German towns (*oppida*), and had no king but only *principes*. But they recovered. They decided to choose a king, like other *gentes,* they developed laws, and after living for a time around a *castellum* they finally took over a series of Roman towns and cities in Belgium and the Rhineland. The writer's conception of their progress after this is limited to the story of Frankish military triumphs. It is on military success that most later boasting of progress rests. The ninth-century monk Otfrid of Weissenburg asserts that his people are as brave and quick-witted as the Romans and have as much innate intelligence as the Greeks; they are backward only in not having written hymns in their native "frenkisg," and Otfrid sees no reason why they should not remedy this.[13] Two centuries later, William the Conqueror's biographer (a cleric of noble birth who had done soldiering) proclaims that his hero is a far better general than Julius Caesar; he had conquered all of England in a few days with a smaller force than Caesar had employed in his only partially successful invasion.[14] For the first declaration that Western prowess surpassed that of the ancient Romans to be a little flamboyant is altogether appropriate. True, there had never been a soldierly equivalent to the scholars' sense of inferiority to the great Roman stylists, for the clergy were always quick to explain defeat at the hands of pagans as due solely to the Christians' sinfulness. Yet the Norman poet's relegation of Caesar to second place is a landmark.

By the eleventh century Western self-confidence was being bolstered also by a rational consciousness of material progress. The disasters of earlier centuries, and the advantage that preachers took of them to exalt spiritual values, had not dampened the desire to live in more security and comfort. The shameless exaggeration of population size and of trading opportunities in early medieval town eulogies testifies to the direction of wishful thinking. In Venice, whose growth from a fishing village to an emporium had been unchecked, and where Cassiodorus's description of its earlier state kept recollection of this alive, there is no ground for doubting that a sense of achieved progress was strong. Nor is there reason to doubt that this was true also of other areas of advancing urbanization in the eleventh century. The vision of the future may well have been limited, on the part alike of kings and other town lords and of townspeople, to the hope of some continued increase of wealth through trade and industry and to immediate political objectives. If any man in the late eleventh century ever speculated on the possibility of an indefinitely continuing surge of material and moral progress he would have been met by the two pessimistic arguments in *The City of God*, that material progress is at the best of times precarious, and that no state can count on being free from invasion.[15] A still harder-headed argument was at hand, in Urban II's explanation of war within Europe as being due to overpopulation.

There was an uneasy idea, with a long tradition behind it, that in the Orient things were better, that people were richer there, and cleverer.[16] Lellia Ruggini, who has proved our tenth-century version of the legends about Alexander to have been copied from a text, long since lost, of the mid-fourth century, has suggested that conservative pagan opinion in Rome was at that time falling back on Alexander and his exploits as a means of defending the glory of the pagan past against Christian denigration.[17] The fact that Alexander outclassed any Roman hero may well in turn have constituted part of his appeal to early medieval Christians growing weary of praise of Rome. If there was a preeminently superior civilization, it was clear by the ninth century, and perhaps earlier, that its genius was Asian: it lay in India, where Alexander had found fabulous natural wealth; it lay in Persia, whose riches could be judged by Haroun-al-Raschid's gifts to Charlemagne; what little was generally known, north of the Alps, of Byzantium, would suggest that it, too, had something of this exotic genius. Jean Lestocquoy has expressed doubt that anyone in Gaul at this time was worried by the thought of superior cities elsewhere; he thinks people were too complacent.[18] Indeed, there is no reason to worry about a superior civilization which leaves one alone. But Islam did not leave the West alone. And Islam had even more of the East about it than Byzantium.

The chansons de geste and romances that bring their heroes into contact with Muslims are our best clue to the views of the various Muslim peoples prevailing among French nobles and their followers and probably also among the upper bourgoisie in the twelfth and thirteenth centuries.[19] The less popular ones were less popular because they are dull and long-winded, and not because they contain idiosyncratic or unpopular observations of Muslims. Descriptive detail falls into a pattern which was obviously designed to interest readers. The elements of the pattern are the cosmopolitanism of the world of Islam, its power and wealth, the splendor of its greater cities, the cleverness of its people, the beauty of its horses and its women. The poets make the French world compete on all these points, but they award it first prize only for courage. Situations are selected to accord with themes that give the French heroes moral grandeur. In the chansons de geste the overarching themes are the problem of order, and the problem of justice seen from the point of view of the noble treated unjustly by his king.[20] In the romances the horizon narrows to the problems of the young noble who has to make his way with little or no income in a competitive age. The Muslim world then ceases to buttress the major theme of dramatic conflict, to become a scene of incidental adventure.

The convention of setting the chansons de geste in the Carolingian age obliges the poets to inflate the Muslim forces, for dramatic effect, to gigantic proportions. In *Ogier de Danemarche* they take all the south of Italy, and Rome; repulsed there by Ogier's prowess, they return and flood north to Hainault; their emir, claiming that his ancestors had held Montmartre, plans to take Paris; Charlemagne's Nestor, Duke Naimes, warns him that all of the churches in France are in danger of going over to worship of the Mohammedan god Tervagant.[21] This inflation gives the writers a chance to parade the diversity of peoples that Islam has brought into alliance, and to try to balance it by the list of vassals and friends who attend Charlemagne's court or come to his aid in the wars. The list of the regions from which he can draw them—from Brittany, the Low Countries, Lorraine, Bavaria, Burgundy, and all of the territories of France—is a long one, but hardly as impressive as the Muslim array. Emirs come from India, Persia, Turkey, Arabia, Egypt, and Spain. Kings, invariably rich, reinforce them. The rank and file of the armies, too, is cosmopolitan. In the *Enfances de Guillaume* the attack on Narbonne is mounted by Slavs, Saracens, and Turks; in *Ogier le Danois* 30,000 Turcople archers terrorize the civilian population of France, with Bedouins forming part of the army at Rome; Almoravides and Berbers (Barbarins) are known. Saracen and pagan are generic terms, though Persians are usually distinguished separately. The ethnic diversity of Islam is well understood. It is proof of might and a cause of wonder; Charlemagne's empire cannot match it.

The Muslims are richer than the French. They go to war better equipped, with vast fleets to transport their armies. The cavalry force of 100,000 that wipes out an inferior French force on the sandy field of Larchamp had come by sail from Saragossa, every man with an Arab horse, a white hauberk, a great shield, and fine weapons.[22] After one of the battles Charlemagne's knights are so dented that they have to reequip themselves by stripping the dead.[23] All of the heroes dress well, but the most elegant man in the whole roster of figures is King Karaheus of Persia, who strolls about Rome in robes of brilliant color fastened with gold buttons.[24]

All of the poets see wealth and power as measured, secured, and symbolized, by the possession of cities. In particular the French counts always identify themselves with their capitals: their lands and castles are secondary. A city stands for gold. When a king or a noble finds a proposal foolhardy or unworthy he dismisses it by crying that he would not yield "for all the gold" of Pavia, Paris, Montpelier, or some other city; in the twelfth century he will usually name a Mediterranean city. Every capital, whether it be Christian or Muslim, is wonderful (*mirabile*) because it has some absolute quality of majesty as a center where justice is administered. But there are degrees of majesty according to the splendor of the ceremony that surrounds the court. Charlemagne's palace at "Ais" is guarded by fourteen counts, and he holds court one Easter *mirabillose*, entertaining seventeen kings and thirty bishops in his palace at Paris.[25] But Charlemagne has only an ordinary throne, while the Emir Gaudisi at Babylon in Egypt (Cairo) delivers justice from a dais raised on fifty golden pillars and planted with a pine tree.[26] The tree, the pillars, and the great tower in Cairo, are all of them ancient cosmological symbols. Cairo is also livelier than Paris. Countless suitors come and go at the palace; thousands of servants are busy training the emir's birds and caring for his horses; thousands of courtiers are playing chess, dallying with young ladies, or sitting over their wine.[27] To reach the palace, moreover, one has to pass over a series of four bridges.

The Saracens are better builders and use more marble, the supreme token of wealth and art, than the French. Charlemagne's palace at Paris is of marble,[28] and Rome holds its own. The Muslim kings who occupy it are happy in a marble palace, and the city is enclosed within a double circuit of marble walls.[29] But Narbonne, Orange, and Cordova in the hands of Saracen captors are transformed. When Charlemagne is able to observe closely, from the shelter of a siege engine, the beautiful Syrian workmanship of the Narbonne walls and towers, he forbids his men to damage them with the engine, and uses scaling-ladders instead.[30] When, through Aymeri's valor—he has fallen in love with the city—the French at last rout its garrison of 20,000 soldiers, they find a rich marble palace, and masses of gold and silver bars stored in the synagogues. The fortifications of Orange are equally strong, and the palace in which four kings hold court there, named Gloriate, is resplendent with vaulted chambers, carvings, and mural paintings.[31] In the *Prise de Cordres et de Sebille* there is less descriptive detail, but obvious wonder at the strength of Cordova—it has a formidable prison—at the store of plate and candelabra to be looted, at the wealth of the surrounding countryside, and at the trade—with England and

Normandy and in Spanish cloth and Syrian silk and war-horses—
that has enriched its bourgeoisie.[32]

The Saracens are better organizers than the French. Notably,
they provision their armies well. The French twice plunge hare-
brained into battle at Larchamp with no provisions at all. Two
surviving heroes, fainting after three days' fighting on an empty
stomach, are fortunately able to rout a band of Saracens who are
dining well at tables set up on the shore, and to revive themselves
with some of their meat and wine.[33] Charlemagne's men do not even
carry bread with them on their way to Rome. The French are
astonished to discover how well Narbonne had been provisioned
against siege. In the Saracen thrust to the north, though the French
become utterly disorganized, the Saracens are able to eat well and
have a number of their ladies with them.[34] King Brehus, whom Ogier
finds sitting comfortably in a tent and challenges to single combat,
first regales him with a meal of Ogier's choice—partridges and other
birds that had been caught.

Apart from building and logistics, the poets try to make the
French at least as shrewd as their opponents. They are very proud
of French army engineers: these men are named, they are in command of teams of carpenters and stonecutters, and are said to know
as much about engines as clerks do of Latin.[35] The Saracens, on
seeing Charlemagne's siege engine rolled up to the walls of Narbonne, are terror-struck, exclaiming, "Molt sont François sachant!"[36]
The engineer whom Charlemagne engages to try to flush Ogier out
of the castle in Tuscany where he has taken refuge as a rebel is
from *Outre-mer;* he had perfected his skill there, had directed the
siege of Alexandria, and had learned to make Greek fire, from sul-
phur and quicksilver.[37] This burns the little town at the foot of the
castle, but Ogier in a sally kills the engineer. Ogier has, however,
the brains to be tricky. He conceals from Charlemagne the fact
that he has been deserted by all his men by propping wooden
dummies against the parapets of his tower. Robert Guiscard's biographer has a similar admiration for his hero's ingenuity, telling
how *per varias artes* he caught a huge fish which though horrible
to look at was edible.[38]

Wisdom (*sagesse*) is also knowledge of the world and its ways,
which in a cosmopolitan world calls for knowledge of languages.
Guillaume d'Orange, who marries a Saracen and lives to be over

one hundred, manages to learn two or three of the Saracen languages—*barbarin, aleis,* and *hermin* (Armenian)—as well as *Sala-
moneis* (Hebrew?), Greek, and two kinds of German (*Teis* and
Allemande).[39] No other French character seems to be able to con-
verse with Saracens in their own language unless he or she has
been in captivity. The heroine of *La Fille de Comte de Pontieu,* who
is taken prisoner and marries the Sultan of Aumarie, is within two
years or so able to understand *sarrasinois* and to speak it "molt
bien."[40] For the most part the poets follow the facile convention of
modern historical novelists, of ignoring language difficulties. But
when, for greater verisimilitude, they face it, the French either
speak their own "latin,"[41] or employ Saracen interpreters (*latiniers*).
Charlemagne in Italy employs one named Jossés, who has spent
fourteen years in France and knows Paris and Beauvais particularly
well.[42] Saracen *latiniers,* in the fourteenth-century romance, *Guillaume de la Barre,* are available in African port towns, where their
role as go-between gives them great influence.[43] It is not specifically
noted that any of the Saracen leaders has troubled to learn European
languages. But it is clear that the advantage, in linguistic ability,
lies on the Saracen side.

The French are vulnerable also because of their superstitious
reverence for astrology and necromancy in which the Jews and
Saracens excel. The old Aymeri, sick and frightened by a dream,
calls on a Jew named Saolin to interpret it for him. Saolin, a *sages
clers,* is apparently attached to Aymeri's household at Narbonne:

> En la cort ot un jui Saolin
> Sajes homs fu et de grant sens porpris;
> Il ot un livre paré de toz latins
> Ou li art sont et li sonje descrit;[44]

His is the only book I have noticed in the chansons de geste that
touch on Islam. Among the Saracens the magic arts are passed on
mysteriously and are especially the property of women. At Orange
the Princess Orable, married by her brothers to King Thiebaut of
Arabia, whom she dislikes, after shattering his nerves at the wedding
feast by staging a kind of magical cinema, turns him for the night
into a little golden ball.[45] The Queen of France continues to suspect
her converted Saracen sister-in-law, Guillaume's countess, of prac-
ticing sorcery:

Dame Guiburc fu nè en paisnisme,
Si set maint art e mainte pute guische.
Ele conuist herbes, ben set temprer mescines [poisons]⁴⁶

The poets do not, however, ascribe Saracen strength to powers of evil origin. True, one of the Saracen giants whom Ogier kills, a man from the kingdom of Cordova, is said to be "de diable engenrés"; he has two pairs of arms and a double head.⁴⁷ But the giants are not devils. One of them, a Cordovan prince named Reneward who is captured as a child and sold by slave merchants to the king's kitchen in Paris, speaks *latin* and becomes a Christian.⁴⁸ He is represented only as a little stupid and awkward. Horrible African giants reflect the dismay created by knowing that the Muslims were able to recruit soldiers of tall and strong physique from a variety of African tribes on the borders of their empire. Hugh of Bordeaux kills two black giants in Egypt; they are brothers, and one of them has offered Hugh his giant black "soeur germaine" in marriage if Hugh will take up land where she lives, "en Orient."⁴⁹ King Brehus, who holds Africa and Syria (*terre de Damas*), is seventeen feet tall, very ugly, and snores in his sleep.⁵⁰ Ogier kills him after a superhuman duel in which both use white magic: Brehus has in his shield a vial of the unguent used in anointing the body of Christ, which heals wounds instantaneously. Ogier steals it for a time, but renews his strength also by prayer (as do all of the dueling heroes). In *Floovant* it is suspected that the Saracens plan to concoct a powder from cremated bodies of Frenchmen they have killed, as medicine to be taken "en bataile";⁵¹ but it is not said that magic is the secret of any of their victories. Nor are they any more cruel than the Christians.

Saracen skills, then, are not devil-inspired; they win admiration because they rest on secret knowledge hidden from the French. Their building secrets are like those of the ancients. One of their own towns in the East, Dunostre, is strong because Julius Caesar built it.⁵² But there are some signs of intelligent interest in Saracen techniques. At Vienne their technique in rebuilding the walls had been to tie the stones with iron and steel. Charlemagne, who is a delighted guest there after Count Girart has held him off, in rebellion, for seven years, has never seen anything like the "richeces" of the two palaces within the walls, nor of the metaled road giving secret access to the town through an artificial cave.⁵³ Saracen occupation of Mainz has not only made the walls impregnable but has given the town marvelous ivory gates.[54] The wonders of Cairo are due partly to its access to waters flowing from the Terrestrial Paradise: an old man who washes his hands in the palace courtyard fountain will be restored to youth; a woman who sips the water will have her youth and her virginity restored.[55] There is also indirect recognition of the obvious fact that Cairo drew its wealth from the fertility of the Nile valley. Hugh of Bordeaux, approaching the city by a vaguely described circuit from the east, passes through the *Terre de Foi*, a land of such plenty that to Hugh's astonishment, people have all the wheat they want.[56]

In contrast to their perception of the sources of Muslim wealth in agriculture and trade, the poets are totally ignorant of the religion of Islam. On this subject they are no better informed than the minor theologians whose distorted accounts of Muslim theology began to circulate early in the twelfth century.[57] They reinforce this hostile propaganda by representing the Saracens as literally worshipping Mahomet's image, along with the images of other gods; the pantheon includes Apollo.[58] But they are at least aware of major points of Christian theology. Christian and Saracen champions who elect to fight duels often have a theological argument beforehand and in rest periods. The Saracens are given both defensive arguments and arguments of attack. They deny Christ's resurrection, scoff at Christian sacraments as worthless, laugh at the god with the twisted neck on the crucifix.[59] Their preference for Anti-Christ is snidely introduced in a quarrel between Gloriande and her brothers.[60] But the poets are at least realistic in realizing that religious debate is futile: it will not convert anyone. Roland breaks off his long and interesting debate with Feragu in a temper:

> Tu ne veus croir en riens que je te die,
> Filz dou Diable.[61]

The poems do not bear out Norman Daniel's impression that moral innuendo and slander—the charge that Mohammed was a drunkard, and stress on the lasciviousness of taking more than one wife—was the most effective weapon in the clergy's armory of anti-Muslim propaganda. In the religious arguments between champions the charge that Mohammed was a drunkard comes up only once,[62] the Christians saving their breath to expound the doctrine of redemption. In fact, the only drunkard in the chansons is a Christian, Count Thiebaut of Bourges.[63] He sins, but only against the warrior's code, in which the virtues are loyalty and courage. The sanction of these is ridicule: Thiebaut is the stock coward; he can kill only a sheep, and that by accident. He is the natural foil to the heroism of his fellows who ride impetuously against overwhelming odds to die on the field of Larchamp. The Saracens, as has been seen, are represented as drinking wine, at the court in Cairo, but not as drinking to excess. The scene there is one of civilized pleasure. Nor are the Saracens cowards. They lack the stoicism of the Christians, who suffer crippling wounds without a groan, while their enemies yelp when they are wounded and scold Mohammed for reverses. But the Saracens fight bravely.

In portraits of the superior Saracen leaders, who are sharply distinct from their less civilized, or uncouth, auxiliaries, what stands out is their courtliness and sophistication. The elegant King Karaheus of Persia plays an ambiguous part in teasing Ogier, trying to undermine his morale by offering him his own fiancée, Gloriande, should the Dane win a duel with another Saracen.[64] The Persian's friend Sadones, son of the King of Nubia, is another courtly figure. "Que vos a dit li paiens mescreant?," he asks the distrustful Ogier, and plies him with flattery: "Preus estes et vaillans."[65] Gloriande, too, flatters him; she is the stock court flirt. Ogier's distrust is soon justified by a treacherous ambush at his duel, planned by Gloriande's brothers. These scenes, set in Rome, are all framed to show the simple Westerner at a disadvantage among sophisticated Easterners. But Karaheus is not base. He has religious integrity. He scorns Ogier's invitation to become a vassal of Charlemagne:

> Ains me lairoie tos les membres ardoir
> Que ja Mahous soit relenquis par moi.[66]

It is to be remarked that Ogier is represented as unusually pure. The single love of his youth is a Northerner, daughter of the chatelaine of Cambrai, who seduces him, conceiving a son, in a one-night affair. He forgets her, and thereafter lives ascetically except for an enormous appetite, and when in late middle age he finally marries, his bride is fittingly an English princess infatuated with his courage, who makes the proposal; she has the prettiness of good health, is brave, and a good horsewoman.

To most of the poets, the moralists' belief that wealth and luxury are necessarily corrupting is utterly wrong-headed. To be sure, in Ogier's story there is an association of luxury with weakness in the character of Carlot, Charlemagne's son, who is alternately timid and rash, a moral coward, jealous of Ogier, and requires an ivory bed in his tent, laid with silk sheets and ermine covers. But in the Guillaume cycle there is frank avowal of the fact that the spur to southern French aggression against the Muslims in the Western Mediterranean is fury at their having annexed the richest territories. As a landless young "bacheler" Guillaume leaps on a tabletop to harangue his young fellow-barons, harping on their ragged appearance and their poverty:

> . . . . povres bachelers
> As menus cops et as dras descirez.

If they will join him in attacking Nimes, he can promise them money, lands, castles, and best of all—Spanish war-horses.[67] Ten thousand men, "la flor de France," arm to follow him. His promise of wealth is quickly confirmed by an encounter with a *vilain* who has prospered (*conquesté*) by remaining, converted to Islam, near St. Gilles. The peasant is returning in his cart from Nimes, where he has been buying salt, to harvest his wheat at home; he assures Guillaume that Nimes is so well "garnie" that bread there is only half the price it is in other towns.[68]

The Muslims are openly envied because they know better even than the French how to live. Nor is this just a conventional attitude of the *trouvères*. Robert Guiscard's biographer, a clerk thought to be of Norman origin, when he comes to the capture of Salerno describes the town as *deliciosa,* and the most delightful in all of Latium. He dwells on the fruit there, on the beauty of the women and brushes aside any suspicions of laxity by noting also the probity of the men.[69] A clerk arriving at an oasis in Syria finds it Paradise. Elie of St. Gilles, hauled through the garden window of the Princess Rosamund and recovering from wounds in the soft bed where she ministers to him, finds that oasis, too, Paradise.

The love of horses is however more eloquently portrayed than the love of women. It rings true; it was probably one of the few grounds of common understanding with the Muslims. The Muslims' horses are bred in Arabia, Syria, Hungary, Africa, and Spain; they are intelligent and fearless, as beautiful as the women, and are caparisoned with as much art. The reins of King Brehus's magnificent mount are of Sardis silk, the bit is an Almoravide one made by fairies on the island of *Caldéys*, the animal's tail is plaited with silver thread, and he wears a headpiece adorned with pictures of birds and fish; King Brunamont of Majorca has a horse "ki vaut une cité"; King Jubien, when Elie by cunning steals his favorite Arab horse, is heartbroken: "C'était las plus grande force de ma valeur et de ma chevalerie"; Ogier's Arab, as strong a character as the hero himself, is his only true love, and wears reins of Syrian silk.[70]

By contrast, the scenes in which Saracen princesses fall in love with Christians are sheer fantasy. The fantasy could be indulged without moral disapproval because the heroes always insist on baptism as a condition of marriage, and because the women make faithful wives. Guiberç, as the Countess Orange, is perhaps the most admirable wife in medieval literature. Rosamund, daughter of the King of Sorbrie, is more of a Hollywood goddess, or a moon goddess. She dons a veil to enter her father's court, but flings it off at once to dazzle the men present with her ravishing dress, jeweled and embroidered.[71] From Elie's point of view her best quality is her accommodating nature. She does not mind at all that because he stood as godparent at her baptism, Elie cannot be her husband but marries the King of France's sister, fobbing Rosamund off on his squire, who is a count's son, but a dwarf. Maugalie, daughter of the Emir Galien, has already set Rosamund an example; she loves Floovant the son of Clovis, but when he decides that Florette, the daughter of a Christian king, would be a more suitable wife for him, Maugalie obligingly marries Floovant's squire Richier.

During the thirteenth century literary comparisons between Muslim and Western civilization gradually become less unfavorable to the West. An example is the spread of marble, the symbol of wealth and status, in the Western scenes described. Its multicolored splendor in the palace hall where Count Julien of St. Gilles holds court might perhaps be interpreted as a legacy of Muslim occupation. But more cities are described as rich, great, "garnie." Doon, a rather dull hero, is able to fortify his little castle town of La Roche ("en son privé demoine qu'il a de Jhesu"), and to provision it against siege, extremely well; his wife has a marble painted chamber, and thirty knights attend her to church.[72] In *Girart de Vienne* Charlemagne's gifts of money and clothing to young knights become lavish. There is a change, too, in the depiction of the bourgeoisie. Whereas formerly in the chansons these have been butchers and tanners unruly in their behavior and subject to their lord's arbitrary justice, now in the romances they are prosperous merchants who are even *courtois* and have beautiful well-dressed wives. In *Doon de la Roche* a citizen of Mainz who is not a knight has a marble staircase; so has a countryman who is on the rise, with flocks of sheep and thousands of cattle, and four of his five sons away as knights.

There is also a belated recognition of the liability of the Muslim world to internal dissension. King Jubien is a bully and insolent; he demands the hand of Rosamund under the threat of destroying her father's kingdom. Her father suffers the humiliation of being saved only by the arrival, in the nick of time, of a French army under King Louis (the Pious), which has come to rescue Elie from his imprisonment with Rosamund (at the hands of her father and brothers) in a tower. These scenes are set in Sorbrie, somewhere in the Eastern Mediterranean: the French arrive by sea. This imaginary victory may be taken as symbolizing an end to the sense of inferiority to Islam that sustains the tension and excitement of the earlier chansons.

In the new literary genres, though French heroes may travel far on adventure, there is a new confidence in their own civilization. The belfries of Paris are its symbol. Girart de Vienne's nephew gazes at them in wonder.[73] Eustache Deschamps in the fourteenth century will be singing that he has seen Jerusalem, Babylon, and Alexandria but Paris is the best of all cities.[74]

NOTES

1. D. C. Munro, "The Western Attitude towards Islam during the Period of the Crusades," *Speculum* 6 (1931): 329–43.

2. Sir Hamilton Gibb, "The Influence of Islamic Culture on Medieval Europe," *Bulletin of the John Ryland's Library* (1955), reprinted in S. L. Thrupp, ed., *Change in Medieval Society* (New York, 1964).

3. *Historia Ecclesiastica Gentis Anglorum*, cap. 14, adapted from Gildas, cap. 17–23, *Monumenta Germanica Historica* (hereafter cited as *MGH*), *Chron. Minora* 3 (1896).

4. On other sermon-writers' use of Caesarius see W. Levison, *England and the Continent in the Eighth Century* (Oxford, 1946), pp. 305–8.

5. There is an immense literature on the incest problem. Eddi's pro-Saxon *Vita* of Bishop Wilfrid (early eighth century, ed. W. Levison, *MGH, Scriptores Rerum Merovingicarum*, 6) imputes bestiality to the Picts.

6. E. Ewig, "Résidence et Capitale dans le haut Moyen Age," *Revue historique* (1963).

7. F. Lot and R. Fawtier, eds., *Institutions Seigneuriales* (Paris, 1957).

8. Edith Ennen, *Frühmittelalterliche Stadt* (Bonn, 1953) and "The Different Types of Formation of Medieval Towns," in *Early Medieval Society*, ed. S. L. Thrupp (New York, 1967). Jean Lestocquoy, "Le paysage urbain en Gaule du Vᵉ au IXᵉ siècle," *Annales: Économies–Sociétés–Civilisations* (April–June 1953).

9. Lewis Mumford, *The City in History* (New York, 1961), esp. chaps. 1–4.

10. *Etymologiarum*, Lib. 15, cap. 2, Migne, *Patrologica Latina* (hereafter cited as *PL*), vol. 82, col. 537.

11. R. Koebner, "Dans les Terres de colonisation: marchés slaves et villes allemandes," *Annales d'histoire économique et sociale*, t. 9 (1937): 547–69, translated in *Change in Medieval Society*, ed. S. L. Thrupp (New York, 1964).

12. As in the *Liber Historiae Francorum*, *MGH, Scriptores Rerum Merovingicarum* 2 (1888), pp. 241–328. Hincmar, in *Vita Remigii Ep.*, *ibid.*, at p. 291, omits reference to the German *oppida*.

13. See R. E. Keller, "The Language of the Franks," *Bulletin of the John Ryland's Library*, vol. 47 (1964), at p. 101; also translated extract in Stewart C. Easton and Helene Wieruszowski, eds., *The Era of Charlemagne* (Princeton, 1961), p. 183, adapted from *Otfrid's Evangielbuch* (ed. Piper, vol. 1, 1882).

14. Guillaume de Poiters, *Gesta Willelmi*, ed. A. Duchesne, *Hist. Norm. Scriptores*, 1619; cf. R. Foreville, "Aux Origines de la Légende épique," *Le Moyen Age*, t. 56 (1950): 195–219.

15. See Theodore Mommsen, "St. Augustine and the Christian Idea of Progress: The Background of the City of God," in his *Medieval and Renaissance Studies*, ed. Eugene F. Rice (Ithaca, N.Y., 1959), pp. 265–98, esp. p. 297.

16. Oliver F. Emerson, "Legends of Cain," *Publication of the Modern Language Association* (hereafter cited as *PMLA*) 21 (1906): 831–929, is one of the best surveys of this tradition.

17. Lellia Ruggini, "L'epitoma Rerum Gestarum Alexandri Magni e il liber de morto testamentoque ejus," *Athenaeum*, n.s. 39 (1961): 285–357.

18. J. Lestocquoy, *loc. cit.*, p. 171.

19. On the audience problem see M. Delbouille, "Les chansons de geste et le livre," in La Technique Littéraire des chansons de geste, *Actes du Colloque de Liège* (Paris, 1959), pp. 295–405.

20. R. Bezzola, in *Actes du Colloque de Liège*, cf. pp. 188–95, n. 32.

21. *Ogier de Danemarche*, par Raimbert de Paris, ed. J. Barrois, 2 vols. (Paris, 1842), ll. 196, 2108, 10610–880.

   Par tote France querra hon Tervagant
   Et Apolin et Jupin le puant
   Et les églises deverront poplicant. [*Ibid.*, ll. 10804–6.]

22. *Chanson de Guillaume*, ed. Duncan McMillan (Paris, 1949), ll. 212–20.

23. *Ogier*, ll. 677–78.

24. *Ibid.*, ll. 1433–38.

25. *Ibid.*, ll. 3485–3503.

26. *Huon de Bordeaux*, ed. P. Ruelle (Paris, 1960), ll. 5448–51. (Ruelle dated poem 1170–1210 but J. Monfrin, in *Romania* t. 83 [1962], pp. 90–101, judges ms. of mid-thirteenth century.)

   Emmi la voie avoit un pin planté
   Qui fu asis sur cinquante pilers
   Qui tout estoient de fin or esmeré
   La tint ses plais Gaudisès l'amire.

27. *Ibid.*, ll. 5431 ff.

28. *Ogier*, l. 3503.

29. *Ibid.*, l. 307, "mur de marbre bis."

30. *Aymeri de Narbonne*, ed. L. Demaison (Paris, 1887), ll. 1104 ff.

31. *Les Enfances Guillaume, chanson de geste du XIIIe siècle*, ed. Patrice Henry (Paris, 1935), ll. 1628, 1271, 1704–29.

32. *La Prise de Cordres et de Sebille, chanson de geste du XIIe siècle*, ed. O. Densusianu (Paris, 1896), ll. 2162–63, 2172–77, 2182–87.

33. *Chanson du Guillaume*, ll. 839, 1735–62. The Saracens have:
   "Pain e vin e char i ad remis assez
   Vaissele d'or e tapiz e dossels" [ll. 1698–99]

34. *Ogier*, ll. 12959–60.

   Soixante dames vestues de bon fus
   Fems de roi, d'amiraux et de dux.

35. *Ogier*, ll. 6693–95; *Doon de la Roche*, ed. P. Meyer and G. Huet (Paris, 1921), l. 3296.

36. *Aymeri*, ll. 1030–51.

37. Constant d'Outre-Marin, *conpains* of Malrin, *Ogier*, ll. 6693–6840.

38. Guillaume de Pouille, *La Geste de Robert Guiscard*, ed. Marguerite Mathieu (Palermo, 1961), ms. dated from end of twelfth century, lib. II, ll. 167 ff.

39. *Chanson de Guillaume*, ll. 2170–72.
40. *La Fille du Comte de Pontieu, Conte en prose*, ed. C. Brunel (Paris, 1923), p. 23. Gériaume, captured on pilgrimage, had "Entre paiens . . . bien conversé" for thirty years, *Huon de Bordeaux*, ll. 3102, 3106.
41. A knight at Narbonne, sent to find out whether an approaching troop is a merchant group or Saracen, speaks "en latin"; they are Saracens and reply in his language. *La Morte Aymeri de Narbonne*, ed. J. Couraye du Parc (Paris, 1884), ll. 1755–60.
42. *Ogier*, ll. 627–31.
43. *Guillaume de la Barre*, roman d'aventures par Arnaut Videl de Castelnauderi, ed. Paul Meyer (Paris, 1895), ll. 224, 410, 442, 461. In the *Saga d'Elie*, a late prose tale, the princess Rosamund reproaches her father, "Vous m'avez promis, à votre retour de France, de ramener pour moi de France un pauvre prisonnier, pour m'apprendre la langue welche." *Elie de Saint Gille*, ed. G. Raynaud (Paris, 1879), includes this tale.
44. *La Mort Aymeri*, ll. 380–83; cf. "Moysès, li clers sachans/ . . . / J'ai hermites esté xxxvi ans: Si sai d'astrenomie le covenant/ Je vos dirai del songe par avenant."
45. *Aiol*, ed. J. Normand and G. Raynaud (Paris, 1877), ll. 390–94.
46. *Chanson de Guillaume*, ll. 2590–92.
47. His name is "Cordaglon le desvé," *Ogier*, ll. 12813–18.
48. *Chanson de Guillaume*, ll. 3518–45; meeting French soldiers, they shout:

"Finement est venu
Un Anticrist u Bagot u Tartarun
U d'enfern le veillard Belzebun."

Reneward then speaks to them "en sun latin," *ibid.*, ll. 3228–48. King Brehus jeers at Charlemagne, that his family were dwarfs: "Pépins tes pères, li malvais nains puant," so the score is evened; *Ogier*, l. 9940.
49. *Huon de Bordeaux*, ll. 6549–61.
50. *Ogier*, ll. 9796, 11006, 11592–94.
51. *Floovant, chanson de geste du XIIe siècle*, ed. Sven Andolf (Uppsala, 1941), ll. 1842–43.
52. The palace has 25 chambers and 300 windows. *Huon de Bordeaux*, ll. 4586–89.
53. *Girart de Vienne*, ed. F. G. Yandle (New York, 1930), ll. 6094–95, 6226 ff., 6500–6503 ("une cave de viel antiquité/Paiens la firent molt a grant tans passé"), 6565 ("chemin ferré").
54. *Doon de la Roche*, ll. 3838–39.
55. *Huon de Bordeaux*, ll. 5574–86.
56. *Ibid.*, 2923–28.
57. Norman A. Daniel, *Islam and the West: The Making of an Image* (Edinburgh, 1960).
58. King Brehus offers Ogier ten cities and other wealth if he will, "croi Tergavant et Mahou/ Et Apolin et mon dieu Barratron/ Et Jupiter

qui croient Esclavon . . . ," *Ogier*, ll. 11749–54. Numerous scenes of idolatory.

59. *Ibid.*, ll. 11316–44. *Le Couronnement de Louis*, ed. E. Langlois (Paris, 1888), ll. 841–43 (charges of the giant Corsolt). *Guillaume de la Barre*, ll. 631 ff. Depiction of the Muslims' worship in this romance is particularly crude.

60. *Ogier:* "Vus atendés la venue Antecrist/Qui par venra od le Deu as Juis," ll. 2074–75.

61. *L'Entree d'Espagne*, ed. A. Thomas (Paris, 1913), ll. 3988–89; the debate, ll. 3579–84.

62. *Le Couronnement de Louis*, l. 851.

63. *Chanson de Guillaume*, ll. 12–45.

64. *Ogier*, ll. 1359–81.

65. *Ibid.*, ll. 750–63, 785, 807.

66. *Ibid.*, ll. 1379–80.

67. *Le Charroi de Nimes, chanson de geste du XIIe siècle*, ed. J-L. Perrier (Paris, 1931), ll. 637–42, 656.

68. *Ibid.*, ll. 875–93, 910–11.

69. Guillaume de Pouille, op. cit., ll. 470 ff.

70. *Ogier*, ll. 1269–79, 2396, 4736; *Saga d'Elie*, p. 152. See Jean Frappier, "Les Destriers et leurs epithètes," *La Technique Littéraire des Chansons de Geste* (1959), pp. 85–104.

71. *Saga d'Elie*, p. 94.

72. *Doon de la Roche*, ll. 2270 ff., 3594, 3532 ff., 3355–56.

73. *Girart de Vienne*, l. 1703.

74. "Ballade sur les beautés de la Ville de Paris," *Poésies morales et historiques* (Paris, 1832), p. 24.

The City as the Idea of
Social Order

Talk about cities is ordinarily of how they strike the eye, of whether life in them is pleasant, and of what makes one more important than another. Writing about them, too, is either of their design and fabric or of the social interaction that goes on against this background; histories of cities touch on both to enliven the story of how power—political, economic or religious—came to be centered in them and how their populations grew. The premise of this paper, that cities are the focal points of a civilization in its aspect of social order, is taken for granted and left implicit. We are as conscious as any people of the visual esthetic order, or lack of it, in our cities; indeed, air travel, especially when night blots out the countryside and leaves only the patterns of street lighting, makes us conscious in a new way of the beauty or defects of their ground plan. Yet few are aware of the part that the esthetic character of the city has played in developing and maintaining the sense of order out of which civilization grew and on which it depends.

Historians have written of its connection with the sense of order in this broader sense only fragmentarily. Yet the theme is a great one. It gives the city moral and intellectual dignity as an idea, but is not to be dismissed to the realm of symbolism. It concerns the practical life and history of every city, the more so when these are regarded, not as insular affairs, but in their relations with the countryside or trading territory out of which a city grew. A brief paper can do no

Reprinted from *The Historian and the City*, ed. O. Handlin and J. Burchard (Cambridge, Mass., 1963), pp. 121–32.

more than try to link together, along the Western historical thread, the disparate ways in which the theme has so far been treated.

The sense of order has a resonance as old as culture; it antedates the city. Culture required continuity and could have it only by inventing the idea of order. Initially this took form in the mind's eye as a spatially structured cosmos with different levels in it for gods and men, connected by a hollow central shaft. The religious leaders of primitive communities persuaded their fellows that the proper location for a settlement was directly beneath the means of access to the home of the supreme gods, that is, at the centre of the universe. At the same time these thinkers devised a simple plan for linking any living-space, even a nomad camp, with this "sacred space," the procedure which Mircea Eliade describes as the "cosmicizing" of an area. A common example was the grouping of village huts about a cultic building embellished with features that made it represent the heavens and the means of access to them.[1] The village was then safe. The first cities in the ancient Near East were planned on a similar system, improved only by the greater impressiveness of the temples at their heart, which were true models of the universe and lent safety to a larger area. These cities, in short, were the supreme living expositions in their time of the idea of cosmological order. The idea was abstract yet visible and tangible in their design. In cosmological thinking there could be many such models; there was no inconsistency in multiplying centres of the universe, no monopoly of right location. For an enemy to destroy one's sacred centre would make defeat the more dangerous, but the centre could be rebuilt. There were not contending orders.

As the ancient cities became the seats of monarchy, consciousness of order rapidly matured in a second form, that of social order, consisting in the deliberate regulation of human relationships through custom corrected by law and by the royal power over a territory that had limits. With empire, the king's capital city stood preeminently for social order over the whole conquered territory. There were also lesser cities, the nodal points of the royal administration.[2] These provincial cities are the places where officials reside, where military levies must report and taxes be deposited. Like the capital city, though to a lesser degree, they are the backdrop for the public ceremonial which makes the idea of social order visible and comprehensible to the illiterate. The distinction between the provincial cities and the smaller places which we would call towns and villages, like the difference between capital and provincial city, is one of status gradient. Although the cities are more closely identified with the idea of social order and with the power that directs it, they are not thereby in logical opposition to rurality. They are simply to a superior degree the source of the order that covers urban and rural areas alike. The only logical opposition is the desolation of barren land where no man lives, not even shepherds or nomads, but only wild beasts, owls and demons—the fate that the prophet Isaiah willed for Babylon.[3] As between rival empires, however, there are now different and contending social orders.

The ancient world bequeathed also the identification of the city with a third form of order, perfect order. In its dialectic this is simply a rational combination of cosmological order conceived as proper formal relations between men and the gods, and social order conceived as authoritatively ordered relations among men. In the heavenly Jerusalem God will make men one with himself and with each other. In Plato's Republic God's place is taken by the idea of justice.

The idea of perfect order was born in the same atmosphere of ferment that gave birth to the idea of moral order. Yet the two are sharply distinct for many centuries. Moral order, as Eric Voegelin traces its emergence in his epic *Order and History*, is essentially subjective, dependent on a sustained conflict within man, and deriving, in his view of the West, from the Greek conception of man as engaged in a struggle against fate.[4] Perfect order on the contrary is by definition static, the creation of divine authority, and requires a spatial location.

The city has therefore never been identified with moral order, and the birth of the latter as an idea to some extent jeopardizes the moral worth of the city's identification with social order. For it brings opposition now not only from without, from a rival empire with a different social order, but from critics within. In the Greek as in the Judaic tradition moral thinkers took a highly derogatory attitude toward the city both as an actual community and as claiming high status over other places through standing in a superior degree for social order, because in both capacities it necessarily embodied what they perceived to be evil as well as good. As a community the city concentrated in itself the best professional skill of the day regardless of the moral level of the profession—star prostitutes and confidence men as well as high priests and the best lawyers. As the idea of social order it justified the rule of the rich over the poor which the prophets denounced. Like many of the authors of the Jewish scriptures, Plato himself believed the pre-urban condition of men to have been morally better.[5] He placed his vision of perfect order in a city not because this form of community was more disposed than others to moral excellence but because of its high place in the status gradient. To have placed perfect order in a village, a camp-site or a farmyard would have been ridiculous.

The cities of the ancient world helped to produce another of the distinctive elements of the Western intellectual tradition, the application of the idea of evolution or progress to societies. The Graeco-Romans limited that criterion to a backward-looking perspective, for they saw their cities as the peak of human evolution. But with the aid of a condescending tolerance for the lower degrees of social order which were all that purely agrarian peoples or nomadic peoples could boast, these other societies could be seen as having at least a potential future. Nomads might become settled cultivators and cultivators might learn to build cities as well as villages. In the Mediterranean world this view passed on from Rome to the men of the medieval world as a way of viewing the course of history and by the late twelfth century was a commonplace among educated men even in northern Europe. Gerald of Wales applies it interestingly in his writings on the ethnology and history of the Welsh and the Irish.[6]

The idea of the city as standing for social order had thus survived the ages of barbarism and early feudalism. In spite of the obvious decline of urban life during these centuries cities had remained architecturally by far the most impressive visible groupings, and through the bishops' powers had remained the most important administrative centres. Moreover, they were indispensable as dramatic and sacred background to the political and religious ceremonial through which kingship retained its hold on men's loyalty. Even in the legendary history that was popularized in the twelfth century a king was unthinkable without a city: Arthur had to have a Camelot.

As they recover economic vitality the medieval cities come to be more and more the dominant expression of civilized order. At the extreme, in Italy, they again govern the countryside and uproot and urbanize the rural nobility. North of the Alps they become the instruments of advancing royal power and the means, along with castle towns and planned market towns, of holding newly conquered and colonized territory. In Germany, owing to the collapse of royal power and the crystallization of urban communities around exclusively commercial interests or in the miniscule towns around petty bourgeois routine, most of the nobility continued to prefer the old-fashioned life of family surrounded by servitors and dependents in castle and hunting lodge. Yet where outside cultural influence penetrated most deeply, as in southern Germany, territorial lords took to ensconcing themselves in strategically located dwarf administrative capitals whose architecture and planning were lucid translations of the ideas of power and social dominance and remained so throughout the age of Baroque rebuilding.

The city's hold on the imagination in the early modern centuries was substantially reinforced not only by the physical expansion of political capitals and centres of economic power but by speculative thought and by-art. Speculative thought played with new patterns of perfect order that had little of the heavenly Jerusalem about them—although in millennial thought Jerusalem shines on—but that under cover of Utopianism advanced a great deal of indirect incitement to social and economic reform. Baroque art completes as it were the counterpoint of the age. The princely capital designed in the geometrical symmetry of the circle or of some other form recognized as perfect is the benevolent despot's reply to the discontented: "See, all is well!"

The thinkers through whom the idea of moral order evolved were incapable of shaking the acceptance of the city as the idea of social order because they too accepted it. Medieval attacks on Paris and Rome as concentrating in themselves carnal temptation, newfangled professional ambition and the avarice of lawyers were motivated by varying mixtures of conservative revulsion against the development of bureaucracy and of fear that loose women and lawyers were heralds of Anti-Christ. A chorus of criticism leaned on Apocalyptic thought to stigmatize Rome as Babylon while offering no alternative plan by which the Church could be governed without Rome.[7] St. Bernard pleading with Paris students to flee this Babylon and enter his austerely reformed monasteries was in effect urging them to flee the social order. The purpose of the monastic rule as he saw it was to maintain a disciplined meditation on the sufferings of Christ throughout the monk's every waking moment, in order the better to prepare him for the hereafter.

With the Enlightenment the career of the city as the idea of social order entered a new phase. Gradually, through recognition of the changing role of cities in the economic order, they are worked into the new scheme of thought in which the idea of progress is forward-looking. Montesquieu strikes a new note in characterizing modern cities as radically different from ancient Rome. Rome, he asserts, grew out of the same type of barbarian fort that could have been found in the Crimea, a retreat for raiders living by pillage. She never really reformed her ways; the fate of the Empire was determined by the pickings of pillage. The modern city, on the contrary, is part of a productive economic order.[8] Voltaire traced the origins of this order to medieval urban industry. Despite his detestation of the middle ages, he saw its craftsmen humbly and obscurely preparing the foundations of a new civilization. His praise of the cities he knew and delighted in as the home of pleasure reflects only one aspect of the city's ancient role of meeting esthetic needs, although aristocratic pleasure was taking on new refinements. His remarks are not very penetrating. A Babylonian or an ancient Roman could also have discoursed on aristocratic city pleasures. What is extraordinary, in a Frenchman, is his infatuation for London, which was already darkening the air with coal smoke. The reason for this enthusiasm was his perception that of all the countries of Europe the England of his day was the only one ideally fitted to become the home of deism.[9] London, for Voltaire, stood for England, for the English social order.

The idea of progress had to contend with as many enemies as the armies of Napoleon, the most lethal being the readiness with which its optimism could be twisted into the pessimism of the cyclic view of history. Adam Smith himself, the apostle of economic progress, was uncertain whether men could become enlightened enough to avert the ultimate decay that had overtaken in succession every civilization of the ancient past; Playfair assumed that they could not; and Ricardo buttressed that assumption by his system of economic reasoning. Economic pessimism sharpened the anxiety with which moralists now watched the disturbing growth of British cities. What little was generally known of the failure of the ancient civilizations was connected through Biblical reading with the moral weakness of their city people. If urban industry was now to add a new cause of breakdown and decay the outlook was poor. Socialists were optimistic because they hoped to take over the cities and re-shape the whole institutional context of industry. No one in Western Europe could envisage a social order devoid of cities. Even the Fourierites and the Owenites in their attempts to make a fresh start on the organization of production were simply making a fresh start in small-scale urban development. The anarchists were more radical in their belief that the status gradient between city, town, and village could be levelled out by means of new cooperative devices that would eliminate social injustices. Only in Russia, under the joint influence of nationalist and populist sentiment, could agrarian socialists think of employing village institutions as the model and nexus of a better social order.

At the start of the nineteenth century moralists on the Continent could still hope to forestall excessive urban growth by attacking Adam Smith's doctrines of free enterprise as calculated to destroy traditional culture. Fichte appealed to small-town German burghers in this vein.[10] Equally characteristic was the call of the cameralist economist Adam Müller, in the post-Jena crisis, for national leader-ship from officialdom and the Junkers. The bitterness and eloquence of his attack on every figure connected with urban credit or money power from the merchants even of the medieval cities through Adam Smith to the bankers of his own day are astounding.[11] Müller ad-vocated strong paternalistic government to restrain free enterprise. In Germany, as he wished to see it, the dominant cities would obviously have been those housing bureaucrats and soldiers, with only such trade and industry as would be needed to serve these. Such cities would have been visible embodiments of the principle of authority. Through the Junkers this same principle would have extended over the villages, where it would somehow be supported by a traditional spirit of community.

Fichte and Müller agreed in desiring more rational use of authority to obstruct the growth of world-market cities. Disciples of Adam Smith wished authority to be used discreetly to the opposite end, to free the way for enterprise. In short, all who took any stand on the kinds of progress that the early phases of nineteenth century industrialism brought, socialists included and anarchists the only group excepted, alike wanted to back by authority some form of organization that they advocated as rational. The one rugged individualist who opposed this trust in rational organization, William Blake, was jeered at by his contemporaries as mad.

To Blake the one issue that mattered was whether life in society left room for individual creativity and spontaneity of feeling. When people lived by a rationally constrained morality, conceived of society as based on rational contract, and in looking at the stars could think only of a mechanism, how could they find joy? He blamed three men—Voltaire, Locke, and Newton—for having pushed life into these loveless habits, and he never tired of railing at them. At the same time he could place true freedom only in the golden age of myth. As to the future, he was not optimistic. Some degree of constraint inhered in the nature of society. Nothing could be done with the social order beyond trying to persuade people to be more tolerant of spontaneity.

Having these convictions Blake was content to accept the conventional connections of the city with social order and with perfect order. London, for which he had the affection of a native, and where as artist-craftsman he found more scope for his talents than provincial cities offered, was to him England, an England whose order had even in ancient times included other cities as well as villages. His "dark Satanic mills," which to the unwary reader conjure up factory walls, were any constructs stemming from the influence of Voltaire, Locke and Newton, and the "marks of woe" he saw in London faces are merely the stamp of the same demonic trinity. His own thought is embedded in the ponderous allegory which makes his long poem *Jerusalem* virtually unreadable. Babylon is a popular woman he beholds "in the opening streets of London"; a few lines further on he explained that she was "Rational Morality." Beside her another woman named Jerusalem wandered the same streets "in ruins." She is the emanation of spiritual man, destined with the awakening of nations in the seventh age of the world to become his resplendent bride in the character of the city of perfect order. She is also the potentiality of London as the city of "Universal Humanity," for it is here in the foggy streets of London that Blake calls for the light of Jerusalem to descend. His scheme demanded also that he furnish even the terrestrial Paradise with a city, which again is London-Jerusalem. By this token his readers were to know that perfect order as an idea had eternal existence and meaning. Yet muffled as it was in Druidic myth, Blake's meaning reached very few.[12] The pre-Raphaelite response came late and loaded with pseudo-medievalism.

But the city never lost vitality as an idea. After the middle of the nineteenth century, when economic pessimism had subsided, poets and novelists of extraordinary sensitivity explored the city-dweller's life as aesthetic experience. This brought the great capitals rather than industrial cities to the fore. Seen in historical perspective, the adventure of city-literature from Baudelaire to the anti-novelists of today has been to carry the early romantic philosophy of individuation through a sequence of new phases. The individual has been dissolved successively into sensation, into fleeting personal relationships, into ignominy and fear. Yet the artist's pursuit of self-awareness has not weakened but has strengthened the idea of the individual in a society avowedly based more and more upon it. The striking contrast between this city-literature and that produced under totalitarian control of the artist brings out very clearly the differing nature of the city as an idea in different social orders.

Following the lead of literature, and of criminologists, sociology also turned to the exploration of great cities, at first mainly in regard to matters of concern to social reformers. The bias of this approach caused "the city" to be conceived as something pathological, the more so as small communities tended to be idealized as healthy. Robert Park's leadership in American urban sociology brought more realistic concepts through precise analysis both of processes of social disorganization and of the complexity inherent in the structure of city occupations, with its inevitable juxtaposition of the reputable and the disreputable. More objective analysis of rural communities and small towns and of the conditions under which they too may present features of disorganization then became possible.

The onrush of industrialism is today fast making any urban-rural dichotomy patently unrealistic. This very fact, however, is likely to refix it in nostalgic views of the past, a new urban romanticism taking the place of the older, agrarian romanticism. The scholar's task is not so much to attack either one or the other but to reconsider the historical validity of the dichotomy. It is preferable to treat all types of community in relation to the intensity of their engagement in the maintenance of the common social order to which they belong. Their degree of engagement is manifest in their share in concentrations of power and of cultural creativeness. It is manifest also in the esthetic sense of order shown in their spatial form and architecture which, in towers, spires, skyscrapers, and domed roofing, still bear traces of their origin in the sense of cosmological order. Although even in a contemporary society the gradations of engagement can never be precisely measured as on a scale, the historian can become aware of changes in the angle of the gradient. For example, in Renaissance Italy the gradient as between city and village grew steeper. Why this was so is still not fully explained, for city society and intercity affairs have virtually monopolized research attention to the neglect of the countryside. American history displays an opposite trend, the peculiar vigor of American democracy having always tended to level the gradient. The truculent criticism of cities as being too civilized in early nineteenth-century American writing is unthinkable in the Europe of that time.[13]

An urban-rural dichotomy can find only tenuous support in moral condemnation of cities, although the record of this in prophecy, sermons and stereotyped images in other literature may perhaps, if it is searched, yield some theories of decadence, some attempts to analyze the processes, apart from the military contingencies, by which city-based empires decayed. More likely, such research will yield only the pervasive influence of the millennial dream. Those who, like early and reformist monks in Buddhist and

Christian cultures, and like Thoreau in New England, retired to meditate in rural peace did so not because they believed rural life to be ultimately satisfying but because they believed nothing on this earth could be satisfying except through the miracle of a new age. Their dreams were of the golden age that lies at the heart of all varieties of millennial thought and that flickers even in the most orthodox Heaven. They were not seeking a viable basis for social order in rurality but rejecting the social order as worthless. It is true that the myth of the terrestrial Paradise did more to make a social order of rurality. But early religious efforts along these lines in Hispanic America foundered and to the extent that the myth may have played some part in the Westward push in North America, it may indirectly through the disillusionments of the frontier have promoted urbanization. A. K. Moore has argued with cogency that disillusionment arose, not merely from hardship, but from the disorder that plagued the frontier, disorder with which settlers found themselves unprepared to deal because they had brought with them no clear conception of how order should be organized in the Paradise they were seeking.[14] Many pioneers may have remigrated for this reason to the small towns that grew up behind the frontier, their children in turn migrating in search of more cultural nourishment to cities, and often not finding enough even there. This sequence of expectations and disappointments may go far to explain the changes in attitudes to city life of which Morton White has written.

There are vast gaps in our knowledge of city history. Yet regional study has gone far to establish the radius of European cities' economic influence at different times and has been examining their social and cultural relations with the countryside. To find planners and sociologists interested may encourage such work and spur comparative study.[15] The chief difficulty at present, if the historian is asked how any given division of economic and cultural functions between different types of community worked, in a given region, is the fact that even when a pattern of this kind might appear to remain fixed, the people involved in it might have been moving from place to place in a highly variable fashion through time. Population has for centuries been more mobile than is generally realized; its migrations are a largely unstudied aspect of any of the older social orders.

Today's planner cannot wait for the long labor that historians have before them on such questions. History can tell him only what he knows already, that his problem is a philosophical one.

NOTES

1. See *City Invincible* (ed. C. Kraeling *et al.*, Chicago, 1960), 363–66; also *Le symbolisme cosmique des monuments religieux* (Rome: Istituto Italiano per il medio ed estremo oriente, XIV, 1957), *passim*, especially Mircea Eliade's "Centre du monde, temple, maison," 57–82.

2. See *City Invincible, passim.*

3. *Isaiah* 13: 20–22.

4. Eric Voegelin, *Order and History* (3 vols., Baton Rouge, Louisiana, 1956–   ).

5. For the view that he also thought earlier types of city, Cretan and Spartan, better than Athens, see G. R. Morrow, *Plato's Cretan City: a historical interpretation of the Laws* (Princeton, 1960).

6. *Opera Giraldi Cambrensis* (ed. J. F. Dimock, Rolls Series, 1867), 151.

7. See John A. Yunck, "Economic Conservatism, Papal Finance, and the Medieval Satires on Rome," *Mediaeval Studies*, XXIII (1961), 334–51.

8. *Esprit des lois,* chap. 12.

9. See Franco Venturi, "L'illuminismo nel settecento Europeo," *Rapports, XIth Congress of Historical Sciences* (Stockholm, 1960), vol. IV.

10. See Carl E. Schorske, "The Idea of the City in European Thought: Voltaire to Spengler," in *The Historian and the City*, ed. O. Handlin and J. Burchard (Cambridge, Mass., 1963).

11. Müller is discussed further, with references, in "The Role of Comparison in the Development of Economic History." [See pp. 274–92 of this volume.]

12. Northrop Frye, *Fearful Symmetry, A Study of William Blake* (Princeton, 1947) is a study of his allegory; see especially Part II and Chapter 11. See also Ruthven Todd, "William Blake and the Eighteenth Century Mythologists," *Tracks in the Snow* (New York, 1947). My quotations from Blake are from his *Jerusalem*, stanza 74.

13. See Morton White, "Two Stages in the Critique of the American City," in *The Historian and the City*, ed. O. Handlin and J. Burchard (Cambridge, Mass., 1963).

14. A. K. Moore, *The Frontier Mind: a cultural analysis of the Kentucky Frontiersman* (Lexington, Kentucky, 1957).

15. See John Friedmann, "Cities in Social Transformation," *Comparative Studies in Society and History*, IV: 1 (Nov. 1961), 86–103.

Aliens in and around London in the Fifteenth Century

London is one of a few great European cities which have been attracting peaceful foreign visitors and immigrants for close to a thousand years. It has conducted, as it were, a remarkable series of experiments in toleration of cultural differences. Continental border towns have done so also but in a more limited way; provincial seaports and university towns have done so but less continuously. Although political historians of post-Norman periods, like the medieval local chroniclers, rarely mention London aliens except when they made news by getting into trouble, romantic historians of London have always painted in a few for atmosphere, and economic historians of any period up to the nineteenth century have made them their stock-in-trade. Their presence is above all a challenge to social historians, whose business is to discover how different types of foreigners have fitted into the network of social relationships through which the City's life has been carried on. This paper will first, as briefly as possible, examine the evidence as to how many aliens there were, in and around fifteenth-century London, and as to how varied they were, ethnically. The main focus is on the kinds of social contact they had with the English and with each other. How far did prejudice of one kind or another, or mere lack of interest, raise barriers? Did London life in that age encourage ready exchange of ideas in a spirit of friendliness?

Reprinted from *Studies in London History,* ed. A. Hollaender and W. Kellaway (London, 1969), pp. 251–72.

Numerical information about the aliens is much better than for
the rest of the City's population, especially in showing the effects of
epidemics. All estimates of the City's total population in this period
are unrealistic if they convey any impression of stability. The proportion who were alien-born, however, was always very small. Making due allowance for reasonable differences of opinion on matters
still uncertain until there is more research on London artisans and
labourers, one would set it at either two or four per cent, and it
probably varied between these limits. As is well known, most of the
few London aliens who were of any high social status came from
Mediterranean areas, the rest of the continental immigrants coming
from within a radius of only some three to four hundred miles. In
refining this picture and in developing the theme of friendly relations, the chief sources used here are two that have not been much
used for London social history—the records of the subsidy on aliens,
and wills proved in the court of the commissary of London.

The exchequer records of the alien subsidy that was introduced
in 1440 form an impressive collection. They constitute the only
nation-wide surveys of immigrants that any European nation pos-
sesses from so early a period. For London they cover the years
1441–4, and run irregularly between 1449 and 1469, with a last set
for the years 1482–4. They contain a few feeble efforts to measure
mortality, the earliest known English efforts of the kind. The tax
itself became a plague casualty in 1445. The statute authorizing it
had expired, parliament was not summoned for two years because
of recurrent epidemics, and pressure of accumulated business prevented renewal of the tax until two more years had passed. During
the interval the City inaugurated a measure of surveillance over the
movements of aliens, requiring innkeepers to conduct all alien guests,
within twenty-four hours of their arrival, to be interviewed by the
mayor.[1] No record of such interviews has survived. Like recent attempts to enforce a statute putting foreign merchants under the
surveillance of official "hosts," it may have fallen flat. Surveillance
of visiting merchants by hosts responsible to city authorities was
mandatory in other commercial cities in northern Europe, and inn-
keepers had police-reporting functions in Italian cities. By comparison, England appears to have been extraordinarily casual about
its aliens.

The writs to the justices of peace and borough authorities who were commissioned to make the first levy of the tax describe it as a means to alleviate popular vexation about the aliens.[2] This rather awkward statement of its political purpose may have been a cue to the commissioners to point out to the aliens the unfairness of the competitive advantage they had been enjoying through freedom from direct taxation; the increase in this over the past decade, and its renewal for 1440, after a brief respite, had possibly been acting as a stimulus to immigration. It may also have been intended to underscore the fact that the new measure had a police aspect. Being a poll tax, it enabled local authorities to find out just how many aliens they had, and to keep track of their numbers. The work of assessment was reduced to enumeration under the two headings of householders, to pay 16d., and non-householders, to pay 6d. This minimized the need for interrogation, for the criteria were objective and there were few borderline cases. Anyone was regarded as a householder who made his living as a merchant or as a craftsman having his own workshop, or by contracting for construction or transport jobs, or by a profession. A non-householder was a servant, usually living with his employer. Some London servants were wage-workers who lived out, and some of these were married, but neither circumstance altered their classification. The low rates of payment minimized the chances for corruption. Until 1449 merchants and their employees were assessed at the same rates as everyone else. The ordinary rates stood unaltered until 1482, when the 16d. was jumped up to 6s. 8d., and the 6d. to 3s. 4d.

Three kinds of allowance for error have to be made in using the records of this tax. First, there has to be some allowance for unavoidable incompleteness, and for carelessness. Second, local opinion affected the way in which instructions were interpreted in different places, and from one period to another, especially as to groups obtaining exemption. Finally, there was some leeway for favour through influence and patronage.

Absolutely accurate head-counting is possible only in a prison, where there is no freedom of movement. Anywhere else, even by census methods applied in a modern Western population, the count may be five per cent short. Catching aliens who were on the move was the chief difficulty throughout the whole history of the tax. In all towns alien artisans, like English artisans, were accustomed to make the circuit of regional fairs and markets or to send trusted servants off to buy and sell. However, the medieval method of relying on local inquisitions was better adapted to cope with this problem of mobility than modern methods. The work of enumeration was entrusted in the counties to local constables and in boroughs to panels of jurymen who met to swear before the commissioners that the lists they had prepared were complete. It is not their oath that justifies confidence in the returns, but the fact that each man had personal knowledge of the district on which he was reporting. In London over the first few years separate inquisitions were held in each ward, each panel consisting of twelve men who swore to the accuracy of their list before their alderman. The jurors were citizens of middling economic status but of local importance in their wards who would have had the help of gild officers' knowledge of alien competitors in their trades if they needed it. Later, when exemptions and the ravages of plague had reduced the amount of work, reports from several adjacent wards were presented together before the mayor.

Local jurors interpreted their instructions as they saw fit, in several directions. Although the minimum age of liability to the tax was twelve, one set of Yorkshire returns made it thirteen.[3] This and other variations of the kind are statistically unimportant, for most of the aliens' children were probably born in England and therefore not liable. The returns from Herefordshire and Leicestershire in 1440 state definitely that there were no sons or daughters liable.[4] It has sometimes been assumed, from the bizarre proofs of an heir's age that are recorded in the inquisitions post mortem for tenants-in-chief, that people were vague about the matter. But town courts assumed that parents and close relatives knew children's exact ages: in the London and Bristol orphanage records they are put down without question, often to within a half-year.[5] In any case the assessors had a rough objective criterion in the fact of employment. Few of the aliens, even in London, were in a position to keep their children at school, or to allow them to play all day, past the age of twelve. As to alien wives of aliens, who were liable, local opinion uniformly overrode the law. The only exceptions are in the last returns from London, in which wives are assessed as non-householders.

In the returns of the first few years, though they are not assessed and therefore not entered into the total numbers reported, wives are commonly listed along with their husbands.

Local jurors had also their own opinion about the wisdom of honouring the various exemptions by place of birth through which the scope of liability was progressively narrowed. After 1442 Channel Islanders and the Irish were exempt; from 1449 immigrants born under the king's allegiance in Normandy, Gascony and Guienne were exempt; the legislation of 1482 extended exemption to most foreign merchants—Spaniards, Bretons, members of the Hanse, Venetians, Florentines and Lucchese.[6] London was one of the places which did not at first consistently honour the exemption of the Irish, and which occasionally put Welsh people, who were never legally liable, on the lists. Again, London jurors could be unwilling to honour the French exemptions. The extent to which they were unwilling is uncertain, for ethnic identifications were entered on the lists only sporadically. A notable case is that of Master Gervais Le Vulre, a former royal servant in the English administration in France who for many years held high office as French secretary to Henry VI.[7] Preferring to live in Bishopsgate rather than in Westminster, he was repeatedly assessed there in spite of a royal mandate of 1440 explaining that he and his wife and servants were exempt because his office gave him the status of a member of the king's household. He was finally left off the lists after the issue of a second royal order in 1456.

Le Vulre's case raises a further problem, that of the bearing of naturalization on liability to the tax. Le Vulre had obtained letters of denization for himself and his French wife in January 1441, but these did not, as has been seen, exempt him in the eyes of London assessors, and a number of other men can be identified who were in like case. There is no point in counting them up, for a man whose name appears on an assessment list might at the last moment have established a claim to be not liable; there were always many non-payers, and they are not ordinarily marked as such. It is possible that some of the London jurors took the stand, logical enough, that since an alien was a person born under foreign allegiance, nothing short of a special act of royal grace or an act of parliament could make him an ex-alien; letters of denization might order that he should be treated as though he were an Englishman, and make it legitimate for him to buy land, but not remove his alienness in the matter of taxation. The issue that concerns us here is a question not of law but of the opinion of rather obscure citizens arguing the matter among themselves. The question was no doubt made more confusing by the fact that letters of denization were not fully standardized in form. They might or might not specify the right to bequeath land to an heir. They might mention the length of time the man had already spent in the country, as though it were an extra recommendation. More important, and this was well known, they might specify that the man who was granted denization must continue to pay customs as an alien. This condition was written into the letters for which Thomas Frank, a Greek physician, paid 5 marks in 1436, but at the king's command it was erased.[8] In the letters granted in 1444 to William Outcamp, a London broiderer from Holland, it stood; he was to be in lot and scot and pay customs and other dues like other strangers (*extranei*).[9] The jurors may have had similar doubts about aliens who became citizens. This act was sometimes preceded, sometimes followed, by obtaining letters of denization, but these were not essential unless the man contemplated buying land.[10]

There had, however, been a rush, during the excitement and disturbances in London in the months following the duke of Burgundy's switch from alliance with England to alliance with France, to demonstrate loyalty by swearing fealty to the king. Loyal Flemings were in March 1436 ordered to do so within two months, but a crowd of miscellaneous Lowlanders, and some Germans, from many parts of the country came forward to do so. Over 400 gave addresses in the London area. In return for swearing allegiance they obtained letters patent certifying that they had done so, and authorizing them to stay in the realm and to enjoy their goods peaceably.[11] These documents were not described as letters of denization and many may have bestowed only a kind of third-class naturalization not necessarily entitling the holder to buy land.[12] Only a few of the Londoners who had obtained them can be identified as appearing on the first City assessment list. This was not made up until five years later, and some of the quota who had sworn allegiance would by then have died either of natural causes or in one of the outbreaks of plague that had intervened; they are likely to have been older immigrants who had more goods to enjoy than others and had felt therefore more vulnerable to looters. Again, some may have moved away and settled in quieter spots on finding themselves still, in the last phase of the military crisis, before the duke of Burgundy was chased away from Calais, being molested in London.[13] Possibly there were up to a couple of hundred of these men in the London area in 1441 who were regarded as not liable to the tax.[14] This is the only period at which there may have been any sizeable group of resident London aliens not visible in the assessment lists.

For favour, in the City, was virtually limited to respect for royal favour to important merchants. Deference to magnates probably kept servants of theirs who were employed in Middlesex or Surrey off the county lists, alien servants in great lay households being conspicuously absent from assessment rolls throughout the country as a whole.[15] But few of these would have been living in the built-up London area.

The interest and effort that was thrown into keeping track of the numbers of aliens did not extend to the work of collecting the tax. No machinery was set up to make them collectively responsible for payment, and because it was realized from the start that the aliens' freedom of movement would present a problem, the tax commissioners were never held liable for uncollectable shortages in their accounts. They were liable to prosecution only for collecting more than they reported. Some details of an investigation that impugned the honesty of the sheriffs' clerks in Middlesex in 1456 are of interest in showing that even corrupt collection was extremely inefficient, and that honest collection depended in part and perhaps very largely on the conscientiousness of individual aliens.[16] Notes scrawled on rough accounts state that the Middlesex officials had reported receiving only £14 16s. 11d. of the £38 10s. 1d. assessed, yet had actually collected, and kept, another £7 3s. 2d. Although the honest and the dishonest collections together had amounted to only sixty per cent of the amount due, the investigators saw no possibility of raising this by more than five per cent. This was hopefully to be extracted from people the collectors had reported as having moved out of the county since the date of the assessment, but who were in fact still there. A non-collectability rate of thirty-five per cent was by no means unusual.[17] Masters were not held responsible for their servants' payments, and it is likely that a large proportion of the servants assessed were mere boys really in the status of apprentices working without pay. The Middlesex investigation shows the élite of the alien artisans to have been most dutiful in making regular payments. Some of the servants who had genuinely moved out of the county had paid an installment of their tax before leaving; one newly arrived servant who made a half-payment was credited with having paid the other half in Essex. In Westminster the investigation entailed summoning alien householders known to be employers of aliens to a court session to testify under oath, before the sheriffs and a bailiff, to the number of their servants. The word of a responsible alien came to be better than the word of minor officials.

The same care for enumeration coupled with leniency in collection as was general in the counties and in towns appears in London City. In 1484, when sixty-two per cent of those assessed had paid up by the close of the tax year, the non-payers were systematically ticked off on the list sent to the exchequer. Entries of surnames of thirty clerks in this year, one or two at the head of each ward list, witness to control by the aldermen, but there is never anything to show whether the aliens were simply left to bring their money to the Guildhall or whether collectors were sent around to dun them.

Even in plague years, the City returns inspire confidence. If an epidemic was on the rise at the time the inquisitions were held for assessment, the normal margin of under-reporting may in fact have been narrowed by the inclusion of people who had just fled or had just died in their homes; the jurors' information could never be up-to-the-hour. The rates of removal reported at the close of accounts in such years are startling. But the City authorities never used removal as an excuse for shortage in the tax accounts except in these years of crisis. Their count of removals cannot in the circumstances have been very accurate, but is plausible, the more so because of the check provided by the next set of inquisitions. In 1443, royal writs demanded a series of three inquisitions, in January, in May, and again in the autumn. These and the returns of 1442 and 1444 give an unrivalled, almost photographic picture of the disruption of personal lives that plague in a city produced. Hundreds of aliens disappeared. Some who fled returned, with new companions, settling down often at a distance from their old homes, only to rush off again because the City was not yet safe. The rhythm of the movements, and the turnover of names, cannot have been peculiar to the alien population. Flight was the only rational course. Faringdon Within lost eighty per cent of its aliens, Dowgate seventy per cent, Broad Street ward nearly sixty per cent, between January and October 1443.

The exact numbers of aliens who were assessed in the London area are set out in the annotated table appended to this paper. In round numbers, excluding married women because in most years they are not reported, the City at the beginning of the 1441 tax year had about 1,500, Southwark about 350, and Westminster and the Middlesex suburbs taken together about the same number. By 1449 the City number had fallen by almost forty per cent. True, the Irish and Channel Islanders and French people entitled to exemption were now invisible, and the Welsh were no longer put on the lists. But these groups, in so far as their members are identifiable by their names, amounted in all to less than two per cent of the city's alien quota in 1441, and French refugee migration to London was thin. Over the next two decades the total fluctuated around still lower levels, recovery not occurring until after 1469. The figures of 1482–4 are still a little below those of 1441. There may have been some new influx in 1483 that is not reported. However, the 1441 figures are also short, through exemption of survivors of the group that swore fealty in 1436. Again, there must have been some loss from mortality in the plague that was spreading in the autumn of 1439. The tax records of six counties in 1440 indicate that this epidemic was quite serious even in villages. To give an example from a district close to London, the constables of Blackheath hundred, who lost touch with twenty-seven of their fifty-nine aliens because they moved away, noted six deaths among the rest.[18] If those who moved away all saved their lives by doing so, the mortality was only ten per cent, but if those who moved carried enough fleas with them to cause continuing infection and some died of it, the rate was somewhere between ten and nineteen per cent. In London, mortality would surely have been close to the upper figure. It is certainly reasonable to conclude that there were more aliens in the area in the late 1430s than in the early 1480s.

The vast majority of the London aliens were classed as *Doche,* a term latinized as *Theutonici* but today untranslatable, since it covered the Flemish as well as those we call Dutch, and Germans

as well. In the last City roll over eighty per cent of the names are
so marked, and the names are so distinctive that there appears to be
only one error—the slip of calling Master John Giles, the papal col-
lector and archdeacon of London, and his household of relatives
Theutonici, whereas Giles was a native of Lucca.[19] The proportion
is a trifle exaggerated, because of exemptions of Italians and French
in the City, but for the London area as a whole the proportion of
Doche must then have been nearer ninety per cent, and had probably been so all along. In the last listing for the Middlesex suburbs
and Westminster the names are solidly *Doche*, and they are marked
as *Omnes Duchemen* in 1467;[20] there had been only a few French
there before their exemption. The same is true of Southwark.

The only available breakdown of the *Doche* by places of birth is
for the group swearing fealty in 1436. More than half of these men,
both those giving London addresses and those in the provinces, were
from Holland or Brabant, the Hollanders being the more numerous
by almost three to two in London and still more so in the provinces.
This truly Dutch preponderance is therefore likely to have held
throughout the century, though the quotas from other Lowland
territories and from Flanders and Germany may have been variable.
In the City only ten per cent of the oath-takers were Flemings and
no Southwark Flemings came forward, but possibly a good many
had moved away to lie low in quieter spots until the war crisis
should blow over. This circumstance helps to raise the proportion
of Germans in Southwark to as much as a quarter, as against only
about nine per cent in the City. In all of the groups the origins are
mostly in small places; Harlem, Utrecht and Middelburgh stand out
among cities of origin for the Dutch, Bruges for the Flemings,
Cologne and Aachen for the Germans. A good many of the Germans were from unspecified places in Westphalia.

The aliens in the City wards were more mixed. The Italians
stand out as maintaining their numbers through the period of decline
in the alien population. The likelihood of personal exemptions, and
the variable chances of including mere visitors, make the tax lists
a poor guide to the actual number of Italian residents. In 1441
twenty were assessed as householders and about the same number
as non-householders; for 1464 there are fifty-seven names. The
French were a still smaller group; there were several thousand of

them in England in 1440, but they preferred small towns and villages to London.[21] Other groups were mere handfuls of strays: three or four Greeks, the odd Portuguese sailor, a few Icelanders of whom the first to appear is the only woman in the lot, and stray Jews.[22] The Icelanders were among the imports brought back on Bristol ships to drift around the country as servants; there are eight of them on the last City list. Two Danes and a Catalan armourer round out the picture then, though there were Spaniards present, invisible through exemption. The only real change over the forty years is in the movement of Scots. A mere handful in the 1440s, they number at the end, with some wives, close to a hundred.

The tax records reflect the social differentiation among the aliens. It is the Mediterranean men who have the influence to get personal exemptions; the Hanseatic merchants remain invisible because of their group privileges; Frenchmen try to get favour but unsuccessfully.[23] The *Doche* are the conscientious servants who bring in their tax before moving, the large employers who sometimes pay their servants' tax, the proprietors of beerhouses whose tax was raised at the end to 20s., the servants who have no money to pay their tax, and the small married householders living too precariously to pay it regularly. But there were few or none in steadily desperate poverty. Only one person in the whole set of London records is described as a beggar—Henry Bem, a labourer living outside Aldgate in 1440.

The Mediterranean group was highly differentiated within itself. Among the most interesting members of it are medical men of high status. Greek, Italian, and Spanish physicians were attracted to England by the known shortage of university-trained men there. Many were appointed as personal physicians to royalty and nobles. Others who lived in London may mainly have treated the foreign merchants there. Thomas Frank, the Greek doctor who took out letters of denization, stood as executor for one Venetian merchant and had business relations with another. These men probably missed in London the stimulus of professional companionship to which they would have been accustomed in a southern city, but they made professional friends in Oxford. Fernand de Melonia, "doctor in medecynes," began his will as though it were a letter to his four Spanish executors: "Sires Because I am nowe in Way to departe for to go to Oxford as many tymes I have told you because to exercise me in my Study and because I am mortal . . . ." He belonged to a prosperous medical family: he ordered his money and plate and his professional books to be sent to his father in Spain, the books to be shared with his two brothers.[24] Master Adam, a Venetian who was being assessed for tax from 1443 through to 1469, was only a surgeon, and therefore of lower status.

The Italian merchants, as everyone knows, formed a commercial and financial aristocracy and had wider social contacts than any other group of London aliens. But they were far from equal among themselves. An agent of a big firm was not the equal of a partner in it, there were small partnerships lacking the resources of the big firms, some men operated independently with varying degrees of success, and the less successful of these might more or less abandon trade for brokerage and moneylending. A man's chances depended in the long run on his business acumen, but his family connections were a part of his business reputation. Where a man stood in the Italian world determined not only the kind of business dealings he had with Londoners but his social relationships with them.

The wills of nineteen Italians who died in London between 1417 and 1492 illustrate this.[25] To the wealthiest men, all that mattered in this world at the end—family, property, reputation—was in Italy. Several had made earlier wills there which they confirmed. Lucius de Vivaldis lay in his house in Billingsgate worrying about his wastrel son in Genoa. Most made a few formal religious bequests in London, but charity was reserved for the poor of their own city. They mention no English people save scriveners who wrote the wills, and one Venetian employed an Italian notary. There is one small gift to a servant named Herman, and Raphaell Ponsola wished Mariona van Bowdon to pray for him. The citizen barber who helped witness the will of Francisco de Aurea had probably just been summoned by the foreign doctor present, Thomas Fatuk, to bleed the wretched man. The only other case in which there were citizen witnesses was an emergency: Fautinus Remondi, citizen and noble of Venice, lay *in extremis* in the great chamber of the Sun Tavern in Lombard Street.

Two reasonably well-off merchants had some attachment to London. John Belevider *alias* Negerepounte de London was the only one of the whole group to leave anything—only £10—to the London poor. Percival Marcosano, merchant of Genoa *ad presens* (1448) living in London, left 20 marks to smarten up the clergy in his London parish church, St. Nicholas Acon, with white damask vestments, and an equal amount to a church near Genoa. His wife Alice, who *juxta morem Anglie* was to receive all of his plate and furnishings and 400 marks, sounds English; the only child with them was an Italian ward, to be turned over to Percival's brother, his executor. There was a £5 bequest to a citizen goldsmith's wife and one of 20 marks and a piece of silver-work to an English servant, Thomas Hyll. This was very probably the future alderman who died as knight and mayor in the epidemic of 1485. Having just completed his apprenticeship and been admitted to the freedom in the Grocers' Company, he would have been useful to Marcosano, who in turn could give him an advanced course in Italian business methods.

Four of the testators had really settled down in London. Though one had inherited some rural property near Pistoia, they were all fairly small men. The Pistoia man, Lewis Antony, made his English housekeeper co-executor with his elder son, had another son serving as chaplain in a London church and a daughter professed as a nun at Clerkenwell; he left the sons London property, acquired possibly through marriage. Benedict Austyn, a social member of the grocers' fraternity, made his English wife his executor, with a citizen fishmonger as co-executor.

Italians doing business with London merchants may not have expected their talk, over the wine that followed a deal, to turn on anything much but business and current events as they affected it. They may not have had the same caustic reservations as the author of *The Italian Relation of England* at the end of the century, who after mixing mostly with courtiers deplored Englishmen's disinterest in love and letters. Yet boredom with unsophisticated or insular clergy may have been one of the reasons why the Italians' favourite religious house in London was the most cosmopolitan one, that of the Austin Friars. Fifteen of the nineteen wills provide for burial in that convent's church. The convent had a room known as Lumbardeshall, which though not reserved exclusively for Italians, may have served as a common social centre.[26] All of the confessors and other non-parish clergy mentioned in the wills, like the physicians, were foreigners.²⁷

Wills of Lowlander merchants who died in London show more easy relationships, both with English citizens and with *Doche* immigrants.²⁸ John Rekys of Antwerp, dying in 1460, had a godson in the Vintners' Company and was friends with an immigrant basketmaker and his wife. John Gyse of Antwerp, dying in 1494, appointed a tailor in Southwark as executor along with an Antwerp merchant, under the supervision of a citizen fishmonger; after making religious bequests in London, they were to dispose the residue of his goods "among my Emes children after the custom of the cuntrey of Brabant." German merchants, though they holed themselves up in the Steelyard during visits to London, also knew immigrants.²⁹

The coming and going of merchants helped to keep *Doche* immigrants in touch with their homelands. At the same time, being thrown together in their various occupations, and having so generally to accept a common label because of similarities of language, the *Doche* began to merge their separate identities in the new broader one. Scores of the poorer Lowlanders, arriving with no name but the one given them at baptism, promptly acquired the surname of *Docheman*. Some changed it later, but some who had a surname clung to it as a status term. Sebet Titillot commended his soul to God in 1447 as that of a "Ducheman de London." It is still more significant that several fraternities used the term in defining their membership: the fraternity of St. Katherine, "founded and ordeyned by Duchemenne" early in the century, others dedicated to St. Antony and to the Holy Blood of Jesus, and a cobblers' group dedicated to SS Crispin and Crispinian.³⁰ These fraternities were supported not just by poorer people but by more substantial immigrants from cities. Egidius de Have, "Beerbruer," left money to the cobblers' fraternity and St. Antony's to pray for him, and Ludwig van Brig and Gysburne de Acon are on the membership lists of the Holy Blood fraternity. In short, England gave these immigrants a new cultural nationality.

The characteristics of that culture were a striving towards piety and economic advancement through honest work and mutual help within the group, in a spirit of neighbourliness towards all. These aspirations had long been set out in religious fraternity rules for artisans and small traders all over Europe. But the London *Doche* invigorated the old tradition.

The wills of their English neighbours express piety, but the *Doche* were stricter. One item of evidence of this is the greater frequency of mention of confessors in their wills. In the many hundreds of wills proved in the court of the commissary of London between 1417 and 1499, the vast majority of which are of English Londoners, I have noticed only five of these referring to a confessor as against ten in the *Doche* wills; several of the confessors were Austin Friars, some were Franciscans.[31] Parish clergy appear occasionally as supervisors of the executors. The *Doche* appear to have been much attached to their parish churches, where some had buried more than one wife or husband, or a father, but some preferred, like the Italians, to be buried in the Austin Friars' church. Evidence of fervour lies in the almost missionary character of the Holy Blood fraternity. Originating at the church of the Crossed Friars, this was an extension of a Saxon cult at Wilsnak, and had the universalist aim "for to norish encrese and engender love and peas amonge gode cristen people." There was religious thinking going on, too. It emerges in vernacular phrases which break right out of the conventional forms of commendation of the soul at death, phrases that were perhaps the last to ring in a dying man's consciousness. Here is the preface to a will dictated in 1495: "I John van Tyke of London goldsmith these words of the prophete havyng in mynde utterly syghing of my mispended tyme this present day of repenting almyghty God thou King of tyme and space . . . ."

In matters of morality the *Doche* were concerned but not hypocritical. The fraternity of St. Katherine was unusually candid about the problem of alcoholic squabbling at its dinners, a problem that was as ancient as Christian gild dinners. Redrafting their rules in 1491, the members decided to invoke the help of the bishop's ordinary in obliging the quarrelsome, if not too hard pressed from loss of working time through sickness, to pay the fines imposed. Another of their problems hinged on the imbalance of the sex ratio, their young men far outnumbering their young women.[32] There were always a few of the latter earning their own living in the usual occupations allocated to women—laundry, spinning and domestic service—and there was one schoolmistress. A Beatrice Kempstere ran a household of her own for a number of years, but there is a high turnover of the single women assessed. The wills give the impression that the immigrants preferred to marry *Doche* women rather than English. There was strong family feeling; mothers, and sometimes a father, lived on with sons, whose wills provide for aunts and sisters, and may remind executors to collect a small debt still owing from a brother. The wills of citizen *Doche* show the same strongly *Doche* family milieu as the others. The immigrants, some of whom retained small pieces of property abroad and went abroad on business, may have included in that business the selection of a wife. William Husman of London, making the parson of Fenchurch supervisor of his will in 1479, directed him to have his wife sent straight home to Hartyngtawe in Brabant where she was born, "unto her fader and moder Eymes and frendes ther for to abyde and dwell"; if she refused to go she was to get nothing whatever from his estate. Perhaps she was not so much incurably flighty as just very young.

It was probably the general custom of the *Doche* artisans, as the Statute of 1484 complained, to employ only *Doche* servants. Occasional lists of the number of these who worked for the same master, in the tax schedules, indicate a few workshops quite large for the time. Cordwainers employed up to nine men, beerbrewers up to eleven. The largest employer in 1484 was a goldsmith in Walbrook, Marcellus Maures, who had fifteen men as well as a woman servant. The *Doche* were indispensable in London goldsmithing, in the leather trades, in tailoring and in making and selling the small wares of haberdashery, took part in many service occupations, and pioneered in making clocks and spectacles as well as beer. There is space here to note only their more celebrated work, in printing. The tax record of 1484 lists all of the printers who are known to have been at work then except Machlinia, who is missing because of imperfection in the suburban lists, and adds the name of John Hawkes, "bokeprynter," a householder in Langbourn. There is also a Richard Hawke listed in that ward with wife Joan and a servant named Rouland. If this Hawke, whose occupation is not given, should prove to have any connection with the citizen and founder of that name, and with John, he may be the link that has been missing, so far, between the printers and the founders. Henry Frankenbury is listed as a householder in the same ward with a woman servant named Katerina and four men servants named Herman Grote and Dedericus Derykson, who paid their tax, and Adrian Derykson and Stephyn Ree, who did not. Bernard, presumably van Stondo (the surname is omitted) is listed, like Frankenbury, as a householder and "boke-prynter," and his name follows immediately after Frankenbury's. John Letowe, "Bokeprynter," is listed as a householder in Dowgate with his wife Elizabeth; William Ravenswald follows as a non-householder, and the names of four men follow as servants of Letowe and Ravenswalde jointly: Peter Martynson, George van Hawyn, Bernard van Dentour, and Joste de Fuller, all of whom paid their tax. All of the printers and their servants are styled *Theutonici*.

The London *Doche* held honesty and good salesmanship in especial regard. When nicknames appear on the tax rolls these are the qualities they advertise, as with Gerard the Gode, John Fairbusshel, John Wyncope, and Antony Popagay. Antony's fine feathers helped to make the Langbourn hat shop where he worked in the 1480s a fashion centre patronized by nobles; through this patronage his master Philip Lecok won royal permission to ignore price ceilings set on aliens' haberdashery.[33]

It was not a duty of the tax assessors to keep a record of the employers of alien servants, but they did so in a sporadic way. The City rolls for the early 1440s add about fifty English employers of aliens and for 1484, when masters' names were added more systematically, close to 120 are English. At both dates the masters include aldermen and other merchants employing all kinds of aliens, but most of the aliens serving Englishmen were of course *Doche*. Some of these—at the later date, Lord Howard's man Tutson, George Cely's three men, and others working under such important merchants as William Pykering and Geoffrey Feldyng—may have been taken on for responsible service in trade, but it is likely that more were employed in workshops. At the later date John Saunders, a draper, had five *Theutonici* running a brewery for him in Portsoken, and other aliens employed by Englishmen included smiths, makers of bows and arrows, joiners, cappers, an occasional weaver and broiderer, caterers, and servants at leading London inns.

Evidence that fifteenth-century Londoners were at all bothered by cultural differences between themselves and the aliens is hard

to come by. In a political-legal context the word "straungier" as
applied to merchants was an equivalent of *extraneus* and *alienigena*,
setting the merchant apart as having special privileges or disabilities.
In London gild records the word "stranger" can apply both to
English non-citizens, the *forinseci*, and to immigrants from abroad,
and gilds in a restrictive mood made quite as much fuss about admitting the one as the other. A special vernacular term for people
of humble status born overseas, perhaps a Dutch term for "stranger,"
occurs in a chancery petition of Edward IV's reign. James le Leche,
"Ducheman," was petitioning from a London prison to which he had
been taken on plaints of trespass laid by Sir Edward Courtney.
James was one of those low-grade medical practitioners who, contrary to professional medical standards of the time, would guarantee
a cure. Sir Edward had been foolish enough to take him into his
service to treat a diseased leg, had dismissed him, and James' self-
help in the matter of rounding out his fee had been regarded as theft.
James was frightened, yet he did not complain of meeting prejudice
as an alien. As he put it to the chancellor, Sir Edward was "of grete
power in London and also wele acqueynted and frended wt ye
queste whiche is sumoned," whereas he, James, was "an outlandlisshe man and litill or nothing acqueynted wtin ye said cite."[34]
He was using "outlandlisshe man" in the same way as we use
"stranger."

Such trouble as fell on London aliens in crises of war and commercial rivalry never lasted long. The only one to affect the Lowlanders was the Burgundian crisis of 1435–6. Although the protection
of the law was for some months inadequate, the royal government
kept pushing the City authorities to do their best, and was greatly
concerned over a boycott of Lowlander breweries through slander
of their product. A proclamation condemning this was issued at the
height of the alarm over the duke of Burgundy's attempt to take
Calais. Its calm must have been reassuring to all: the slanderous
rumours are malevolent, beer is a wholesome drink, and the Lowlanders are to get back to work producing a supply for the summer.[35]
The gross literary caricatures of Flemings that were published at this
time may have let off some of the current head of steam, but are
hardly a valid guide to London feeling. When the citizen inn-keepers
petitioned in 1446 for the right to collect fines under moral police
regulations and to keep a share of them, they did not imply that the

shady characters "luskyng a boute" in the city were Flemings or any other kind of alien immigrant.[36] There were some attacks on *Duchemen* in the early 1480s by young men,[37] occasioned perhaps by increase in immigration; the attackers would have done well to keep away from one definitely shady character in St. John's Street, an "apilier," in the degraded occupation of a professional trial champion. But the large well-organized gilds of goldsmiths and tailors, under merchant control, and the gilds in the leather trades, had always maintained friendly relations with their aliens and continued to do so.

The story of the anti-Italian agitation in London in the 1450s has a double plot—commercial rivalry among merchants, and heady excitement among young men who were by no means mere instruments of the mercers, as chroniclers charged. The story has the makings of a comic opera. The merchants play out running altercation, there is English complicity in an act of piracy, both sides break trade regulations and see through each other all along; at the end there is a shower of cheap pardons for all, and increased royal favour for the great Italians, which the English have to stomach.[38] The young men are seen in action first in a sword-play club and in a suburban drinking-club. Men in small trades following two mercers' servants of bad reputation, excited by the sword-play instruction they get from a wiredrawer, they thirst to avenge a companion, a shearman's servant whose wife has preferred a Lombard named Galiot Scot. To kill Scot and his associates as "fals extorcioners, common lechours and avoutrers" will be a good deed. They think all they need do is stir up tempers in Cheap. Yet they have great difficulty in angering a crowd, even though they provide a collection of weapons, wooden staves. They have to fall back on a lying report that a Lombard has killed an Englishman.[39] Even then, the band they muster achieves nothing but damage to Italian houses in one street. The net effect of the incident was to make merchants curb tempers, keep a tighter control over wild young men. Violence at sea, commercial war in the Baltic, was one thing; violence at home in the streets was too dangerous. Crises in commercial rivalry did nothing to alter social relations with alien merchants.

Unconstrained talk on matters of common interest to English and alien Londoners had normally to be in English, even among merchants. This general situation was not peculiar to London, and an Englishman who had made a long stay in the Lowlands might have an advantage over a visitor new to England. Northern foreign trade was managed without language schools, through native intelligence and with the help, no doubt, of interpreters. Although it was the fashion among wealthy merchants to send sons to grammar school, the years they spent on Latin did not give them a means of spoken communication.[40]

As to the alien craftsmen and small merchants in London, the evidence refers mainly to the *Doche* and it indicates that English became the means of communication within this group. The fact that the Holy Blood fraternity, which had a mixed membership, drafted its rules in English, would seem to prove this. But the reliance on English may be much older than the gild, and older, too, than the date of the first alien will in English to be proved in the court of the commissary. This date is 1430, and most English people's wills were still being drafted in Latin. The testator is Hary van Sandwyk, a poor man who cannot afford to be buried inside his parish church, St. Clement's Eastcheap, so asks to be buried in its churchyard. He had very little to leave, so very little to say. Half a mark was to go to "frere John de Colyne" and another half mark, with "all myn houshold," to his executor's wife Troyde.

There were a number of small professional people among the aliens who would have had special need of English. Most of these entitled *Magister* on the tax rolls turn out to be physicians. There were also chaplains, who could have supplemented the teaching of Elizabeth Scolemaystres in Cripplegate in 1441 and of the one *Theutonicus* schoolmaster of 1484. There may of course have been some women who never acquired English—the young wives brought over from the Lowlands, and the old mothers living with their sons.

Parish and neighbourhood life, and taverns and workshops and merchants' offices were the settings in which most talk between English and *Doche* would take place. There was matter enough of mutual interest in ordinary people's puzzling over religious concepts, in techniques and workmanship, in health problems, and in music. In Westminster there was always a *Doche* organmaker or two, and Walter, one of the two *Doche* minstrels in the City that year seems to have had a family orchestra or choir. How else could he have paid his full tax, as he did, on six children, his wife and his mother? There were dreams of innovation. John Tate, the London mercer who had the initiative to set up a paper mill near Hertford,[41] may already have been talking about this with his servant Adrian Water. Other merchants had tile or brick kilns, and may have employed Dutch or Flemings at these, in the country. An unusual Essex commendation of Dutch and Flemish masons comes in a letter written in 1469 at Havering atte Bower,[42] a highly commercialized village much frequented by Londoners, as was nearby Romford. The villager is asking a friend who lives in the direction of London to oblige him by engaging "a mason that ys a ducheman or a flemyng that canne make a dowbell chemeney of Brykks for they canne best fare there wt & I wold have seche as cowde maket wele to voyde smoke." He continues, "3yf ye may no flemynge have then I wold have an enkelesche man & he were a 3onge man for a 3onge man ys scharpest of Witte & of one mynde & cane as wolle undyr take to make it fettly." This pragmatic temper, judging a person not by his origins but by his practical intelligence, gave aliens a meeting-ground with Englishmen on terms of mutual respect as individuals. Perhaps it was stronger in villages, but it was strong also among merchants and among the more enterprising craftsmen. It was London's true strength. The rhetoric of prejudice which parliamentary lobbying fostered in a spirit of envy and restrictionism should not be permitted to obscure it.

Appendix

Numerical information in alien lay subsidy records for London area.
N.B. See p. 105 above for group exemptions from 1443 and 1449.

I. *Numbers assessed, reported fall in numbers through removal or death during tax periods, numbers of merchants and their clerks and factors included in first total when assessed at higher rates.*

Public Record Office references are to Exchequer Lay Subsidies, E. 179. "Inq." means record of inquisitions; "Acct." means there is no list of names. When nature of documents is not specified, there is a schedule of names without actual record of the inquisitions held. Easter and Michaelmas dating abbreviated to "E" and "M."

Tax period	Area covered	Total assessed (wives excluded)	Fall in numbers through removal	death	Merchants, their clerks and factors	P.R.O. ref. within E. 179
1440 Spring	co. Midd.	661	280	7		141/69
1440 July-Sept.	co. Midd.	396	71	2		Inq. 141/68
1440 E-M	co. Surrey	597	308			184/212

Tax period	Area covered	Total assessed (wives excluded)	Fall in numbers through		Merchants, their clerks and factors	P.R.O. ref. within E. 179
			removal	death		
1441 E-M	co. Midd.	397	96	2		141/67
1441 E-M	City wards	1506				Inq. 144/42
1442 E-M	City wards	1512	1382 (removal plus death)			Inq. 144/47
1443 Jan. Feb.	City wards	1650				Inq. 144/52
1443 E	City wards	1005	742	22		Acct. 144/48
1443 May	City wards	968				Inq. 144/53
1443 E-M	City wards	1512	1308	74		Acct. 144/43
1443 Oct.	City wards	866				Inq. 144/50
1443 Jan.	co. Surrey	333				235/17
1443 Jan. Feb.	co. Midd.	355				Inq. 141/71
1443 Spring	co. Midd.	415	129	7		Inq. 141/72, 74
1443 E-M	co. Midd.	296	53	2		Inq. 269/38
1444 Oct.	City wards	927				Inq. 144/54, 57, 58
1444 M	City wards	921	680	53		Acct. 144/49
1449 Sept.	City wards	907			72	Inq. 235/23
1449 Sept.	co. Midd.	296				Inq. 235/23
1449 Sept.	co. Surrey	272				242/126
1451 Aug.	City wards	566			46	Inq. 144/64
1451 Aug.	co. Midd.	132				Inq. 235/36
1451 Aug.	co. Surrey	139				Inq. 235/40
1452 Sept.	co. Midd.	118				Inq. 235/24
1453-5	co. Midd.	c. 290				235/57, 141/89, 35*
1455-6 Nov.-Aug.	City wards	750	114	20	c. 115	Inq. Aug. 235/58
1457 Aug.	City wards	593	25	15	c. 113	Inq. 236/74
1457 E-M	co. Midd.	258				Inq. 235/69
1457 May	co. Surrey	c. 65				Inq. 184/106
1458 E-M	City wards	521	54	12	472	Acct. 236/76
1462-3 M-yr.	City wards	400			58	Apr. 1464 Inq. 144/68
1464 Apr.-M	City wards	565	67	39	57	Apr. 1464 Inq. 144/69
1464 July	co. Midd.	188				Inq. 141/88
1465 July	co. Midd.	c. 184				Inq. 236/96
1465 July	City wards	460				Acct. 236/96
1466	co. Midd.	219				Inq. 236/102A
1466	co. Surrey	67				Inq. 184/110
1467 May	co. Midd.	262				Inq. 236/107
1467 July	City wards	650			72	Inq. 236/107
1466-7 M-yr.	City wards	668			90	Acct. 236/107
1468 May	co. Surrey	77				Acct. 236/116
1468	co. Midd.	204				Inq. 141/85
1469 June	City wards	569			65	Inq. 144/67
1469 E-M	City wards	504			38	Acct. 236/123
1469 E-M	co. Midd.	202				Acct. 236/123
1483 Jan.	City wards	1349			15	144/75A
1483 June	City wards	1349			15	Inq. 242/25
1483-4	co. Midd.	439				Inq. 141/94, 95
1483-4	co. Surrey	273				Acct. 276/64
1483-4	City wards, schedule from 242/25.					

(*141/35 erroneously catalogued as t. Ric. II)

II. *Aliens assessed in Westminster and suburbs and Southwark*

Area	1440	1456	1483
Westminster	83	40	91
Western suburbs	91	43	139
Northern suburbs	77	55	31
Eastern suburbs (including Stratford)	111	103	176
Southwark	353 (plus 79 wives)		
Other places in Surrey	244 (plus 4 wives)		

N.B. Other small places in today's Greater London area in 1440 had from one or two to a dozen aliens assessed, but few had wives, and many were perhaps itinerant. For example, three of the four at Hendon in that year moved, including Blak John, who may have been either an intinerant smith or the Johanna West who bore that nickname and was fined 2s. as a "Comynwoman" in Southwark in 1436 (Surrey Estreats, E 137/44/1). There were similar scatterings in adjoining Kentish hundreds and smaller ones in Essex. Gravesend and Greenwich together usually accounted for less than twenty. The total in nearby places in Essex in 1459 was fifty-six and was no higher in 1483 (E 179, 108/124, 130). Southwark, including Bermondsey, clearly had the greatest concentration of aliens in the whole area, but they were still a minority there. The only clue to the size and character of the English population of Southwark is in the poll tax returns for 1381, which list 844 people, including 125 married couples, in fifty male occupations and thirteen for women. The 844 include sixteen with alien names: e.g. John Champayne, Thomazyn Spynell, Gerard de Borgh, and six women named Frowe (Anghis, or Gece, Frowe, etc.) E. 179/184/30. In the city wards the greatest concentrations of aliens were simply in the more densely populated areas, i.e. where there were also most English living.

III. *Shortage of women among the aliens*

Area	Date	Alien men married to alien women	Alien men not so married		Single alien women (including a few widows)
			Householders	Non-householders	
City	1441	203	303	832	131
City	1444	184	222	456	65
City	1451	107	142	240	31

Taking City and suburbs together, the proportion of alien men to alien women was still higher in 1484, because very few single women appear in the lists for the Middlesex suburbs in that year. In the City 247 of the aliens had alien wives, and two *Doche* women are listed as married to Englishmen. There is no means of knowing how many alien men were married to English women; one can, however, eliminate the possibility of this as unlikely for the non-householders.

NOTES

1. C[alendar of] L[etter] B[ook] K, 316–18 (Dec. 1446).

2. The writs are included with many of the returns. For calendaring of the writs see C[alendar of] P[atent] R[olls], *1436–41*, 409–11. A typical phrasing is *ex causa vexacionis popularis*.

3. P.R.O. Exchequer, Lay Subsidies, E 179/270/31.

4. Herefordshire, E 179/117/51. Leicestershire, E 179/133/71; the non-householders here were put down as all "Singilmen."

5. Assignments of London orphans to guardians are recorded in the Letter-Books and Journals of the Court of Common Council, of Bristol orphans in the City of Bristol Archives, Tolzey Court Records, Orphans' Recognizances.

6. *Rotuli Parliamentorum*, v. 38b–39a, 144; vi. 197b–198a.

7. On Le Vulre's career see J. Otway-Ruthven, *The King's Secretary and the Signet Office in the XV Century* (1939), 89, 93n, 94–103, 105, 138, 156.

8. *C.P.R., 1429–36*, 604.

9. Printed from the patent roll of 23 Henry VI in Rymer, *Foedera*, xi (1710), 74. He may be the William Browderer who was assessed that year in the ward of Broad Street.

10. Aliens seeking citizenship were supposed to be admitted through the husting court. I was unable to recheck my notes of admissions for this paper, and the record itself may not be complete. It can be checked only from gild records of admissions, and for the majority of London gilds these are missing or broken. The entries of denization on the patent rolls may also be incomplete. See case of Adrian Grome, born in Bruges, who was said to have broken his allegiance by taking a pro-Burgundy stand but claimed to have sworn allegiance again and done liege homage in 1440; no oath is on record. *C.P.R., 1429–1436*, 612 and *London Possessory Assizes*, ed. H. M. Chew (London Record Soc., i. 1965), 119–20.

11. The names are listed in the *C.P.R., 1429–36*, 537–9, 541–88. A Gelderland smith living in Sussex who is listed there in entries made on 18 April 1436 had already obtained his letters patent by 8 Aug. the year before, when they entitled him to restitution of the value of goods taken from him by a swindler representing himself to be a bailiff, *ibid.*, 611.

12. Unless the letters specified this privilege. The content may have varied, for extra payments. Fealty and homage accompanying privileges granted by royal grace, sometimes through petition to parliament, presumably resulted in the fullest degree of naturalization. Some letters of denization specifying full privileges were conditional on liege homage and fealty, e.g. the grant of 1442 to the Venetian merchant Jeronimo Dandulo and his son (Rymer, *Foedera*, xi. 2), who were nevertheless still to pay customs as aliens; others say a man has sworn fealty and allegiance, or refer only to fealty or only to allegiance. The distinction between the terms, in the context of denization of craftsmen and merchants, was irrelevant.

13. A royal proclamation in July deplored such incidents and ordered the arrest of offenders, *C.L.B.K.*, 206.

14. Dr. N. J. M. Kerling's research on Norwich discloses the same problem there. See her "Aliens in the County of Norfolk (1436–1485),"

Norfolk Archaeology, xxxiii (1963), 200–14. It arises in other places I have checked. The extent to which it was due to removal can be shown only when the entire set of records can be printed or put on tape for collation.

15. Dr. Kerling (*op. cit.,* 208–9) tells of two tax-collectors being thrown out of one locality; she suspects that magnate influence may have made for appreciable underlisting of names sent up with Norfolk accounts.

16. E 179/235/57, E 141/35/89. Collection was especially difficult in that year since after being waived for two years, three years' payments were demanded.

17. This statement rests only on a reading of the accounts. A search of the record of these on the Pipe Rolls and Memoranda Rolls would be needed to show what rates of non-collection were regarded as reasonable.

18. E 179/124/107.

19. Eight of his servants and clerks were possibly *Doche;* the relatives were his servant Silvester and a merchant, Sebastian, both surnamed Giles; all lived in his household in Coleman Street ward and were exempt by writ.

20. E 179/236/102 A.

21. See my paper on the tax records of 1440, "A Survey of the Alien Population of England in 1440," pp. 133–49 of this volume.

22. The Jews in the 1440s are James Gentyll, a broker (*Calendar of Plea and Memoranda Rolls, 1413–37,* 225), Simon Jude, servant of an Englishman named Archer; Petr' a Jewe and Gerardus Jude, non-householders in 1449; and a married couple named Salomon at the end who could not pay all of their tax.

23. John Frank in Holborn reported four servants in 1456 but was found on investigation to have six, *juvenes;* and there is the case of Le Vulre.

24. Date of 1492. Unless otherwise noted, all the wills referred to are from the registers of the commissary of London (Guildhall Library MSS. 9171/3–8).

25. In chronological order (by dates of probate given in the court of the commissary of London): Conrad de Melidie, Alessandria, 1418. Fautinus Remondi, Venice, 1420. Lodowicus Antonii de Crimonensibus, Pistoia, 1431. Jeronomo de Ernualdis, Genoa, 1438. Jeronimus Centuriono, Genoa, 1439. Franciscus de Moline, Venice, 1440. Franciscus de Aurea, Genoa, 1445. John Belevider (executors Venetian), 1447. Benedict Augustin de London Grocerus, 1448. Percivalus Marchexan, Genoa, 1448. Marinus de Regla, Venice, 1449. Raphaell Ponsola, Genoa, 1451. Lucius de Vivaldis, Genoa, 1456. Nicholas Frankyn de Bononia grassa, 1466 (living in parish of All Hallows, Barking, with wife Grace; bequest of 50 marks to daughter Avicia, son Laurence executor, Franciscus de Christianis, *consanguineus,* supervisor; Frankyn is probably the Nicholas Boleyn assessed through the '50s). Georgius Spinilla, Genoa, 1471. Augustinus de Cumo, Genoa, 1470.

Robert de Prato, Savona, 1480 (all goods to his master Ruffino de Prato). John de Sermano, Milan, 1491. Franciscus Massacorty, Milan, 1493.

26. Mentioned as the place where the shearmen's gild drew up its rules in 1457. Court of the commissary of London, Register Sharpe, MS. 9171/5, f. 101v.

27. Nicholas, Venetian priest at the Austin Friars, named by Moline; Fr. Tyson, to pray for Benedict Austyn; Fr. Mayne de Swetia, to pray for Ponsola; witnessing will of Robert de Prato with his confessor, Angelo de Costaciis, was Fr. Angelo Melchiorus de Ferrara, of the order of hermits of St. Paul; Fr. John Antony of Milan, Austin Friar, witnessing will of Massacorty.

28. Wills of Rekys and Gyse, John Berman of Bruges (1431), Henry van Nivell of Brussels, only ones found.

29. Arnald Soderman, mercator Alman, 1441, will witnessed by Henry Overbaryk, alderman of the merchants of Germany and by a goldsmith and tailor of Dowgate long assessed in that ward, Magnus a Wardon and Henry Cruspyn, both names variously spelt in assessment lists. Executors of will of Jonas Schenk, licentiate in canon law and secretary of the merchants "de hanza Alemania," were citizens of Cologne, 1488.

30. Ordinances of St. Katherine's and of the Holy Blood fraternity were registered with the commissary of London, and are printed in H. C. Coote, *Ordinances of Secular Guilds, 1354–1496* (1871); and see will of Egidius de Have, 1442.

31. Austin friars confessors: Fr. George, will of Gisbertus van Diste, 1431, and of Arnald Soderman, merchant, 1441; Fr. Alard, for Sebet Titillot, 1447; since Eva van Styvtogh, 1445, left money to each *Duche* brother in the house, her confessor, Matthew van Prusen, was probably there, as also Nicholas (will of Walter Eveldagh, goldsmith, 1445). Fr. Henry Wydebak, Franciscan, for Herman Johnson, glasier (1481) and for Lucas Ratenhole, goldsmith (1445). Unidentified: John Candelesby, Frederic Herbert, and John, confessors of John Berman and John Rekys, merchants of Bruges and Antwerp, and of Arnold Steyvert, goldsmith (1464). There may be more among both alien and English wills in the commissary court; a good many pages of the registers are too stained for complete legibility.

32. For the sex ratio, see the Appendix, p. 123.

33. *C.P.R., 1485–94,* 371.

34. *Calendars of Proceedings in Chancery,* [ed. J. Bayley], i (Record Commissioners, 1827), p. civ.

35. *C.L.B.K.,* 205.

36. See note 1, p. 123.

37. *Acts of Court of the Mercers' Company, 1453–1527,* ed. L. Lyell and F. D. Watney (1936), reference to royal proclamation making masters responsible for servants involved. Under date of 1482.

38. See I. W. Haward's account in *Studies in English Trade in the Fifteenth Century*, ed. Eileen Power and M. M. Postan (1933), 309–15.

39. These details are from the City's report of its investigation into the riot of June 1457, *C.L.B.K*, 316–18. A Lewis Scot of Genoa had been assessed in 1451. In that year, as always, the Italians were scattered in several different wards. Dr. Alwyn A. Ruddock has interpreted the whole thing in terms of commercial rivalry, but has also demonstrated admirably, for Southampton, that feuding over trade advantages did not affect fundamental social relationships there. See her *Italian Merchants and Shipping in Southampton, 1270–1600* (1951), 162–8 and ch. vi.

40. For discussion of the linguistic problem in trade see N. J. M. Kerling, *Commercial Relations of Holland and Zeeland with England from the late 13th century to the close of the Middle Ages* (Leiden, 1954), 167–9.

41. D. C. Coleman, *The British Paper Industry, 1495–1860* (1958), 40–1.

42. Essex Record Office, manor court rolls, D/DU 102. Drafts of two letters written for this man come between the manor court entries for the years 9 and 10 Edward IV and are of such interest that I propose to print them in full elsewhere.

III

Historical Demography

Introduction

M. M. Postan

To try to assess Sylvia Thrupp's demographic studies by themselves is to do her injustice. Her contribution to the history of medieval populations owes much of its importance to the ease with which it fits into the overall story of economic and social change. There is of course no gainsaying the purely professional excellence of her demographic work or of her command of the appropriate terminology and technique. She may not be the first medievalist so equipped; she, like all the other workers in this field, has been preceded by J. C. Russell, whose book on the medieval English population is the first major study of the subject employing the full intellectual panoply of modern demography. Sylvia Thrupp, who could at times be highly critical of Russell's individual arguments, as in her article on the effects of plagues, would be the first to acknowledge her debt to Russell's pioneering treatise. Where she differs from him and from some other demographers who followed him, and excels over them, is in her ability to integrate her demographic findings into the total pattern of contemporary historical situations. For she is above all a social historian, or perhaps a historically oriented sociologist. Her demographic studies have obviously been undertaken with the intention of plugging gaps in the accepted versions of social history, and the success with which she has conducted this gap-plugging enterprise measures her true contribution to knowledge.

From this point of view Sylvia Thrupp's essay on replacement rates is the most characteristic and the most valuable. Allowing for the imperfections of her evidence (these she herself recognizes and allows for) the replacement rates she has derived from manorial court rolls are not only the most complete series so far constructed but are also the most pertinent. What makes them so pertinent is their perfect agreement with what most historians now believe to have been the general trend of medieval development. They move upward until some time in the first quarter of the fourteenth century and then enter on a declining course which continues well into the first half of the fifteenth century. A further series derived from wills suggests that the rates were recovering in the last quarter of that century. The concordance between Sylvia Thrupp's trend and the general direction of medieval development is thus complete; and she seals it by her discussion of the underlying causes. In that discussion she, unlike most demographers, draws upon the entire gamut of contemporary developments: wealth, social structure, migrations, and even bacterial mutations.

Equally well integrated and therefore equally conclusive is Sylvia Thrupp's study of alien immigration. Even a historian as familiar with her evidence of alien subsidies as I happen to be, may be surprised to discover how large in fact were the numbers of immigrants and how wide was the spread of their settlement and occupations. But unexpected as the facts may at first sight appear, they fit snugly into the general configuration of medieval economy and society.

Needless to say Sylvia Thrupp's determination and ability to present her demographic argument as part of an entire social pattern goes together with historic scholarship at its most exciting. The sources she uses may be well known but they have not so far been employed in demographic study to the extent she employs them and with comparable acumen and imagination. It would not therefore be an exaggeration to claim for her yet another achievement. By combining the global view of a general sociologist with a full command of demographic expertise and with all the demands of medieval scholarship, she has overridden the mutual disparagement of generalizers and scholars. By her own example she has proved that research, however exacting, can be conducted in the pursuit of a social generalization, and that sociological generalization, however comprehensive, does not inhibit, indeed requires, scholarly attention to all the minutiae of historical facts and evidence.

A Survey of the Alien Population of England in 1440

The extent to which mediaeval civilization favored peaceful migration about Europe is known only in broad outline. The scene is clearest in the central age of population growth, from the eleventh century into the thirteenth, when the influx into towns, and the organization of internal and frontier colonization, bring the main directions of movement into focus. Even so, we know little as to the numbers of those who moved in relation to those who may have vegetated in one spot all their lives. Later, migration is harder to trace because it was less organized, more simply dependent on individual decisions to leave one town for another or to abandon a declining industry or a war-devastated region. For the most part the people who made these decisions were too unimportant either to leave any personal record of their wandering or to make much impress on public records. Any full interpretation of the degree of movement and of its economic or cultural significance must wait on the progress of local research.

England's place in the final picture will be remarkable by reason of her long-continuing capacity to absorb immigrants from all sides. This may be illustrated, in a haphazard way, from almost every generation in her history, but there is little quantitative information on the subject before the fifteenth century. There is then a voluminous collection of Exchequer documents, surviving from the so-called alien subsidy, a poll tax that was granted in 1440, ran for five years, was revived in 1449, and from 1453 became an annual institu-

Reprinted from *Speculum*, 32 (1957): 262–73.

tion, granted for the king's lifetime. This paper will attempt to evaluate the records of the first year's experience with the alien subsidy, those of 1440, as evidence relating to the amount and character of immigration into early fifteenth-century England.[1]

The circumstances in which the tax was imposed were, it will be recalled, those of wartime emergency. The proceeds were earmarked for naval defence. The parliament that met in the winter of 1439–40 seems vaguely to have realized that the government's chronically wretched financial position was deteriorating. It granted a subsidy and a half and renewed the customs. The idea of taxing the unnaturalized alien-born, perhaps the only group in the country who would not have risen in rebellion at a new form of tax, was a feeble gesture in the direction of increasing the sources of revenue.[2] If the commons had expected to raise any substantial sum from the new tax, they must have been greatly exaggerating both the numbers of the alien-born and their amenability to pressure. Had all who were assessed at the rates set, 16d. for householders and 6d. for non-householders, paid up, the navy would have benefited by a little over £700. Actually, the tax could have realized not much more than half its potential maximum. To judge from the record of eleven counties, the sums collected averaged between fifty and sixty per cent of assessments. Cumberland, paying up less than a fifth of the £11 14s. 6d. reckoned as due, was the worst offender in this group. Northamptonshire paid up a quarter of the sums assessed, Northumberland, Westmoreland and Shropshire about a third, Surrey not quite a half, Devon and Hertfordshire about two thirds. Worcester, Wiltshire and Hampshire, the most responsive counties in the group, paid about three quarters of what was due. Rates of default among non-householders, especially in country districts, were staggering. In Devon nearly seventy per cent of those who were assessed at 6d. failed to pay.

Who were assessed? Very few merchants appear on the rolls and very few servants of great households. It seems to have been implicitly understood that the tax was not designed for these two groups, whose members were almost certain to obtain special favor. The people for whom the tax was intended were artificers and laborers, and servants employed in small households. Few if any of these could have enjoyed sufficient special favor or protection to enable them to avoid assessment. There was certainly a genuine effort on the part of the authorities to have all members of these classes placed on the assessment rolls. Prepared from testimony given by local constables and other jurors empanelled by the justices of the peace at various dates from April onward, the rolls show evidence of careful house-to-house enquiry. Usually the names of the employers of non-householding alien servants were included in the record. The rolls may therefore be regarded as approaching the character of a census. They do not profess to be a true census, for certain groups were explicitly left out—regular clergy, children under twelve, and alien women married to Englishmen.

It should be pointed out here that there was no legal ground on which an alien could contest payment or assessment. True, the fullest fifteenth-century letters of denization were so phrased as to make the obligation to be in lot and scot appear contingent on the rights to hold land in fee simple, to plead and be impleaded in the courts, and sometimes also on the right to receive special franchises. But to infer that aliens could exercise none of these rights prior to denization and were therefore liable to no taxation save the customs on their merchandise in foreign trade would be absurd. In matters of personal safety, contract, and title to leasehold property they still enjoyed, as Miss Beardwood showed to be the case in the fourteenth century, as much protection from the courts as anyone else.[3] Those who had the means and could find sponsors could be admitted to the freedom of boroughs. The vast majority of those who settled in and about the towns, however, were in a position similar to that of the native *forinseci* of the neighborhood. In important respects this was a semi-privileged position. Immune from direct borough taxation falling on citizens they were yet able to compete with citizens in petty trade. Borough charters barring non-freemen from retail trade were never enforceable once the latter had won customers' goodwill. But there was nothing in the situation to exempt the aliens among them from national taxation.

As to the local officials in charge of assessment, there could have been no generally valid motives for under-enumeration. It must have been extremely difficult to track down casual labor that was perpetually on the move, and some proportion of this element must have escaped the jurors' count. Yet there was a genuine effort to trace the floating population. All of the alien laborers and servants reported from Northumberland, numbering over 400, are described as *vacabundi*. Obviously, it must have been still more difficult to collect money from such people than to learn their names. This point had been foreseen. County officials were in no fear of being penalized if collection fell short of assessments, the collectors being guaranteed beforehand that a sworn explanation of shortages in the accounts as due to the death or removal of people assessed earlier in the year would be accepted.[4] In order to minimize defaults by removal collection was supposed to be in two instalments, one counted as an Easter payment and one due at Michaelmas. Actually, owing to delays in setting the machinery of administration to work, the two collections must often have been taken close together or at one time. They could not have been pressed very hard. Some collectors specified poverty as the chief reason for non-payment. Most fell back on the official formula *amoti sunt*. As often as not, this may have been a mere laconic euphemism for passive resistance.

Although collection was lax, there is no reason to suspect laxity or apathy in the work of enumeration for assessment. It may well have had a police aspect. The political situation was tense. Many of the alien-born were known to have come from countries and territories with which England was unfriendly or at war. That they were still able to find employment or were permitted to set up shop may seem to argue popular indifference to their origins, but in more likelihood it argues only the economic value of their services. The English were at the time painfully aware of their vulnerability to attack, and under conditions of such strain their attitude to strangers was apt to be anything but stolid or complacent. Parliament had early made itself an outlet for xenophobia, going to the lengths of demanding the banishment of one group after another. Alien friars had been so singled out in 1345, charged with sending secrets abroad. The Good Parliament had demanded the banishment of Lombard brokers on the grounds that they practised usury and unmentionable vice and that there were Jews, Saracens, and "privy spies" in their ranks. Richard II had been put under pressure to banish Bohemian courtiers, and Henry IV, in his turn, to send Bretons home. The stresses of the fifteenth century made fear of spies endemic. On renewal of open war with France the commons petitioned for a screening of all immigrants, those already in the country as well as those newly arriving, in order to test their intentions and their loyalty. In 1413 they proposed that the Irish be sent back to Ireland. Perturbation of this kind was not confined to talk in Parliament. It led to the harassment of refugees from Guienne who had managed to settle down and acquire lands. Local persecutors challenged them as "alliaunts" without a right to lands.[5]

The most serious crisis of the century occurred shortly before the adoption of the alien subsidy. After the breach of relations with Burgundy, Flemish immigrants, along with all others from neighboring territories who on account of similarity of language were popularly lumped together as "Duchemen," were now suddenly regarded as a danger. They were, indeed, in the strategic position of virtually surrounding London, many hundreds of them being massed there in slum and suburban dwellings. During 1436 the rumor spread that Dutch beer was poisonous, and some London breweries belonging to Hollanders and Zeelanders were attacked.[6] The government gave Flemings two months in which to prove their loyalty by taking an oath of fealty. The patent rolls contain a list of over 1,800 names of those who took the oath, not Flemings alone but men also from Brabant and from neighboring territories. Mandates were then issued to local authorities to allow these men to enjoy their goods and to inhabit the realm peaceably.[7] Given the possibilities of panic, it is hard to believe that the government's interest in the first alien subsidy was solely fiscal. The police check on the total numbers and the whereabouts of the alien-born for which it offered opportunity was probably welcome to all authorities, local and central.

Still another reason for believing the records of the 1440 subsidy to represent an honest attempt at enumeration should be mentioned. This is the simple fact that the tax was new. There had to be genuine enquiry at first hand, if only because there were no old lists of the kind on file from which they could have been made up.[8]

The table on pages 144–47 gives the totals, by counties, of the figures that are available. There are none from Cheshire or Durham and returns are missing from Oxford until ten years later. Lancashire, too, may be regarded as a blank. The figure of 5, sworn to as a county total in 1441, is suspiciously low. For Bedfordshire also one has to use the figures of 1441, which may be a little low. In neighboring Buckinghamshire the figures drop from 258 in 1440 to 204 in 1441. A more serious gap is in London, where one has to skip two years and use, for what they are worth, the figures of 1442. With Oxford and the palatinates missing, and with the 1441 and 1442 substitutions for Bedford and London, the table gives us a conservative minimum estimate for the total alien-born working population, of a little over 16,000. Men outnumber women in the lists by about ten to one.

The margin of error in our present estimates of the population of late medieval England is still so elastic that it is futile to attempt to assert precisely what proportion the aliens liable to the subsidy represented. If the rate of evasion of the poll tax of 1377 was anything like as high as the alien rate of evasion in 1440, then estimates of the national population that stem from the fiscal returns of 1377 have been decidedly too low. In any case, the aliens assessed in 1440 could hardly have represented one per cent of the population.

Contemporary impressions of the extent of early fifteenth century immigration may have had a strong bias to exaggeration. This would have been due to the peculiar distribution of the aliens. They were not only heavily concentrated along the coastal areas that were most open to enemy invasion, but were very widely scattered throughout the south and west. About a third of them were in these regions. They were found in over 120 communities in Devon and in twice this number of Kentish communities. They were disproportionately numerous in London, which, counting the suburbs, must have harbored well over ten per cent of the alien population of the country. Excluding the suburbs, and without counting married women, the London figures for 1442 come to over 1,500. The four county areas with the largest alien quotas were Hampshire, Kent, Gloucester and York, each with over 1,000.

There was no universal pattern of concentration in towns. The high proportions in London, and also in Bristol, must have been due partly to a constant swarm of travellers and sailors laid over between ships, and partly to an abnormally high demand for casual labor and petty hucksters. In Norfolk almost half the aliens reported were in the three towns of Lynn, Yarmouth and Norwich. Those in Suffolk were more scattered.

Classified by the information that is given in the rolls as to their origins, the immigrants fall into four main groups. They were Irish, or born in Scotland, or from Normandy or Picardy, or they fell into the contemporary blanket category of "Duche." Precise testimony as to their nationality or place of birth can be eked out by reference to the more distinctively national surnames and personal names that occur, such as Janyn or Peryn Frensheman, Patrick Yrish, Alexander Scot, or Clays Claysson. The procedures of assessment caught also a few stray aliens of more exotic origin. Portuguese and Icelandic sailors were found in the ports. There were a few Aragonese and Gascons. Beerne, *natus in Fynmerk,* ashore at Stokisley in Yorkshire, is almost the only Scandinavian on the lists. Isabella Manswoman, vagabond in Yorkshire, was one of the few Manx.

This information as to origins is too incomplete to be added into aggregates for the country as a whole, yet it illustrates, more fully than any other source of the time, the general character of immigration into each main area. East Anglia, for example, was a zone of Lowlander predominance, with a few Irish appearing on the scene in Cambridgeshire. In Kent the French begin to predominate, with Lowlanders second, and the Irish in third place. London was the zone of greatest attraction for the Dutch and the Flemish. As for the south, and the west country, and the inland counties north of London, the question is mainly one of mapping the bounds and the overlap of what was French immigrant territory, as it were, or Irish. Berkshire was Irish territory, Wiltshire and Staffordshire French. In each of these counties there were some Flemish and German craftsmen, mostly in the towns. There were strong French quotas also in Lincolnshire and Yorkshire. Not quite a quarter of the Yorkshire aliens are classifiable. Of this fraction half were Scottish, a third French, and the rest "Duche." The Northumberland lists show only one French name, and one Brabanter; the rest are stated to have been "nati in regnum Scotiae." As would be expected, the Scots had also infiltrated Cumberland. Almost half the aliens listed there have the surname "Scot."

As between town and country, the distribution is very clearly marked. Scots and Irish preferred the country, Lowlanders and Westphalians preferred the towns, the French were more divided.

The rolls contain important information as to the occupations of the immigrants. This helps to explain their distribution about the country. Their zones of settlement were not determined, as might appear at first sight to be the case, solely by ease of geographical access. They depended at least as much on opportunity for work in lines that were common in their home countries. The Scots and the Irish, familiar at home with cattle and sheep, had reason to stay mostly in the north and west because this was pastoral country, where they could find work as herders. When they moved on it was often to serve as swineherds or biremen or else to do the heavy work of sawyers. Otherwise they made use of schooling rather than of craftsmanship. There were a good many Irish parish priests and parish clerks. The French were more versatile. They could do herding, work on the land as general laborers, and, particularly those from Normandy, contribute skill in construction trades, in iron-smithing, in milling, in weaving, and in brewing. They were also, already, much in demand as domestic servants. As has been indicated, the evidence of the rolls does not cover the households of magnates, but it touches those of a few country knights and it describes many Frenchmen as servants at small monasteries and with village clergy.

The Flemish, Dutch, Brabanters, and Germans, on the other hand, were almost exclusively in skilled crafts in the leather and textile industries or in other highly specialized lines. They were tailors, goldsmiths, and glasiers, and made barrels as well as beer. They carried many of these skills into very small towns, but they gravitated naturally to the larger towns rather than to villages.

The local distribution of the aliens' occupations as shown in the rolls makes a substantial contribution to knowledge of the development of English consumers' demand. The evidence, grounded here on specific description of the occupation, may be extended by some use, with caution, of specialized trade surnames. Caution is needed, because men could turn from one trade to another without changing their name, and because the more common trade names are not necessarily evidence of occupation at all. Tailor, already a common name, is no evidence of a man's trade: Peter Taillour of Boston was a brewer. Even less common trade surnames may be deceptive. William Maserere of Newton in Kent did not live by making masers (wooden cups) but was a tailor. Robert Cork of St. Albans was a falconer, while Fauconer as a name is found in other trades. John Tilemaker, however, when one can check him, will always turn out to be a tilemaker, Herman Mulward to be a miller, and Mathew Goldsmith, or Glasier, to be in those trades. Arnold Belrynger of Sutton Hoo disconcertingly turns out to be a weaver, but perhaps he was in demand as an expert at the bells on holidays.

The Continental immigrants were far from being concentrated in clothmaking. Many Flemish and Brabantine weavers were to be found, and some from Normandy, but there were probably more skilled men of these origins in the leather trades and in making other small finished wares designed to tempt the English into living more comfortably. While the English were busy working for foreign markets, exploiting their cost advantages in woollen supply, foreigners from the regions that suffered from their competition were moving in to push on the development of the English home market. Adam Smith, who so deplored the frictions that human irrationality tends to impose on the free movement of labor, would have been delighted to find so many fifteenth-century French and Dutch, in his terms, relatively rational.

The situation is of cultural as well as economic interest. The immigrants may or may not have contributed much to the popular stock of ideas on politics or religion. Yet, through their crafts, which were all, in a sense, forms of art, they were slowly altering the everyday conditions of life. Again, to put more of the English into proper shoes and stockings, to familiarize them with popular continental styles of tailoring, to coax them into wearing warm knitted caps—surely these alone were changes of at least potential cultural significance.

The aspect of fifteenth-century immigration that is of widest interest concerns the problem of assimilation. A late seventeenth-century pamphleteer who advocated bringing in more foreigners to develop English industry assured his readers that in a generation they would be indistinguishable from the English.[9] Were second generation immigrants in the fifteenth century so quickly assimilated? The subsidy rolls offer a great deal of auxiliary evidence that helps in breaking this question down into manageable proportions. There is no single easy answer to it. The problem of security of land-holding and inheritance, for example, has little relevance to the situation in which the great mass of the people on these rolls found themselves.

The poor wage-workers among the immigrants may conceivably have been very isolated, even from their kind among the English poor. They were unmarried, and many may have remained in the condition of unmarried servants all their lives. An illegitimate second generation may have been in no better case.

On this matter of isolation there is one invaluable source in the personal names on the subsidy rolls. The evidence of the nondescript ones—Janyn Frensh, Peter Iryssh and the like—is negative: the workers so dubbed may or may not have had an identity, a personality, in the eyes of English neighbors, or have had friends among them. But many of the names, instinct with the poetry, the banality, and the crudities of popular culture, show anything but a negative reaction. Arnold Wanderfayn and Willy the vagabond could be strolling across an Elizabethan stage, with Joanna Coteye (Cat-eye?) and Joanna Wall-Eye dragging along behind them. The name of Josy the Gentlewoman, keeping house alone in Boston, stirs curiosity, as does Artur the Roy, servant in Chichester, and Katerina Inkepottis, householder in Canterbury.

The established householders with a good trade, anxious to provide well for their children and considering full denization as a means to acquiring secure title to land, would have been drawn into wider relationships with the English, if only through their customers. But they too could remain culturally isolated. Some were providing services mainly for their own fellow countrymen, some may have intended to return in time to their homeland. The commons' petition for a protective customs duty on small ware, in 1484, complains that some of the Dutch and Flemish came to England only temporarily, to make money.[10]

Evidence as to intermarriage, in the rolls, is slight, since neither alien wives of Englishmen nor English wives of aliens were liable to the subsidy. Alien wives of aliens were not clearly liable. At all events, they seldom paid, and may often have been omitted from the assessment lists. The Rutland jurors gave unusually full information about their own small inland sample, in which most of the family men, Lowlanders and Frenchmen, were married to Englishwomen. On the other hand, in thirty out of thirty-one cases scattered about Cambridgeshire, Northamptonshire, and Warwickshire, in which the wife's origin is specified, she is of the same alien group as her husband, either Irish or "Duche." There are a few notices of mixed intermarriage among aliens. Two in Exeter refer to a Breton married to a woman from Normandy and a Ducheman to a woman of Bayonne.

The unmarried alien women were mostly in unspecified service, often perhaps domestic. Some had trades by which they supported themselves as independent householders, spinning, weaving, knitting caps. One woman householder in Canterbury is described as the nurse of a local merchant's children. A number of the hardy Scottish girls who tramped across the border are set down as laborers.

The town parish addresses of aliens that are given in the rolls show that they were not segregated from the English and did not cling together physically in national groups. They might be at one end of a very small town but they would be there together with English *forinseci.*

This survey, based on one year's records, can do no more than point to a few of the problems presented by the alien elements in fifteenth-century English society. The records of 1440 are reliable in the sense that they may be regarded as an honest if not an absolutely complete survey of the alien working population of that year. They help to explain how this element, although forming only a very small fraction of the population, could yet, through its distribution and its mobility, be an occasional source of tension. Few of the questions that they raise can be answered from fiscal records alone, however, certainly not from the records of one year alone. The question of the ease or difficulty with which immigrants of different national origins came to be assimilated, to be regarded, with or without formal denization, as English, can be answered only through continuous tracing of the lives of individuals and of the experience of particular communities in dealing with the various alien elements, floating and settled.

The records of later levies of the alien subsidy are useful chiefly in tracing the fortunes and the contributions of the more prosperous members of the German and Lowlander groups. The scope of the tax was reduced in 1443 and 1444 by exemption of the Irish and the

NUMBERS, DISTRIBUTION, AND ORIGINS OF ALIENS ASSESSED FOR SUBSIDY IN 1440

(N.B. Assessment of 16 d. indicates classification as householder, of 6d. as non-householder. P.R.O. references to rolls used within class E179 at left.)

| | Figures from Inquisitions and Accounts | | | | | | | Origins Stated or Inferred from Personal Names | | | | | |
| | 1 | 2 | 3 | 4 | 5 | 6 | 7 | 8 | 9 | 10 | 11 | 12 | 13 |
	Total at 16d.	Total at 6d.	Single Women	Wives	Total Men	Total Women	Total Men and Women	Total	"Duche"	French	Irish	Scots	Other
West													
CORNWALL 87/77, 78, 80	124	156	5	7	275	12	287	149 (c. 50%)	15	61	65	1	3 Portuguese 1 Guernseyman
DEVON 95/100, 102	342	333	20	2	655	22	677	630	71	435	92	1	1 Spaniard 1 Portuguese 4 Manx 25 Channel Is.
DORSET 103/83, 235/9	243	515	12	—	c. 746	12	c. 758	84	6	47	—	—	30 Channel Is. 1 Portuguese
GLOUCESTER Co. excluding Bristol 113/100, 102	83	76	2	4	157	6	163	84 (c. 50%)	12	37	33	2	
Bristol 113/103 Total from 7 parishes plus double the total of remaining 11 parishes in return of 1442	289	496	87	68	698	155	853	26	11	4	11		
Total for Glouc.	372	572	89	72	855	161	1016						
HEREFORD 117/51, 52, 50	34	24	2	2	56	4	60	57	6	44	7		
SOMERSET 235/9, 169/92	180	197	5	2	c. 372	5	c. 377	59 (15%)	6	33	16		4 Channel Is.
East													
CAMBRIDGESHIRE Co. 235/4, 81/85, 87	58	39	—	7	97	7	104	72	26	39	7		1 "de regno Sweth."
	..	..	..	.6	6.	.8	8.	78	58	58	10		

	1	2	3	4	5	6	7	8	9	10	11	12	13
	Total at 16d.	Total at 6d.	Single Women	Wives	Total Men	Total Women	Total Men and Women	Total	"Duche"	French	Irish	Scots	Other
LINCS. 136/206, 270/32, 269/28 Hundred of Holland only, and towns of Lincoln and Boston	141	111	15	1	237	16	253	34 (13%)	20	11	2	1	
NORFOLK 149/124, 125, 126, 130	119	112	12	14	219	26	245	90 (36%)	66	21	1		1 Orkeney Is. 1 Icelander
SUFFOLK 180/92	247	249	8	29	488	37	525	240 (45%)	160	71	3	4	1 Icelander 1 Spaniard
Midlands													
BEDFORD 235/11 (1441)	40	17					c. 57						
DERBYSHIRE Figures arrived at by subtracting returns for Notts., 1440 from joint returns 1441 (235/13)	12	45					c. 57						
HUNTINGDON 235/3	36	34	—	2	70	2	72	43	11	28	3	1	
LEICESTER 133/71	52	45	1	1	96	2	98	90	13	51	19	7	
OXON No returns													
NORTHANTS 155/80	178	170	60	24	288	84	372	261 (73%)	45	87	135	5	1 Icelander 1 Aragonese
NOTTS 159/73	57	44	1	2	100	3	103	46	7	30	5	4	
South													
HANTS 176/585, 586 173/98, 99, 100, 102	289	832	65	3	1056	68	1124	154 (13%)	46	82	10	1	10 Italians 1 Portuguese 2 Guernseymen

NUMBERS, DISTRIBUTION, AND ORIGINS OF ALIENS ASSESSED FOR SUBSIDY IN 1440—(Continued)

	Figures from Inquisitions and Accounts							Origins Stated or Inferred from Personal Names					
	1	2	3	4	5	6	7	8	9	10	11	12	13
	Total at 16d.	Total at 6d.	Single Women	Wives	Total Men	Total Women	Total Men and Women	Total	"Duche"	French	Irish	Scots	Other
SUSSEX 184/212	281	580	42	3	819	45	867	245 (28%)	42	200		1	
WILTS 196/100	204	273	1	1	476		478	369 (77%)	30	214	125		
CINQUE PORTS 235/2	126	91	14	15	202	29	231	68	9	59			
London and Home Counties													
BERKS 73/91	93	104	5	21	182	36	218	172 (78%)	8	30	134	1	
BUCKS 77/159	112	155	9	8	258	17	275	82 (29%)	22	41	19		
ESSEX 108/113	203	199	10	1	392	11	403	114 (28%)	65	42	7		1 Italian
HERTS 120/83	162	146	4	1	304	5	309	101 (32%)	36	57	8		
KENT 124/107, 105	446	683	44	59	1085	103	1144	453 (38%)	192	218	42	1	
SURREY 184/212	96	407	39	87	462	126	588	216 (36%)	152	61	3		
MIDD 141/69	406	256	c. 30	65	c. 631	c. 95	c. 726	178 (24%)	112	53	11	2	
LONDON 144/43 Returns of 1442	528	984					c. 1512						

146

	1	2	3	4	5	6	7	8	9	10	11	12	13
	Total at 16d.	Total at 6d.	Single Women	Wives	Total Men	Total Women	Total Men and Women	Total	"Duche"	French	Irish	Scots	Other
RUTLAND 165/68	16	10	2	—	24	2	26	19 (73%)	8	9	1	1	
SALOP. 269/53	30	42	3	3	69	6	75	17 (22%)	3	9	5		
STAFFS 117/56	68	70	3	—	135	3	138	62 (45%)	2	50	10		
WARWICK Co. 192/65, 66, 235/8	49	40	4	8	85	12	97	86	7	28	51		
Coventry from 192/67 (1441)	62	55	10	—	107	10	117	17	—	4	13		
Totals	111	95	14	8	192	22	214	103	7	32	64		
WORC. 200/75, 76	57	67	4	—	120	4	124	55 (44%)	4	41	10		
North CHESTER CUMBERLAND DURHAM LANCS. 132/367 (1441)	96	213	119	1	190	120	310					142	
	3	2					5						
NORTHUMBERLAND 158/115, 39, 41	203	501	113	40	591	153	744	c. 100%	2		1	c. 741	3 Icelanders 3 Orkeney Is. 2 Manx
WESTMORELAND 195/33	15	90	22	—	83	22	105	18	11	2			
YORKS Co. (270/31)	265	745	133	12	877	145	1022	263	33	90	—	132	8
York City (217/46)	45	37	7	—	77	7	82	18	11	2	—	5	
Hull in 1441 (202/112)	18	41	10	3	46	13	59	7	5	1	—	1	
Yorks totals	328	823	150	15	1000	165	1163	288	49	93	—	138	

Channel Islanders. It then lapsed for five years and when it was revived there was additional exemption for all who had been born in the duchies of Normandy, Gascony or Guienne. Further, the principle was enunciated that the king's liege men born in any place under his obeisance could claim exemption. This gave a broad exemption to Normans. To compensate for these surrenders the tax was more steeply graduated. Merchants were drawn in at rates that by 1453 reached 40s. Under Richard III the original notion of trying to raise money from the poor was dropped entirely. The minimum rates set for servants and householders were raised to 2s. and half a mark, and proprietors of brewhouses were made liable at 20s.

Both the records of 1440 and the returns from later levies of the alien subsidy require to be collated with town records and with court records of all kinds. The experience of the various bodies of aliens in the country bears on important problems of economic innovation as well as on the legal aspects of the developing concept of nationality. Together with questions of the kind that have been touched on here, relating to cultural assimilation at the lower levels of society, these are all rather neglected aspects of that well-worn theme, the national consciousness in the fifteenth century.

NOTES

1. The documents, including writs, commissions, inquisitions, assessment rolls made up from the latter, and accounts of the sums actually collected, some of these containing copies of the names assessed, form a sub-class of the Public Record Office Exchequer K. R. Lay Subsidies. A number of items from other classes of subsidy return have been misclassified as alien subsidies. It is to be hoped that some of the missing alien subsidy returns will be discovered within other classifications, so that gaps in the table appended to this article may be filled.

2. *Rot. Parl.* v, 6b; see Anthony Steele, *The Receipt of the Exchequer, 1377–1485* (Cambridge, England, 1954), pp. 214–215.

3. Alice Beardwood, *Alien Merchants in England, 1350–1377: Their Legal and Economic Position* (Cambridge, Massachusetts, 1931), especially Chapter v.

4. "... if any such persone ... chargeable ... dye or voyde so that Levye ... maye not be made ... ," *Rot. Parl.* v, 6b.

5. *Rot. Parl.* II, 163a; III, 332a; *id.*, 242a, 247a (1387); *id.*, 527b, 569b, 571b–572a (1403–04); *id.*, 578b, 588b (1406); *id.*, 627a (1409); *id.*, 656b (Petition from immigrants from Guienne, 1411); IV, 5b–6a, 13a (petition regarding the Irish, 1413).

6. *Calendar of the Letter Books of the City of London*, ed. R. Sharpe, K, p. 205.

7. *Cal. Pat. Rolls, 1429–36*, pp. 537–39, 541–88; *cf. id., 1436–41*, p. 37. It is not clear whether taking the oath under these conditions gave these men the privileges of denizens in regard to land-holding. A study of the group will be required.

8. Cf. E. M. Carus-Wilson's discussion of the alnager's returns, reprinted in her *Medieval Merchant Venturers* (London, 1954).

9. "Strangers pay neither scot nor lot, 'tis true, but 'tis because they are disturb'd, and are hardly suffered (or at least encourag'd) to take houses, but otherwise they'd quickly be like us, and the next generation would not be known from English." "England's Great Happiness" (1677), printed in *Early English Tracts on Commerce*, ed. J. R. McCulloch (London, 1856), p. 264.

10. 1 Ric. 3, c. 9.

Plague Effects in Medieval Europe

DEMOGRAPHIC EFFECTS OF PLAGUE: A COMMENT ON
J. C. RUSSELL'S VIEWS

Professor Russell was the first historian to try to apply statistical
methods to analysis of the effects of epidemic plague on the composition, not just on the total size, of medieval population. He argues
now that general plagues differed from the type of the disease that
became epidemic after the crop failures of 1315–1317, in sharply
lowering the sex ratio and in greatly increasing the burden of
child-rearing.

He uses two main bodies of evidence. The first is the detail contained in English inquisitions post mortem and converted by him
into generational life-tables measuring male life-expectancies between the mid-13th century and 1500.[1] The tables rest on some
3000 cases of tenants-in-chief, a category biased towards high
landed wealth though not forming a homogeneous social group.[2] In
the absence of other work of the kind, there is naturally a temptation to use these tables as though they applied to the English population at large, but Russell has repeatedly reminded his readers that
one can do so only hypothetically.

His second body of evidence is a trial tabulation of data reported from examination of the skeletons on 77 burial sites, mostly
central European but including a few from Sweden and other west-

Reprinted from *Comparative Studies in Society and History* 8, no. 4
(1966): 474–83.

ern areas not identified. He has not told us in what centuries (more exact dating is usually not possible) these particular sites were in use. In Sweden and in central Europe, especially in Poland, systematic excavation both of early medieval burial sites and of those used in later centuries has been going on for many years, but elsewhere in Europe cemetery archeology has been mainly occupied with the more exotic societies of the early middle ages. Its chief value is in giving more and better information about the ages at which women died than can be found in written sources. Medieval archeologists have not all been expert at ascertaining the age of a skeleton, experts may be frustrated by damaged remains, and in the case of infants and young children damage to bones is likely to be too extreme to allow of reliable verdicts on either sex or age. But to have the approximate ages of the adults buried, ghoulish as this evidence may be, is a gain.

There is good enough reason to believe that after the worst of the medieval plagues the adult sex ratio was fairly even. For example, the English poll-tax returns of 1377 suggest that although towns might have more women than men, and villages more men than women, the ratio over the age of 14 in the country as a whole was only slightly in favor of men.[3] On the other hand, if we accept Russell's skeletal evidence as forming valid aggregative data, there is no denying that in pre-plague periods in central Europe the ratio was higher. After 14, women were the more fragile sex. However, Russell appears to have no ground for stating, as he does in his table, that the ratio *at age 14* was already 114. This is sheer guesswork, for the ages at death of these skeletons can be ascertained only approximately. Russell then calculates, on the basis of years lived by each sex, that the ratio rose progressively in higher age-groups to a maximum of 140, with an average, over 14, of 138. Again, such a calculation would be feasible only for cases in which skeletons were in good condition and were examined by up-to-date techniques. For purposes of crude comparison with live populations at a given point of time it is better simply to take the ratio among all skeletons in a sample. In Russell's sample it is 114. When younger children whose sex can be identified are included, as in 35 other site-reports mentioned in his appendix, the ratio falls to 106. The case for a

spectacular difference between pre-plague and post-plague conditions therefore collapses.

But should we accept burials scattered chronologically over
several centuries as valid aggregative data? The assumption that
abnormalities will be cancelled out, as is the case in a census population for a whole country, does not hold. There will be changes
brought about by currents of migration, by war, by economic circumstances, that can be understood only historically. Some attention
to these may set the central European core of Russell's evidence in a
different light. In the first place, owing to the influx of predominantly
male German and Flemish colonists in the 12th and 13th centuries,
one would expect to find a high sex ratio over most of that period.[4]
But one would not expect to find this fully reflected in all settlement
cemeteries: the pull of non-agricultural occupations—the gathering
of fur and forest products for trade, river and coastal fishing, mining,
trading and warlike expeditions—would ensure that not all men
would die in settlements. Many young men leading a frontier life
may have died in circumstances not permitting of Christian burial
at all. By the late 13th century immigration had slackened, and the
spread of little towns had widened opportunity in non-agricultural
occupations that were more sedentary. In this perspective, Russell's
general sex ratio should for the 12th and earlier 13th centuries
probably be higher than 114. There could still have been higher
ratios in some of the age-groups between 20 and 40, but allowance
for young men dying in hazardous occupations away from any
churchyard would cut down the dramatic increase that Russell so en-
thusiastically proposes. Finally, the lower ratios found in cemeteries
in use in the 14th century, which he thinks are due to plague, can
be explained well enough by the decline of eastward migration and
in the case of urban cemeteries by the migration of more peasant
women than men, from the countryside into the towns.

Russell is in error in stating that English evidence shows the sex
ratio to have been as high as he claims it was in his cemetery populations. His calculations on this point were foiled by underenumeration of women in his sources, the tenant-in-chief inquisitions. These,
following the custom of primogeniture, name daughters only when
in default of a direct male heir they became heiresses or co-heiresses.
But not all living daughters in these cases are so named. Daughters

who had been professed as nuns, either voluntarily or under pressure from some male relative who wanted to grab the inheritance, could not inherit.[5] This factor of omission is erratic but a serious one, for the classes represented among the tenants-in-chief supplied the vast majority of English nuns.[6]

At present there is actually no good work on the sex ratio in western countries before the plague and none after it except for towns, where it is distorted by migration: centers of ecclesiastical life, and some industries, attracted more men; otherwise towns had more women than men.[7] The only possibilities of checking plague effect on the sex ratio must be sought in other periods. Records from Catholic countries in the 16th and 17th centuries serve this purpose rather well because they cover rural areas as well as towns, and in both they cover religious celibates. Although plague was still endemic in these centuries, general epidemics were infrequent enough for one to be able to see their immediate effects and how these faded out. When the records are not distorted by migration, and when there had been no recent epidemic of plague, they point to a sex ratio that was only very slightly in favor of males. In Florentine territory outside the city of Florence, Beloch's figures show the sex ratio in a lay population of over half a million as 104 over the age of 15 and among children as even; when religious celibates are added, the adult ratio falls to 101.[8] Daniele Beltrami states that in the villages of the Venetian Terra Firma the ratio was traditionally in favor of men, but his 18th-century figure is only 103;[9] he does not state the ratio among those who emigrated from the villages. One way of being certain that there is no distortion by migration is to use the method of reconstruction of families, which Pierre Goubert has patiently applied in the Beauvaisis. Here, down through the latter half of the 17th century and into the early 18th, children born in the little rural town of Auneuil show a sex ratio at age 20 of 97, i.e., favoring women.[10] This was clearly the outcome of high infant and child mortality, for at birth the ratio was the normal 105. The mortality rate in the first year of life was 28.8%, and half as many again died over the next three years; barely 49% reached the age of 20.[11]

The Italian records prove also that plague had no distinctive influence on sex ratio. Severe epidemics of any kind affected it, though in opposite directions among children and adults. Venetian data show an appreciable rise in the proportion of male births after any epidemic, as also after hardship crises.[12] The Florentine census-taking, under house-quarantine conditions, as the two waves of plagues in the years 1630–32 subsided, confirms this effect and shows also a substantial fall in the adult sex ratio among the laity. The latter, however, seems to have been due chiefly to differential recruitment into the ranks of religious celibates.[13]

Other comparisons make it highly improbable that the pre-plague sex ratio in medieval Europe, when not distorted by migration, was so peculiar as Russell claims. In countries where rural poverty is widespread today and where infant mortality in consequence is high, statisticians find a rough equality in the life expectancy of the sexes measured from birth.[14] Reporting of a sex ratio even so high as to maintain the normal numerical superiority of males at birth would be suspect. In some of Russell's earlier cemetery communities selective infanticide may conceivably have been a factor. There is indirect evidence of infanticide in the very early middle ages, though not of it being selective by sex. Again, differential nutrition may in times of hardship have weakened some self-sacrificing mothers. But there is really no need to look beyond the factors of migration and of unreported male casualties in hazardous occupations. Medieval war casualties can never be measured accurately, but their historical incidence can at least be dated. In England during the plague period the French campaigns were helping to lower the sex ratio not only through the death of soldiers in battle and from wounds and fever, but through the recruiting also of civilian artisan personnel.

At present it seems likely that where infanticide and migration effects can be ruled out, the medieval sex ratio would have fluctuated irregularly between quite narrow margins. There might normally have been a slight edge in favor of males, certainly so after famine and epidemic, and a variable edge against them after heavy losses in war. The need to replenish the priesthood after epidemics, and any heightened wave of recruitment into religious orders or lay celibate groups, would alter the significance of our measures.

To turn to the question of age-grouping. Russell suggests that plague raised the proportion of children under 14 in the population under

60, from 34% to 46%.[15] These estimates are no better than the various assumptions which he built into his life-tables in order to fill them out at the lower levels of the age-scale. They seem not to allow for the contemporary impression that the second and third epidemics cut down the proportion of children; the fourth might well have raised it again, but hardly by so much. Nor has Russell's impression that the epidemic following the crop failures of 1315–1317 improved health by killing only the weak, and had no effect on the proportion of children, any adequate evidence behind it. The Venetian data from the 17th century prove that severe epidemics of any kind raised the proportion of children, though only slightly and not by any regular ratio to total mortality.[16] Russell is right in drawing attention to the increased burden of child-rearing, but he exaggerates both its extent and the aspect of economic cost. Medieval children among the poorer classes were already contributing to their keep before the age of 10.[17] The more important factor was perhaps the imponderable one of nervous strain. Among parents too poor to feed infants properly, they intensified daily anxieties; on the other hand, there was intense grief at the death of a child.[18]

Russell is much to be admired for his persistent pioneering in so difficult a field; both his valid findings and his errors are alike a stimulus to other new research. But new methods combining statistical care with careful screening of the historical context of our material are called for. In the first place, more use could be made of the excellent data furnished by Italian census-taking and registration of births and deaths, in the 16th and 17th centuries. For example, the Venetian data are able to show precisely how age-structures differed between villages and a great city. The average age in Venice was some seven to eight years higher than in the countryside:[19] a third of a village population might be under 10 and only 3%, as against from 10 to 12% in Venice itself, over 60.[20] The Italian data demonstrate, all the better because as economic development waned there was probably an increasing drift into religious orders, the effects of such recruitment in lowering marriage rates and therefore birth rates. The Venetian data could in fact be recast into a model providing enough of the major demographic indices to clarify the probable upper and lower limits of the remainder. Russell has been trying to do something of the sort for medieval demography, but work which kept the actual evidence more cleanly separate from assumptions would inspire more confidence. Assumptions could then be ordered into purely abstract models. Goran Ohlin has already designed a mathematical model designed to show the automatic deceleration of growth, even though mortality might be lessened, in a peasant population which through arrival at the limits of land supply is forced to raise the age of marriage.[21] At the conference he cast doubt on the assumption that the age of marriage could be so automatic a control, but the model could be reinterpreted simply in terms of shifting birth rates. Models could also clarify and order hypotheses as to medieval population structure in regions with differing degrees of urbanization and migration. They could demonstrate the range of consequences, after epidemics of varying severity, of depletion of the ranks of men of marriageable age by demand for replenishing the priesthood. This factor, combined as it was with demands for army service, may well have provided the chief cumulative effect of the first four general plagues in England.

SOCIAL RESPONSES TO PLAGUE: A COMMENT ON ROSENBERG'S VIEW OF 19TH-CENTURY RESPONSES TO CHOLERA

The last point reminds us that statistics of disease effects are hardly self-explanatory. A society confronting epidemics, even of a new disease introduced from outside, is not, as a population of wild animals may be, a wholly passive agent. It seems always . . . to react in part by fear, guilt, and recourse to placating supernatural power; it may also take steps that will limit the spread of the disease and may hasten the discovery of preventive measures and cure. The balance between these two types of reaction, Professor Rosenberg insists, will reveal the nature of the fundamental values of the age.[22] His analysis of 19th-century responses to the menace of cholera emphasizes the lack of conflict between the two types of reaction; he implies that the lack of conflict was historically new. A comparison with responses to plague in medieval Italy will show that any such supposition is mistaken.

In Rosenberg's analysis the prime conditions of the activist response to cholera were the pre-existence of melioristic attitudes, of effective municipal organization, of a medical profession with at least a minority of clever minds, and of scientific progress in chemistry and in biology. All of these existed in Italian cities, in varying degrees, before the arrival of plague except the sciences of chemistry and biology. Cholera, as Rosenberg says, catalyzed the union of medicine with these sciences. In the 14th century, medicine was trapped in the theory of humors and of astral influence on them.[23] It could cope with plague only by empirical methods and had no aid from microscopes. Even so, medical men recognized the role of contagion in a plague-struck environment, advocated better sanitation and invented quarantine measures. Religious feelings did not hinder their efforts: no one would have suggested that prayer would clean up the streets or make dirty water pure.

In Italy the medical profession was held in particular honor, had influence with city governments, and was already cooperating with these in socializing some part of its services: there was a recognized obligation to serve the poor, and one of the more eminent physicians of the city was a public official, on salary, for this sole purpose.[24] The immediate response to plague was for cities to compete for the services of doctors.[25] The general effect of plague crises was to heighten individual concern about all diseases, to make people deeply dependent on their doctors, and to promote an increase in the supply of university-trained doctors by including medical faculties in new universities, by offering special privileges to compensate for the expense of the education, and through scholarships to medical students.[26] The prestige of doctors was not weakened by heavy plague mortality, for they could take credit for cases of recovery and by personal concern and courage they eased the atmosphere of fear. Popular devotion to a favorite doctor was expressed in terms of love and of the honor due a father by a son.[27] This relationship was strengthened by the fact that medieval doctors were interested in advising people how to preserve their health, and understood the pernicious role of fear. What they learned in plague crises was carried over into combat against other diseases. Writing to Duke Borso of Ferrara, who had engaged him as communal physician, John Martin recommended house quarantine rules be imposed against a summer epidemic of fever which he considered to be spread more by contagion than by air-borne infection; he added that he found many people were falling ill through fear.[28]

It took time to devise effective quarantine systems, because the devastating effects of the first plague in many Italian cities complicated an already existing state of political crisis.[29] The only other hindrance to doctors encountered was complacency in intervals of fair health. Early 15th-century city council minutes in Modena show conflicting and shifting opinions; some councillors would say that people were dying every day "for want of doctors," others that the city had plenty of doctors, or, when the epidemic had passed, that the city was very healthy.[30] It had always been a point of local patriotism to boast that one's city had fine air and water and was a healthy place.

Failure to improve systems of water supply and sanitation was due partly to the reduction of population by the first plague, which automatically made water supply more ample than before, and partly to the fact that the owners of slaughter-houses and workshops producing the worse sanitation problems inside cities had political influence.[31] But the main reason lay in the lack of any chemical or biological science. Medical theory looked more to the air as a source of infection than to water: it was the smelly industries that were earliest removed to suburbs. For the same reason, although doctors urged personal cleanliness they did not campaign for it: warm bathing, especially in winter, was likely to leave the pores open to air-borne infection. It was best to wash moderately, and to sniff medicinal herbs for protection against infected air.

To say that if the 14th century had had chemistry and biology then medieval Italians would have eliminated plague as quickly as the 19th century eliminated cholera, would be idiotic. Quite apart from the fact that the etiology of plague is more complex, the conditions which ultimately made it possible for chemistry and biology to emerge as sciences were not yet present. But to blame religious feeling for medieval helplessness merely muddles the problem. It would be better to look into the material values of the age. For one thing, these kept morality very class-bound. As plague of its own accord diminished the virulence of its attacks and retreated to the more rat-infested town tenements, public concern about it waned. Whenever it flared up, the rich could escape to their country estates;[32] it did not frighten them so much as cholera frightened the new town-bound business classes of early 19th-century England. The Renaissance rich had their own diseases, and worried constantly about their health. But plague, for them, tended to recede into the cloud of afflictions which they took for granted as the lot of the poorer classes. Although the Italian medical profession managed to keep public authorities alert to the importance of quarantine measures in epidemics of any disease thought to be contagious, expenditure on public health remained picayune. When Duke Borso ordered the communal physician of Ferrara to look after the poor in the country as well as in town, he forgot to provide him with a horse.[33] This duke is said to have had a stable of 700 costly thoroughbreds.[34]

PLAGUE AND THE PEASANT ECONOMY

The economic effects of plague, through reducing total population by close to 40% within 30 years, are far from self-evident: they depended in part on the vigor with which survivors coped with problems of readjustment. Robert Lopez believes that the volume of international trade shrank even more than population,[35] but no measure of the consequences for the sectors of local and regional trade have been worked out. Peasants, to the extent that they were able systematically to abandon poorer land, would in areas where industry survived well have been able to sell more and in other areas at least to eat or drink more.

The problem that is most relevant to this symposium is the peasants' health. It is agreed that in England there was no marked or sustained recovery either of trade or population until a hundred years after the first waves of plague subsided. Russell's impression that life expectancy improved early in the 15th century is not borne out by my own sampling of family histories among either peasants or merchants, from sources with better data on child mortality than he has for the tenants-in-chief.[36] Whether or not the peasants were eating more, their health and working efficiency must have remained low. The reasons for the coincidence of economic and demographic recovery in the 1470's and 1480's may lie in improved health and energy through greater immunity to some of the current diseases, but this in turn may have been the result of the availability of more protein in the form of meat. In the form of mutton, this was a byproduct, as it were, of the woollen cloth industry that was extending its markets, and the prosperity of graziers and butchers may indicate that consumption of beef and veal also was growing. Quantitative study is needed, for most of the meat supply may have gone to the towns.

Qualitative improvement in peasant diet may have occurred for a time in Italy, where Herlihy finds rural credit cheapened in consequence of the plagues.[37] But in Italy population growth then outran economic recovery. We have it on the word of the great Italian physician Bernardo Ramazzini, who wrote at the end of a career in practice and teaching from the 1650's to 1713, that peasant health was miserable.[38] In his opinion peasants were healthier than town craftsmen in at least not suffering the lung infections and toxic effects that arose from the still medieval conditions under which craftsmen worked. But the annual cycle of peasant life as he knew it in the Campagna and in the Po valley ran through fever in the summer, dysentery in the autumn, pleurisy and pneumonia in the winter. At all seasons, peasants regularly suffered from asthma, quinsy, erysipelas, from depressing digestive and intestinal ailments and bad teeth. Ramazzini attributed their troubles to overexposure, overwork, and to their diet of bread, garlic, onions and fruit. They reserved strong wine for medicine against quartain fever in the winter, and their small store of protein in the form of eggs and chicken for cheering the last days of those who were fatally ill. This state of protein-starvation is likely to have been the lot of peasants also in the 13th century. Plague reduction of their numbers could have substantially improved their health only where there was plenty of fish or where it became possible to raise more animals for the home dinner-table. So long as plague continued to break out here and there, even though its virulence might be lessening, it added one more hazard, one more cause of strain and weakness, to shorten life and keep working efficiency low.

NOTES

1. J. C. Russell, *British Medieval Population* (Albuquerque, 1948), ch. VIII–X; "Effects of Pestilence and Plague, 1315–1385," *Comparative Studies in Society and History*, 8, no. 4 (1966), 464–73.

2. The category includes the great nobility along with many lesser landowners and some of the wealthy city merchants who invested in land.

3. Russell, *op. cit.*, pp. 149–54. The data in the returns still await checking against other local records; the returns may under-enumerate both the elderly and servants.

4. Roger Mols, *Introduction à la démographie historique* (Louvain, 1954–56), vol. II, pp. 196–97, draws attention to this as regards the towns founded by Germans.

5. Eileen Power, *Medieval English Nunneries* (Cambridge, 1922), pp. 31–38.

6. *Ibid.*, pp. 4–7.

7. Mols, *op. cit.*, pp. 197–208, surveys most of the evidence that is in print.

8. Karl Julius Beloch, *Bevölkerungsgeschichte Italiens,* Bd. 2 (Berlin, 1940), pp. 212–13.

9. Daniele Beltrami, *Storia della popolazione di Venezia dalla fine del secolo XVI alla caduta della republica* (Padua, 1954), pp. 82, 85.

10. Pierre Goubert, *Beauvais et le Beauvaisis de 1600 à 1730* (Paris, 1960), p. 41.

11. *Ibid.*, p. 39.

12. Beltrami, *op. cit.*, p. 81.

13. Beloch, *op. cit.*, pp. 143–45.

14. Bruce M. Russett et al., *World Handbook of Political and Social Indicators* (New Haven and London, 1964), pp. 22–27.

15. A conversion of his ratios in "Pestilence and Plague," p. 471.

16. This effect of the plague of 1630 in Florence and Venice is very similar although the mortality in Venice was far higher.

17. Their occupation at the time of an accident, whether playing or at work, is given in accounts of miracles. Some boys were apprenticed at 7 or soon after.

18. This is described in accounts of miracles when a child who became unconscious had been presumed dead. It is described also in coroners' reports of fatal accidents.

19. Beltrami, *op. cit.*, p. 97.

20. *Ibid.*, pp. 91–94.

21. G. Ohlin, "Mortality, Marriage and Growth in Pre-Industrial Population," *Population Studies,* vol. 14 (1961), pp. 190–97.

22. Charles E. Rosenberg, "Cholera in 19th-century Europe: A Tool for Social and Economic Analysis," *Comparative Studies in Society and History* 8, no. 4 (1966), 452–63.

23. For some account of contemporary plague treatises see Séraphine Guerchberg, "The Controversy over the Alleged Sowers of Black Death in the Contemporary Treatises on Plague" in Sylvia L. Thrupp, ed., *Change in Medieval Society* (New York, 1964), pp. 208–26 (translated from the French in *Revue des Etudes Juives,* 1948).

24. For Florentine detail and more general bibliography see Raffaele Ciasca, *L'Arte dei Medici e Speziali nella storia e nel commercio fiorentino* (Florence, 1927). There is no full study of the institution of public city physicians, which spread beyond Italy.

25. E. Carpentier, *Une Ville devant la Peste: Orvieto et la Peste Noire de 1348* (Paris, 1962), gives details and shows how much better Florence handled the first crisis than Orvieto.

26. See Ciasca, *op. cit.*, pp. 291–95.

27. A. Chiappelli, "Medici e Chirurghi in Pistoia nel medio evo," *Bolletino Storico Pistoiese*, VIII (1906), at p. 137, IX, at p. 198, X, at p. 1.

28. The letter, from Johannes Martinus de Garbatiis de Parma, and dated July, 1463, is printed by C. Foucard, in *Espozione di Documenti Storici dall' VIII al XIX secolo di une speciale raccolta di altri spettanti alla medicina ed alla chirurgia dal XIV al XVIII secolo* (Modena, 1882), pp. 9–10; there is a slightly different version of the text in the Archivio di Stato at Modena.

29. Illustrated in E. Carpentier *op. cit.*

30. Archivio communale, Modena, *Provisioni, 1423–30*, ff. 120, 132, 169–70; *1431–39*, ff. 3, 165.

31. Popular histories of medicine often malign medieval sanitation. For some facts and better bibliography see my *Merchant Class of Medieval London* (Chicago, 1948 and Ann Arbor, 1962), pp. 136–39.

32. In Catalonia, when the poor attempted to escape, like the government officials and the rich, they were driven back: J. Nadal and E. Giralt, *La population catalane de 1553 à 1717* (Paris, 1960), p. 35.

33. By letter (see n. 28), the doctor requested one.

34. E. Noyes, *The Story of Ferrara* (London, 1904), p. 93.

35. R. S. Lopez and H. A. Miskimin, "The Economic Depression of the Renaissance," *The Economic History Review*, 2nd series, XIV (1962), pp. 397–407.

36. Sylvia L. Thrupp, "The Problem of Replacement-Rates in Late Medieval English Population," pp. 163–89 in this volume, and *Merchant Class of Medieval London*, pp. 203–4.

37. David Herlihy, "Population, Plague and Social Change in Rural Pistoia, 1201–1430," *The Economic History Review*, 2nd series, XVIII (1965), 225–44, at pp. 240–44.

38. Bernardo Ramazzini, *De Morbis Artificiorum*, ed. with Latin text and translation, from the revised and enlarged edition of 1713, by W. Cave Wright (Chicago, 1940), ch. 39 and *passim*.

The Problem of
Replacement-Rates in Late
Medieval English Population

Medieval population research would profit by assembling comparable information from as many different social groups as possible, information bearing on their capacity to reproduce themselves through given periods of time. The comparisons that H. E. Hallam presented in the *Economic History Review* in 1958 between certain Lincolnshire Fenland communities in the third quarter of the thirteenth century gave an encouraging fresh lead in this direction.[1] For two groups he was able to measure the rate of increase over one generation in terms of the ratio between married couples and the numbers both of their sons and of their daughters who grew up. He was able also to prove that the rate of increase varied directly, and the rate of emigration inversely, with the prevalence of partible inheritance and ample land. The material to be presented here is thinner; it lacks census data and, though based on study of families, it for the most part ignores daughters. The aim is to establish a crude measure of replacement through the number of sons, per adult male of the successive generations, who survived to maturity. The evidence has been gleaned as a by-product of research dealing with the social structure and trading relationships of various types of village and small town in several parts of the country. It is capable of large-scale extension, which in turn will facilitate refinements of the method.

Hallam's replacement-rates refer to two groups of families in which, if I interpret his description correctly, reproduction was completed some time before 1270; at that date they had no minor chil-

Reprinted from *Economic History Review*, 2d ser. 18 (1965): 101–19.

dren living. In the village of Weston 36 families, and in the village of Moulton 24, had produced respectively an average of 1.86 and 2.5 sons who were alive and adult in 1270.[2] As a measure, this of course rests on the assumption that the marriage-rate, for males, was 100 per cent. Hallam does not discuss the marriage-rate, but he discloses that 6.7 per cent of the young men of 1270 born in Moulton became ordained (not counting several who went abroad as clerks); in Weston, where life was harder, the attraction of clerical careers was still stronger, 12.2 per cent of the sons (or 17.6 per cent, if several who became clerks were later ordained) becoming priests or monks. If celibacy had been equally attractive to the men of the fathers' generation, the replacement-rates given above would have to be reduced, for the Weston group to 1.6, and for the Moulton group to 2.34.[3] With fuller information, some further slight reductions might be in order, to allow for men who had come of age but died before marrying, and for those who went abroad soldiering or on pilgrimage before marriage and never returned. Hallam's figures, however, standing as they do for communities that were still growing, Weston only slowly but Moulton rapidly, as well as exporting manpower and womanpower,[4] serve as an excellent reference point.

The first sets of figures below are derived from manorial court rolls. As all who have worked with these sources know, the original notes taken in court have come down to us in various stages of editing. At their worst, they are edited down to a bare conveyancing record, which may reveal little or nothing about the people who were actually living on the manor. At their best—in the first formal redaction—they indicate the reasons for every amercement and fine, and the names of those who pledged for payments due by others. They give the names not only of heads of tithings, and of people owing suit to the court who were absent but of residents empanelled on special juries. They give rather full reports of litigation, including the genealogical evidence required in pleas of land and the historical evidence required in disputes as to whether particular holdings were partible or impartible. They give details of guardianship arrangements even for villein heirs under age, they may state the ages of these children at the date of the next court after the father's death, and may note the dates at which, if they survived, they took up their patrimony. They may give the names of both free and unfree immigrants who owed the chevage tax for the privilege of living on the manor as under-tenants or as labourers, the names of all males over the age of 12 who had failed to join a tithing, and the names of bond fugitives—often tracing their movements about the country and whether or not they had married. They may give the names of members of bond families who married on or off the manor by licence or without. Court leet sessions, variously styled, regularly list the names both of residents and visitors who flagrantly offended against any law: the value of these lists, for the purpose in hand, is in helping to round out the record as to young people who did not yet hold land from the lord but were staying on with their parents, or as servants of neighbours, or as under-tenants. Manorial accounts may supplement the court rolls in this respect by showing whether these young men were getting their start by leasing bits of demesne land or by working as manor servants.

Population research has so far used manor court rolls and accounts mainly to illustrate fluctuations and trends in tenant mortality, or to help measure changes in a total manorial population, in terms of heads of households or of families, without relying solely on surveys that may or may not include under-tenants. The attempt here is a more modest one. Its value depends, in the first instance, on the completeness of the information available as to the number of sons alive at the time of the father's death. The immediate notice of a tenant's death may fail to give the total number of sons for one or more of the following reasons: the patrimony was impartible, so that there was no occasion for any son but the one marked as heir to be mentioned; the patrimony was partible but was for the time being divided only among sons already of age; the father died young enough to have left a child or twins still in the mother's womb; the father was old, and died after having assigned his sons their patrimony and retired to a cottage tenement. For these reasons it is futile to race through court rolls taking out only the notices of tenant deaths; the entire record has to be sifted. In rolls that are detailed and run continuously, sons who for any of the above reasons are not named at the time of the father's death are almost certain to turn up either in earlier or later courts. To consider the first category of omission, that of the extra sons ineligible to inherit an impartible patrimony: these sons frequently turn up in the record receiving other pieces of property that their father had acquired and could dispose of, either during his lifetime or at death, as he pleased, or pieces of property that their mother inherited and passed on to them, or pieces of property that they were somehow able to buy or lease from other tenants. Impartible inheritance customs contributed pressure to emigrate only when competition for land became stiff. Free emigrants, it is true, escape the record of the home manor, but unfree emigrants do not. The second and third categories of omission, those of minors not mentioned at the first division of a partible inheritance, and those of heirs born posthumously, are taken care of by the record of later litigation, and the case of the elderly father whose sons had all been provided for before his death is in turn taken care of by the earlier conveyancing record. The one category of tenants' sons that may ordinarily be under-enumerated in manorial records is the group recruited into the Church. Yet, as Hallam has amply demonstrated, this group can be tracked down through research in local ecclesiastical sources.

The risk of incompleteness in the count of sons is considerable, however, if court rolls do not run continuously. The conveyancing by which older sons were provided for before the father's death, and the claims brought by younger sons later, may have disappeared. Small gaps in a series are in part compensated for by the slow pace of court procedure and the repetitious nature of its record. Information lost through the loss of part or all of one annual record may in part reappear in restatements of the family relationships of the parties to a suit. Lists of fugitive serfs, too, are repeated year after year, occasionally with notes of their marriages off the manor without licence or of increases in an emigrant's family. Failures to pay heriots or reliefs due from an heir or fines due from transactions in land are also repeated in the record. The risk of incompleteness in the count of sons will be minimized by taking cases of mortality only from some middle stretch of years within continuous records. Since the reasons for losses and damage of court rolls are quite unrelated to demographic trends, this solution amounts to the method of random sampling. Since it reduces the size of samples, it makes them liable to skew by abnormal circumstances. This problem in turn can be surmounted by using very large numbers of samples. The value of such work will depend, in the second place, on the amount of information that is available as to the age of sons at the father's death, the age of majority, the ages at which men married and died, and the marriage-rate among men. All of these varied with the time, the region, the form of land tenure, and the customs of a social group, and will be discussed only for the particular groups represented below.

The bulk of the records used here are from eight eastern manors: Long Bennington in Lincolnshire; Northwold and Thorney in Norfolk; Wyverstone, Redgrave, Hinderclay and Brandon in Suffolk; Wilberton on the edge of the Isle of Ely.[5] For a pilot study and for the purpose of comparison with Hallam's figures, it seemed best to keep to heavily settled areas where both partible and impartible inheritance were practised, and to represent both purely agricultural settlements and manors embracing markets. Except in the case of Long Bennington, most of the original records used happen to have crossed the Atlantic; this circumstance, and the excellent condition of the manuscripts, helped to determine the selection of these particular manors. Wilberton and Brandon manors were each contained within a single vill, although Brandon embraced twin settlements, one of them the market settlement at Brandon Ferry on the river Ouse; the other manors sprawled from a central vill into several others. Density of settlement in the whole region is likely to be correlated with concentrations of cottage textile and leather industry.

One of the advantages of selecting these particular manors is the possibility that they followed a fairly uniform custom as to age of majority among unfree tenantry. In Redgrave in 1398 and in Long Bennington in 1439 this was declared to be 16.[6] On all of the seven manors, as was indeed general throughout the country, an unfree minor could be "admitted" to his patrimony on finding pledges for payment of the requisite heriot or *gersuma,* but another Long Bennington statement makes it clear that he could not make his oath of fealty until he was of age, and that until then someone else had to be responsible for the proper upkeep of the holding.[7] Since the taking of these oaths was not uniformly recorded, and since the age of sons at their father's death is given only in a minority of cases, it has been assumed here that unless a son "admitted" to land was placed in the custody of his mother or of some other guardian or obliged to find pledges for the upkeep of the property, he was of the age of 16 or above. Large absentee freeholders, among whom the age of majority after 1300 was likely to have been shifting to 21, have been excluded from the cases of mortality used. The exclusion leaves the evidence definitely biased towards unfree cultivators and to craftsmen, although small and middling freeholders are represented. It is indeed likely that small cultivators and craftsmen, whether they were free or unfree, took a similarly practical attitude to the question of age of majority, judging a boy to be of age when he was sturdy and responsible enough to work on his own. In one instance when a boy of nine was placed under guardianship, this was said to be because he was not strong enough to work his holding of 16½ acres, and in another instance an heir was judged simply to be "of sufficient age" to perform the labour services due from his land.[8] Custom was perhaps no more than a rough guide to actual practice, but it allows us to assume that on the average a male serf was considered to be of age at 16.

The rolls from the second half of the thirteenth century show Redgrave and Hinderclay rates of replacement within tenant families very close to Hallam's figures from Lincolnshire. The rolls are chronologically too broken to permit the ideal procedure of taking samples only from a middle stretch of years within consecutive records. At the start there is no more than a few months' leeway for sleuthing backwards after hypothetically forgotten grown sons. Yet the first portion of the Hinderclay court record, which runs only from 1257 into 1260, is surprisingly informative. It reveals that emigration, even emigration abroad, did not break communication with the manor. A man living *ultra mare* arranged for his share in a small-holding to be transferred to his brother, a son and daughter heard of their father's death *in partibus extraneis,* and two heirs living in London waived their rights in favour of sisters, one temporarily, one permanently. In the last case the court's communication was with the mother, who sent word from London that she would bring one of the sons (they were living with her) to take up the land the next August. On learning that she had to bring the right heir she changed her mind. Although aware that the tenement

was impartible, she was seemingly unaware that the heir was designated by order of birth. Or perhaps the son who was willing to
return was illegitimate, and she had only just learned that a bas-
tard could not inherit. At all events the story suggests that people
might be confused about their rights. Genuine doubt, as well as
fraternal jealousies, may have lain behind some of the disputes
over whether a tenement was partible or impartible or over the
nature of the father's title to land he had acquired, that recur in
later rolls. Reports of such disputes rarely show more than three
grown brothers alive at the same time. Of the 10 men in this first
sample of Hinderclay tenant deaths, two left only sisters to inherit,
one left a son and grandson and a parson brother, one definitely left
three sons and two others, including the father of the boys in
London, may have left three. Whether all the sons were of age
at the time of the father's death is not clear, but if they all attained
majority, and if we include the grandson, then our 10 men were
succeeded by 17: a replacement-rate of 1.7, or 1.6 without the
grandson.

The figures in Table 1 show Hinderclay sustaining this high
rate into the 1280's, and Redgrave through the first decade of the
fourteenth century. Thorney may have been already trailing by
1280, and all of the manors examined show lower rates well before
the plague period. The samples used could be enlarged if it were
feasible to add, to the mortality cases, those of tenants retiring.
Only two such cases have been added, in the first two Hinderclay
periods. The first is of a man who ceded his land to two sons, on
condition that he should live with them; two more sons then turned
up to claim shares in the land. The second man retired to live with
a son because of near blindness. Once a man surrendered his land
in such circumstances and heriot had been paid, the court had
no reason to record his death. Otherwise retirements are excluded, for if a worn-out man settled down with a married daughter, it is usually less easy to discover whether he had sons than if
his death were on record. In the tabulations, all sons who attained
majority are for simplicity's sake grouped together. For some, the
only evidence of majority is that on claiming their inheritance they
were not placed in custody; for others, the evidence is in their continued appearance in court in a variety of adult roles—many ap-

TABLE 1

Manor	Dates	Male deaths	Cases no sons	Sons of age or coming of age	Minors, survival uncertain	Replacement rate	Other male heirs	Marriages	Child-wyte fines
Redgrave	1259–65 1280–90 and	15	1	26		1.7		39	6
″	1296–1300	10	1	20	4	1.6			
″	1303–13	15	3	27	1 (aet. 14)	1.8	4 (brothers)		
″	1330–37	11	3	18	2 (1 aet. 4)	1.45	1 (nephew aet. 10)		
″	1340–46	5	1	6		1.2	2 (brothers)		
Hinderclay	1268–84 (8 years only)	14	2	24		1.7	3 (brothers)	37	6
″	1289–1300	12	1	18		1.5		68	20
″	1303–07	14	2	17	(in one family, no. uncertain)	1.2	4 (brothers)	39	3
″	1335–48 (Feb.)	22	7	22	2	1.0	9 (3 brothers, 4 nephews, 1 grandson)	30	11
Thorney	1278–81 and 1285	19	3	14	3	0.7	1 (brother)		
Great Bromley	1311–26	7	2	6	1 family of 4 children, sex uncertain	0.85	1		
Brandon	1317–34	22	6	18	1	0.85	3		
Wyverstone	1332–40	12	5	5	3 (1 aet. 12 1 aet. 6 mos.)	0.4			

pear in the record of marriages; some of the minors placed in custody are on record as emerging from it. To avoid building in any element of guess work about child mortality, the replacement-rates are calculated solely on the basis of sons who came of age. Grandsons named as heirs are placed under "other male heirs," as are brothers of the deceased so designated. The number of marriages on record through the levying of licence fees or of fines for marrying without licence, on the unfree, and of childwyte fines due from serf women producing illegitimate children, are also given. The few girls noted as marrying shortly after such an event are, however, listed only in the *Marriages* column. Bastards are, of course, excluded from the deaths listed, since their sons escape the inheritance record. Clergy are excluded, except for married parish clerks.

The downward drift of the replacement-rates in the pre-plague period is unmistakable and not to be explained away by defects in the sources, for these are constant in nature. Communication with emigrants remained firm. In 1305 only one of a Hinderclay family of six sons stayed away when the father was dying; in the 1335–48 period an only son returned, and two brothers whose whereabouts was at first unknown came home after an interval of two years. Recruitment into the church does not entirely escape the record: at Redgrave in 1334 a man newly professed as a monk at Leiston Abbey came into court to cede some land to a brother, and in 1346 a chaplain became sole heir to a shop, which he promptly sold. There is little reason to believe that the count of minors who were not recruited into the Church is short. When the widow of one of the Redgrave tenants who died in 1337 was rumoured to be pregnant she was examined and found to be not pregnant; she had only one son, under age. Few of the widows who died had more than one or two boys under age. The possibility of an incomplete count of sons becomes more crucial as the replacement-rate begins to sag below unity. Yet the records for the periods in which this occurs (barring the first short run for Thorney) are if anything rather better than for the earlier periods. The· downward trend may therefore have been even sharper than the figures indicate. Illegitimate children, whose sex and fate is hard to discover, could have compensated for it only temporarily.

The grimly dramatic episode of the Black Death, in its first appearance, is the one point at which historians in general have puzzled over the problem of replacement. Yet local researchers have seldom reported the information to be found in court rolls in such a way that it can be used for this purpose. In its raw form the information is a mixed list of male tenant heads of families, of women tenants who had been widowed before the plague, of women who succeeded husbands dying of plague only to become victims of it themselves, and of sons and daughters of age and under age who succeeded their parents but in turn succumbed. The lists usually include many cases in which the heirs could not be ascertained immediately because they had fled the locality or were perhaps ill. Some of these turn up later but escape the researcher who does not follow the record through to check the names and relationships; the latter are often difficult to determine. Again, the first mortality lists include men who would have had no sons, or none that could be designated as legal heirs to their tenement. Usually more priests than have appeared among the tenants noted as dying in earlier years are in the 1349–50 lists. This in itself is not without significance. There are usually also more bastards and sometimes more men holding only by right of their wife, *ex lege Anglie;* their sons, even if they survived, would not be named as having a legal right of inheritance. In spite of J. C. Russell's warning as to some of these pitfalls in the use of Black Death court rolls,[9] they have still not been utilized in any uniform way. Russell's handling of his sample of tenants in chief is still, therefore, our soundest guide to the effects of the first four general outbreaks of plague in England.

To isolate the ratio between the number of male tenants who died only of plague and of sons born to this group who survived to majority, manor by manor, is often impossible and in any case not the best approach to the general problem of population replacement in the mid-fourteenth century. Even for the sole purpose of picking up heirs who were ill or had fled during the panic year but survived and returned, whatever material is available for the decade of the 1350's should be included, and a still more valid picture would be obtained by including material from the whole decade of the 1340's.

The difference in results according to the method used may be illustrated from Hinderclay. Here male tenant mortality from the plague period as reported through the court of January 1350, when we exclude two categories—men whose sons would not have had a legal claim to the holding, and sons who briefly succeeded a father only to die during the epidemic—amounted to 66. Although this group had only five sons who came of age during the epidemic and survived it, there were two infants and a boy of four who may conceivably have survived it, and in 22 other cases it is almost certain, from the subsequent record of tenants and fugitives, that at least one son survived. In 26 other cases it is certain that no son survived. For the 66 cases of death during the epidemic, the maximum replacement-rate that can be calculated in terms of infant and grown sons is .45, a very sharp drop below any earlier figures. The proportion dying without sons—39 per cent—is also much higher than in any earlier period illustrated for Hinderclay. If we include similarly screened information from the courts between December 1341 and 1349, and from those between March 1351 and February 1354, we get 80 male tenant deaths and 43 sons. The replacement-rate is then .53, a slightly higher figure. The picture in which most historians have been interested, however, that of the immediately available pool of male heirs who were in any way related to the plague victims, is considerably brighter. Careful inquiries made in the Hinderclay courts during the epidemic discovered 14 cousins, five brothers, two uncles and a nephew who could inherit. In the earlier 1340's, and in the early courts of the 1350's, inquiry was less successful, or perhaps less careful. In terms of all available male heirs between 1341 and 1354 the replacements for the group of 80 deceased male tenants noted above totalled 74, giving a rate of .9. As Miss F. M. Page implied long ago in her study of the Crowland Abbey estates, the availability of cousins and other male heirs goes far to explain the fact that many fewer tenements lay vacant after the plague than one's impressions of the mortality would lead one to expect.[10]

The size of the total pool of male heirs available to take up tenements vacated by the first wave of plague mortality, important though it is for manorial history and for the history of families, is relevant to the more general problem of the trend of population replacement only in so far as the court inquiries were so scrupulous as to add to our too slight knowledge of the age-structure of local groups. Again, and the fact is emphasized here because it becomes particularly plain at this juncture, the male replacement-rate in tenant families is not by itself an adequate clue to changes in the size of total population. Even if further research should prove that the Hinderclay male replacement-rate for the 1340's and 1350's—.53—is representative for tenant families in similar communities throughout the country, it would not follow that the total population staying in or migrating away from these communities fell, in that period, by 47 per cent. Change in the size of total population depended also on the variables affecting survival of daughters and the illegitimacy rate. Even for the male groups represented, the replacement-rates being traced here are significant merely as indicators of direction, as arrows tilting up or down. The tilt could alter at any time through change in the male child mortality rate, and its significance as an indicator depends also on change in the ages at which men married and died. As an indicator it needs also to be supplemented by study of illegitimacy. These points will be considered in turn, but first let us follow the indicators into the fifteenth century.

From the point of view of replacement-rates, the immediate aftermath of the second general plague, that of 1361, looks almost worse than that of the first plague.[11] Combined figures from the three manors of Brandon, Redgrave and Thorney show 21 men (including three chaplains) who died between 1362 and 1370 leaving, as male heirs, only four sons, two brothers, and two cousins; one of the sons died a year after his father, leaving only a daughter. There were female heirs, but continuing mortality depleted these too. One Thorney man at the time of his death had two daughters and a granddaughter by a third daughter who had died; three months later it is stated that there are no heirs. In only two cases did the court admit uncertainty as to the existence of heirs, one being the case of a Brandon smith who had gone to London. Two of the male heirs named at Redgrave did not come to claim their property. They may have migrated, and fugitive lists for this decade may not be quite complete. Again, the figures refer mostly to poor cottagers. But on all three manors these were an important class.

On Thorney manor the situation improved in the 1370's, 46 men leaving 26 sons who were either of age or came of age within a few years, and four who were younger, one of them aged eight. There were four other male heirs. In five cases the court did not know whether heirs existed, in four others it knew there were none, and in nine cases there were daughters only. In short, 31 per cent of a group of 41 were dying without sons. Some of the daughters were already of age; one was 14, another five; one man's family consisted of twin girls aged three months and a little girl who died just after the father. These figures are not biased by departures from the manor. One of the men in the group was himself an emigrant; it was known that he had taken his two sons with him, but only one had survived to be named as heir. In another case three brothers had emigrated together, but only one, still away at the time the father died, was named as an heir. The death of the other sons in these cases may be presumed, for the small holdings in question were normally partible on this manor. As for the next two decades, those of the 1380's and 1390's, improvement was still insufficient to bring about a stable equilibrium between losses and replacements. For example, against eight losses in 1397 there were only three sons aged 16 or up and two who may have been minors; one boy of 16, a free tenant, may have had younger brothers. The record then breaks off until 1414, when it becomes worse, a sinister proportion of the male tenant deaths being of men who left no sons or were childless. Excluding a cleric and a knight, we find 21 Thorney men dying between 1414 and 1422; eight left no sons and only two of the eight left daughters. In six other cases the court was either uncertain as to the existence of heirs or failed to note, in transferring land to the widow, whether she had young children or not. If we assume that the percentages of the childless and the sonless were constant for the whole group of 21, then 29 per cent were childless and 38 per cent were without sons. If we exclude the indeterminate cases, the percentages for the remaining group of 15 stand at 40 per cent childless and 53 per cent dying without sons. One son was *leprosus*. Such were the conditions of life in one corner, at least, of the England of Henry V.

In another corner of England, Long Bennington manor, which reached into five vills, the demographic situation also remained poor. Between 1377 and 1392 there were 22 losses by death here, excluding a chaplain but including both substantial tenants and smallholders. In eight of these cases there is record only of uncertainty regarding the existence of heirs. The other 14 cases show seven men leaving seven sons who may have been of age, five leaving minors, and two leaving no sons. Excluding two of the sons because they died within a few months of the father, we have 10 replacements for 14 men—a rate of .7. The rate stands at the same level in the period 1414-20, again for a group of 14 losses. Over the years 1431 through 1440 it may have risen to .8. Excluding from the 27 deaths in that decade a cleric who committed suicide and five cases in which detail as to the heirs is lacking, we find 18 sons left to replace 21 men. Two of the replacements were said to be aged 16; one was a boy of eight. Conditions look brighter in that only three of the men (14 per cent) left no sons. Over the next two decades, from 1441 through 1460, there may have been further improvement. Excluding a suicide (of a layman, this time) and 13 other cases in which information as to the heirs is lacking, we find 18 men leaving 18 sons. There is detail as to ages in only two cases: one heir was a boy of nine, and another was a child too young to work his land, whose father had died from falling off a cartload of peas.

On Northwold manor, in Norfolk, the picture between 1414 and 1459 is truly shocking, the more so because although the sample available includes such smallholders as a baker with half a rod of land and a weaver with 5 acres, many of the deaths were of virgaters or free tenants with 24 acres. The sample numbers 31 cases, eight of which have to be excluded for lack of detail as to the heirs: either there were widows who might have had young children, or else the property was transferred to feoffees or executors for sale, or was sold to someone else who is not described as heir. Of the 23 cases remaining, seven are definitely stated to have had no heir and in four more the heir was the daughter, brother, father, or male cousin of the deceased. For the other 12 there were 12 sons, and if these tenements were impartible, there may have been other sons—the court record is not full enough to enable one to check this. The shocking fact is that no less than 10 of the 23, or 43 per cent, died childless, and that 11, or 47 per cent, left no sons. It is just possible that in two of the cases in which a man is said to have died without heirs the point is a legality, for the property was in one instance a leasehold and in the other may have been a leasehold. Even if we allow for doubt on this point by reducing the sample to 21, with only eight dying childless and nine without sons, the percentages still stand at 38 per cent and 43 per cent respectively.

On two of our manors, however, the population showed more resilience. At Brandon, for 12 deaths in the decade of the 1390's, the replacement-rate rose to unity. In the first decade of the fifteenth century there were four sons to replace four married men, but another man died unmarried. Between 1414 and 1425 the replacement-rate for a group of seven rose to 1.4, and three men who died in the 1430's each left a son. Wilberton, a small, purely agricultural settlement secluded on a ridge bordering fenland, experienced an earlier recovery, but sustained it less well. The affairs of this little village are especially well documented in the late fourteenth century, the clerk who kept the court record having taken a real interest in the people around him. Virgaters and half-virgaters outnumbered the cottagers. The first group was the most stable, but there was movement in and out of all three groups, all of it well chronicled. Between 1379 and 1390 the replacement-rate, for seven deaths, was at least 1.6: 10 sons of the deceased and a stepson are known to have come of age, and another son had been sent away to school at the age of eight. Then, during the 1390's, though one half-virgater left four sons, two virgaters died childless. The replacement-rate for nine deaths sank to unity and remained at this level through the first two decades of the fifteenth century. Tenements here were impartible, but this situation was alleviated by sub-letting, as well as by the leasing of bits of demesne land, or by setting up a son in a cottage tenement that happened to fall vacant. On occasion families kept two or three grown sons in the village.

The bare facts as to the trend of replacement-rates on the

manors examined do not by any means exhaust the relevant demographic information that lies in the court rolls and accounts.
Change in the average age at death can, of course, be reckoned,
from continuous accounting of heriots, by change in the span of
time required for complete turnover of a given tenant population, but this method breaks down at the point when owing to
population shrinkage the number of tenements let is variable.
A slower method is to accumulate samples of tenant biographies
and genealogies in which the dates when men first took up land—
perhaps not from the lord but by sublet from a tenant—and the
dates of death, can be filled in. By adding the customary age of
majority to the period of land-holding one should then come within
a year or two of the length of life. Conveyancing by which a father
first arranges that a son who is named shares title with him to a
given piece of land was sometimes, as can be shown from cases
in which that son's age at the father's death is recorded, carried
out within a year of the child's birth, though inference that this
was always so may not be valid. It is my impression, without using
any such inferences but only lengths of tenure in some 60 cases in
Brandon, Thorney and Wilberton records, that the median age at
death fell, between the first decade of the fourteenth and the first
of the fifteenth centuries, by some ten years—from the forties into
the thirties. Very large-scale research is needed to establish the
nature of the trend. Cottagers probably on the whole died earlier
than men more prosperous, and in the post-plague era the increase
in migration from one manor to another makes it difficult to gather
adequate samples.

Information as to ages at marriage is not hard to come by, the
record of licencing suggesting that most men married as soon as
they had some land. Impartible inheritance of the main family
tenement did not, in Wilberton, necessarily delay it, though a
widow's quarrels with a son might. Information as to the dura-
tion of marriage is harder to come by, since the deaths of women
whose husband was still living rarely reach the court record. The
Wilberton record gives the impression that there was some lassitude on the part of village men of the late fourteenth and early
fifteenth centuries about remarrying after a first spouse had died.
Between 1379 and 1411, out of 27 cases there are 12 in which a

man appears to have had no wife at the time of death or retirement. One of the 12 was a virgater who may possibly never have married because his mother and aunt had lived on his land for many years, the other was a young cottager who died before marriage. Wilberton was a secluded place where men could enjoy the consolations of fishing and there was no industry to attract young women migrants. The other manor records give the impression that the increase in migration from one manor to another and from one little town to another in the post-plague era and throughout the fifteenth century must have reduced the fecundity of marriage. It may sometimes have been a way of escaping the responsibilities of marriage. Though the record of fugitive serfs does not state the whereabouts of the wife and though, as in the case of one man who went off with his two babies and other cases in which it was known that more children were born after a family's flight, the wife surely must have gone with the husband, in other cases it seems likely that she and the daughters were left behind to fend for themselves as best they could. For many men left with one or two sons only. If they took daughters these are named, but this occurred less often. Of course, both sons and daughters went off singly or together on their own. When this happened the parents may have gone on begetting more children on the manor.

Again, the availability of education exercised some downward pressure on the birth-rate. Education did not necessarily lead a village boy on into the condition of celibacy through ordination as a priest or profession as a monk, for it could open alternative opportunities in the careers of parish clerk and village scrivener or in the lower echelons of estate adminstration, and would have raised a boy's value as a prospective town apprentice. Opportunities for education seem to have been particularly good in Lincolnshire. When the lord of Long Bennington in 1378 demanded the names of all serfs who had lately sent sons to school without paying for licence to do so, he was met with a blank refusal on the grounds that by ancient custom the serfs had a right to send their sons to school without asking permission.[12] Certainly some lords were liberal in the matter. The Abbot of Bury in 1389 appointed Richard Brok, *capellanus,* to conduct a grammar school in Botlesdale, the market community on the abbot's manor of Redgrave. There was the usual proclamation of monopoly, which was to run within the manor.[13] Some elementary teaching may have been available on many manors. A Wilberton serf in this period allowed a clerk who was a cousin of his wife to settle down in a hut in their yard. If such a man was doing anything at all, it is likely to have been a little teaching. The increase in the number of chaplains named in the court rolls as tenants or heirs to tenants in the post-plague era suggests that education was leading more villagers into the priesthood.

On the other hand, the illegitimacy-rate may have risen in the immediate post-plague era. The extent to which this was true cannot be tested from childwyte fines alone, for free women who were not liable to the fine produced illegitimate children. Given the number of free tenant families in the lowest economic class, one could estimate their proportionate contribution to illegitimacy by comparison with the number of serf families and of childwyte fines.

To convert an illegitimacy-rate into a contribution to the replacement-rate one needs the mortality-rate among children and adolescents. The only direct statistical information as to this that exists, to my knowledge, is contained in the London citizen orphanage records.[14] These are not as systematic in noting what happened to girls as they are in regard to boys. But they could illustrate the trend of survival of male members of a mixed pool of orphans of both sexes, through the fourteenth and fifteenth centuries, both for merchants' children and for craftsmen's children. The rates would be lower if they could be obtained for mortality before the age of 16, our serfs' age of majority, but only a little lower.[15]

There can be little doubt that child mortality was the main reason why manorial replacement-rates remained so long in a precarious condition. Why did Wilberton not maintain the recovery it shows for the 1380's? The clerk noted that certain people were ill during the next decade; the illness was not fatal to these persons, but it must have been fatal to several boys nearing the age of 16. The village was not deteriorating from an economic point of view. On the contrary, the fall in the replacement-rate during the 1390's was accompanied by a mild rise in economic activity. This had made for more contacts with outside markets, possibly for more exposure to new infections.

Manorial records tend to become disappointingly thin over precisely those decades of the latter half of the fifteenth century in which replacement-rates may have begun to stay on an upward curve. For the whole of the fifteenth century, however, there is a vast and virtually untapped source of information in the registers containing copies of the wills of villagers and provincial townsmen. Not all men, and very few women, made wills that were registered. The bias, among the men, may have been simply towards piety, the clergy having desired to make sure that executors would carry out a dying man's desire to leave money to his parish church or to have masses sung for his soul. Pious donations are sometimes only of a few pence, so that they do not make for any obvious bias towards the more prosperous. Like most medieval sources these wills are biased towards a record of the male sex. Daughters who had already received a dowry could usually expect nothing more from the parents than some part of the household goods. Among these humble people, the household goods were normally too few to allow of depletion while the family still held together, but were distributed only by the will of the widow, or by the will of a man whose wife had predeceased him. These two classes of will usually enumerate more daughters, and often, for the same reason, more sons than the wills of men whose wife survived. Taken as a single body of source material, therefore, the wills of these humble people are not a valid index to the actual numbers of sons surviving a father's last illness. But since the factors making for underenumeration of sons may be taken as a constant; they are at least a valid clue to the *trend* of the replacement-rate.

Wills from the region of the manors examined above being not at the moment available to me, the registers examined are from two other parts of the country—Essex and Hertfordshire. The Archdeaconry of Essex and the Archdeaconry of St Albans between them supply over a thousand examples, mostly from country parishes but including the town of St Albans and the semi-town of Barnet.[16] There is a gap in the Essex record between 1435 and 1479, but the Archdeaconry of St Albans register runs continuously from 1411 to 1470. The figures as set out in Table 2 exclude wills of clergy and of women, the will of Janyn Frenscheman who after living in Buckinghamshire wandered in to St Albans,[17] all cases

TABLE 2

	Male Testators				Sons			
	Single	Married	Widowers	Total	Adult	Other	Total	Sons per male testator
Archdeaconry of Essex								
1420–35	19	67	7	93	18	32	50	.54
1477–79	4	30		34	3	22	25	.7
1480–92	6	242	36	284	276	60	336	1.18
Archdeaconry of St Albans								
(1) Town of St Albans								
1415–30	12	33		45	8	5	13	.29
1431–40	18	76	4	98	29		29	.30
1441–50	11	66	4	81	26		26	.32
1451–60	29	70	7	106	36	7	43	.40
1461–70	13	73	6	92	41	4	45	.48
(2) Rural								
1412–30	16	35	1	52	22		22	.42
1431–40	23	74	8	105	48		48	.45
1441–50	7	100	7	114	44	6	50	.43
1451–60	20	121	17	158	66	6	72	.45
1461–70	14	66	15	95	56	2	58	.61
(3) Barnet								
1416–20		10					11	1.1
1461–70		7					12	1.7

182

of doubtful date, a few stray gentlemen, and all cases of intestacy. They include everything else, even brief bequests of all possessions to the wife as executor and residuary legatee, in which there may very well have been children. Omission of children in this way, as stated above, is taken to be a constant. Another problem, that of failure of a testator to specify the number or sex of young children, and occasionally even to specify the exact number of those who may have been adult, has been treated in a uniform way by the assumption that one of these omissions was a son. The chances of new pregnancy or births in between the date of drafting of the will and the date of death have further been ignored, given the large numbers of cases, as a constant. The date of probate is not stated except in the later Essex wills. These show some gaps of a year or even more, which may suggest that people were now sometimes recovering from illnesses they feared at first would be fatal. But any student of medieval wills can see that they were normally made only on a premonition of death that was fulfilled within a few months.

The evidence of these wills as to replacement trends falls into three patterns. Comparing the Archdeaconry of Essex wills as three blocks—those of 1420–35, 1477–79, and 1480–92—there is a sharp contrast between the first and the two later blocks. In the first period the number of sons mentioned per male testator is only .54, in the second it rises to .7, a lift of 29 per cent, in the third it rises again to 1.1, a lift of 51 per cent over the starting-point in the first period. In the first period 20 per cent of the wills are classified as those of unmarried men since they make no mention of wives or children living or deceased. Some of these were obviously young men. They have few possessions and leave them to brothers, sisters, or even to the father who is still living. In one case at Havering atte Bower, one of the men so included turns out from a check of the court rolls of the manor, to have been 70. His age is on record because he applied for exemption from jury work. Further checking of court rolls may reveal some more exceptional cases of this kind. But in general the proportion of the testators who fail to mention deceased wives must be small. Some mention two, though they had a third wife living. The margin of error in taking the proportion of men naming no wife as an index to the incidence of early death lowering the replacement-rate must be slight. In 1477–79 all but 12 per cent of the Essex men had wives at the date of drafting of the will, in the third period all but 2 per cent. In the first period 36 per cent of the sons named were adult. The two criteria used for this classification are appointment as executor or co-executor, and marriage. In 1477–79 only 12 per cent of the sons are so described, in the third period 79 per cent. The pattern, therefore, is one of a rising marriage-rate due to better chances of survival, and of a markedly better survival of male children reaching back into the 1470's.

The town of St Albans and the rural St Albans wills, excluding Barnet, illustrate variants of a second pattern. In St Albans improvement was steady through the decades, the ratio of all sons named, to all testators, being 65 per cent better in the 1460's than in the initial period 1415–30. In the rural parishes the improvement is only 41 per cent and is not quite steady, showing a drop in the 1440's. On the other hand the rural figures are, as one would expect, consistently higher.

Barnet was separated as a test case of a market community which would have had an attraction for semi-agrarian craftsmen and traders rather than, as St Albans, attracting a mixed group of more specialized craftsmen and of men looking for employment as abbey servants. It is also a case in which the court rolls are particularly good for the fourteenth century and survive in part for the fifteenth century. They will be used in a later publication to help elucidate the pattern that the wills show—that of a much higher number of sons surviving than in other rural parts of the archdeaconry, with an improvement of 55 per cent over the period covered. The improvement is greater than that of the rural areas but less than that of the town of St Albans.

The wills do not give an altogether unrealistic impression of family size. In the first block for Essex two men in the 1430's left three sons apiece and another left two adult sons and two daughters. The largest family in the whole record is one of five sons and three daughters at Havering atte Bower in 1477. The widows do not consistently name more children than the men do. One at Hockley in 1433 names two more sons than her husband did at his death two years before, but there is a possibility that they were hers only, by a previous husband. They have not been counted and would in any event not affect the trend.

The wills of these obscure people are nevertheless not in the same class, as source material for family size, as those of wealthy merchants either in the provinces or in London. Wealthy merchants amassed plate and finery from which they made long lists of bequests not only to sons and daughters who were already established in life but to their children under age, to godchildren and to friends. For London it is also easier to confirm the family history from deeds by which property was conveyed. Due to the "parchment" trade and to migrations of family papers, no English collections of deeds are complete, but the provincial deeds are more widely scattered within England. The evidence of wills and deeds as to the low rates of survival among sons of London merchant families which I presented in an early work, has proved repellent to two readers who apparently skipped my account of the methods used.[18] Their own method of raising the rates is the method of loaded samples, by which one can readily prove either that everyone left two sons, or three sons, or that no one left any. The most rational method of handling the huge body of economic and demographic information contained in the London and provincial wills is obviously to use modern statistical sampling methods, applying them in such a way that correlations of family size with wealth, occupation, and types of rural community, can be worked out.

To economic historians the facts presented here merely confirm what is already apparent from economic evidence. There is however some advantage in establishing demographic trends independently, by methods immune to the charge of circular reasoning. The problem now is to discover how general these trends were, by examining wills from other parts of the country and making studies in depth of still other types of community. Only then can we attain a full understanding of the variables that were affecting birth-rates and death-rates respectively. Although there are grounds for a Malthusian interpretation of the downward drift of replacement-rates in the pre-plague period, this interpretation is plainly redundant in the post-plague era. Again, although in the late fourteenth century and at certain points later, plague must have radically altered the age-structure of the population—J. C. Russell's reasoning as to this is essentially sound and not invalidated by criticism of his life tables—it is converting history into grand opera to make the macabre character of plague responsible for the long sluggishness of replacement-rates in the fifteenth century. Chroniclers were not medical diagnosticians. Now that medical science is learning so much about bacterial and viral mutation, historians should be prepared to consider this as a factor in the situation. New types of infection are always dangerous. As we know only too well today, travel and communication are their best friends. It follows that the migratory habits of the poorer peasantry and the customary movements of village traders and craftsmen among the markets of their district maximized opportunities for infections to spread. It is not even necessary to prove that this spatial mobility was any greater in the post-plague era than it had been in the thirteenth century, or in the twelfth century. To the extent that migration was motivated either by "push," in seats of economic stagnation, or by "pull" towards centres of greater economic activity, we have an element of economic interpretation of the demographic trends on our hands.[19] To the extent that migrations were aimless, or motivated by moods of fear, despair, desire to enter the Church or otherwise to evade family responsibilities, we have a cultural interpretation. In either case, the period from 1349 to the 1470's, if it was a golden age, was the golden age of bacteria.

APPENDIX

Location of Court Rolls Used

Brandon. University of Chicago, Harper Library, Rare Books Department, Bacon Collection. Other Brandon records are scattered about England. I have examined all of these but they did not contribute data for this paper.

Great Bromley. Essex County Record Office, Chelmsford, Microfilm supplied me by courtesy of the Archivist.

Havering atte Bower. As above.

Hinderclay. University of Chicago, Bacon Collection. Long series of accounts there also.

Long Bennington. British Museum Additional Rolls, 54990 *et seq.* Microfilm of this series supplied me by courtesy of the Manuscript Department. The stitching of the rolls is such that it is impossible for the photographer always to indicate the numbering. References by court date are, however, sufficient.

Northwold. Norwich Public Library, MS. 18,629.

Redgrave. University of Chicago, Bacon Collection. Accounts also.

Thorney. As above.

Wilberton. The court rolls used by Maitland in his classic study, "The History of a Cambridgeshire Manor," reproduced in *Selected Historical Essays of F. W. Maitland,* ed. Helen M. Cam (Cambridge, 1957), are in excellent condition in the Library of the University of Wisconsin, Rare Books Department. Other Wilberton records are scattered about England. As in the similar case of Brandon records, I have consulted all these but the information presented here rests on the main set in Madison, Wisconsin.

Wyverstone. University of Chicago, Bacon Collection.

NOTES

1. H. E. Hallam, "Some Thirteenth-Century Censuses," *Economic History Review,* 2nd ser. X, 340–61.

2. *Op. cit.* p. 354. The average for daughters was 2.33 for Weston, 1.88 for Moulton.

3. *Op. cit.* p. 356. In this reduction, those of Hallam's clerks who might have married, as parish clerks normally did, have been omitted.

4. Emigration rates, including clergy, are given as 38.2 per cent of sons and 53.5 per cent of daughters in Weston, 23.3 per cent of sons and 44 per cent of daughters in Moulton, Moulton having to import a few brides. *Op. cit.* pp. 356–57.

5. A complete list of the location and nature of all the manorial records used in this paper is given in the Appendix of this essay.

6. Redgrave Court Roll, 29, m. 22; Long Bennington, Easter Court, 1439. Custom for free tenants may have generally set the age higher: in 1397 the heir to a free tenement in Briston, part of Thornes manor, although he was said to be 16, was declared *infra etatem.* Thorney Court Rolls, Feast of St James the Apostle, 21 Richard II.

7. Long Bennington, Pentecost, 1 Ric. II.
8. Hinderclay, Jan. 1301.
9. J. C. Russell, *Medieval British Population* (Albuquerque, 1948), pp. 214–31.
10. F. M. Page, *The Estates of Crowland Abbey* (Cambridge, 1934), ch. X. Miss Levett's figures for St Albans manors, excluding cases in which the existence of an heir was uncertain and those of orders for distraint of an heir not named, show 334 male tenants replaced by 61 sons of age, a replacement-rate of .18, with 61 more sons under age, 11 whose age is not indicated, 37 other male heirs of age, 22 under age and 21 of uncertain age. Here, since harvest work was not disrupted, the women may have pitched in to a greater extent than usual. A. E. Levett, *Studies in Manorial History* (Oxford, 1938), tabulations.
11. Redgrave data on all four of the first general plagues are particularly good and will be presented elsewhere.
12. Court of Exaltation of the Holy Cross, 2 Ric. II, Long Bennington.
13. Redgrave Court Roll 28, m. 6, Easter, 12 Ric. II.
14. Incompletely calendared in Sharpe's *Calendars of the Letter Books* . . . and not calendared at all for the *Journals* of the City of London. Not used except by me in *The Merchant Class of London* (Chicago, 1948, re-issued by University of Michigan Press, 1961), ch. V. Orphanage records exist also for Bristol but with less full information as to what happened to the children.
15. On child mortality at different ages in a stagnating population in the seventeenth century, worked out with the help of excellent parish records, see Pierre Goubert, *Beauvais et le Beauvaisis de 1600 à 1750* (Paris, 1960), pp. 30–59.
16. The information, from registers *Wynterbourne* and *Stoneham*, was taken partly by me and completed with the kind assistance of Dr. Nellie Kerling, from the registers at Somerset House. All the registered wills and many original wills of the period now are preserved also in microfilm at Salt Lake City.
17. Immigration from abroad had been making some minor net additions to population, mostly of adult males. For the numbers of aliens taxed in 1440 see my "A Survey of the Alien Population of England in 1440," pp. 144–47. Sex ratios are shown there. By accident a portion of the figures for Norwich were omitted in this publication, but the error will be rectified in a further publication analyzing the taxed aliens of that date in the environs of London and for the later fifteenth century. Dr. Kerling has in a recent article attempted to rectify the omission from the Norfolk figures, but omitting sex ratios, so that the material is not demographically comparable and making an incorrect allegation that I discounted the figures of aliens making a loyalty oath in 1436.
18. The answer to misunderstandings of my procedure on the part of E. Ekwall in his publication of *Two Early London Subsidy Rolls* (Lund,

1951), misunderstandings compounded with further irrelevant observations and guesswork by G. A. Williams in his *Medieval London from Commune to Capital* (London, 1963), is contained in footnote 15 to p. 199 of my *Merchant Class of Medieval London*. My esteem for Prof. Ekwall's philological work is so great—his *Dictionary of English Place Names* is my daily staff—that I can forgive him anything. Mr. Williams has yet to learn that admissions to citizenship do not constitute evidence that the city in question is growing. This was discovered long ago in German urban research and is illustrated in my recent editing (with the collaboration of Harold B. Johnson) of the admissions to citizenship in Canterbury ("The Earliest Canterbury Freemen's Rolls, 1298–1363," *Kent Records*, XVIII, ed. F. Du Boulay, 1964). Admissions there will be seen to have risen after the first plague, when property was thrown on the market. Whether those who took up citizenship to buy such property were immigrants or previous residents of the city, the rise hardly proves a rise in population. Further admissions to citizenship in Maldon and in Reading are in my possession and will be published.

19. Much further evidence on the causes of mobility is contained in J. A. Raftis, *Tenure and Mobility* (Toronto, 1965), which at the time of writing has not yet reached me.

IV

Social Change

Introduction

ERIC R. WOLF

Our understandings of how men establish modes of life appropriate to their circumstances, or of how they cleave to them and alter them, undergo continuous oscillations—between phases of particularism and generalization; between the historian's fascination with the stream of events and the sociologist's use of conceptual models from which both time and space have been strained; between an emphasis on intellectual or governing elites and approaches which credit the labor of the common people; between views which underline the importance of material circumstances and views which grant priority to the play of ideas; between perspectives which emphasize institutional constraints and interpretations which see men as agents, exercising choice in the selection of means for man-made ends.

Such changes of phase, such oscillations, are potentially productive; each shift can complete the work done by its predecessors, bringing new information to bear on old questions, or asking new questions demanding new information. Yet this dialectic of inquiry is never self-evident: at its center there always stands the question of how one can relate old work to new work, new data to old understandings, old data to new models. It is easy enough to upset the constructions of those who have gone before, to violate the contextual boundaries of space and time, to sacrifice complexities to a single-minded *rage à concluir*. And how can we be truly comparative, without converting human populations inhabiting determinate territories in space and time into the disembodied shadows of Economic Man or Political Man or of the Self-Realization of the Universal Idea? Furthermore, can we hold on to the sharpness of detail and outline of our material, when we immerse it in the acid bath of all the social sciences: anthropology, sociology, economics, politics, ecology? It is difficult enough to know even a little about an individual or a small population. Can we be truly comparative about human groups, and can we be truly comparative, furthermore, standing between disciplines and fields of study, open enough to gain diverse kinds of new knowledge, capable of producing further knowledge and further inquiry?

There are certainly those who now slip back the safety on their intellectual armament whenever they hear the words "cross-cultural," "comparative," and "interdisciplinary"; and even directors of interdisciplinary studies seem to despair sooner or later of realizing the promises held out in their brochures to sponsoring foundations and eager students. Yet whether or not comparative studies are possible is not an issue which can be settled by taking thought or hoping against hope; it can only be resolved by doing work. And it has been Sylvia Thrupp's special distinction that she has attempted to furnish an answer, both by doing her own work as a social historian, and by working on our common behalf as editor of *Comparative Studies in Society and History*.

The readers of the essays collected in this volume and in this section will soon understand why Thrupp was so preeminently fitted to carry on a task of such magnitude. It is essentially her intrinsic realism, her lively sense of what is possible and probable, that has brought her undertaking to fruition. The reader can do no better than to glance at her essay on "Medieval Gilds Reconsidered," for it transcends quickly the stereotyped picture of gild life and organization on which many of us have been raised. There were regional differences between gilds, and differences between gilds located in small and in large towns. Gilds could have combined trading and handicraft functions only where raw materials were immediately at hand. Gilds rarely represented homogeneous interests; they were congeries of a wide variation of special interests, and these interests varied from place to place. They were not always restrictive and conservative; they could restrict output or access to membership only where factors of production were limited or markets stagnant and stationary. They were not economic organizations only: they need to be understood also in the context of a social order chronically disordered by warfare, epidemics, crop failures, lack of insurance, shortages of capital. After reading Thrupp's essay, we come away with a new sense of heterogeneity, adaptability, differentiation, flexibility—and with new questions.

Or take her discussion of the characteristics of social classes and of their boundaries in the essay on "The Problem of Conservatism in

Fifteenth-Century England." Any picture we might have entertained about static medieval society yields to a portrayal of much greater mobility and ambiguity, of "a lively degree of social mobility, of movement not only from one community to another, but from one social class to another." Differential rates of fertility and mortality affected class continuity as well. Class boundaries were often am- biguous, but grew more sharply defined as men granted greater prestige to the possession of property, or as various groups faced diminution in inherited status. In this treatment, classes are no longer treated as fixed categories, but as fluid and shifting "regions" of the social structure, each region not so much separate and distinct from the others as interrelated with the others and shifting and changing as they shift and change.

Medieval society thus appears no longer as changeless and im- mobile; "adaptive change occurred everywhere, custom and tradition were flexible," she says in her Preface to *Change in Medieval So- ciety*. But if tradition is flexible, then it cannot be thought of any longer as opposed and antithetical to "modernization." Tradition can be flexible enough to respond to change, to accommodate to change, even to underwrite it. If "modernization" is understood as state-mak- ing, the creation of bureaucracies, the onset of rational planning, the universalization of legal and philosophical norms, then these characteristics appear, in one form or another, with lesser or greater intensity, in any society above the tribal level. Tradition and mod- ernity appear as a dialectic, not as successive stages in an evolution- ary process. The model of a modernized society—created by a de- mand for planned change which converts all elements of life into "passion-less" means for "passion-less" ends—is thus nothing but a form of rationalist irrationality. "A moment's reflection," says Thrupp (in the review article, "Tradition and Development"), "would remind them that a society is not a society and human beings are not human, unless there is some element of ceremony within the institutions that embody common values and some refreshing of energies through conviviality. Ceremony and conviviality are among the first charges on the resources of any community."

Ceremony and conviviality, however, are expressions of a so- ciety's values, and societies are not only engaged in ongoing ecologi- cal changes and in the ordering and reordering of social relations: they also codify perceptions and cognitions in values, and continu- ously produce new values and distributions of values. Cities, pre- eminently, are loci for the generation and distribution of values. The differential relations of cities to their hinterlands—economic, social, political, and intellectual—produce differential and changing fields of force. But the ability of cities to generate and distribute values can also shrink and atrophy. The result is often a "yielding to futilities, to organization without purpose and hence to obsession with destruction." Yet there is also a dialectic of lassitude and of innovation, of *accidie* and creativity, in human affairs. Men not only adapt to an external environment, they innovate and evoke new visions of the world to spur a new creative effort, to achieve a different level of tension. Hence also Sylvia Thrupp's interest in the innovative thrusts of millenarianism, and in the topic of cultural innovation in general. Two conferences, sponsored by *Comparative Studies in Society and History*, grew out of this concern.

What qualities do we therefore demand of the models which we employ for comparison? They must not be too abstract and they must not be too rigid. Not too abstract, for too much abstraction would strain out much of the stuff of life and movement. Not too rigid, so that the mental nets we cast will always be able to accommodate change and shifting boundaries.

Much of Thrupp's approach to conceptualization and comparison is illuminated, in her essay on "The Creativity of Cities," by her critique of Gideon Sjoberg. Sjoberg, author of *The Preindustrial City, Past and Present*, presented us with a "constructed type" of the city before the onset of industrialism, constructing it with data drawn primarily from descriptively integrated sketches of Peking, Mecca, Cairo, Fez, Bokhara, Lhasa, and Renaissance Florence. Yet such sketches, argues Thrupp, are not enough: description and analysis requires a thorough inquiry into economic history, more sensitive handling of the processes of social mobility, and, above all, a proper regard to the ways in which values are generated and distributed among the population. Types should be "real," not "constructed." Premature abstraction and rigidity in defining the characteristics and outlines of the model preclude an understanding of similarities, in the context of diversities. "The lines of advance," she argues, "are through study of the ways in which cultural change (understood broadly as including political and economic change) affects the workings of a system even when the structural elements here emphasized may not be fundamentally altered, and of the ways in which through creation of new values and new roles it significantly alters these elements." Otherwise, we are left only with fixed images of the past, which, Professor Thrupp avers, are "essentially an effort to support an image of ourselves."

We thus need careful case studies of places and times, steeped in rich data and informed by empathy for the people studied, before we embark on comparison. But comparison is essential for an understanding of each case, for we cannot know its uniqueness or its differences from other cases until we do compare. But comparison is neither an endless digging for more information, nor a trip to the moon: it needs to proceed slowly and cautiously along a middle ground of understanding and theory. Nor is it work which can be carried on by a single scholar: it requires a collective process of work and communication. Sylvia Thrupp's essays represent a notable contribution to such work, and *Comparative Studies in Society and History* will stand as an enduring monument to the process of scholarship and communication. We are all in her debt.

Tradition and Development:
A Choice of Views

If a citizen of the Roman Empire were to attend a conference of to-day's development experts, he could readily grasp much of its subject matter. The spread of new engineering and military technology, of new techniques of government and rational law, of trade, of formal education and a wider moral sense of community, all emanating from cities, would be familiar to him. He would doubtless rise to speak, and his remarks on the theme, "We too had Modernization," might well have been printed in either of the volumes of conference reports listed in the note below.

For development studies have jolted the social sciences into omnivorous curiosity. They are at grips with a bewildering variety of novel scenes. The very status of the expert, his power to help the peoples he is studying, depends on imaginative use of the scarce resources available for research. He is under urgent pressure to devise new hypotheses, new rational generalizations. This pressure to generalize has led in three main directions. It has first led a retreat to existing schools of general theory, either to Talcott Parsons' systematic sociology or to cultural theory. Both of these are endlessly expounded. The next move is towards the construction of models of the economic and political systems found to be engaged in the process that is rather awkwardly styled political and socio-economic

Reprinted from *Comparative Studies in Society and History* 6, no. 1 (1963): 84–90. A review of Ralph Braibanti and Joseph J. Spengler, eds., *Tradition, Values, and Socio-Economic Development* (Durham, N.C., 1961), and of Bert F. Hoselitz and Wilbert E. Moore, *Industrialization and Society* (The Hague, 1963).

development. David Apter's paper in the Unesco volume distinguishes between a mobilization system and a reconciliation system as models of differing relationships between political and social structure.[1] In the first, political parties or governments start rapid programs of change. In the second, initiative is more diffused, with the result that progress is slower. S. N. Eisenstadt, in the same book, summarizes some of his work on the kinds of social and economic power that different systems of bureaucracy may exercise.[2] Neither book contains any more comprehensive model that would clearly exemplify how the development process may alter as it advances nor how, apart from statistics of per capita income, it may in any precise way be recognized as advancing.[3] In both, the emphasis is on the promotion of attitudes of readiness for change, of readiness to break, if necessary, with tradition.

The third direction in which the pressure to generalize leads is towards the past, towards historical study of the origins of development. Some would be content to stop at a fairly recent past, conceiving the process of development as a unique set of events stemming from the desire and the power to control environment. It must then on each scene have had a definite starting-point or starting-zone in time, and we should understand the social structure of that time. Alternatively, if development is thought of as continuous with the whole civilizational process, one might still need to mark off relevant cutting-points. So far, the main tool in use for marking out these points or zones has been Max Weber's distinction between the traditional and the rational as ideal types of society. This distinction is now realized to be so loose that elements of rationality of rather large significance for development might escape notice simply because an age had been labelled Traditional, Undeveloped. Research on the Development Age would then start off on the wrong foot, with erroneous assumptions. At all events, the experts are tapping on the historian's door, if only in hope of salvaging as much as possible of their generalizations about "traditional" civilizations.

But several conflicting views of the nature and of the function of tradition enter into these discussions. As Hoselitz points out, experts have long taken for granted many points that demand detailed enquiry.[4] Uncritical use of Max Weber's rather casual definition of traditional behavior, which covers both blind and selfconscious at-

tachment to daily routine, has again and again led writers to berate
a tradition-ridden peasantry or artisanry as obstacles to development. Hoselitz is able to show that as regards unconscious habitua-
tion to particular postures or rhythms of work, which differ among
artisans from culture to culture, this impression is illusory. Factory
managers are easily able to make adjustments, to make efficient industrial workers out of artisans of any culture. He is able also to
show how even selfconscious attachment to routine pattern need not
impede economic or political development, once this has succeeded
in introducing new milieus of activity. Weber never studied the
norms of attachment to routine. Content to describe them, most un-
realistically, as "inviolable," he did not perceive the need of distinguishing, as Hoselitz now does, between the differing degrees of
selfconsciousness and formality they may display, and consequently
failed to see that they are not necessarily carried over from one milieu of activity to another. As to the function of tradition, Hoselitz
stresses the stabilizing function, and the fact that, once rapid economic growth is under way, tradition is therefore an aid rather than
an impediment. Certainly in the sphere of family relationships and
religion, tradition has everywhere helped to safeguard new industrial centres against the drawbacks of their own tendency to disorga-
nize the society around them.

A longer view will be found in the late M. J. Herskovits' paper,
which calls for cautious comparative study that would probe more
deeply.[5] Tradition is here virtually equated with the dynamic aspect
of culture, conceived as an ever-continuing process of change. By
definition this is far too complex ever to be brought entirely under
the control of the explicitly formulated norms, ends and values that
the economic sociologist associates with rational action. Herskovits
made a genial effort to set aside the contradiction between the cultural and the rationalist theories by conceding the latter the field of
static analysis of social relationships at any given point in time.

This solution does not satisfy a theorist who sees choice between
ends, norms and values becoming more rational through wider communication and discussion. Joseph J. Spengler, who takes this view,
favors a solution of the contradiction between the theories by postulating a division of history into two eras, one in which the content of
culture is primarily irrational, in which individuals cling to continu-

ity, and one in which they become increasingly rational and attuned to fresh starts, to discontinuities.[6] In the West he sees the transition from one to the other as having been gradual, and still far from complete. For societies and civilizations in which the scientific attitude is not indigenous he sets himself to justify the need of a cultural shock, a planned transition. He feels—and being not only an economist but also a distinguished historian of population problems, he speaks on this point with some authority—that this is the only alternative to Malthusian disaster. His argument, which rests on the theory of system analysis as this is currently applied in biology as well as in economics, makes his essay by far the most tightly reasoned and challenging in either of these conference reports.

Spengler combines cultural and societal theory into a single, pluralistic, theory. His philosophical starting-point is F. A. Hayek's description of the individual mind as a selective and classifying apparatus, conditioned in its response to stimulus by the classificatory map of the world that it builds up, yet at any given moment having "great autonomy" in "dealing selectively and authoritatively with current events, stimuli and situations." Individual autonomy is of course hedged about by institutionalized sets of social relations, constituting subsystems within the broader groups and systems held together by common values. Spengler's concern is to use this scheme to differentiate between two types of change. The one type may be limited to a single subsystem. The other is the kind that will fan out and transform a whole society. Both arise (he raises but leaves aside the question of pressure from external changes in the physical environment) primarily from changes in the way in which people perceive their physical or their social environment. Change is however likely to be contained within a single subsystem, or set of institutions. Even though it may lead to cultural borrowing, he argues on the basis of both system theory and historical examples that innovations so borrowed will tend to be contained within a subsystem, where they may or may not survive. The type of change that will resist containment, that will fan out and transform a whole society, has to come with a jolt affecting all of its subsystems.

Spengler identifies the jolt required for successful long-run development with the inculcation in the elite of what Veblen called a "passionless matter-of-fact" attitude to human affairs. Spengler describes this more precisely as a driving rationality that will search out and wherever possible resolve conflicts between ends or values, when these inhibit new forms of action. Its chief obstacle is ideology, which he redefines for his purpose as non-rational habits of mind that tend to obstruct the resolution of inter-value conflict either by interfering with a rational weighing-up of situations or by concealing the existence of the conflict. In his conclusion he advocates research aimed to identify and classify the values present in local communities. Values favorable to development and susceptible to outside influence could then be reinforced.

A Japanese historian might observe that Spengler could have expanded his conclusions, and supported them, by reference to the last century of Japan's history. The first reaction of a Western historian, especially of an intellectual historian, would be to place the whole of the debate between cultural theory and rationalist value-theory in the light of its own history, which goes back to the debate between romantics and rationalists in the French revolutionary era. That debate, like today's, was essentially about how change occurs. Does it come through tradition, never quite letting go of the immediate past, or does it come by conscious decision that there ought to be a break with this or that custom? Like the cultural theorists of today, the romantics accused the rationalists of not understanding the facts of life, of being too enamoured with their own ideas of what *ought* to be, of what *ought* to happen.

The debate is now moribund, its utility reduced to pointing up the differences between the simple kin-based societies that have been the preserve of ethnology, and complex civilizations, which are never wholly integrated. If the training of social scientists ever comes to include a seminar on some aspect or period in the history of a pre-modern civilization, the debate would expire. To one trained only in theory and contemporary research, the more remote past is inevitably foreshortened. Even to modernist historians it appears as little more than a sleepy contrast with our own explosive century. Read in capsule form, though changes in the literate traditions of philosophy and religion may stand out, history is distorted. The restructuring of economic and social life that urbanization, from the start, sets on foot, is lost. In reality all civilizations appear to have known spurts of planned change along with sectors of continuing sleepiness.

Cultural theory might spur historians to try to find out more about the ultimate results of planned change in the past. There is a vast scope for comparative study both of peaceful expansion through colonization, trade, and missions, and of imperialist expansion. The written record is however biassed towards successful acculturation. We almost never have the underdog's view of imperialism, never a full record of how cultures die. Yet we can see, both in the more remote and the recent past, how they may be pushed into retreat, regressing economically and clinging in the process to kinship customs, as to a lifebelt, and to religious beliefs, which may be all they have left to nourish dignity and pride. In the world of today these phenomena of retreat and regression, one of the legacies of Western imperialism, have been aggravated by the unprecedented population pressure which is the first gift, hardly a clear benefit, of modern medicine. It is by this situation, unique in history, that social scientists are judging the character of "traditional" peoples.

Rationalist theory can provide other cues for new historical research. The development experts are dealing only obliquely with the central problem of how social cohesion is to be maintained if change is accelerated. They grudge the diversion of resources to uses that are not in a material sense productive. Yet a moment's reflection would remind them that a society is not a society and human beings are not human, unless there is some element of ceremony within the institutions that embody common values and some refreshing of energies through conviviality. Ceremony and conviviality are among the first charges on the resources of any community. In a rich society the outlay on these is considerable, but is hardly noticed. In a poor society the cost necessarily absorbs a much higher proportion of each community's total resources. Yet an observer from a rich society is almost always impatient about a poor society's expenditure for these purposes, condemning it as waste. Spengler takes this attitude. Mark Twain's fable of the Yankees at the court of King Arthur who vainly tried to persuade the king's subjects to divert their customary tribute to the court and to the priests into the building of better houses for their families and the improvement of their land, is to him a work of wisdom, the Yankees' failure demonstrating the power and the irrationality of tradition. The irrationality is actually in the rationalist. This might come to be more generally understood if economic historians would occupy themselves with the costs, including costs in time, of the ceremonial and convivial "overhead" of different societies. The proportion that these bear to total resources is admittedly hard to calculate, the more so because the affirmation of cohesion that ceremony provides, and the stimulus of conviviality, may bring people to raise their levels of production. Yet no model of development process will be of much use unless it can incorporate some attack on this problem.

Historical study could in many other ways help the rationalist to realize that the function of tradition goes far beyond the matter of stabilization. Most traditions have been positively correlated both with social cohesion and with innovation. They can change yet continue to enjoy the same kind of anonymous social sanction as before. As the chapter on the history of Islamic political thought shows, in the Duke University volume, flexibility may in a period of general regression freeze into rigidity, only to revive again.[7] Tradition may provide useful niches for the absorption of changes required by development, quietly and without fuss. An Indian anthropologist has described how public health workers, if they are trained to envisage Indian village practices of ritual purity as a system of actions directed to the end of health, a system which at some points overlaps a scientific set of means directed to this end, may at these points slip standards of sanitation into the traditional system, "in a phased scheme."[8] Spengler clearly appreciates such possibilities in stressing a matter that is obvious to him as an economist but has been too little used as a research tool, namely that some element of rational calculation is present in all cultures. It must in some degree enter into the allocation of resources between competing ends. Historians of science are now helping economic historians recover the phases through which the West acquired its interest in measurement and calculation. This is another field in which comparative study would be illuminating.

It is astonishing how little attention these conference volumes pay to the all-important question, for a developing economy, of how to build rural prosperity. The Unesco book leaves it to Arnold C. Anderson, whose specialty is comparative education, to assure us that migration to towns is not enough, that the productivity of labor staying on the land must rise. To most agrarian reformers in Africa it has appeared to be obvious that this can occur only through introducing Western patterns of individualized land tenure, and they have been surprised when their measures meet with resistance. Herskovits pointed out rather wearily how absurd it was not to have foreseen this, not to have prepared people better for the change. In cultural theory it is axiomatic that to add a novel practice, such as literacy, is much easier than to substitute new practices for old, especially when the old, as in the case of land tenures, are enmeshed in the kinship structure and its attendant obligations.[9] In regard to the adoption of technical innovations, the opinion is offered that peasant traditions are not a major obstacle. It has been remarked that when peasants distrust the advice of officials it may be because their advice has often been bad. None of these writers proposes that agricultural officials study the logic of peasant thinking about soil or plant and animal life in order to locate points through which, as in the case of health practices in India, new ideas might be slipped into practice. Anderson's proposals are confined to the setting up of technical schools for farm children. No one raises the question of how Asian agricultural skills came to be developed, through innovations, to their present high level. Unfortunately Asian economic history is still too backward to answer the question.

NOTES

1. David E. Apter, "System, Process, and Politics of Economic Development," Hoselitz and Moore, *Industrialization and Society*, pp. 135–58.

2. S. N. Eisenstadt, "Problems of Emerging Bureaucracies in Developing Areas and New States," *loc. cit.*, pp. 159–174.

3. For a move towards a comprehensive model based on measurable indices, see Karl W. Deutsch, "Social Mobilization and Political Development," *The American Political Science Review*, LV (1961), pp. 493–514.

4. Bert F. Hoselitz, "Tradition and Economic Growth," in Braibanti and Spengler, *Tradition, Values, and Socio-Economic Development*, pp. 83–114.

5. M. J. Herskovits, "Economic Change and Cultural Dynamics," *loc. cit.*, pp. 114–138.

6. Joseph J. Spengler, "Theory, Ideology, Non-Economic Values, and Politico-Economic Development," *loc. cit.*, pp. 3–56.

7. Ishtiaq Husain Qureshi, "The Background of Some Trends in the Political Thought of Pakistan," *loc. cit.*, pp. 181–211.

8. R. S. Khare, "Ritual Purity and Pollution in Relation to Domestic Sanitation," *The Eastern Anthropologist*, XV (1962), pp. 125–39.

9. M. J. Herskovits, in Braibanti and Spengler, p. 133.

Preface to Change in Medieval Society: Europe North of the Alps, 1050-1500

The civilization of Western Europe in the latter half of the middle ages, from the late eleventh to the late fifteenth century, is the earliest for which we have written records relating to almost all aspects of life. Our picture of civilizations older than this is drawn from the work of their more successful political and religious leaders and lawmakers, and from the ideas of their philosophers, men of letters, and artists. Skilled archaeologists, and economic and legal historians can round out the picture, in some cases very considerably. Yet the patterns of loyalty and organization among the people who built and ran the cities of the ancient and classical civilizations, who made the tools and worked the land, whose sons willingly or unwillingly manned the armies, remain very much of a blank. We interpret, in the main, the rise and fate of these civilizations through their forms of political power. We have to assume that the ideas and ideals in the writing and art that has survived were influential.

But the last four centuries of the Medieval West have left enough administrative, legal, economic, and personal records to bring the middling and lower ranks of people before us objectively. When people of this kind appear in the literary sources, they are likely to be caricatured or shown only as a moralist thought they ought to behave. The nonliterary sources provide a check. These sources are vast, but they are accessible to any scholar, and they are not, like the records of the recent past, so bulky as to be unmanage-

Reprinted from *Change in Medieval Society: Europe North of the Alps, 1050–1500*, ed. Sylvia L. Thrupp (New York, 1964), pp. v–viii.

able. Research in them has opened up many new perspectives that are not yet fully explored and raised new questions to be asked of the literary sources and the chronicles.

The new research makes older attempts to simplify medieval history by reducing it to a single theme, suggestive and dramatic though they may be, unsatisfactory. The interpretations of this kind that have been most influential have been based either on politics or on philosophy. To many writers, the key theme of medieval history has been the rise of the nation-state, or of middle-class liberties and the principles that these invoked. The other most popular type of interpretation rested on the overriding medieval faith in God, and on the curious survival of the idea of one Empire. The leading characteristic of the age then becomes the quest for unity. A variant of this view makes the idea of law the driving force of the age. This is more subtle, since the idea made for debate over the sources of authority.

Brilliant use has been made of such interpretations. Without them, medieval history would hardly exist for us. It would be no more than the chaos of wars, intrigue, and local disaster which is all that the chronicles, at first sight, seem to contain. The historians' ideas may often have been one-sided. They may have represented medieval men as owing everything to ancient Rome, or to idealized ancient Germans. They may have shown them too much in the light of religion, or of nineteenth-century liberalism or romanticism. But they made the age interesting, they aroused curiosity, and they opened up the documents to research. Stress on the middle class, for example, led to research into the development of urban life and the economy. Nor is it really fair to complain of their one-sidedness, for none of these interpretations ever professed to do more than describe certain aspects of medieval life or to show more than a few links of causation. Their causal analysis may sometimes have leaned too heavily on the influence of heroes. But it led also to study of the development of institutions, and of the bearing of abstract principles on political action.

If medievalists have been turning away from older interpretations, it is from curiosity about matters that these passed over. There had been at least a tacit implication that apart from the movement of politics, law, philosophy, and art, the medieval world was simple and more or less static. Now that we know more about its scientific effort, its technology, medicine, music, diplomacy, finance, population problems, and opportunities for social mobility, this impression is seen to be illusory. On all sides there is evidence of change. This came either through slight but cumulative adaptations to new circumstances, or through the influence and spread of imaginative innovations.

Change of course occurred within a framework of order which, if we contrast it with our own, had certain fixed characteristics. But a medieval man, if he could have read a general history of the future, would similarly have found certain fixed characteristics in the modern world. The contours of change in a remote time are always foreshortened, just as in a remote landscape, even in rolling country, the contours around the more striking landmarks blur into an impression of flatness. It is only through detailed research that historians discover how the conditions of life and thought in a past age were actually altering. This is not to say that the pace of change is always the same. In the medieval world communications were slow, population being small and for the most part scattered in small villages and tiny towns. England's population at the time of the Norman Conquest could be housed in Detroit, and the population of medieval France at its height was not very much greater than New York's. This in itself made for regional diversity. Innovations were more likely to arise in centers of discussion, that is, in the larger cities, in universities, among the upper echelons of government servants, or in reformist circles in the Church. Adaptive change, however, occurred everywhere. Custom and tradition were flexible. Handicraftmen had always to be ready to adapt their techniques to changes in the quality or nature of their materials and also to changes in demand, as their customers' standards of living rose. They were inventive in devising new uses of waterpower, wind power and animal-power. The peasantry, too, even in backward regions, used their small resources rationally and adapted as best they could to long-run economic trends. It is a libel to stereotype them as cabbages. In short, though change was in many directions slow, and was contained always within limits that are clear, there could have been few men in the last half of the middle ages who faced quite the same life situation as their fathers did.

Obviously it is becoming harder now to give any ordered picture of the medieval world that will do justice to its diversity and complexity. But this is a chronic problem in all fields of historical knowledge as specialist research advances. There are three ways of dealing with it. Some writers are temperamentally able only to take an artist's view, putting what interests them personally at the center, and leaving out or treating only vaguely what bores or confuses them. Others try to be scientific in the sense of applying broad theoretical generalizations, leaving out exceptional situations or regions. Certainly a few exceptions need not invalidate a generalization. These writers try to unify the picture by leaning on the type of cultural theory that insists on the interrelatedness of all aspects of a society. Marxism is one form of such theory. In any form this type of theory leads one to look for interconnections between the development of thought and institutions, and to take account of environmental influences. Yet social anthropology found long ago that even in very simple societies, though there may be some environmental influence, for example, on religion, it cannot explain the variety of religious customs one meets. People's response to a physical environment depends on the way in which they perceive it, and the same is true of their response to the traditions that have shaped their social environment. These perceptions alter in subtle ways and by no means necessarily all at the same time. One can discover important interconnections between the development of medieval philosophy, art, political leadership, and the economy, yet change in these different spheres went on very unevenly.

A third and more hopeful way of advance is along the lines mapped out by the French scholar, Marc Bloch. Only one of Bloch's major books—*Feudal Society*—has been translated into English, and much of his most important work is scattered through the files of the magazine that he and Lucien Febvre founded, the *Annales d'histoire économique et sociale,* now entitled *Annales: Economies—Sociétés—Civilisations.* But he has exercised a profound influence on medievalists everywhere. Both he and Febvre seem to have felt that the heart of the historian's problem lies in understanding the social influences by which, in any age, people's perception of natural and social phenomena is shaped, and also their consciousness of a past, of values that maintain a sense of continuity. Only in this way can we grasp the quality of experience in another age, discover the starting points of any type of change, the reasons for readiness or unreadiness to accept change, the reasons for borrowing from other cultures, the reasons for the success or failure of innovations originating in creative minds.

This view calls for a still further extension of research interests. At the same time it holds out some promise of unifying them, not through straining to discover connections between the course of different types of change—connections that may or may not exist—but in relation to a common denominator, a common base. Interest in the influence of social experience on perception and readiness to change can never become a narrow specialty, for it is equally important to the understanding of all aspects of an age; all alert imaginative scholars share in it. Every medieval historian and biographer is aware that members of the upper classes and elites were steeped, at least in their childhood, in the popular culture of the localities where they grew up. Their horizon was extended by the discussion that went on in the universities, the courts, and the councils into which their careers led, yet their outlook usually retained much in common with that of humbler people. . . .

The Creativity of Cities

Cities have led high civilization for so long that one can scarcely imagine one without the other.[1] Yet it is not easy to delimit their place in the creation of values and the organizing power to implement them that constitute a developing civilization. They can be described in innumerable ways, for as is true also of small towns and villages each city has a unique personality. The existing literature leans either to extreme particularity of detail or to an unconvincing generality. The two articles that follow are the first of a series in which common general questions will be brought to bear on the rise of different types of city in different societies and on the conditions under which they play particular creative and organizing roles. Since three recent books have attempted large-scale comparison along these lines our own series had best open with an attempt to review their contributions.

Lewis Mumford's *The City in History*[2] is a work of art. Its superbly annotated photographs, beginning with primitive man's meeting-places in bush and cave and ending with the challenge of "Hive or City?", would stand alone as an imaginative contribution. To him it is self-evident that the story of cities is the story of civilization because in its character as a meeting-place the city both polarizes a culture and raises its potential. The city has also the character of tangible record, giving continuity to life. In this aspect it can become a burden, its form being difficult to readapt to new purposes and tending to perpetuate any given misdirection of energies. But

Reprinted from *Comparative Studies in Society and History* 4, no. 1 (1961): 53–63. A review article.

the emphasis of the book is less on the containing form than on the people contained, on their capacity through the ages of Western civilization to rise above constricting influences. The ancient Near Eastern city was a magnificent achievement that became ultimately stultifying. Hypnotized by the material power and wealth they had symbolized in its massive form, its people in dissatisfaction had nothing to fall back upon but a dreary parochialism. The people of Athens were incapable of sanitary planning yet built the Parthenon. Thereafter cities come to pay some tribute to beauty in their order. Hellenistic cities were "the modern town-planner's dream" and its public buildings lent dignity even to the sprawl of Imperial Rome. But the monotonies of power, wealth and leisure as ends in themselves had the victory, thinning out Hellenistic culture and reducing Rome to degradation. The indictment of Rome has the ring of Old Testament prophecy. It is an indictment of our own yielding to futilities, to organization without purpose and hence to obsession with destruction.

From this climax the book slows to etch the various types of city that have arisen successively in Western Europe and North America, down to England's New Towns and Scandinavian urban planning, each type being presented in the main as a product of changes in our civilization. As in Mumford's earlier work, *The Culture of Cities*, the medieval town though not cleaned up for its portrait is brightened up and quietened—we hear none of the noise that bedevilled its cobbled and workshop-lined streets from dawn to dark. In opposition to Pirenne "the revival of the protected town" is given credit for the revival of international trade, rather than the reverse. The theme of the revival of organizing power, in royal as well as in ecclesiastical hands, which preceded the expansion of the episcopal cities and the founding of new towns, is recognized as the heart of the problem, but is left something of a mystery. Despite reliance on out-of-date descriptions of the nature of medieval trade and of the great fairs it is recognized that the medieval town gave birth to capitalism, to incipient "power economics," and to the Renaissance despots who perfected power politics. The baroque capital is portrayed as the sinister outcome of these two ideas and of their servants, the centralizing bureaucracy and the great standing army. Here the rapid narrative assumes the quality of a nightmare switchback ride. We pass the huge barracks of Berlin in 1740 and see "this mass of mechanized and obedience-conditioned human beings" hastening the enslavement of the once free citizen:

> The army supplied the model for other forms of political coercion: people got into the habit of accepting the aggressive bark of the drill sergeant and the arrogant brutal manners of the upper classes: they were copied by the new industrialists, who governed their factories like absolute despots.

For a gentle moment we pause in the residential square, noted as the one constructive contribution of the urban planning of this age to civilized living. We do not pause long enough to ask why this rather than the barracks characterized England, which invented the smoking factory chimneys ahead. It is enough that everywhere "beneath the superficial polish of baroque upper-class manners there is the constant threat of an ugly coercive discipline."

Via the new "Ideology of Power" we plunge at once into the horrors of Coketown, with Dickens, not Professor Ashton, as auxiliary guide. If Manchester, New Hampshire, was brighter than its namesake the difference is one only of degree. A shrewd touch notes how even the air the urban upper and middle classes breathed and their own living-space were adversely affected by the indubitably squalid overcrowding of the industrial workers. Comfort in the fact that misery brought nascent civic conscience to bear at last on a problem never before faced in history, that of public hygiene through adequate water supply for all, comes sadly. The cult of cleanliness was inadequate for "the total reconstruction of the social environment" which now our absurd entanglement with transportation problems, through the cult of the automobile, makes essential for the survival of civilized living.

Either to praise or criticize this book would be to display the spirit of complacence it is designed to jar. It halts abruptly at the alternatives before us. If Russia has not yet overtaken America in traffic fatalities it is equally acquiescent in the current surrender to Megalopolis and to Moloch. "Post-historic man" is ready and conditioned to swarm meekly over the precipice of total war. The struggle of historic man can be maintained only through recall of its meaning. Mumford is no romantic impotently cursing modern technology but has spent his life advancing solutions of the problems involved in reconstruction of our environment. In every trend to regional decentralization that will allow the city to become primarily a place of "easy encounter," liberating friendship, he sees hope. Moreover, he would set technology the task of organizing the whole world into one "invisible city," not only by spreading the appurtenances that electricity can provide, but by making books and art available at will to every citizen in the remotest little town or village.

It was a token of respect to Lewis Mumford that he was invited to open and close a symposium held at the Oriental Institute of the University of Chicago in December 1958. The record of this symposium, *City Invincible,*[3] borrows its title from Walt Whitman's visionary symbol of an ideal civilization of Friends. The book is a debate among specialists in nearly fifty different lines of study on how and why civilization, cities and empire were born in the ancient Near East. Its argument moves with a verve that in conference publications is all too rare; it is an exciting guide to recent advances in Near Eastern research and to the kind of reformulation of problems that is spurred by interdisciplinary cooperation in thinking about long-run cultural change.

In the first place, the interpretation of man's response to physical environment as not direct but mediated through culture is being pushed well back into pre-history, nature being demoted from a determinant of culture to little more than a set of opportunities and limiting conditions. Robert Braidwood draws on a vast range of archeological research to demonstrate how and at what points a theory of natural causality breaks down, and Robert Adams goes on to show why the rise of civilization in the Near East cannot be explained simply by soil fertility. He has space to indicate only a few of the many factors besides quality of soil, most of them dependent on social organization, that govern productivity. The chief of these in the alluvial zone of southern Mesopotamia was hard work. In Adams' opinion it is "highly debatable" whether grain production in relation to labor input, including the labor required for maintenance of irrigation canals, would have been any higher in the south than in the northern uplands. Other factors helping to account for the economic lead that the south gained were the widespread addition of fish to the diet, and certain localized forms of specialization resulting in trade. It seems clear that the over-rating of soil fertility as a factor has persisted through mere habit, through using the term as an ambiguous catch-all. In short, an interest in culture now requires the archeologist to learn the elements of economics.

Cultural explanation of the origins of civilization relies on a functional type of causal explanation, that is, on ability to perceive the interconnectedness of all of a people's activities, from the economy to religion. In all of these it discovers a trend to more deliberate and self-conscious choice of the norms or standards of action by which one culture comes to be distinct from another. From this point of view it was never satisfactory to identify the advent of civilization with any specific technical inventions. The significance even of the inventions of enumeration and writing depends on the uses made of them, which in turn depend on the social structure. It is in the delineation of this, and hence in the knowledge of when specialized elites appear, that archeology is still most handicapped. But there is agreement that the pre-civilized Mesopotamia consisted of isolated village communities, cooperating perhaps only in emergencies and within a very limited radius, and that this condition was succeeded by continuous cooperation, the building of temple towns, and the institutionalization of local chieftainship, at least for temporary leadership in war. These changes posit a high degree of self-conscious direction. If a growing perception of the value of wider cooperation for more and more purposes spells civilization, then in Mesopotamia it antedates the rise of cities. However in Milton Singer's formulation of the problem (pp. 255, 259), the point of critical change falls in the phase in which "ideas become forces in history." On this view civilization could be regarded as a product of city life.

For the city plays a climactic role. In becoming the first seat of dynastic authority it exercises a new organizing force which takes form also as the idea of legitimate power. The earliest cities of southern Mesopotamia, even though none of them has been excavated in entirety, are already distinguishable from the towns of the age by greater complexity. A city combines the institutions of temple and market, is a political capital for villages that have decided on union, and acquires a palace. Thorkild Jacobsen (pp. 65–67) sees the political assembly gradually waning, while the figure to whom leadership in war is delegated gathers power until he and the advisers he recruits are in control not only of military organization but of the civil affairs of a city-state territory. This process of concentration of power is so familiar, seemingly so readily explicable by the need of permanent defence measures against aggressive outsiders and by the need, as people from different localities have regular dealings together, of a common legal order, that one might perhaps ask no further question. But the explanation offered has another dimension, reaching into religious and moral consciousness. At some point in the evolution of war leader into king the major gods also begin to evolve from nature deities into rulers surrounded by majesty and responsible for justice. This parallel transformation probably has its roots, Jacobsen suggests, in new attitudes induced by increasing social differentiation within the city. But it is not a mere reflection of this, as Marx would have insisted. The wholly new conception of a moral world order is a part of the social process that culminates in the establishment of dynasties.

Lewis Mumford underlines the significance of the fusion of the sacred and the secular in bestowing legitimacy, in Max Weber's sense of the term, on royal power, that is, in preparing people to accept it. Being free of the chronic tendency of historians to side with the winner or at least to assume that whatever happens had to happen, he is able to see mystery in creative steps and so to freshen the whole problem. The solution he offers is at the same time sound ecology and sheer poetry. The early city quickened sensibility through making daily life for the first time dramatic. It made daily life dramatic because it brought into proximity things formerly remote, above all the temple and the palace. It seems to be uncertain when the city palace appeared, but the thesis cannot be overthrown.

John Wilson enlivens the debate by arguing that Egypt attained and maintained civilization without benefit of the all-containing city. The slow progress of Egyptian excavation leaves this thesis doubtful. Yet the notion that communication among villages and towns could build up civilizing stimulus might apply in areas of political security anywhere. In Mesopotamia there was the additional stimulus of temple and manorial organization, which developed small-scale planned economy before the cities promoted the growth of market economy.

The members of the symposium are however loth to accept advances in organizing power as sufficient explanation of the expansive drive of civilization. They distinguish two types of expansion. One is based on a moral vision of wider community. It results at first in small "national" states unified by common cultural traditions and later produces the sweeping spread of Hellenistic civilization and of Islam. The other thrusts on impatiently to empire, defined here rather vaguely as based on force, and engenders a kind of stress within the separate cultural traditions that it dominates which is damaging to them. Within this general scheme we are given a running analysis of five thousand years of Near Eastern history with attention to the conditions under which cities make for expansion of "the human unit." That city life aided this drive within Hellenistic civilization and gave it still greater impetus within Islam needs no new proof. But the exposition given here is a sociological one, and it extends to the more difficult problem of why the drive was arrested. At some point the city elites lose all flexibility of mind and become content merely to preserve what has been handed down to them. Carl Kraeling finds the Hellenistic city finally reverting to the same "traditional" type, the same grooves into which the ancient cities of the area had already sunk a thousand years before.

The reasons for believing that the moral energies of Mesopotamian civilization were concentrated in the cities up to the end of the Babylonian periods, i.e., up to about 1600 B.C., lie in evidence of their activity in elaborating cultural traditions. In artistic expression their work shows greater profundity as it turns from the theme of the nature god to the majestic god. In the Gilgamesh epic the king-hero exemplifies not mere strength but nobility of character. Strong likelihood that the story was recast after the city of Agade had launched on the building of an empire far beyond the valley zones would suggest that dramatic conquest helped, at least at first, to enlarge men's image even of their moral potentialities. But monarchy loses the power to guide moral growth. Agade organizing power seems to have been unimaginatively coercive, limited to the garrisoning of subject towns. Centralized civil administration under a chancellery in which professionally trained scribes could rise to high office appears only as this first empire shrank, and even so a period of dissolution into petty city monarchies ensues before the Babylonian and Assyrian kingdoms take shape. Meanwhile the expansion of a common culture proceeds independently of political arrangements. A Sumerian-Akkadian culture, officially bilingual, absorbs later contributions into a common whole with Aramaic as the dominant language, and with a Babylonian dialect of this becoming a "lingua franca of Western Asia" (Ignace J. Gelb, pp. 327–8). Further clues to the nature of the changes are found in Benno Landsberger's lively sketch of the curricula of the city schools in which professional scribes were educated. Respect for folk-lore gives way to a fascination with the uses of language. But there is no means of knowing whether this attitude penetrated the various occupational groups that the scribes served, or the upper classes, nor of telling the extent of literacy. From the occurrence of words standing for the idea of a gentleman, and for good judgment, we may infer that the upper classes valued honor and practicality. A landed class can train its sons in honor and practicality as well in the country as in town, and without formal literary education. We are given no information as to styles of life, but since cities did not grow up spontaneously except in the southern and central valley zones and their northern peripheries it would seem that outside these regions landed proprietors must have been deeply attached to a country.style of life. Later, as cities become necessary instruments of royal power, nodal points through which taxes and troops are levied, each expanding kingdom spreads them more widely. The landed classes then presumably lived in them for at least part of the year, for though new foundations were peopled partly by compulsion Leo Oppenheim assures us (p. 81) that "the city was always accepted as the basic institution for civilized living."

The case for the concentration of cultural influence within the cities might be stronger if more use could be made of the evidence, slim though it may be, as to the legal, the administrative, and the economic order. These spheres of record are less congenial to the humanistic scholar than religious and literary texts, but are likely to hold more of the information about social structure for which he is groping. Any detail about the type of case that came before government courts, if examined in the perspective of comparative law as Max Rheinstein urges (pp. 152–5, 405–18), might be helpful.

When evidence as to the social context of ancient urban cultural growth is rounded out it may become easier to do the same for the later processes of atrophy, and to compare these. As they are pre-

sented here each is seen from a different angle. G. E. von Grune-
baum connects the decline of Muslim intellectual life with pessimism and with the decision of religious leaders in the course of the
11th century A.D. to favor the emotional tone of popular piety.
Kraeling connects the decline of culture in the Graeco-Roman Orient
with long inbreeding of local schools. Discussion of the loss of vitality in the older Mesopotamian culture dealt chiefly with external
pressures that would tend to push provincial cities in upon themselves. The aggrandizement of Babylon and Nineveh is mentioned as
a factor adverse to the cultural life of the smaller places. Another
was the frequent absorption of local energies in dispute and clashes
with the central government. Far from being subservient to authority, Mesopotamian cities never ceased to show a robust aversion to
the payment of taxes and the furnishing of troops. In consequence
they were liable to be punished by dispersal of their population
among new foundations. This policy of enforced migration as a safeguard against regional separatism was followed also by the Byzantine and the Ottoman Empires; its effects in different ages could be
compared.[4] Newer cities founded by fiat were at a disadvantage
politically as well as in being culturally divided. Older Mesopotamian cities had a sufficient pride in their own continuity to institu-
tionalize this in corporate unity (pp. 79–80). The spread of Islam
produced the same two types of "organic" and "arbitrary" cities, but
Muslim skill in absorbing diverse groups into a common social order
makes the distinction then of lesser import.

   Lewis Mumford explicitly sets city, town and village, given a civilized society that advances communication through writing and social circulation, in a continuum. But the degree of such communication among them could vary significantly. For example, the decline
of creativity in the intellectual life of Islam through concessions to
mystic piety altered urban-rural relations by giving country-dwellers
a greater share in the religious culture of their time. No precedent is
mentioned for such an alteration of rhythm elsewhere. Indeed, except for Mircea Eliade's fine exposition of the universal role of religions in evolving the vision of the cosmos as order, the symposium
gave less time to religion as a unifying or divisive force than to secular education and political forces. Under Assyria local religious cults
are interpreted as primarily expressing political separatism, and the

Persian policy of toleration is seen as generally tending to weaken urban religious culture. Village life presumably escapes record, and the distinction between town and city seems to become blurred. Like the discourse of modern geographers who see merely "agglomerations" of different size cluttering the landscape, the ancient languages of the Near East do not distinguish between different types of community. Jacobsen observes that this impression may be due only to a bias of the religious and literary texts. Another clue that eludes us in the ancient Near East is that of differences in size. No member of the symposium would hazard an estimate of the population of a single place. It is perhaps presumptuous of a non-specialist to suggest that there must be by now enough knowledge of the differing areas of urban residential quarters to allow, if not an estimate of upper and lower limits of population, at least some estimate of proportionate differences. Smallness of provincial cities and any shrinkage through time would surely reinforce tendencies to parochialism.

These comments on *City Invincible* select only a few of the problems with which the book deals and give little idea of its richness. If the interpretations reviewed are not well reported the only excuse, misunderstanding through ignorance being no excuse, is the difficulty of doing justice to a book that has no index.

Gideon Sjoberg, author of *The Preindustrial City, Past and Present*,[5] feels that Western efforts to understand the rest of the world have been overdoing appreciation of cultural diversity and losing sight of structural uniformities. In particular he proposes that cities in non-industrialized civilizations all belong to the same genus, that in respect of social structure they lie in a tradition that runs back to antiquity. The uniformities to which he refers could well be summarized in terms of Weber's conception of a society organized around kinship and other particularist social relations. He has however tried to be more systematic than Weber and since his work bears importantly on comparative study it is his method that primarily demands attention.

In order to take up a firm position on the problem of historical change Sjoberg discards both the empiricism of modern American sociology and the influence of Comte and Durkheim and revives the stage mechanism of early German economic sociology. To grasp change one must freeze it in a sequence of stages and since the only consistent progress man shows is technological, stages must be based primarily on technology. Foolish though this appears to a cultural anthropologist, in the context of the evolutionary thought to which Sjoberg returns it was sensible. His preindustrial society differs from folk society in having invented writing and from industrial society in not having inanimate sources of power (except water and wind).

As soon as we turn to the city this scheme can be ignored, for the city being only a part of its society is not a stage and can be characterized quickly only through some form of typology. The method now adopted, if it were under better control, would resemble Arthur Spiethoff's.[6] Spiethoff employed "real types," intended to represent the historical reality of a recurrent phenomenon such as an economic style by including all of its essential elements. Some of these were invariably present, some were occasionally lacking but had to be included in the model; other elements might play an essential role but only in rare exceptions and for this reason could be left out of the model. Sjoberg's material is quantitatively so vast that he cannot follow this procedure. Nor can he use ideal types, because he regards them as "fictional." He calls his preindustrial city a "constructed type." It is a synthetic picture put together from elements which, because they are mentioned in accounts of a number of different cultures, he feels to be representative or typical and therefore capable of being extrapolated backwards. The criteria by which particular elements were included or left out are not made explicit but lie presumably in their functional consistency. Sjoberg claims no more for his constructed type than "objective probability," and he offers it only as having possible utility in further research.

The reader is not shown any single "typical" preindustrial city as a functioning whole. Instead, we are given a number of short sketches of different aspects of the life of the genus, illustrated at random. Sjoberg was afraid to start with case studies lest he should light on examples that were atypical, and for some reason he does not admit to studying any particular cases in depth. He says that he concentrated "heavily" on eight examples—Seoul, Peking, Mecca, Cairo, Fez, Bokhara, Lhasa, and Renaissance Florence—and corrected his impressions by information culled very widely. Such bibliography on these eight cities as appears in his notes is lamentably

thin, and like the sources of his corrective data is a mixture of travellers' tales, the writings of missionaries, historical work some of which
is far from up to date, and recent work by social scientists. He also
used the observations of unnamed students in his classes. Information so culled is to begin with of uneven value and when torn out of
context is at best dubious evidence of how a social structure func-
tioned. Moreover Sjoberg seems to have had no alternative hypotheses to save him from the danger of being always right. When the
evidence of eminent Orientalists is uncooperative he doubts or con-
tradicts it.[7]

The case for extrapolation to antiquity rests on the supposition
that all historical change between the rise of cities and industrialization is cultural and therefore irrelevant to the hypothesis. The book's
central point, that prior to industrialization societies are organized
more by kinship and other particularist relations has long been generally agreed upon. Nothing is gained by exaggerating the impression.
The lines of advance are through study of the ways in which cultural
change (understood broadly as including political and economic
change) affects the working of a system even when the structural
elements here emphasized may not be fundamentally altered, and of
the ways in which through creation of new values and new roles it
significantly alters these elements. The freezing of change, the reduction of time to the dimensions of a space flat as a pancake and
monotonous as a prairie, is as primitive a technique as early photog-
raphy. With the formulations and research of Talcott Parsons and
his school sociology has left this far behind. Sjoberg is well aware
that cultural change alters the working of a society, but he is insensi-
tive to the extent to which economic and political development alter
the society by introducing more universalist elements. He makes no
serious use of economic history. For example in an unfortunate passage on credit he innocently misreads Iris Origo as quoting interest
rates for a 14th century Italian city equal to those which he has
heard prevail in present-day Iran.[8] If he knew more about medieval
Italy he would doubtless dismiss it, along with the whole Mediterranean area, as atypical. Ironically, in insisting that all preindustrial
elites are urban, he is making the Mediterranean area typical and
incidentally does great violence to northern Europe.

Like all fixed images of the past, Sjoberg's constructed type is essentially an effort to support an image of ourselves. The obverse of the coin is a generalized type of industrial civilization. This type is not made explicit, but clearly contains elements which comparative study of the different forms and phases of industrialism tends to modify. One point in question is the unsubtle treatment of social mobility. Industrialism and the introduction or expansion of modern bureaucratic government obviously make for striking changes in the quantitative degree of ascent from low to high position. But when this rate slows down the rewards of the social system have to consist more in the creation of new values by which as it were every man rises. The stagnating preindustrial cities of the recent past from which Sjoberg constructed his type—Timbuctoo is one of them—were doing neither of these things. But in their great days they did both. Comparison demands both better quantitative techniques for the handling of social mobility and attention to the processes of creativity.

The spirit of this book is nevertheless one of genuine effort to broaden horizons and to make the concept of a traditional city more tidy. If Sjoberg does not get beyond Max Weber (he can hardly do so while he shies away from legal structures and comparative law) he at least honors him in the best way, by trying to get beyond him.

. . . Better description is needed, and comparison directed to the generalization of regional differences, as a first step, is an aid to this. Different phases of development and atrophy need to be delineated more clearly. The universalist-particularist dichotomy has long been a guide to common questions, but since one always finds combinations of the two kinds of relationship, it does not necessarily give a sense of the direction of change. The perspectives of comparative law help to reveal the direction more concretely and cannot be neglected. But they are not sufficient alone. The Redfield-Singer distinction between orthogenetic and heterogenetic types of city,[9] which fastens attention on the extent to which a city in shaping cultural tradition draws on its own region or more widely, the extent to which it isolates alien groups in enclaves or absorbs them into its life to enrich it, introduces further criteria that are pertinent to the theme of the expansion of a city's influence. . . .

NOTES

1. On the variant uses of the term "civilization" see E. de Dampierre, "Note sur 'Culture' et 'Civilisation,' " *Comparative Studies in Society and History*, III (April, 1961), pp. 328–340.

2. *The City in History, its Origins, its Transformations, and its Prospects* (Harcourt Brace, New York, 1961), xi, 657 pp.

3. *City Invincible. A Symposium on Urbanization and Cultural Development in the Ancient Near East.* Edited by Carl H. Kraeling and Robert M. Adams (Chicago, 1960), xiv, 448 pp.

4. See Peter Charanis, "The Transfer of Population as a Policy in the Byzantine Empire," *Comparative Studies in Society and History*, III (January, 1961), pp. 140–154.

5. *The Preindustrial City, Past and Present* (Glencoe, Illinois, 1960), xii, 353 pp.

6. See Frederic C. Lane and Jelle C. Riemersma, "Introduction to Arthur Spiethoff" and Arthur Spiethoff, "Pure Theory and Economic Gestalt Theory; Ideal Types and Real Types," translated by Fritz Redlich, in *Enterprise and Secular Change*, ed. Frederic C. Lane and Jelle C. Riemersma (Homewood, Illinois, 1953), pp. 431–63.

7. Gideon Sjoberg, *op. cit.*, pp. 81–2, 138–9. For further discussion of the matters raised see Vernon K. Dibble and Ping-ti Ho, "The Comparative Study of Social Mobility," *Comparative Studies in Society and History*, III (April, 1961), pp. 315–27.

8. Gideon Sjoberg, *op. cit.*, p. 215, cites a range of 20 to 40%, whereas business rates were from 5 to 10% at the time. See A. Sapori, *Studi di Storia Economica*, 3rd ed. (Firenze, 1955), I, pp. 223–43.

9. For applications see Milton Singer in *City Invincible*, pp. 260–7.

Medieval Gilds Reconsidered

I

Present-day economic historians display an uneasy feeling that medieval gilds have enjoyed much more attention than they deserve. Professor Heckscher compares them unfavorably with later gilds,[1] Professor Gras grudges them credit for anything save the keeping of records to mislead historians,[2] and the authors of a recent textbook almost apologize for pausing to describe them.[3] In general, this reaction from former attitudes reflects a shift of interest from the interpretation of economic policy to other problems that now appear more fundamental. We have a quantity of information about gild policies, but it leaves us uncertain whether or not the gilds were of any real importance in the history of economic development.

There is relatively little work in English on the question, English gilds having long been treated mainly in relation to institutional or political history. Brentano's brilliant essay aroused interest, but chiefly in its political aspects.[4] His central thesis, that gilds had everywhere been an instrument of class struggle, was never thoroughly explored, and controversy on the point died down without leading to any deeper investigation of the differences between English and Continental conditions. Gross applied Continental theory to the study of English gilds more cautiously. His familiar doctrine of the early formation of a heterogeneous merchant gild with a monopoly of trade in the borough, of the gradual evolution of specialized crafts within this body, and of the later evolution of mercantile in-

---

Reprinted from *Journal of Economic History* 2 (1942): 164–73.

terests within the crafts traces a most attractive abstract pattern. Gross himself realized that it did not apply to all towns in its entirety, since many lacked any record of a gild merchant.[5] But, notwithstanding the exceptions to the first part of the theory, there has been a temptation to follow its second part quite blindly, without reference to the possible effects of differences in regional setting.

Thus it has been assumed that the separate crafts, conventionally but unhistorically described by the hybrid term "craft gilds,"[6] were evolved at the simplest stage of development compatible with a market, and that the later appearance of mercantile interests altered and finally broke up the gild system. "The essence of the craft gild," according to Mr. Lipson, lay in the combination of trading and handicraft functions in the hands of the master craftsman, who bought his raw material direct from the producer and sold his finished goods direct to the consumer.[7] But this arrangement would obviously not have been convenient except when the raw materials in question were produced in the immediate vicinity of the town. In most places, then, it would have been characteristic only of the brewers, butchers, bakers, pastry cooks, and tallow chandlers, and of trades selling articles made of wood, leather, or wool, when these commodities were not in the hands of merchants. The situation was slightly different in the tailoring shops, where customers ordinarily brought their own cloth; other customers probably often saved other craftsmen, too, the trouble of procuring materials. This plan allowed the craftsman to operate with less capital. What is more important, it also allowed the general merchant to build up a business in raw materials. But it did not directly impair the independence of the master craftsman. In very small towns off the main highways of commerce it is well known that this elementary organization of industry persisted for centuries. Any one wanting goods not produced locally would have to seek them, either in the stock of merchants traveling or living in the neighborhood, or else at a fair.

But in the larger centers of consumption there were not sufficient supplies obtainable locally for the craftsman to be able to buy at firsthand from the producer. Moreover, in the larger towns craftsmen who worked on materials that were imported from a distance, as was usually the case with wax and metals, certainly did not rely upon their customers for supplies. They bought from native or for-

eign merchants or their agents or through other middlemen. Malt-
mongers, cornmongers, and mealmen came to the assistance of the
brewers and bakers. These two trades were under too close surveillance in the Middle Ages for any of their members to profit by buying supplies for their fellows. But in other crafts, especially if they
produced wares that could be sold at country fairs, there was a tendency for some of the masters to specialize in dealing.[8] Finally,
there was a third set of conditions, under which craftsmen had no
direct contact with either producer or consumer, but bought and
sold through the agents of a local capitalist entrepreneur.

Far too little is known of the origins of gilds for any one to assert
that they arose only under conditions that assured the handicrafts-
man's complete economic independence.[9] It is certain, however, that
at the earliest periods of which there is any definite record of their
existence they were adapted to the varying circumstances of different types of trade and of cities differing widely in the size and nature of their population. For merchants to intervene in the organization of industry in the smaller and more remote places may have been
an abnormal or late development, but in the larger medieval towns
it was neither. In the great industrial cities of the Continent it must
have coincided with the rise of their export trade. No English city
could rank with the more famous manufacturing centers of Italy or
the Low Countries, so that one would not expect the role of English
merchants in regard to industry to have attained the same early importance. Yet the London weavers of the late thirteenth century
were working on orders from local cloth merchants; this is known
only because of friction between the two groups at that time, and it
is stated that there had been a previous quarrel "in time whereof
memory does not run."[10] A list of London gilds amerced by the king
in 1180 included several that, being assessed at a high rate and
headed by prominent citizens, were presumably composed of
wealthy merchants.[11] Among them, paying the highest sum of all,
were the goldsmiths. More likely than not they were already, as we
know their successors to have been in the fourteenth century,
wealthy merchant manufacturers controlling the conditions under
which poorer workmen carried on their art.

Mercantile influence on English town industries may have been
on the increase in the later Middle Ages, and it no doubt contributed

to the splitting of companies into sections distinguished by the wearing of a livery. But to assume that every aspect of its activity in that period was then necessarily new is unjustified and will remain so until there has been fuller research into conditions of the twelfth and thirteenth centuries. To imply that it was undermining the gild system of industry is absurd, for there was no such thing. The only sense in which one can speak of the gilds as forming a system is in regard to urban economic administration.

II

The gilds everywhere represented congeries of special interests, loosely bound together, under the aegis of municipal authorities, by a common care for the quality of goods sold. To assess their influence upon economic development requires a more detailed knowledge of industry, trade and finance, and also of urban politics, than is yet generally available either for England or continental Europe. A good deal of interest has been shown in the problems of their potential influence in critical phases of transition, but the results are on the whole inconclusive.

The change with which they are perhaps chiefly associated is the increasing tendency, at the end of the Middle Ages, for industry to be located in the country. It is apparent that many gilds became obstinately conservative and exclusive, and hence may have helped to deflect new enterprise from their town. Yet they are not necessarily to blame for every case of urban decline before village competition, for in any large-scale diversion of industry to the country other factors would surely have been at work.

Another problem is that of their influence upon technological progress. Here the negative character of the findings may be illustrated from the story of the introduction of the fulling mill, run by water power, in the neighborhood of London. There is no evidence of the reactions of the townsmen during the first phase of this innovation but it may be surmised that the cloth merchants were quick to make use of it and impatient with opposition from the city fullers. Sir John Pulteney, a rich draper, ten years an alderman and four times mayor of London, is known to have acquired one of the mills, at Stepney, early in the fourteenth century.[12] In 1298 the civic authorities reluctantly allowed the fullers the right of making search at the city gates with the object of preventing either fullers, weavers, or dyers from sending cloth to the mills; they were not to interfere, however, if the sender swore that the cloth was his own.[13] Efforts to enforce the ban were renewed in 1311 and 1342,[14] but the cloth-making crafts were plainly so permeated by mercantile interest that they were soon able to adapt themselves to the use of the mills. In 1376 both the fullers and the drapers are found disapproving of the practice of fulling caps at the mills, on the grounds that the fulling mills damaged their cloth.[15] Further action and controversy in London over mechanical fulling related solely to this question of caps, the hurers, "men of low degree and simple," having intermittent success in opposing the desire of the hatters and haberdashers, a mercantile craft, to patronize the mills.[16]

To discuss whether or not gilds hindered the rise of entrepreneurial activity is clearly useless. They embodied all of the diverse interests concerned in the movement. The greater merchants, having ordinarily a dominant influence in town government, tended sometimes to abuse their power, but the situation varied from place to place and at different periods. In the lesser trades, those in which there was very little capital invested, the mutual jealousies of the masters tended to hinder the rational combination of related industrial processes under one management.[17] Yet it is doubtful whether in the smaller towns, where there were too few men in the minor crafts to keep up efficient gild organizations, there would have been many hindrances of the kind.

III

The hardest work that lies ahead of gild historians is in studying the question of monopoly. The most involved of all their problems, it is at the same time the only one to which reasonably exact answers, as expressed in price trends, might ultimately be expected. Meanwhile a certain sifting of theories advanced and facts available is in order.

The idea that gilds passed through two phases,[18] an early phase in which they were anxious to throw their ranks wide open, and a later one in which they became exclusive and monopolistic, though probably in a great many cases true, needs to be qualified. On the one hand, in trades that were obnoxious, such as butchering and tanning, or in which equipment was limited, as in baking, there was often a natural tendency, from a very early date, to keep member-ship down.[19] In all victualing trades monopolistic tendencies were chronic. That was one of the reasons why they were kept under closer supervision than other crafts. Wyclif denounced merchant victualers as "false conspiratours . . . cursed of God and man," be-cause they manipulated prices by secret agreements.[20] There is no reason at all to imagine either that the practice was new in his time, or that it was ever seriously checked, for price control was attempted only through the retailer.[21] Fifteenth-century records show that breach of price agreements among merchants, though naturally not one of the offenses punishable by a term in the city prison, was sub-ject to heavy fines and disciplinary boycott.[22] In industry, again, when the raw materials used were found locally in great abundance, or when there was an expanding market for the goods produced, or when the capital of merchants was attracted for these or other rea-sons, it is highly improbable that craftsmen could ever have suc-ceeded in attaining a monopoly within an exclusive gild.

On the other hand, although the fact that many gilds tended to become more exclusive as time passed cannot be contested, open claims to monopoly need not be taken at their face value. In indus-try it was always difficult to enforce them. When the tailors of Namur in the later Middle Ages forbade mothers to teach their girls to sew, they no doubt encountered trouble.[23] Again, statements im-plying that there was an increasing tendency for gilds to become hereditary or caste-like in character in the later Middle Ages may be taken with a grain of salt unless they are supported by actual genealogical research. Chances of family survival were less favorable in the fourteenth and fifteenth centuries than in the thirteenth century.

The most important aspect of the whole problem is to judge how far craftsmen deliberately restricted output; it is probable that the practice was in inverse ratio to the influence of merchants over their trade.[24] Gild control over the recruiting of masters and the training of labor, however, was general. Conceded in the interests of maintaining high technical standards of work, it obviously lent itself to abuse. But ordinances controlling the number of apprentices and journeymen that a master might employ were not necessarily effec-tive. In the fourteenth century there appears to have been a general shortage of labor, and in later fifteenth-century London, where population may have been on the increase again, the rules were in some cases invoked only when there was already considerable unemployment in the trade. There were many ways of evading the rules. Men could join a gild temporarily, simply for the purpose of registering apprentices whose terms of service would presently be sold.[25] It is very unlikely that a gild could restrain members from expanding their workshops when they had the capital to do so. A merchant who had dual membership in the companies of mercers and pewterers in mid-fifteenth century London employed eleven apprentices and seven hired workers in his pewter business; the average per member in the company at that time was two apprentices and about three-quarters of a servant, and later regulations permitted a maximum of three apprentices.[26]

Another difficult question that bears upon the problem of gild control over prices is that of the ownership of transport facilities. Members of merchant companies coöperated both in hiring convoys for their overseas trade and in arranging for the services of porters to convey their goods from waterfront to warehouse. But the organization of inland and coastal transport is a very obscure subject.

IV

Gilds were of obvious service to their members in a number of other ways that have been so often described one hardly dares mention them again in a journal devoted to research. They restrained competitive bidding that threatened to raise rents;[27] they maintained extensive loan funds;[28] they dispensed relief in sickness and poverty. The right of taking a part of fellow gildsmen's purchases at the original price, on which Gross laid so much stress, may refer less to the conscious fostering of coöperative policies in trade than to the common and convenient practice of buying in small groups in order to obtain better terms of credit. Coöperative purchase of industrial supplies was resorted to only in emergencies.[29] Despite these qualifications, the usefulness of the gild should not be underestimated. Indeed historians and economists unfamiliar with the contours of the medieval scene may not always fully appreciate it. Especially in the later Middle Ages, medieval townsmen had incessantly to contend with the disasters of war, epidemics, and local crop failures;

they suffered at the best of times from shortage of capital; moreover, outside the Mediterranean area, the custom of insurance had not established itself. In these circumstances the gilds may have been of invaluable help in maintaining the continuity of economic activity on as even a keel as possible.

To any one sharing Marshall's broad-minded interest in whatever aspects of history throw light upon human nature,[30] the gilds are of still further importance. It has often been remarked that many trade gilds were based upon a fraternity life similar to that of the parish gilds. In common with the latter they gave expression not only to religious faith and conviviality but also to certain social needs and ideals and forms of class consciousness. Industrial gilds, for example, were at pains to cultivate a spirit of thrift and temperance and to discourage idleness. Brethren of their fraternities were eligible for relief only if their need were the result of circumstances beyond their control. No skinner in Norwich could expect alms in any misfortune resulting from "his foly," nor could any carpenter there risk indulging in "ryoutous lyvyng."[31] Parish gilds, which in London drew the majority of their members from people of middling social rank, showed the same strictness. One withheld alms from any who had suffered "through plunder by harlots or any other bad way of life";[32] and the ordinances of another paint a most beguiling picture of the temptations that beset the weak-willed townsman:

> If ony man . . . use hym to ly long in bed; and at rising of his bed ne will not work ne wyn his sustenaunce and keep his house, and go to the tavern, to the wyne, to the ale, to wrastling, to schetyng, and this manner falleth poor, and left his cattel in his defaut for succour; and trust to be holpen by the fraternity: that man shal never have good, ne help of companie, neither in his lyfe, ne at his dethe; but he shal be put off for evermore of the companie.[33]

In these and in the ordinances seeking to restrain apprentices from gambling and journeymen from coming to work still stupid from their "drinkings" of the night before, one sees the petty bourgeois master, the only medieval figure who cherished any love of the economic virtues for their own sake, fighting an uncertain battle for some measure of efficiency in industry.

The spirit of the great merchant companies was differently keyed. It set a high value on the qualities of dignity, decency, and courtesy and also held the economic virtue of prudence in esteem. But with the passage of time, as the history of innumerable towns will tell, the prudence of the merchants gave way before habits of ostentation and luxury. Pride in their gild led them on. The cost of membership of gilds mounted with the cost of building and maintaining fine halls, wearing liveries of startling color, and holding splendid banquets. All the gilds alike, by giving office to their wealthier members, encouraged the custom of showing respect to the rich. Snobbery flourished among them. Spurred on to imitate their social superiors, the greater merchants, the members of the lesser gilds strained their resources to outshine each other in magnificence, and gradually relaxed their hold on the humble economic virtues on which they might have built a greater industrial prosperity. Snobbery and extravagance made for exclusiveness and deadened enterprise. By this road, the gilds leading the way, medieval urban culture strayed into an economic and social cul-de-sac.

Notes

1. Eli F. Heckscher, *Mercantilism* (1935), I, 142–143. *See also* his "The Aspects of Economic History," *Economic Essays in Honor of Gustav Cassel* (1933), 709.

2. N. S. B. Gras, *Business and Capitalism* (1939), 31–32. The further remark here that gilds have been studied "almost to the neglect of the real business of the men who established them" is a tacit admission of the fact that the influence of gilds in medieval business is still largely an open question.

3. S. B. Clough and C. W. Cole, *Economic History of Europe* (1941).

4. "On the History and Development of Gilds," Toulmin Smith, ed., *English Gilds*, Early English Text Society, Original Series, 40 (1870), xlix–cxcix.

5. C. Gross, *The Gild Merchant* (1890), I, 20–22.

6. Possibly invented by Dr. F. J. Furnivall, when he was assisting Brentano in the translation of his essay. *See English Gilds*, lv. Furnivall, like Carlyle, was fond of compounding eccentric terms of his own; he described himself as the "foolometer" of the Early English Text Society.

Early English Meals and Manners, Early English Text Society, Original Series, 32 (1868), lxvii. Carlyle, as the Oxford English Dictionary notes, had coined the term "craftbrother."

7. E. Lipson, *The Economic History of England* (5th ed., 1929), I, 374. But *see* p. 295, where it is stated that "the craftsman *usually* [italics mine] worked on materials supplied by his customer." The only examples given (pp. 295n., 298) are from the trades of tailors, skinners, and dyers; the customers of the last may frequently have been merchants.

8. For a London example *see* G. Unwin, *The Gilds and Companies of London* (2d ed., 1925), 74. The custom need not, as Unwin assumed, have been new in the late thirteenth century. The sale of town goods at fairs unless monopolized by the richer craftsmen who could afford to travel to the fairs in person, would early have necessitated the rise of a class of middlemen.

9. For bibliography and brief summary of different schools of conjecture as to gild origins, *see* J. Kulischer, *Allgemeine Wirtschaftsgeschichte* (1928), I, 165, 181–192.

10. F. Consitt, *The London Weavers' Company* (1933), I, 7 ff.

11. Unwin, 47–49.

12. *Calendar of Inquisitions Miscellaneous*, III, Inquisition No. 189.

13. F. Consitt, I, 6–7. On the whole subject *see* E. M. Carus-Wilson, "An Industrial Revolution of the Thirteenth Century," *Economic History Review*, XI (1941), 39–60.

14. Consitt, I, 21; A. H. Thomas, ed., *Calendar of Plea and Memoranda Rolls of the City of London, 1323–1364*, 153.

15. T. Riley, ed., *Memorials of London and London Life* (1868), 400–404.

16. *Ibid.*, 529–530, 558–559, 667–668; *Calendar of Plea and Memoranda Rolls, 1364–1381*, 230; *Calendar of Letter Books of the City of London*, I, 176–177, K, 220; *Journals of the Court of Common Council of the City of London*, 7, f. 73v. The ordinances of the fullers, when examined in 1488, provided for official inspection of cloth on its way to the mills, *Calendar of Letter Books, L*, 262. Lipson gives the impression that opposition to the fulling of cloth continued in London for two hundred odd years, *Economic History of England*, I, 426.

17. As in the trades using wire, in London and Coventry. *See Calendar of the Letter Books of the City of London, K*, 42–43, and *The Coventry Leet Book*, Early English Text Society, Original Series, 134, pp. 115, 181–183, 185. The specialization enjoined was less extreme in Coventry than in London.

18. Lipson, I, 310; E. F. Meyer, "English Craft Gilds and Borough Governments of the Later Middle Ages," *University of Colorado Studies*, XVI (1929), 356–357.

19. E. Martin Saint-Leon, *Histoire des Corporations de Métiers* (1922), 57, 98. Levasseur, *Histoire des classes ouvrières et de l'industrie*

en France avant 1789 (1900), I, 330, 345–347. In London tanners' selds were carefully bequeathed by will.

20. T. Arnold, ed., *Select English Works of John Wyclif* (1869–1871), III, 332–334.

21. For interesting data in this connection *see* P. E. Jones, *The Worshipful Company of Poulters* (1939), 102–109. The record of London fishmongers, as Unwin showed, *Gilds and Companies of London*, 38–39, was not good. Yet see Levasseur's impression that food was relatively cheaper, and shoes and clothing dearer, than in his own time, *Histoire des classes ouvrières*, I, 420.

22. *See* J. A. Kingdon, ed., *Facsimile of First Volume of MS. Archives of the Worshipful Company of Grocers of the City of London, A.D. 1345–1463* (1886), *passim*. Fines ran up to ten pounds.

23. Pirenne, *Histoire de Belgique* (1909), II, 320.

24. *See* account of friction between weavers and cloth merchants over destruction of looms and other attempts to limit output, Consitt, 8–25.

25. Levasseur, I, 307–308.

26. C. Welch, *History of the Pewterers' Company* (1902), I, records of 1456–1457, and p. 111.

27. Ordinances of this kind were enforced. *See* threat of a fine of ten pounds in a case of "ousting" a man from premises in Eastcheap, Kingdon, 93. The London butchers sought to keep down the rent of pastures, *Calendar of Letter Books of the City of London, L,* 216.

28. *See* notices of the Trinity Gild of Lynn, *Historical Manuscripts Commission*, Eleventh Report, Appendix, Pt. III, 228–230; also my study of "The Grocers of London," *English Trade in the Fifteenth Century*, Eileen Power and M. Postan, eds. (1933), 253.

29. *See* the summary of extensive research, Erich Wege, "Die Zünfte als Trager wirtschaftlicher Kollektivmassnahmen," *Vierteljahrschrift für Social- und Wirtschaftgeschichte, Beiheft* 20 (1930).

30. "The Old Generation of Economists and the New," *Quarterly Journal of Economics*, XI, 120.

31. Toulmin Smith, ed., *English Gilds*, 31, 38.

32. *Ibid.*, 269–270.

33. *Ibid.*, xl.

The Problem of Conservatism in Fifteenth-Century England

Most modern misconceptions of mediaeval society are due to a distorted notion of the rigidity of its structure. In the circumstances of the last century, it was perhaps inevitable that such an idea should have arisen. The capitalist economy, in its phases of rapid expansion, was creating new occupations and ways of life, radically altering the position of the older social classes and bringing new ones into existence. Society in the middle ages, largely agrarian and slow-moving, indubitably offered an extreme contrast to these fluid conditions. By an easy and natural process, aided by prejudices of eighteenth-century and Renaissance lineage, the contrast was exaggerated. The middle ages therefore came to stand, in the mind of the average educated reader, as the very type and symbol of immobility.

But the days of dynamic expansion are now long past, and the various political and social movements of today all tend alike towards congealing the social system in some mould or other that will ensure security and respect for all citizens. If these desires for a more static system persist, the mediaeval world will take on a much less alien aspect. More sympathetic readers will more readily appreciate that it, too, underwent periods of expansion and of contraction, and, as it comes to be seen in its true colors, the popular legend of its immobility will die.

At the same time, specialists should find themselves in a better position to analyze the nature of the conservative influences in mediaeval society. It is undeniable that very strong forces were periodically at work, opposing change. For example, one cannot but be

Reprinted from *Speculum* 18 (1943): 363–68.

struck by the apparent willingness of mediaeval people to accept as divinely ordained whatever social order the economic and military situation might impose. A brief paper can do no more than point out one of the problems that would be raised by a study of this attitude of mind. The problem may be illustrated by considering the question, how far, in fifteenth-century England, conscious acceptance of class divisions was a conservative force. Fifteenth-century England provides a setting in which one would expect to find class divisions mature and class consciousness assuming stereotyped forms, for, until the economic and political revival under the Tudors at the end of the century, the age was for the most part one of decline, with population either static or receding.

A few of the difficulties that beset this type of enquiry must be mentioned at the outset. In the first place, it is imperative to be specific in the use of terms; yet there is an immediate danger of becoming doctrinaire, and of begging one's major questions. Thus, in referring to a society as stratified one is presupposing that its members were conscious of being grouped in social classes distinguished by typical sources of income and cultural standards, and that these classes were in the common judgment ranked in a certain order. But these suppositions must be put to the test of facts, and the relevant facts are elusive. They are contained mainly in literature and in the more intimate documents of private life, such as letters, wills, marriage settlements, which reveal the extent of circles of friendship on terms of equality, and give expression to attitudes of superiority and inferiority. To speak of social classes unless there is proof of this kind that their division issued in attitudes affecting people's conduct of their lives is merely to invent political or economic abstractions. A further difficulty lies in the fact that in respect of these matters England was not a homogeneous unit. The only true picture of the situation would be a composite one, based on comparison of many local studies. And adequate local studies have not yet been carried out.[1]

Yet although shadows of obscurity hang over many sides of fifteenth-century social life, the broad outlines of a class system bulk fairly clear, and may be hastily called to mind. Whatever local variations may have affected the rating of groups in the middle and lower ranks of society, the uppermost class, that of the lords, was held in uniform esteem throughout the nation. Its supremacy was the prod-

uct of a number of factors. As a seventeenth-century writer remarked, "Honor sprang originally from the Field, for it being the
effect of Power."[2] The fifteenth-century English had not forgotten
that their background was in part that of a society organized for
military service, in which prestige was measured by capacity for
such service. The people's attitude of deference toward the nobility
was rooted in the tradition that made them leaders in the organization of war and defence. That they were still able to fill this rôle was
obviously due to their wealth. As a class the nobles had no distinctive
source of income, living on the rents and produce of their estates,
augmented in some cases by pensions granted by the Crown, but
they were individually wealthier than any of their inferiors. They
were thus able to employ wealth in a unique manner, maintaining
their famous liveried staffs of servants and soldiers, which were at
once symbols and instruments of power.

The foundation of "the estate of a lord" was the power that
made his patronage a boon eagerly solicited by lesser men. In theory
the dignity pertained only to barons or those of still higher rank,[3]
but in practice, as Stubbs pointed out,[4] the wealthier and more influential of the knights were also regarded by their neighbors as lords.
Formerly there may have been a great deal of ambiguity in the de-
limitation of the class, but in the fifteenth century it was coming to
be much more clearly marked. The larger groupings of estates were
concentrated in very few hands.[5]

The gentry, numbering several thousand families, shared with
the lords the distinction of being regarded as noble, or gentle. They
were a composite class, formed of a series of groups whose members
derived their income and their prestige from different sources. Some
were rich and leisured landowners. Some were satellites of the lords,
serving them for wages in the administration of their estates, as
armed retainers, or as menial servants in their households. A smaller
group, but one growing in importance, served in the royal households or in various branches of the civil service. Still another group
was made up of the leading members of the legal profession. These
groups roughly paralleled each other in rank. From the point of view
of precedence their members were divided into knights, esquires
and ordinary gentlemen, but these titles did not in any sense denote
separate classes. That of knight carried heavy and expensive military
responsibilities that most people were anxious to avoid. That of es-

quire marked a degree of promotion in military or household service, but outside these it was often self-assumed, and often the same
man might be described either as esquire or gentleman.

Three criteria determined whether a man was gentle. It was
essential either to have security of fortune, which meant to have
wealth in the form of lands, or else to be able to claim descent from
a landed family. In both cases it was desirable to live up to certain
cultural standards. Those who combined all three qualifications
stood highest in the public esteem. They had inherited estates, and
were able to live at leisure in the style that was considered fitting for
men of rank, with servants about them. Their property gave them
power, their birth gave them influence through connection with
other families of note, and their way of living, which imitated, on a
humbler scale, the ceremony and luxury of lordly households,
seemed a visible demonstration of power and influence.

Birth was honored, independently of wealth, not only because it
might spell influence, but because of the very strong belief in the
inheritance of superior gifts, and because it was realized that pride
in family traditions, especially traditions of military service, gave a
man spirit and ambition. Yet younger sons had a struggle to maintain their position as gentlemen. Often they received little or no inheritance, having to be satisfied, as an Elizabethan cadet lamented,
with "that which the cat left on the malt heap." Poverty would in
time obliterate gentility. The easiest way for the younger son to
maintain his status was probably by entering the service of a lord.
But there is no evidence of prejudice against any occupation save
that of retail trade. It was requisite only that one continue to live
"like a gentleman."

Wealth, too, was honored, independently of birth, on condition
that the man of property lived "like a gentleman." To live "like a
gentleman" meant to incline towards certain cultural ideals rather
than to live in luxury or to spend any fixed amount of money. The
ideals were aristocratic in quality, colored by love of country life, by
the rudiments of a classical education, and by an interest in romances. But there were no specific customs peculiar to the gentry,
nor did they have any elaborate code of manners.

The more successful members of the merchant class, particularly those in London, were to all intents and purposes regarded as
the equals of gentlemen. This merchant class was composed of men

with capital who handled foreign trade and wholesale distribution. Forming the governing class of the towns, they exercised great political power locally; as an important source of loans to the Crown they were frequently in touch with the central government; as authorities on foreign trade they were sometimes sent abroad on embassies. Intensely proud of their unique position, they kept themselves, at least in the larger towns, very much aloof from the retail traders, artisans and workers. But in London and in several other parts of the country, the century saw a growing rapprochement between them and the gentry. There are many instances of men who called themselves indiscriminately "merchant" or "gentleman," or "merchant and gentleman."

The structure of the rural classes is not at all clear. It probably differed greatly in different regions. One can draw a line of economic distinction between freeholders and tenant farmers, but there is no evidence of any social distinction between them. Both came under the heading of yeoman, an ambiguous term which also described menial and military servants below the rank of gentleman and man-at-arms. Some of the yeomen were quite as well off as the poorer country gentry, and there could have been only very small differences between them in their way of life. The yeoman's wife, if Bishop Latimer's recollections of his home were correct, milked the cows; the gentlewoman may have rebelled at this. But there are instances of men who were described in legal documents as "gentleman and yeoman."

As on their upper level the yeomanry merged into the lesser landed gentry, so on the other hand they merged into the copyholders, who in turn merged into the landless agricultural laborers, and together with the proletarian workers of the towns made up the bulk of the nation. Contemporary writers dismissed them as "the common people," and condescendingly described them as "simple." They lived in huts or tenements and had few personal possessions. Although something might be gleaned from manorial records, we know very little of their social relations among themselves, and we can only surmise what their attitudes were to the higher classes.

When so little is known of the masses of the people is one justified in affirming that the whole of English society at this time was rigidly stratified and pervaded by deference to social superiors? It must be admitted that there is much to support an impression of rig-

idity of structure—the power of the lords, the value set by the gentry
on birth, the exclusiveness of the merchants, the poverty of the
workers, and the general religious orthodoxy of the age. Again, it
seems as though the power that normally flowed from possession of
property must have been abnormally magnified by the regard that
men of the fifteenth century had for property. Whoever has money,
Peter Idley advised his son, is "as a Godde under God."[6] If gentlemen held views of this kind, there is at least a presumption that their
attitudes were reflected among the lower classes.

Among the gentry class-consciousness was indeed highly conservative in tone. Its more extreme forms were evoked by resentment
of the economic and social trends of the time. Throughout the century agricultural depression kept landlords under a cloud of anxiety.[7] Their troubles were increased, from Edward IV's reign on-
wards, by the rising cost of keeping up with luxurious fashions in
dress. The situation was the more irritating in that gentlemen could
see the standard of living of the peasantry slowly improving. Furthermore, *nouveaux-riches*, climbing out of the ranks of the merchant
class and the lesser officials and the yeomanry, were buying land
and laying claim to the title of gentleman. These circumstances
naturally swelled the pride which the older families took in their
pedigrees and their ancestral coats of arms, and also made them re-
ceptive to the new currents of aristocratic culture coming from
France and from Italy. The doctrines of courtesy were welcomed
the more because they might widen the gulf between the older
gentry and their inferiors. Pedantic and snobbish doctrines of gentility were formulated and were bequeathed, a legacy of ultra-con-
servatism, to the sixteenth and seventeenth centuries.

The merchant class, too, was conservative in thought, and, like
the gentry, was made so by difficulties. Shrinking foreign markets
made it all the more desirable to check competition in the home
market, and a means to this end was found in strict company organization. Merchants guarded the entrance to their gilds by the re-
quirement of long terms of apprenticeship or high premiums, and
they also jealously tightened their grip of local political powers.

Class-consciousness was certainly, at these levels, bound up with
strong forces of conservatism. But while it lent weight to desires for
a static world, it had also an opposite character and opposite effects.
Satisfaction with the social system and an attitude of deference

towards superiors did not, for the individual, necessarily mean contentment with the state to which he was born. An exaggerated respect for power and wealth made them objects so much the more to be coveted; in other words, a great deal of energy was generated in the shape of social ambition. This is evident on every hand—in the marriage settlements of the gentry, in the provision that merchants made for education of their sons, in the family histories of gentlemen and of merchants, which frequently run back to humble and obscure origins.

That there was so much freedom to rise in the social scale was partly due to a difference in fertility between the upper classes and the lower rural classes. The former consistently failed to maintain their numbers, so that there was continuous opportunity for new men to establish themselves beside the proud old families of rank. There is reason to believe that the average baronial family died out, in the male line, in its third generation.[8] This was not because the barons did not wish to perpetuate their families. On the contrary, they might have up to twenty-two children. But only the strong survived childhood, and not all marriages were fertile. Thus, even without the casualties suffered in the civil wars and on Tudor scaffolds, the old aristocracy would gradually have made way for new men. The wealthy landed gentry, leading less strenuous lives, may have made a slightly better showing. Their families ran up to twenty-five. But, just as was the case among the lords, the rate of child mortality was pathetically high, and not all marriages were fertile. As to the gentlemen in menial or military service, they could not marry young nor lead a normal family life. In the merchant class gild regulations and a preference for rich wives combined to lower the birth rate by delaying the age of marriage. Families of over twenty nevertheless occurred, but a very high proportion of men died either childless or leaving daughters only. All these matters demand statistical treatment, and are to some extent, by methods of sampling, capable of being measured.

The late Professor Eileen Power used to say when people spoke of the immobility of the mediaeval scene, that it always looked to her as lively as an ant-heap. Fifteenth-century England was one of the less rapidly changing corners of that scene, yet it displayed a lively degree of social mobility, of movement not only from one community to another, but from one social class to another. This movement was as characteristic a feature of the class system as were the various exhibitions of class pride and class prejudice that have been emphasized.

One of the basic problems, then, of which the student of mediaeval conservatism must take account, is the coincidence and interlocking of forces of change with forces opposed to change. Since the subject is a broad one, it can be approached from many angles. Attitudes of prejudice and conservatism in regard to the social system being as a rule closely related to similar attitudes in regard to religion and government, a study of religious and political thought is indispensable. From the point of view of the social historian, however, there is a direct line of attack through the laborious analysis of class structure as it varied in one region and locality after another. Tension set up by chance variations from the normal manner and rate of social mobility may have had much to do with stiffening or relaxing attitudes of conservatism in regard to every type of change.

NOTES

1. Information in this paper is based on research into the social relationships of the merchants of London, which extended through the country at large. Full documentation cannot be attempted here.

2. Edward Waterhous, *A Discourse and Defence of Arms and Armoury* (London, 1660), p. 101.

3. *Rotuli Parliamentorum*, v. 268.

4. W. Stubbs, *The Constitutional History of England* (Oxford, 5th edition, 1898), III, 568.

5. See H. L. Gray, "Incomes from Land in England in 1436," *English Historical Review*, 49, pp. 619, 621.

6. *Peter Idle's Instructions to his Son*, C. d'Evelyn, ed. (1935), lib. I, l. 690.

7. See, on this and on trade depression, M. Postan's preliminary report of his investigations into manorial profits, "The Fifteenth Century," *Economic History Review*, IX, 160–167.

8. A surmise of Colonel Wedgewood's, not yet statistically worked out: *A History of Parliament, 1439–1509, Register of Members*, p. lxxi. Cf. P. E. Fahlbeck, *Der Adel Schwedens* (1903), pp. 55–56.

V

On Historical Method

Introduction

Thomas C. Cochran

Probably few historians of any nation have ranged as widely and expertly over both history and the social sciences as Sylvia Thrupp. Her interest in the past of the Western World stretches from the early Middle Ages to the present, and while she has generally been categorized as an economic historian, her interest in the behavioral sciences has been, at least, equally great. Moreover, creation and editorship of *Comparative Studies in Society and History* has perforce broadened her knowledge to include the Eastern as well as the Western World. In addition to her own writing, and the editing of *CSSH,* she has tried continually to bring scholars from different disciplines and fields closer together by judicious personal appeals.

The essays of one who brings such wide knowledge to every subject are hard to categorize. The reader who has started at the beginning of this book and proceeded in an orderly manner, knows by now a great deal about Professor Thrupp's historiographic ideas. What seems appropriate at this point is to summarize some of her basic methodological views and offer a more extended discussion stemming from her present interest in comparative method.

A generation ago, when local history was just beginning to gain professional respectability in Europe and America, and urban history had not yet spawned all the specialized chairs, groups, and publications that exist today, Professor Thrupp wrote "The Pedigree and Prospects of Local History." The pedigree is a long and varied one that reflects the development of Western World historiography. Medieval monks and town burghers in glorifying their foundation, or their city, incidentally supplied material that may be regarded as the origin of European social history. As national interests obscured those of the town, monastery, or manor, local history lost importance, although British county histories and those of Italian cities continued. "The serious interest in the evolution of community life," she writes, "is essentially modern," induced by rapid social and industrial change. Through her own work, included in the present volume, and by publishing numerous articles by others in *CSSH*, Professor Thrupp has done much to bring local history to its present stage of disciplinary interest.

Moving, as she does so readily, to an opposite historiographic pole, she reviewed from the "bird's-eye" view of "spatial and social," rather than topical or temporal horizons, the writing of West European history in the first five years of the 1960s.[1] As an editor, she was also in a position to contrast European with American work on similar themes. In intellectual history, for example, she found that Europeans were more interested than we in the channels by which ideas are communicated and diffused, and in contrast to a degree of American provincialism these foreign scholars often disregarded national boundaries. She also saw economic history, with its series of international conferences that were inaugurated at Stockholm in 1960, as a force for spatial integration of Continental and even world history.[2] Yet she was forced to conclude that "The majority of historians in Europe as in America continue, nevertheless, to work within national boundaries."

The union of history with the social sciences has been her lifelong aim and the remaining articles in this section all directly involve this theme. The first of these is distinguished from the others by being a review of the attempt of some other historians to make progress in interdisciplinary unity rather than representing her own exhortations. As a member of the group involved, I think a few words are necessary to explain the apparent limitations or failings of the book, *Generalization in the Writing of History* (Chicago, 1963). This was the third report in two decades by successive committees on historiography appointed by the Social Science Research Council. The first committee report (SSRC, Bulletin 54) emphasized the limitations of historical statements and methods; the second report (Bulletin 64) dealt exclusively with history and the social sciences; and for a third report the committee thought it most persuasive to let historians speak for themselves about the key problem of generalization, rather than arranging further dialogues with social scientists. The contributors, however, were given a quite detailed outline or model of what questions the committee wanted answered and in what order. At this point, however, the literary tradition of the profession seems to have become dominant. Some of the selected contributors concealed the structure of the model so completely in their well-written essays that the reader would not suspect its existence. Therefore, no specific pattern of either agreement or disagreement emerges. Committee members perhaps added to the apparent lack of structure by contributing essays on points that each felt had been neglected in the general essays. Consequently one may agree with Professor Thrupp's criticisms that

> The one sphere in which we would expect historians to be better equipped to generalize than anyone else is that of the processes of long-term change. Here the social sciences, so strong in structural analysis, are weak, for they are not accustomed to examining processes of change in detail over more than short periods. . . . Strangely enough, the book fails to bring out this contrast.

I feel sure the other living committee members would join me in rephrasing FDR: "We didn't plan it that way."

Professor Thrupp's broad scholarship makes her particularly conscious of the history of the various social disciplines, an understanding which necessarily includes the elements that have kept them apart. In Western Europe in the late nineteenth century, there was a strong historical influence in economics, political science, and sociology manifest in such major figures as Karl Marx, Max Weber, Emile Durkheim, and Henri Pirenne. But, except for history, the twentieth-century trend in each discipline was for greater emphasis on theory based on either deduction or short term data. In the new theoretical contexts the historical approach was troublesome or divisive and was generally minimized. Therefore, although Thomas D. Eliot in the *American Journal of Sociology* (Vol. 27) for 1922 called for a broader sociological approach that would include "all human behavior in groups," in the succeeding generation the non- or anti-historical bent, in United States sociology particularly, gained rather than lost strength.

This situation inspired Professor Thrupp's "What History and Sociology Can Learn from Each Other" (1956). Basically, she hoped that common interest in comparative studies and methods could lead the way. Quantitative methods obviously provided a meeting ground for history and all the other social sciences, but she thought that urban study, social stratification, demography, and family and inheritance patterns might also be of interest to both historians and sociologists.

Society and History

Neither this article nor its successor of the following year, "History and Sociology: New Opportunities for Cooperation," underestimate the formidable obstacles to be overcome in interdisciplinary research. In part the differences are philosophical or psychological and may be minimized through better understanding; but in part they are professional or market-oriented and these obstacles will not be eliminated by sweet reasonableness.

The first group of differences stems from the fact that sociologists (or economists or psychologists) start by relating the problem to be investigated to their theories, whereas the historian, by training, starts with records and merely looks for a logical or inferred progression of causes and effects. Professor Thrupp astutely notes another difference: qualitative evidence for sociological conclusions comes largely from interviews and polling that emphasize numbers of people without regard to their social influence; whereas historical records are usually created by past leaders of the society. Hence each group can criticize the meanings to be attached to the findings of the other. While sociologists think that most historical writing leads to no useful social hypotheses, historians resist any paradigms for social determinism. They have seen so many cases of unpredictable innovation or rapid change in institutions that historians put a scientifically frustrating emphasis on what appear to be random events.

The methodological differences, elucidated further and more clearly in Professor Thrupp's two essays, have been reduced in the succeeding years through the influence of *CSSH* and the writing of a new generation of scholars, but the professional and academic barriers remain formidable. Young scholars want to write theses that will win them maximum recognition in their chosen profession, which means, obviously, that existing divergences are perpetuated. Those who spread their efforts over two or more fields are likely to be regarded by dedicated specialists as superficial. The important audience from the standpoint of promotion and academic honors is in one's major discipline.

This brings up another problem. The sociologist's audience is likely to be other theoretically minded social scientists, the historian's is the whole range of academicians and students plus a part of the literate public. As disciplines, therefore, sociology tends to honor theoretical, and history literary ability. Put another way, the "market" rewards historians for skillful presentation of the unique, colorful, and individual; it rewards sociologists for analyzing groups and formulating theory.

At the time Professor Thrupp was laying out the difficulties of interdisciplinary cooperation, she was planning her main strategy for overcoming them: a journal to publish articles from all disciplines limited by the theme of comparative study. The "Role of Comparison in the Development of Economic Theory" was read at the September, 1957, meeting of the Economic History Association, when her plans for the first issue of *CSSH* were already well advanced. The paper is a preview of some of the ideas she would bring to its editorship, such as "intensive comparison," meaning "any judicious comparison of complex wholes, for example, two styles of art, or two periods of history."

Like her predecessor Marc Bloch, who had done much to spread the idea of comparison through his editorship of the *Annales: Économies—Sociétés—Civilisations* from 1929 on, she would "not be directed by any dogmatic system that would be unresponsive to new findings . . ." and would hope to link all social research "into an ultimately world-wide cooperative enterprise." To a few of her friends, such as me, this made the initial conception of *CSSH* seem somewhat hazy, but time has abundantly demonstrated the wisdom of this broad nondoctrinaire approach.

In the body of this article she traces the vicissitudes of the concept of comparison in the field of economic history from the mid-eighteenth-century work of Adam Ferguson (*Essay on the History of Civil Society, 1757*). Classic theorists and nineteenth-century stage theorists were interested in comparison only to demonstrate the operation of their deductive systems. But the rapid changes of industrialism in the twentieth century, reinforced by a new interest in economic growth, brought constructive, rather than exemplary, comparison back into the main stream of economic history. A very lively discussion of the paper at the meeting emphasized that "the comparative method is the process of putting the same question to different sets of facts," and that the difficulty is just how to formulate and phrase the question.[3]

Not only is the difficulty of valid comparison greater than appears on the surface, but it presents particular problems for the historian. It was said by Professor Thrupp that "Comparative method can be no more than a tool in the service of hypothesis," yet most historians do not start their research with a set of hypotheses. Therefore, a pursuit of comparisons that can satisfy social scientists or philosophers of history calls for more than the unstudied comparative statements which abound in historical literature.[4]

The most frequent and unstudied use of comparison is between different time periods in the same culture or complex of cultures. It would be almost impossible to give meaning to history without using this device. The Grant administration was a period of unusual corruption, the 1920s were a "jazz age," or the New Deal created a break with past traditions, are common assertions involving cross-temporal comparison within the United States. To explain, whenever such off-hand comparisons are used, all the indices and theoretical assumptions involved would be extremely pedantic, yet in the third of the preceding statements such definitions are obviously called for. Furthermore, a really systematic use of internal cross-temporal comparison might yield new insights.

A less used, and therefore potentially more rewarding, type of comparison is between developments in different nations or cultures. Here, because the variables are presumably more numerous and their functions more diverse, only a systematic approach can be convincing.

Selection of problems or types of behavior to be compared requires explicit theoretical assumptions about what is important and why, as well as what data can be found for comparison. Determining the questions to be asked and their implications, therefore, are the major problems of comparison. Even when a coherent and promising set of questions has been framed there are many dangers in application to the data. It is easy to confuse abstract concepts with real facts, or to select aspects of reality that appear to support the concept to the exclusion of those that do not. For example, if one starts with the concept that American management has been more efficient than European, comparative evidence can be found to support the assumption, while if exactly the opposite concept is adopted as a guide evidence will also be found to support it. Thus, comparison usually suffers from too few illustrative cases and too few clear indices.

The fact that historians are more interested in explaining change over time than in current cross-sectional analysis raises another problem: there is a tension between the logical requirements of comparability and the kind of explanations found in the records. Even if superficially similar and reliable statistical series are available, for example, they are likely not to measure exactly the same things either in two different countries or periods. Furthermore, culture is no longer regarded by anthropologists as a collection of traits and patterns susceptible to separate or individual comparison between two areas. Rather, culture is seen more as an organization of diversity, a series of implied contracts to behave certain ways, or a highest common denominator of what to expect in social situations. Consequently, individual customs or traits cannot be compared without due regard to the influence of the entire system. Even when with great analytical care an apparently similar case is found in two different nations, it proves only feasibility, not probability. Negative cases or contrasts are likely, therefore, to be more revealing than similarities, because they are clues to further differences.

In practice international or intercultural comparison works best when two or more contemporaneous societies have similar physical environments, and the same stage of technology, as, for example, Western nations in the Great Depression of the 1930s. A commonly used alternative is to select different periods of time in each country that appear to embrace the same types of development as, for example, industrialism in late eighteenth-century England and early nineteenth-century France. Comparison becomes less tangible or measureable, but still useful, when applied to social characteristics, values, or ideas. Here both national or temporal differences have to be observed in the varying quality or meaning of the intangible factor selected as well as differences in its social application or development.

In her brief "Editorial" introducing the first issue of *CSSH* (October, 1958), Professor Thrupp posed the problem that individual scholars could not, as a rule, be theorists or generalists and at the same time specialists in more than one period or geographic area. What was needed, therefore, was to urge "that specialists in related fields compare notes more frequently." *CSSH* was based on the proposition that "interaction occurs in every society between cultural traditions, social organization, and new ideas, new aspirations and new wants." By getting the specialist to set his discussion in such a broad framework, the journal could bridge a "real gap in our system of communications, and allow those in other disciplines or areas to see relationships to their own specialized work."

The final article "Comparative Studies in Society and History: A Working Alliance among Specialists" is an editorial comment on the first half dozen years of the new journal. The opening statement that the quarterly sought "to find out whether historians and social scientists have anything much to say to each other," indicates a broadening of scope beyond merely comparative method. This came, in part, from the nature of contributions and the editor's desire to publish the best, and, in part, because the techniques of comparative study tap a large pool of interdisciplinary common knowledge which may be used in many ways. In fact, comparative data were frequently used to substantiate general propositions. Observing the contributions as a whole, Professor Thrupp concludes that "the methods of the social sciences are much more adaptable to the study of change over long periods than was at first realized."

To try to maintain comparability, Professor Thrupp and her editorial group initially sent questionnaires to prospective contributors, but as the accumulating articles themselves indicated what was desired of authors, the practice was abandoned. The two-thirds of the writers for the quarterly who were scholars in fields other than history, brought their own definitions of comparability.

Even to some historians, comparative method has divergent meanings. Fernand Braudel, for example, says: "Comparative history is the bringing together of history and contiguous disciplines, the exchange of services between them and their convergence on selected problems, whether these be problems in toponymy or geography, in sociology or psychology, or in political economy."[5] Here the emphasis is shifted to comparing methods and theoretical approaches rather than different bodies of data. In practice this calls either for research by teams or theoretical knowledge beyond that possessed by most historians. In *CSSH* many of the articles using such multidisciplinary approaches have been by other social scientists, particularly sociologists.

Thus, as illustrated in the quarterly, "intensive comparison" includes methodological, temporal, and spatial use of the approach. Because of the indivisibility of culture some interdisciplinary spread is essential. For example, in studying a social institution such as courtship before marriage, it must be thoroughly understood in each culture by use of all social science methods before it can be compared across cultural boundaries. A historian, unwilling to attempt this and content with merely observing superficial events, may easily be seriously misled.

The message of *CSSH* and comparative history, therefore, calls for greater depth of interdisciplinary research and more explicit hypotheses in temporal or spatial comparisons or in those which are both. Without such meticulous interdisciplinary approaches comparisons are more likely to be wrong than right, to be a support for polemical argument rather than the advancement of knowledge.

NOTES

1. "The Writing of West European History: A Bird's-Eye View of Trends between 1960 and 1964," *The Annals of the American Academy of Political and Social Science* 359 (May 1965): 157–64.

2. *First International Conference of Economic History,* Ecole des Hautes Etudes (Paris, 1960).

3. *Journal of Economic History* 17 (December 1957): 500 and 598, Barry E. Supple and Bert F. Hoselitz, respectively.

4. For examples, see: Vann Woodward, ed., *The Comparative Approach to American History* (New York, 1968).

5. *International Encyclopedia of the Social Sciences,* s.v. "Marc Bloch."

The Pedigree and Prospects of
Local History

The writer of local history is to-day deservedly receiving more and more recognition. Thanks to the part that his more dramatic findings can play in arousing the historical imagination of children at school, and to the attention that is paid to his subject in research-work directed from universities, a growing number of people now take an interest in the background of the communities in which they live. The subject has always a certain romantic colour; it appeals to local patriotism, and it has also, to students of history and sociology, a more serious appeal.

This serious interest in the evolution of community life is essentially modern. The writing of history was for many centuries guided by quite different ideas. One can therefore best appreciate and understand the position and importance of the study of local history by looking backward over the long procession of writers and thinkers who throughout the ages have sought to interpret past experience.

Men's outlook upon history has always been conditioned by the attitudes and interests of their own time; this has been so from the very beginning. When a consciousness of the past first began to dawn within our Western civilization warlike and predatory peoples were playing a dominant role. Tales of adventure—recited either in prose, or in verse, which was more easily memorized—were everywhere popular. In the circumstances any one who wished to arouse interest in the past naturally tended to fasten upon the adventures

Reprinted from *British Columbia Historical Quarterly* 4, no. 4 (October 1940): 253–65.

and deeds of great heroes and leaders. Memories of the past were inevitably shaped into stories, and were handed down in the form given them by the more dramatic story-tellers.

When professional story-tellers and poets appeared, another influence was brought to bear upon the shaping of historical traditions. For the audiences best able to reward these men were to be found at the courts of kings and chieftains, and here the subjects most in favour were the valour of the leader and his nobles and their ancestors. Since in all warlike and aristocratic societies people have held blood and ancestry in more or less superstitious reverence, the minstrel who could spread abroad the fame of a leader's ancestors might very greatly enhance his prestige. Thus early written history inevitably came to focus upon the fortunes of the great, the holders of power.

Historical narrative was not at first clearly distinguished from mere story. It was only very gradually and painfully that the idea of founding history upon what had actually occurred assumed the force of an ideal; and had the relating of history been left entirely to the poets and minstrels of the courts, this ideal might never have arisen at all. But fortunately, early in the development of the great kingdoms and empires of the ancient world, the poetic monopoly was broken by prosaic competitors, for it became the duty of certain officials to compile a record of major public events as they took place, year by year. Such annals made dull reading, but their value grew with their length. They preserved and symbolized, for governments and dynasties, the accumulating dignity of age and lineage; besides, they were of practical use. To be able to refer back to exact records was a convenience, and sooner or later a necessity, in the work of government. Hence a care for truthful records of many kinds arose.

Mythology and religion also exercised an immense influence in moulding the traditions of the historian's craft. Indeed, it was through mythology that the historical imagination was originally stimulated. The idea of supernatural intervention in human affairs was carried over from mythology and remained for many ages the chief means of explaining critical turns in the course of events. Priesthoods in many cults had much the same attitude towards the past as noble families and royal dynasties, feeling that records en-

hanced their dignity. They made efforts, with varying degrees of
success, to develop the science of chronology. Moreover, the priests,
unlike the kings, could embrace a vision not only of the past but of
the future. The Hebrew and the Christian religions gave to the
whole sweep of history one single meaningful pattern. As early
Christian writers viewed it, the history of the world was that of a
sequence of empires rising and falling in turn; of these the Roman
Empire was to be the last, and in some form it would endure until
the world's end, when men would be gathered in for judgment upon
the fate of their immortal souls. In this vast prospect all issues but
moral issues were dwarfed into insignificance. Such a philosophy of
history obviously gave little direct encouragement to concentration
upon accuracy of detail for its own sake. Nor did it have any tendency to turn attention to the study of local communities.

In the Greek and Roman worlds a number of intellectual and
emotional interests opened on to the past. Among the wealthy nobility, family pride fostered the art of constructing flattering genealogies, that sometimes ran back to divine ancestors. Religious cults
kept a medley of myths in circulation. Nevertheless, an educated
and sophisticated reading public gradually emerged, among the ruling classes, that was deeply interested in the political history of its
own time. Both in Greece and in Rome the art of tracing the fortunes
of empire in vivid political narrative was carried to a high point of
excellence. History came in fact to be viewed as a way of studying
politics. As such its scope was limited by the scope of popular political theory. And since political theory as yet took little account of
economic and social problems, there was no need to delve into the
details of local history, as is the fashion to-day. The histories of
Rome deal less with the city itself than with the successes of its armies and the expansion of its power. The pages of most of the classical
historians echo, often monotonously, with the clash of arms and the
ringing periods of great political orations.

Like all other intellectual pursuits in Western Europe, the art
of writing history sank to a low ebb during the early Middle Ages.
With the decline of Roman civilization the sophisticated reading
public disappeared. A limited circle of ill-educated readers remained, confined for the most part within the ranks of the clergy and
the monks. These kept alive among themselves some knowledge of

ancient historical writing and of Church history with its Biblical background. But new historical composition was inevitably conditioned by the tastes of the public at large, consisting now mainly of a boorish military and landowning aristocracy and an utterly ignorant and superstitious mass of peasants. In such an environment historical traditions could live and develop only in story and epic form. Ancient times were viewed through the curious perspective of the poetry of Virgil, and memories of more recent times tended to recede into a kaleidoscopic confusion of romantic adventure, abounding in supernatural occurrences and supernatural creatures, both pagan and Christian. A few men of superior intellect—a Gregory of Tours, a Bede—wrote faithful accounts of the careers of kings and bishops, but their work was not nearly so popular as the dramatic short stories, encrusted with legend, that told of the lives of saints, or the long poetic romances about the exploits of Alexander the Great, Charlemagne, King Arthur, and their warriors. On so colourful a stage there was no room for the drab figures of the humble and obscure, with which truthful local history would largely have had to deal.

In time the Church succeeded in gradually raising the level of education among the clergy, and from the tenth century onward, with reviving prosperity and longer periods of peace, more and more members of the richer laity found leisure to read or to listen to reading. Romances, religious treatises, and legends of the saints were still their chief fare, but there was some demand for genuine history. Interest centred naturally in matters which the nobility best understood, and in which they or their ancestors had played a part; that is, in political conflicts and in the fortunes of aggressive leaders. Writers among the clergy supplied what was wanted, producing lively narratives of the Crusades, biographies of kings, and national chronicles.

The chronicles grew out of the files of notes on important events which many monasteries made it their business to keep. It became customary for the abbot to assign a capable monk the task of working the notes into a connected narrative. The monastic writers were often well-read in scriptural and classical history, and well-informed on contemporary politics. In any case their interests tended to stretch far beyond their monastery walls, for the property which monasteries accumulated through the gifts of the pious was often

widely scattered. Furthermore, the chances of retaining the whole
of the property securely depended upon the state of law and order,
and this depended increasingly upon the power of the king, his
character, and ability. At the same time there were religious and
moral reasons why churchmen should follow the fortunes of monarchy with eagerness, for it was regarded as an institution divinely
sanctioned, and each king at his consecration was sworn to the maintenance of justice. For the one reason or the other most of the monk-
historians followed the plan of concentrating upon the development
of royal power. Thus they created national history.

Some of the monks who were assigned to historical writing attempted little more than the compilation of a history of their own
house. The result was a kind of local history, but a kind that suffered
from the defects of a narrow and partisan spirit. The purpose of this
type of chronicle was simply to magnify the importance of a monastery and the power of its abbots. The writers took no interest in
their neighbours outside the precincts of the cloister, and rarely
mentioned them except when they proved to be unsatisfactory or
rebellious tenants. In the Peterborough chronicle, for example, one
learns of the development of industry in the district only through an
account of the abbot's action in seizing the stones of mills that had
been set up by tenants in defiance of his monopoly rights as feudal
lord. The monk always took the point of view of a lord intent on his
feudal rights. In short, he was incapable of viewing local developments objectively.

The cult of local history grew up among the bourgeoisie of the
mediaeval towns. The people of the mediaeval towns, crowding together for security, century after century, behind their encircling
walls and moats, generated among themselves an extraordinarily
intense spirit of community. It grew and found expression in long
and tenacious struggles to win rights of self-government from feudal
overlords, in the adoption of laws and customs different from those
of the countryside, in the triumphant enforcement of the custom
that all residents of the town acquired the status of free men. Pride
in local traditions was in the very atmosphere. Every street and market-place, every church tower, had its dramatic associations with the
past. For a time these traditions would be handed down orally. But
those townsmen who were engaged in trade were obliged for busi-

ness reasons to learn to read. Hence there was sooner or later—sooner in the South of Europe, later in the North, which was economically more backward—a bourgeois public eager to read histories in which the bourgeoisie would figure.

The earlier town chronicles can scarcely be regarded as models of good historical writing. They are crude in form and unpolished in style. Their authors, who were usually of the merchant class, the ruling class in the towns, looked down upon the humbler inhabitants. They often concentrated rather narrowly upon the fortunes of the town government, and they were not free from bias in discussing quarrels among the magistrates. Their interest in national development, like that of the monk-historians, was restricted to the surface of political events. Although they were obviously more skeptical of stories of miracles than were the monks, they were not above relating entertaining fables about the founding of their city by the descendants of gods or mythical heroes. Yet, despite all these limitations, the vigorous and neighbourly sense of community which was a part of their character as townsmen enabled them to portray a wider sector of local life than any other historians had yet had the power to describe.

For example, here and there they would fill in a few lines with journalistic jottings of matters of human interest that had evidently been the talk of the town. They note the bolder local crimes, crimes committed by women, sensational damage done by storms in the neighbourhood, the nature of local epidemics, as how one summer many people were ill of a flux that came from eating too much fruit. They introduced anecdotes of eccentric characters, such as the story of a musician in London who superintended his own funeral, coming to the service and making offerings at masses sung for his soul, because, as he said, he could not trust executors to do this for him liberally enough. With all their faults, the town chroniclers had their feet planted squarely on the common earth on which the common people lived.

From another point of view their work became of the highest importance. The interest in town history that had been aroused in Italy by the time of the Renaissance helped to make possible a marked improvement in historical writing. One of the results of the vogue that classical studies enjoyed at that period was a renewed enthusiasm for the writing of history. Scholars were anxious to prove that they could write in as elegant a style, and with as much political shrewdness, as had historians in ancient Greece and Rome. They chose to write of their own cities, partly because they could often obtain commissions to do so, and could therefore be assured of readers and pecuniary reward, and also because the wars and revolutions in which the Italian cities so constantly indulged made them a fascinating field in which to study political rivalries and factions. The Italian scholars sought, in the spirit of the ancient Greek and Roman historians, to produce books that would be useful to rulers by pointing out mistakes made by their predecessors. As Machiavelli expressed it in his own book on Florence, rulers might be "thus taught wisdom at the cost of others." Whether or not the new histories achieved this end, the emphasis that they laid upon the political development of the Italian city-states had the effect of giving educated people a better historical perspective. The way was opened for scholars to modify the early Christian view of world history, which had been based upon exaggeration of the rôle played by the ancient empires and by the Hebrews, and upon a faulty chronology; and the old pessimistic assumption that all hope of progress on earth had died with the decline of Rome began to yield before a new spirit of optimism. Wherever the culture of the Italian Renaissance radiated, these new views of history spread.

Outside Italy, historians in the fifteenth and sixteenth centuries were naturally more preoccupied with the writing of national history. Intelligent kings, realizing that knowledge of and pride in a people's common traditions could be of invaluable help to them in the work of national unification, wisely encouraged the scholars. The cult of local history also received a fresh impetus from the growing sentiment of national patriotism, for it was soon realized that only through the winnowing of local traditions and records could sound and reliable national history be written. John Leland, who was appointed official historiographer by Henry VIII., toiled up and down England amassing notes on local institutions of all kinds—monasteries, churches, families, towns. So ambitious was his programme and so severely did he drive himself that he ruined his health and collapsed into insanity before his researches were nearly completed. But a succession of scholars arose to carry on the labour of research in the same spirit of excitement, inspired partly by local patriotism, by love for their own city or county, and partly by national feeling. John Stow, who, to quote his own word, "consecrated" forty-five years of his life and much of a modest bourgeois fortune to research, is best known for his *Survey* of Elizabethan London and its monuments, which he felt himself "bound in love" to undertake, but he worked also to popularize the reading of national chronicles. It is evident that history, both local and national alike, was a means of enriching and widening the sense of citizenship.

No one nowadays could sit down and read very far at one time in the books of John Stow and his successors for pleasure. Their works are still indispensable to the specialist, but they were compiled for the most part with complete disregard of literary style or artistic form; they were in essence merely encyclopaedias of local antiquities. Modern scholarship, having at its command a much greater volume of sources, can pick out inaccuracies, but the authors were unquestionably guided by scrupulous zeal for accuracy of detail. In setting themselves this ideal, as also in their indifference to artistic canons, the early English antiquaries breathe the Puritanism of their age. The heavy yoke of discipline under which they bent their shoulders, however, was lightened daily by the sheer delight that they experienced in the turning-up of ancient yellowed records and in the exploration of the long-forgotten details of past events. John Stow liked to think of himself as one of the great explorers: "I have attempted the discovery of London, my native soyle and Countrey," he wrote.

In course of time this first enthusiasm waned. It received little encouragement from the universities and less and less, as the years wore on into the eighteenth century, from the reading public. It was not that the reading public of the eighteenth century was uninterested in the trend of history. Gibbon's philosophical and controversial manner of treating the story of the Roman Empire and the Church won him sensational success, and partisan political histories of England found a ready market. The antiquaries were neglected because they lagged behind contemporary thought; they were not discovering or discussing anything that appeared to bear upon vital interests of the day. They became absorbed in detail for its own sake, never pausing to consider whether one fact was not more significant than another in illustrating the direction of social change. Moreover, they busied themselves chiefly with the Middle Ages, a period which the fashionable wits and intellectuals of the day, following the lead of Voltaire, chose to view as an era of ridiculous and debased superstition, best buried in oblivion. Yet under the banner of the Society of Antiquaries, founded in 1717 with barely two dozen members, a small group of enthusiasts ploughed obstinately on in the observation and study of miscellaneous mediaeval antiquities. Monumental county histories, representing monumental labours and of immense value to later historians, continued to appear at intervals until late in the nineteenth century. For a long period, however, there was little progress in the art of writing local history.

The cultivation of local history did not come into its own again until the rapid social and economic changes of the nineteenth century aroused an interest in the social and economic aspects of the past. In many places amateur historians had come to realize the great importance of economic changes in their own localities long before the professional historians had grasped their importance in the national life. Societies, such as the Camden Society and county archaeological societies, were formed for the publication of documents and descriptive notes bearing on local questions, and were increasingly active from the third decade of the century. Their work gradually made available a great variety of records that dealt in one way or another with economic life, or with gossipy details of private social life in past generations. Thus when some of the professional historians finally decided to turn aside from political and constitutional history to consider economic matters, they found quantities of raw material conveniently at hand in print, and it was clear that there were masses more in manuscript. It is probable that without the work of pioneer local historians the appearance of any satisfactory interpretations of national economic development would have been very considerably delayed.

It is not merely in connection with specialized economic studies that historians have found it necessary to take account of local changes. The old idea that the political and constitutional history of a nation could be written satisfactorily on the basis of the records of its wars and its laws, its parliaments, revolutions and reforms, died hard, but is now safely in its coffin. New laws are a clue to the wishes of those who framed them, but one cannot necessarily assume that they were enforced. Much of the legislation of mediaeval and early modern times fell as far short of its aim as the Eighteenth Amendment to the constitution of the United States. Local opposition decided its fate. Nor, even when enforced, did it necessarily produce the effects that its architects intended. Local conditions again were decisive. Even the significance of important constitutional changes had often been dependent upon the state of repair of the machinery of local government.

Even the more popular type of historical writing, the kind that bases itself on biography, cannot afford to ignore the work of the local historian. The notion that the gist of a nation's story is contained in the life and character of its great statesmen and generals is true only in a superficial way. It is true that the lives of such men as Cromwell, Danton, Robespierre, and all the great colourful leaders of movements, not only changed the course of many other men's lives but also expressed in some degree the spirit of their time, since they would not have become leaders had they not been capable of dramatizing the aspirations and hopes of many of their contemporaries. Yet, since great numbers of their fellows hated, loathed, and despised them, one may still ask why such men were thrown upon the central stage of power. And to answer that question one must turn to the little country towns and villages, to scenes where there were probably no great figures at all, but where the impact of unwise government policies, of official corruption, of sacrifice in war, or of gradually changing conditions—the rise of new occupations, new families and classes, and the decadence of old, were creating social tension and cutting channels for new ideas. Every aspect of general history is inevitably bound up with the slow currents of change at work in the local community.

Most modern corrections of the errors in fact or interpretation that are to be found in the work of the older historians are based upon increased knowledge and understanding of the diversity of local conditions. Scholarly modern accounts of the rise of the great national states of Western Europe rest upon hundreds of patient investigations into the duties and efficiency of local officials, the organization of local industries, the trade of ports, the fortunes of the peasant under the different agrarian systems of different regions, the spread of education and ideas among different sections of the people. Every type of record that survives from the past is pressed into service—not only the vast files of government and municipal records in public archives, but the intimate letters and diaries of private people; family housekeeping accounts; the business letters and accounts of merchants, bankers, industrialists, and stewards of landed estates; wills, inscriptions on tombs; the inventories of old libraries long scattered; ecclesiastical records; school and hospital records; not to mention early newspapers and handbills and literary material of every kind. It is beyond the powers of a single scholar to master all the materials that are needed to illustrate truthfully the varied aspects of life in any historical period. The writing of history is therefore now essentially a co-operative enterprise. It progresses only by virtue of a working partnership between the general historian and the specialist in local research.

Looking back over the evolution of his craft, the local historian may well feel proud of the long cultural traditions that he inherits and represents. Mediaeval townsmen, politicians and patriots of the Renaissance, seventeenth and eighteenth century seekers after truth, and nineteenth century social philosophers, have each in turn practised it with similar and perpetual delight, but guided by ever-widening horizons of thought and aspiration.

On this continent the local historian has had the advantage of enjoying the whole of this heritage with almost none of the trouble that was involved in creating it. He has been spared the heavy labour of research in damaged mediaeval records written in bad, semi-legible abbreviated Latin, and has been spared the reproaches of those who have no patience save for modern history. He has been able to avoid the antiquary's temptation to concentrate upon the genealogy of long-dead aristocrats or the architecture of ruined buildings. It has been much easier for him to gain the respectful co-operation of the general historian because the striking diversity of different regions on this continent has made it essential for the latter to seek the assistance of his special knowledge. Again, economic factors have played so obvious a part in shaping national life that the value of the economic and social data which form so large a proportion of the local historian's stock-in-trade is readily recognized. Although a very great amount of work remains to be done, it should not, in these circumstances, take very much longer to round out the history of national development. But when this task is approximately finished, when all the documents in all the archives have been made to yield up all the economic, political, constitutional or biographical facts that bear upon the national development, when all the important sources now mouldering in the cupboards and basements of lawyers' offices and business firms have been tapped, what will the local historian do? What will become of him? Will he be regarded as a useless relic of the past?

It is sincerely to be hoped that he himself will never take this view, for there will always be vital and absorbing work for local historians. New horizons and new goals will always be appearing. The idea of writing national history will in all probability be succeeded by the idea of writing international history. This will entail far more than the analysis of diplomatic negotiations and the conduct of foreign policies. It will have to include a study of all those movements that transcend national boundaries, not matters of world trade alone, but also cultural changes, currents of opinion, the rise of new attitudes and ideologies, new objects of ambition, changes in the social structure.

Rapid changes of this order in many quarters of the world have been reshaping the lives of our own generation. We live in a day of mass movements, of unprecedented possibilities for good or evil through the mobilization of public opinion. The study of shifting attitudes, opinions, and values is already of far more than abstract academic interest: it is essential for any one who professes to have a realistic approach to the political problems of the day. As time passes it will become more and more necessary for those who are in charge of the planning and administration of government policies to understand the forces that are at work in the formation of public opinion. To whom will they turn for guidance? The journalists, no doubt, will be at hand with advice. We have already floods of journalistic comment on such questions. But journalistic generalizations about the ideas and interests of the average man in this or that corner of the world are of necessity often based on haphazard guesswork, and often biased by prejudice and the desire to be impressive. What is needed is expert intimate knowledge of local conditions. The sociologists, again, will offer help in the form of detailed surveys of so-

cial conditions in typical communities. These are useful and important. Yet what is needed is not only a knowledge of the material
conditions under which people live, but a grasp of the varied elements in the traditions of their community which will help to determine their attitude to new ideas and policies. For this reason a full
understanding of local conditions can only be gained through an
historical approach.

It is not likely, therefore, that the local historian will wish to
fold his hands when present tasks are completed. He will find instead
more and more occasion to cultivate the skill and insight of the
gifted sociologist. It may be that enlightened governments of the
future will find work for him. He may become able to develop the
art of forecasting, as it were, the social and political weather. In any
case, his unique understanding of tradition, of its lasting influence
and its ways of change, cannot fail to find useful application.

Some Historians on
Generalization

For a political historian to invite a group of his colleagues to write about the use of generalization in their own work is something new. Because it tells a story and portrays individual leaders, political history has always been the star witness of those who insist that "the historian" moves in a world of purely particularist thinking. This would of course be a logical impossibility. It is equally obvious that no one can make all of his general assumptions explicit. The choice is among degrees of explicitness. The traditional choice, in much historical writing, is to play down explicit statement even of the main organizing ideas. The reasons for this are in part aesthetic. But whatever the reasons may be, Louis Gottschalk, in his editorial summary of this symposium, is of the opinion that the tradition is ripe for reform, that it hinders historians from making their due contribution to the generalizing thought of our time.

The contributors were left free to define their terms as they chose. If the results at times drove their consulting philosopher (Hans Meyerhoff) to offer footnotes of despair, the essays are at least wittier than is the rule in more systematic methodological discussion, and are full of interesting illustrations both of folly and of wisdom. They deal with generalization in many forms: as built into unit "facts," as hypothesis guiding the selection and ordering and re-

---

Reprinted from *Comparative Studies in Society and History* 7, no. 1 (1964): 98–101. A review of Louis Gottschalk, ed., *Generalization in the Writing of History*. Chicago, 1963.

ordering of fact, as classificatory concepts, abstract concepts, as explanation, as statements of observed regularities, and as evaluative criteria both open and concealed. The argument is always for openness as safer, and for borrowing structural concepts that have been well tested in the social sciences as safer than using the home-made variety or doing without any. Not that such borrowing is held up as a panacea for all the ills of historical writing. While there has been under-borrowing in ancient history, in some areas of Chinese history it would almost seem that the concepts outnumber the ascertained facts. These arguments for explicitness and for better communication with the social sciences are perhaps more familiar to the younger generation of historians than the Committee on Historical Analysis supposes. What damps the fledgling is the severe caution of his professional seniors. What might encourage him to spread his wings more boldly would be more examples of the skillful use of bold generalization in new discovery. From this point of view T. C. Cochran's paper on use of the concept of social role, and W. P. Metzger's on national character studies, are the most encouraging. In its scheme and in many of its pages, the book is a monument of caution.

The one sphere in which we would expect historians to be better equipped to generalize than anyone else is that of the processes of long-term change. Here the social sciences, so strong in structural analysis, are weak, for they are not accustomed to examining processes of change in detail over more than short periods, they cannot check their speculative generalizations about the sweep of time. Strangely enough, the book fails to bring out this contrast. M. I. Finley does however take two pages of the brief space allotted him to expose the weakness of the traditional tool for classifying long-term change, that is, the habit of delimiting "periods" solely by reference to changes in political regime. In Roman history, as he shows, these political periods have no connection even with so important a matter as the development of law. It is true that Ibn Khaldun, who was a great pioneering social theorist as well as an historian, found reasons for centering his view of Islamic history around dynastic breaks.[1] But in European history the effort to do so has no theory behind it and is often very forced. The political delimitations are often no more than red ink markings on the chronological measuring tape.

The nineteenth-century philosophical vision of *Geist* introduced a concept of periodization which in its own terms was more meaningful, since the spirit of an age unfolded a given range of cultural potentialities between one time-zone of critical change and another. This view has faded with its philosophy but its legacies are still with us: the still-debated counterpoint of Renaissance and Reformation, the still-debated concept of culture in anthropology, a stimulus to widen the historian's "past"[2] in such a way as to relate politics to the larger scene, and a stimulus to the comparative study of European nations.

The historian who widens his "past" has of necessity to reduce it in depth by sub-periodization. His problems are then at his starting-point defined by his interpretation of work done on the sub-periods preceding his. It is at this point that hidden assumptions may be particularly insidious. One of the purposes of the critical discourse in the professional journals is to ferret them out. The hardest to dislodge have been those contained in the conventional idea of a break between the medieval and the modern, and frozen into a reified ideal type of medieval society or pre-industrial economy. But even this is being modified. The normal give-and-take of professional criticism has been rendered more active in this direction through explicit generalization. For example, Walt Rostow's dramatic revival of "stages" has helped to focus more attention on pre-industrial economic activity. And the formulation of models of modernization and of "traditional society" is helping to bring major historical variants to wider notice.[3]

This brings us to comparative study, which is no longer a matter of European history alone. As several of the contributors to the book have magnificently demonstrated elsewhere, comparative study attracts and nourishes the very kind of vigor that they are advocating. Arthur Wright's paper here on Chinese history raises, from a different angle, the same problem that Marc Bloch encountered in trying to persuade European historians to look beyond national boundaries before making up their minds about supposedly unique characteristics of their country's evolution. Wright observes that the special descriptive terms, or "labeling generalizations," as he calls them, which arise in a given historical tradition "may be based on a complex of assumptions that a people make about themselves and on notions of causation that are embedded in their world-view." Like a fine local wine, the terminology of a particular historical tradition may not travel well. Wright and his commentator, Derk Bodde, reach essentially the same conclusion as Bloch, that the confrontation of different terminologies is useful in obliging the historian to re-examine and re-order his basic facts. In Chinese studies at least four terminologies now contend: the highly complex one of its traditional historiography, the Marxist, the language of the ordinary liberal Western historian, and the systematized language of Talcott Parsons. On the especially contentious issue of feudalism, the ordinary non-Marxist historian himself is not always consistent,[4] nor, if he emphasizes contract and liberty, is he quite free from ideology. If Bloch's own example of reducing feudalism to relations of dependency were followed, their study in differing contexts might lead to fresher generalization.

One of the defences against the argument of this book may conceivably be a sense that historians are doing at least some of the things that are urged on them, and doing them as well as is feasible, on their own steam. Another recent essay, by an historian turned agricultural economist, was certainly less demanding. In *History as a Social Science, an Essay on the Nature and Purpose of Historical Studies,*[5] Folke Dovring proposed that not much can be expected in the way of empirical generalization in history outside the study of "mass phenomena." For the rest, he is charitable. Detailed political narrative may not be of very long-lasting interest, but in its own time may wield immense moral influence. The profession's emphasis on accuracy as a moral duty is thus seen as ample justification. "Take away the historian," says Dovring, "and there will soon be the most fantastic jungle of myths to inspire hatred between peoples and classes; it takes less than Orwellian imagination to grasp the consequence of falsified history." (p. 91)

Yet even on the moral score, *Generalization in the Writing of History* aims to invade the historian's peace of mind. Finley's remarks on the futility of reducing the problem of war in history to the simple one of studying the causes of particular wars (pp. 27–28) can hardly be ignored.

Notes

1. For recent comment on this, see Joseph J. Spengler, "Economic Thought of Islam: Ibn Khaldun," *Comparative Studies in Society and History* 6, no. 3 (1964), esp. pp. 287–93.

2. See J. G. A. Pocock, "The Origins of Study of the Past: a Comparative Approach," *Comparative Studies in Society and History* 4, no. 2 (1962), esp. p. 213.

3. See Robert E. Ward and Dankwart A. Rustow, ed., *Political Modernization in Japan and Turkey* (Princeton, 1964), esp. pp. 464–68.

4. See John W. Hall, "Feudalism in Japan—a Reassessment," *Comparative Studies in Society and History* 5, no. 1 (1962), pp. 15–51, for some discussion of applications of the concept.

5. The Hague, Martinus Nijhoff, 1960.

The Role of Comparison in the
Development of Economic History

Our conference today on comparative economic history is in some danger of rushing into the wide-open spaces of ambiguity, for the term is new, and to agree too quickly on its meaning and implications may not even be desirable. In order to avoid engaging in a mere game of definitions, this paper will deal first with three general types of comparison in relation to their bearing on problems of evidence. It will then review some of the chief uses to which these types of comparison have been put in building up our body of knowledge about Western economic history. The survey will close with particular reference to our own preindustrial stages of economic growth, when western Europe was, in our uncomplimentary phrase, an underdeveloped or backward area.

It may seem superfluous to emphasize that all empirical knowledge, whether of individuality or generality, is contingent on acts of comparison, and becomes relatively more certain as these are extended. We take this experience for granted every day of our lives. For that very reason everyday language is loose and casual in the matter. It tends to focus on one type of comparison alone, that between things that are in some respect identical or in general closely similar. If two things paired for comparison are not very similar, someone will object that they are not comparable. Yet a recognition

Reprinted from "The Role of Comparison in the Development of Economic Theory," *Journal of Economic History* 17 (1957): 554–70.

of extreme difference with regard to a given quality, as, for example, between the climate at the equator and at the North Pole, is accepted as a second type of comparison, one that is sometimes, but not necessarily, distinguished as a contrast. Sometimes the preposition "to" is reserved for the first type, the meaning of "to compare to" being then assimilated to that of the verb "to liken to." The readiest way in which to explain to a child or a foreigner any of the metaphors that enliven poetry and speech would be through using one or other of these. We liken or compare, we might say, the state of a man much vexed *to* that of a live fish in a frying pan. Yet even poetic sensibility makes no flat rule here. To compare "to" and to compare "with" are both used of both the first and second types of comparison, and also of a third type. The third type refers to the range intermediate between close similarity and sharp contrast, in which two things may be somewhat alike in one particular or in one aspect of their total construction, and in others different. It was once sometimes distinguished by the term "to compare together," but this never became mandatory. Any judicious comparison of two complex wholes, for example, two styles in art, or two periods of history, has obviously to be of this third type. I propose to call it intensive comparison.

It is clear that the first type of comparison, between things that are very similar, is helpful both in probing the similarities and in the discovery of slight differences. Yet if we permit our attention to drop anchor here too long, to the neglect of other qualities, comparison of this type may indirectly become a serious source of error. The man who "thought he saw an elephant a-climbing off a bus" discovered his mistake by looking again. The animal was, of course, a hippopotamus. The man, his attention caught by the first similarity that struck him in associating and hence comparing the two species, then went on his way absorbed in worrying about the hippo's large appetite if it should come to dine, to the neglect of other possible dangers in that situation.

Small differences newly discovered or heightened by comparison may likewise ensnare the attention. In the sonnet that begins,

> Shall I compare thee to a summer's day?
> Thou art more lovely and more temperate,

the poet undeniably advanced in knowledge of his love. Yet dwelling on newly appreciated enchantment he failed to notice other qualities that were no less crucial. He perceived these only later through sorrowful experience.

Again, when we use the second type of comparison, distinguishing sharp contrasts, these too are limiting as well as illuminating. The limitations are not only emotional in origin, as in the above examples, but may be cultural. A broad contrast, in particular, may strike one through some cultural prejudice of which one is not even aware.

It may be argued that in the early stage of any branch of knowledge comparison may lead to these kinds of error, but that a cure can always be found through the construction and application of theory. Since the only form of theory that is not itself liable to error consists simply in the logical relations between general propositions, this view would be illusory. Wherever theory is elaborated into propositions calling for empirical verification, it becomes liable to error from many causes, including those that arise from use of that indispensable but tricky tool, comparison. If the natural sciences handle this tool better than we do in the social sciences, it is because of refinement in their working methods. Yet they do not escape error, and they can never long afford to subordinate problems in the handling of evidence to problems in the construction of theory. In the social sciences the chief way of discovering and reducing the kind of error that arises from sporadic comparison of similarities and drawing of contrasts is to extend these to more cases, and preferably to check further by careful comparison of units large enough to permit of intensive comparison.

These conclusions coincide closely with the logical position on which Marc Bloch sought to establish comparative historical study, especially in his own field of interest, that of social structures.[1] The tendency to confine comparisons to the two poles of close similarity and sharp contrast is not confined to those who think in English. Bloch found it ingrained in the thinking of historians in Europe at large and he pointed out that it did not fulfill the proper purposes of comparison in refining our knowledge.

Bloch's conception of comparative history was in part negatively defined. It was emphatically not to be directed by any dogmatic system that would be unresponsive to new findings or would force them into a preconceived design. Nor could it be identified with any single method, such as the genetic method that has worked with such superlative success in historical linguistics. Social forms are essentially too eclectic. The pioneers in comparative history were to be content with creating and testing a set of informed formulations of recurrent problems. In doing so they would gradually dissolve the compartmentalization of historical terminology that had grown up within separate national traditions of scholarship. Analytic and descriptive work, that might otherwise continue to proliferate at cross-purposes, would thus be able to proceed in harmony with the aims of general synthesis. Bloch by no means intended that all historians should engage in writing comparative studies, but only that the progress of these would help to link all social research into an ultimately world-wide co-operative enterprise. The term "comparative history" remained a little ambiguous in that it could apply both to broad synthesis and to the piecemeal studies of related situations out of which synthesis would have to grow.

This program is no longer, in any branch of historical study, revolutionary in outlook. To economic historians, who have always had a common body of theory at their disposal and profess a common allegiance to scientific method, one would expect it to be congenial. Although the title comparative has hardly yet been applied except to works on the comparison of economic systems whose history is relatively short, our accepted body of literature contains examples of comparative history in both Bloch's senses of the term. Many of our textbooks have aimed at synthesis, and the German concept of *Weltwirtschaft* is directed to the same end through study of the spatial expansion of interrelated market forces. Also we have a number of monographs and articles that have sought to apply as rigorously as possible the method of controlled comparison. Some of these are pieces of intensive comparison of large units, as in John Nef's work on France and England. There are also two other ways in which comparison enters our work, and with these we may be less satisfied. Many writers indulge in sporadic comparisons at random, and some use stereotyped comparisons to buttress their premises or their conclusions. In this connection I am reminded that in Middle English one meaning of the word compare, or "compere," was "to buy." One might say that such writers "compere" their comparisons, much as they buy other products of the mass media.

What, then, does our current interest in the term comparative signify? How deep does it go? Our resistances to extending the scope of comparison are at the moment weakened by the pressures that are flying economists all over the world as consultants and driving them pell-mell into study of the so-called underdeveloped countries. But are we simply excited, as every generation has been, over writing the new chapter on contemporary affairs?

To put the question more bluntly, do we now want a fresh label on the old bottle merely to smarten it up? Does the adding of a few fingers of new material from the Dead Sea or the Congo, or even from the Volga, really call for a new label? Or are we learning so much from the experience of more intensive comparison with new regions as to be ready to re-examine our old accepted materials by more intensive comparison up and down the centuries? In that event, but only in that event, we may look forward to making the whole contents of the bottle a better brew. The prospect is challenging, and to many it may appear alarming in its magnitude. For as a survey of the record will show, the comparisons we have drawn are seldom organized by reference to economic theory alone, but derive also from differing social philosophies and from philosophies of history.

II

This point may be made most clearly by going back two hundred years to Adam Ferguson. In his *Essay on the History of Civil Society*, first published in 1757, he examined the stock of broad inter-cultural comparisons that his age had accumulated, with an eye to bringing them under a consistent interpretation. Although he professed to be "not much conversant" with political economy, he paid particular attention to the relation of economic life to other aspects of civilization.

Ferguson was dubious of most other writers' principles of organization, which he found often inadequately squaring with the facts. "We are loth to be embarrassed by a multiplicity of particulars," he observed, "and in order to bring the matter of our inquires within the reach of our comprehension, are disposed to adopt any system."[2] For a preliminary trial run of the data available from his reading, he adopted the principle of man's propensity to social union, and then developed this into a theory of constant interaction between man and his environment. Provided that the natural environment presented some challenge, but not too stiff a one, society itself became the decisive environmental factor.[3]

At this point he felt obliged to attack both the prevailing philosophies of history, that of progress and the cyclical theory. Study of the rise and collapse of Rome, which was his major scholarly preoccupation, prevented him from believing in unilinear progress, except as regards technology, and he was sharply critical of those who argued from biological analogy that every civilization must necessarily decline. Although he found the latter to be a "general apprehension," he exposed the argument as fallacious both on rational grounds[4] and by factual demonstration. Small nations, in which for sociological reasons the spirit of democracy was likely to escape the creeping political apathy that overtook the Roman Empire, seldom declined.[5] Apathy or corruption overtook India and China only as a form of acquiescence in repeated subjection to new conquerors.[6]

In attributing decline to apathy, Ferguson expressed a belief that this could be prevented not only by statesmen encouraging institutions that would have this effect[7] but through intelligent self-interest. As an epicure consults a physician to learn how to restore failing appetites, he "might at least with an equal regard to himself, consult how he might strengthen his affection to a parent or a child, to his country or to mankind."[8]

Again, Ferguson held that except insofar as the worship of money in a democracy constituted a danger to public spirit, the economy had no part in the process of decline. He believed production and trade under the Romans to have been depressed below their potential maximum by unwise policies in taxation and by monopolies, but he did not see in them any inherent tendency to decline.[9] And although he regarded the barbarian conquest as catastrophic for Western civilization in general, including its economic life, he did not find that conquest necessarily had this effect. He gave India the credit for the earliest development of manufacture and com-

merce and noted the continuance there of "opulent cities" undis-
turbed by military conquests.[10] As to the Chinese, he applauded
them for still holding the world record, after some thousands of
years' application, for hard work.[11]

The development of classical economics brought two changes of
perspective. In the first place, Ferguson's hardheaded criticism of
prevailing philosophies of history somehow dropped below the horizon. Adam Smith's stress on education as an object of public policy
was but a pale reflection of the hope that man might learn in some
measure to control his destiny. Instead of Ferguson's critical social-
environmental theory, Smith adopted the pessimistic a priori cyclical
theory. Instead of being prepared to distinguish between economic
development on the one hand and political history or the course of a
civilization on the other, he assimilated the two; in sketching the
outlines of economic progress he had in mind its inevitable cessation.
Playfair, filling out the picture with his comparative chronological
charts, felt that Britain might perhaps escape the general fate of
nations through one accident and one policy. The accident, or god-
send, was the American market. The policy was vegetarianism, as a
means of preserving the national vigor. The high wartime prices of
bread and meat should be perpetuated, and care taken to ensure an
abundant supply of cheap vegetables.[12] Finally, Ricardo's ingenious
working of stagnation and decay into his system of principles left the
road wide open for Comte and Marx to ride as heroes to the rescue
of a humanity otherwise recurrently doomed.

To the adherents of the new orthodoxy in the generation following Ricardo, comparison was less a research tool than a means of em-
bellishing argument on matters of which they were already certain.
The world was a racecourse, with the British horse out in front. Bet-
ting on other Western entries depended on their governments' commercial policies. There were no bets on Eastern entries, which
shortly after starting had all lost interest in the race and gone to
sleep.

The romantics kept the same frame of reference, with a reversal
of values as between progress and immobility. Since they idealized
the latter and wished to check the spread of the new ideas among
landowners, they lodged their contrast with Britain not in the Far
East but in the Western feudal age. Immediately after Jena the

agrarian aristocrat Adam Müller began his long campaign to rally his class about the notion that it had always stood for the true interests of the people, as these were summed up in stable, *Gemeinschaftliche*, personal relationships.[13] *Burgerliche Gesellschaft* had been a ghastly mistake ever since medieval townsmen first ventured beyond petty local trade. It had no sense of community save through the market, no achievement save through debt, no guide but the slogan "Money is power." Adam Smith, a man as deluded as Faust, was nothing but its oracle. The polemic was of a kind that dispenses with evidence, yet contrives somehow to convey the impression that all the evidence is on the right side. The comparison that Müller established, identifying the feudal age with economic immobility, was of profound disservice to economic history. Its discouragement of study of the early influence of market forces was reinforced by his reputation as an economist. Borrowing Lauderdale's distinction between public and private economy, he restricted his attention to the former. This alone, he held, concerned itself with true wealth, which did not consist in commodities. Public policy, rather than individual decisions in relation to the market, therefore caught the highlight. Müller's perception of the basic antinomy between *Gemeinschaft* and *Gesellschaft*, serviceable though this may have been to sociology,[14] was also, in the setting he gave it, of disservice to economic history. The middle ages, brimming with *Gemeinschaft*, became a dream shop for reformers from Carlyle to the Guild Socialists.[15] While the middle ages were thus theatrically oversimplified, the succeeding centuries, especially the sixteenth, were correspondingly overcomplicated, having to answer for most of the innovations that made a market economy possible and habituated the people to trade and enterprise.

In proportion as they were free from romantic influence, the historical economists made comparison a genuine research tool. In Germany their movement grew naturally out of the interests of the cameralists and was at first free of the intellectual imperialism that afflicted it later. Common to all the participants here was a desire to set the new economic developments of the nineteenth century in a general evolutionary scheme into which somehow or other all mankind could be fitted. In 1830 G. F. Krause triumphantly compressed world economic history, which, as he pointed out, had never been written before, into sixty small pages. He stated the general thesis that production is dependent on the state of culture quite as clearly as Cliffe Leslie did in 1876.[16]

The bent to comparison arose partly from enthusiasm over the advances that other studies were making through various forms of comparative method. The latter appealed even to those who were interested mainly in contemporary Western progress. Karl Heinrich Rau, for example, who launched the first journal of economic history, the *Archiv der politische Oekonomie und Polizeiwissenschaft*, at Heidelberg in 1835, was much intrigued by the new science of comparative anatomy. In his first volume he ran an announcement of the foundation of the Statistical Society in Saxony under the heading *Comparative Statistics*, adding an editorial comment that the aim of the society was probably drawn from the example of comparative anatomy. As this had deepened knowledge of developmental stages in the animal kingdom, so comparative statistics, dealing with different territorial states, would illuminate differences in social conditions.[17] The *Archiv*, which was issued irregularly until 1853, was amiably eclectic. It discussed current contributions to theory and applications of it, reached out as far as the Phillippines for statistical material on the problem of population growth, and carried a classification of historical forms of colonization policies, contributed by Roscher.[18] One general aim was to reduce misunderstanding over the meaning of theoretical terms by applying them to concrete situations.[19] In respect of comparative economic history the aims were conservative. The function of the journal was to assemble data that would aid comparative study of a limited set of problems, drawn chiefly from cameralist tradition, within the historically related contexts of the western European states since the seventeenth century. There was a cautious sifting of evidence that came preferably from official statistical sources.

Mingled with the influence of natural science was that of the historical jurists; indeed, von Below regarded the entire school of historical economics as simply an offshoot of the juristic school.[20] Although this influence was heavily loaded with Adam Müller's romanticism, it became progressively an incentive to research and comparison.

The same influences were at work, more feebly, in England. Rau's contemporary Richard Jones called on the example of physical science as an inspiration to patient study of statistical material and the use of the methods of controlled comparison. His irritation with the Ricardians was couched in terms of their neglect of these methods. He was aware of the work of the German jurists, and his study of peasant tenures, undertaken to demonstrate his belief that the Ricardian premise of the mobility of labor and capital was virtually inapplicable outside England and France, ended with emphasis on the legal factors in economic development; it introduced no new economic concepts. It is unfortunate that Jones was simply a robust English dilettante, fond of offering advice but lacking even the desire for Rau's solid erudition. For evidence on peasant conditions he was content to rely on Todd's work for India and for the rest on travelers' reports, which, as Marshall observed, give too thin a thread of information to support rounded conclusions.[21] He never took the trouble to master the techniques of documentary historical research, merely exhorting "scholars and antiquaries," a breed apart that he had no wish to join, to dig for "unsunned treasure."[22]

A third stimulus to comparative study was the comparative method being developed by the historical linguists, which carried a particularly exciting appeal to Anglo-Saxon racial pride and to all who were drawn to organic social philosophy as this was embodied in the romantic concept of the *Volk*. The story of the quest for the *Ureigentum*, intended to parallel the quest for the *Ursprache* and the Aryan *Urvolk*, would fill a large display case in any museum exhibit of the errors of social science. Hanssen,[23] who became a co-editor of Rau's *Archiv*, was a participant, and Bruno Hildebrand ran an article on the economic and social life of the *Urvolk* in the first issue of his *Jahrbuch*, which in 1863 picked up the work of the defunct *Archiv*. Roscher was long reluctant to recognize the errors that his colleagues were committing.[24] These were due to leaping at apparent similarities, conceived as analogous phases in the evolution of the institution of property, without intensive comparison, and without the aid of the structural check on the evidence which was the secret of the historical linguists' ultimate success.

A fourth stimulus to comparative study arose from the wish to cut up the scheme of evolution into clearly differentiated stages that would be capable of arrangement in a logical progression of universal validity. Here again, as in the quest for the original form of property, the historical economists set themselves a wild-goose chase.

The romantic thought under whose sway they had grown up had itself made the problem insoluble by emphasizing, in its play with the
Chain of Being, the root of all Western thought on evolution, the
principle of the infinitely growing richness and diversification of the
universe. As Lovejoy has put it, there is then necessarily "at every
point an abrupt passage to something different, and there is no
purely logical principle determining—out of all the infinitely various
'possible' kinds of differentness—which shall come next."[25]

In the circumstances, what is surprising about Roscher is not
that he became involved in some confusion in stating his principles
but that he clung to a sound basis for comparative study, thus doing
more than anyone else to preserve it from the discredit with which
misuse of the genetic comparative method of the anatomists and the
linguists, and the more absurd forms of the theory of stages, threatened to overwhelm it. More than anything else, his passion for statistical information helped to keep him on a sound course. He collected this from his vast reading as a bee collects honey, or as J. C.
Frazer collected stray items of mythology. Unlike Frazer, however,
he fitted the pieces not into any novel framework but into one whose
lines coincided at least in part with those laid down by Adam Smith.
His "parallelisms"—generalizations through comparison—were restricted in the main to the Western states since the seventeenth century, when statistical material begins to be more readily available.

III

Nevertheless the reputation of comparative study hung precariously
in the balance in the new era that may be reckoned as opening, with
the spread of the influence of German scholarship to France and
England, in the 1870's. Rigorous documentary research then became
the prerequisite for any academically acceptable historical writing.[26]
Comparisons were drawn inevitably, but were often implicit, without deliberate use as a research tool and therefore without control.
The chief subject of generalization, and the chief means to deliberate comparison, was the period. The period was analogous to the
concept of culture in twentieth-century anthropology, often in part
intuitively apprehended, although not necessarily so. Like cultures,
each period as a whole was conceived as essentially different, so that
some concept of evolution was necessary as a guard against extreme

relativism. Many men who lived on into the twentieth century still held to the twist that romantic philosophy had given evolutionary thought. To them, alike in economic as well as political history, the work of the historian consisted simply in tracing the manifold diversity of events, institutions, and ideas. As such it was an art. Scrupulous criticism of the evidence was at the same time sufficient to make it scientific.

On the other hand were those whom von Below styled the *Systematiker*,[27] who drew from historical evidence only what would fit their notion of well-defined stages, sometimes conceived as analogous to physical or chemical states of equilibrium. To some this alone was scientific. The study of process, of how events occurred or how institutions changed, except insofar as it could be caught in the pincers of the Marxian dialectic, was not. Marxian influence was so strong in sociological quarters that stages, if not taken directly from the Communist Manifesto, were at least primarily economic. Rickert's distinction between science and history came to both the historians of the research guild and the systematizers as a boon, since neither side wished to be associated with the other. The latter were delighted to decide that study of how one stage turned into another could safely be disregarded as unscientific, since it led only into essentially unique detail. Although Rickert's views adequately describe only the extreme relativist position, which denied the utility of any comparison between one period and another, a position which no historian ever held consistently, they have remained one of the sacred cows of sociology.

The wave of polemic over historical method that ensued did much, by setting up discussion over the role of generalization in history, to loosen the hold of romantic philosophy. But it could do so only to the extent that viable analytic concepts and theory, capable of promoting and controlling comparative study in widening empirical spheres, were at hand. Preindustrial economic history in particular was so poorly served in this regard that it remained the last stronghold of romanticism. In all fields the chief constructive stimulus came from legal history, whose journals of comparative study date in France from 1855, in Germany from 1878. The new schools of national economic history that grew up under Roscher's leadership were strongest in their legal aspect.

The charge that the new schools of economic history neglected economic theory is correct, but only because the theory available was of limited use. Ashley's statement to this effect in 1907 was certainly not based on ignorance.[28] The economists in turn had the same attitude toward history, which they regarded as useful only as it could illustrate, in static situations or short-term monetary and market movements, points of general theory. John Neville Keynes, writing in 1890, preferred to restrict his horizon to the previous hundred years, which could offer the best illustrations of current economic theories. Earlier economic history, he added, could be equally important, but only insofar as it would also illustrate through price movements the theory of values and the working of competition.[29] Marshall takes us no farther. It is true that Keynes admitted the possibility of new generalization, based, if need be, on other abstractions than that of economic man, through classification of historical frictions interfering with competition.[30] The point was suggestive, but no theoretical lead was forthcoming. Any medieval peasant who ever sold a cow could have told the historian as much or more about the forces of supply and demand as was to be learned from nineteenth-century theory. So far as the economists were effectively concerned, the preindustrial world was but a jungle suburb to their own small ordered city, a slum where only sentimental antiquaries and anthropologists would seriously think of operating. Even the contemporary part of the suburb was not of much interest, for the city would shortly here effect a slum clearance. Richard Jones himself in 1833 had assumed that the rest of the world would in time follow France and England into industrialism, and the process had soon appeared to be daily accelerating.

By far the most genuinely historically minded of the economists, and to my knowledge the first scholar among them to face the need of explaining all possible consequences of all forms of exploitation of resources, as the task of theory, was Knies. But Knies, feeling his way to the position that economic life depends on the sum total of all the regulative norms, legal and moral, written and unwritten, by which social life in general is ordered, passed the ball to sociology rather than to his contemporaries in economics.[31] Moreover, he did so without firmly attaching the condition that the complex equilibrium among these regulative norms, and change in it, be the focus of study. To be fruitful, comparative study of regulative norms has to go very deeply into the evidence, permitting it, in Marshall's phrase, to cross-examine itself; otherwise the possibilities of error are boundless. While Max Weber's campaign for greater objectivity through the refining of general concepts into ideal types was recognized as a major contribution, his popularizing of Knies's emphasis on the role of religion in shaping the sanctions of economic activity yet in practice led many, for lack of sufficient awareness of the unwritten norms, and of the coexistence of positive and negative sanctions, into as crude an interpretation of the medieval phases of preindustrial economy as any pre-Weberian romantic could have produced.

IV

Comparative study has therefore made most headway along the lines that Roscher and his predecessors pioneered, that is, in the modern history of the Western nations. Instead of writing of parallels and analogies, terms that Roscher preferred as indicating that his discoveries did not exemplify invariant law, we write of types or patterns of industrialization or of long waves. This change of terminology indicates a shift of interest from institutional morphology to a general desire to understand how capital growth occurs, and it requires much more intensive use of more kinds of evidence, evidence of individual decisions as well as of aggregate advances. Yet our concepts are not yet linked into any single generally accepted theory of growth. The demand for such a theory is perhaps largely motivated by the desire to give our work more aesthetic elegance and ourselves the prestige of philosophers, always an aid in the classroom. At all events, an elegantly formulated theory of growth seems more likely to come at the end of a long new phase of comparative research than as a preface to it.

No theory of growth will represent much of an advance unless it attempts the task that Knies tried to pose, that of dealing with all forms of exploitation of resources. The preindustrial obtrudes on us now not only in the far past, which those who are culture-bound in the present can so readily dismiss, but as contemporary phenomena that may or may not yield everywhere to the system with which theory has traditionally dealt. The reactions of contemporary pre-

industrial men not being predictable, it is now obligatory to do more
than subsume their economies under the single rubric of "static." In
the circumstances it may become feasible to link new research in
the two vast areas of the modern and the historic preindustrial
through discussion of general problems that arise in common, and
thereby to avoid some duplications of effort.

In rounding this review to a close a few brief illustrations may
be drawn from points on which comparative study within western
Europe is advancing knowledge of our own medieval phase of pre-
industrial economy, points which have their analogies elsewhere.
They do not fit into a pattern of straightforward growth but into a
long slow climb in total production, population, and trade, reaching
its peak in the thirteenth century, followed by a century or more of
regression. The nature of this pattern was first disclosed by comparative study of the economic activity of the larger towns. Decline in
their trade and population, however, does not measure the exact
amplitude of the change, for this was accompanied by migrations
and by new diffusions and concentrations of trade. The search for an
explanation of the change therefore drives us back to the little market town and the village household, whose responses to conditions
favorable or hostile to the maintenance of family units, to the increase of production for the market, to an increase of consumption
or of saving, and to innovations of any kind, now become of more
significance than was formerly recognized and require much further
comparative study. In this connection research in the modern peasant economies, especially in regard to the extent of production for
the market, the bases of credit, and the growth of wants, is of great
interest to a medievalist. Particularly remarkable is the circumstance
that the same type of initial error may occur both among historians
working from records and among observers of a living scene. An example comes from Peter Bauer's correction of his predecessors' work
on Nigeria, which had so greatly underestimated the role of trade
and individual economic calculation in that economy.[32] Bauer's remarks on the natural ubiquity of these could be echoed even in many
rural parts of fourteenth-century England, which was a relatively
backward area of medieval Europe, and then in a phase of regression. The pervasiveness of the habit of trade was not always realized, since it finds no place in the series of land surveys, on the

model of the Domesday Book, on which historians first leaned for their information on agrarian life, but it appears clearly enough in court records.

Discovery of the ubiquity of trade in a peasant economy appears to sharpen the problem of why there is not more accumulation of capital from its profit and skills. Medieval study would suggest that this question may be posed too impatiently. The overhead of government, the construction and upkeep of the physical plant of towns, the disposition of animal power for land transport, not to mention the squandering of resources in war, in every medieval area represented so many preliminary burdens that tended to increase more rapidly than basic agricultural production, and that, once institutionalized, could not readily be reduced when production fell. In such a situation it is unnecessary to lay the blame for lack of new business or industrial enterprise on lack of skill; what is lacking is a market large enough to sustain innovations in this direction. Where a market was in sight, through medieval military ventures or the needs of ecclesiastical or political government, flexible enterprise sprang up readily enough.

The late medieval economy obviously offers no answer as to how a vicious circle of stagnation can break into rapid advance. It does, however, show widespread response to any potential market for better food, in the form of meat and especially for beer. Confronted with fewer choices than the modern African, the medieval consumer voted overwhelmingly for these. Study of the brewing industry as a source of accumulation of capital has been neglected.

Nor can the medieval economy as a whole be drawn into comparison with any backward area that is subject to the new population pressures, which are unprecedented in history. To lead to valid conclusions, comparison must be of problems capable of isolation in contexts that are being studied intensively. The same technique can be extended to the postmedieval preindustrial centuries.[33]

v

It is by no means the intent of this paper to advocate the indiscriminate use of comparative study in all forms of problems. One could indeed argue from the record that while it remained the ruling passion, up to the last quarter of the nineteenth century, it accomplished very little in what now appears to be the central task of economic history, that of accounting for the existence or nonexistence of growth, and for the varying rates at which increase of per capita capital may occur, and that far more progress was made in this direction later through intensive study of isolated national or regional cases. The reason for this, however, lies in the philosophies of history that made most nineteenth-century comparativists beg the question of growth, in the limited use that they made of continuous series of documentary evidence, and in their consequent frequent failure to identify the agencies that were responsible for new turns of development.

At the same time it has to be admitted that the study of isolated cases in time exposes itself to a high risk of assuming that a certain situation which may be quite atypical is typical. We are now becoming so hypersensitive to this danger that, for better or for worse, the next generation is likely to be wedded to comparative study in the hope of finding in it a sure prophylactic. Such a hope, if it became overconfident, if "loth to be embarrassed by a multiplicity of particulars," it snatched at systems based on cursory leaping at apparent similarities and contrasts without intensive study, could be an even greater danger. Deliberate intensive comparison is the best insurance we can have against the tendency of our minds so to leap.

NOTES

1. This summary of Bloch's views is based on his long series of critical reviews in the journal that he and Lucien Febvre founded in 1929, now known as the *Annales,* and on his article on comparative history, published in the *Revue de Synthèse,* 1928 and translated in Lane and Riemersma, *Enterprise and Secular Change* (Homewood, Illinois: Richard D. Irwin, Inc., 1953), pp. 494–521.

2. Adam Ferguson, An *Essay on the History of Civil Society* (1783), Part I, Sec. III.

3. *Ibid.,* Part III, Sec. 1.

4. *Ibid.,* Part V, Sec. I.

5. *Ibid.,* Part III, Sec. II.

6. *Ibid.,* Part III, Sec. I.

7. *Ibid.*, Part V, Sec. III.

8. *Ibid.*, Part I, Sec. II.

9. Adam Ferguson, *The History of the Progress and Termination of the Roman Republic*, Book VI, ch. ii.

10. Adam Ferguson, *Civil Society*, Part II, Sec. I.

11. *Ibid.*, Part V, Sec. III.

12. William Playfair, *An Inquiry into the Permanent Causes of the Decline and Fall of Powerful and Wealthy Nations* (London, 1805); cf. H. Grossman, "William Playfair, the Earliest Theorist of Capitalist Development," *Ec. Hist. Rev.*, XVIII (1948), 65–83.

13. Adam Müller, *Ausgewählte Abhandlungen*, ed. Jakob Baxa, 2d. ed. (Jena: Gustav Fischer, 1931), *passim*, especially, *Agronomische Briefe* (1812), pp. 134–87. Also *Vorlesungen über die deutsche Wissenschaft und Literatur*, 2d. ed. (Dresden: 1807), especially the *zweite Vorlesung*.

14. Tönnies declared that he evolved these concepts in 1887 from reflection on the older political theorists. See his "Entwicklung der Soziologie in Deutschland im 19 Jahrhundert," in *Die Entwicklung der deutschen Volkswirtschaftslehre* (Schmoller Festschrift, Leipzig: Duncker and Humblot), ch. xiv, p. 36.

15. See Aldous Huxley's essay, "The Future of the Past," in *Music at Night* (Garden City, N. Y.: Garden City Press, 1931).

16. G. F. Krause, *Versuch eines Systems der National- und Staatsökonomie* (2 vols., Leipzig: 1830); cf. T. E. C. Leslie, *Essays in Political and Moral Philosophy* (London: Longmans Green, 1879), pp. 216–50.

17. Rau, *Archiv*, I, 54–7.

18. W. Roscher, "Untersuchungen über das Colonialwesen," *Archiv der politische Oekonomie und Polizeiwissenschaft*, N. F., Bd. 6–7 (1847–48), pp. 1–80, 1–43.

19. K. H. Rau, "Ueber den Nutzen, den gegenwartigen Zustand, und die neuste Literatur der National-Oekonomie," *Archiv*, I (1835), 1–42.

20. Georg von Below, *Die deutsche Geschichtschreibung von den Befreiungskriegen bis zu unseren Tagen* (Leipzig: E. Meyer, 1916), p. 16.

21. A. C. Pigou, *Memorials of Alfred Marshall* (London: Macmillan, 1925), p. 168; Richard Jones, *An Essay on the Distribution of Wealth* (London: 1831); reprinted 1895 as *Peasant Rents*.

22. Richard Jones, *Literary Remains*, ed. W. Whewell (London: 1859), p. 571.

23. G. von Below, "Das kurze Leben einer viel genannten Theorie," in *Probleme der Wirtschaftsgeschichte* (Tubingen: J. C. B. Mohr, 1920), pp. 1–26.

24. G. von Below, "Das kurze Leben. . . ," p. 13.

25. Arthur O. Lovejoy, *The Great Chain of Being* (Cambridge: Harvard University Press, 1936), p. 332.

26. See M. F. Bond, "Record Offices Today, Facts for Historians," *Bulletin of the Institute of Historical Research*, XXX (May 1957), 1–16.

27. G. von Below, "Das kurze Leben . . . ," p. 23.

28. W. J. Ashley, "The Present Position of Political Economy in England," *Schmoller Festschrift*, ch. xv (n. 14).

29. J. N. Keynes, *The Scope and Method of Political Economy* (London: 1891), pp. 256 ff.

30. *Ibid.*, p. 114.

31. Karl Knies, *Die politischen Oekonomie vom geschichtlichen Standpunkte* (2d ed., of 1883, reprinted by Buske, Leipzig: 1930), pp. 126–56.

32. P. T. Bauer, *West African Trade* (Cambridge: The University Press, 1954).

33. See F. J. Fisher, "The Sixteenth and Seventeenth Centuries: The Dark Ages in English Economic History?" *Economica*, n.s., XXIV (Feb. 1957), 2–18.

History and Sociology: New Opportunities for Cooperation

While taking an inventory of what history and sociology may have to offer each other, it is pertinent to ask in what context there is likely to be any strong demand for the offerings. The ideal context would be one of pure rationality. There, if history be defined as the search for a synthesis of human experience as reflected in the course of events including the propagation of ideas, and sociology as the search for regularity, for structure, in human relations, we would co-operate actively both in methodological advance and in empirical comparative studies. It would be evident that, since regular types of structure—families, communities—are actors in events, and since events affect their structure, we should all be both historians and so-ciologists, divided only by our individual decisions to specialize in one period or aspect of human experience. The question of what the one discipline has to offer the other would then be seen as identical with that of ordering our individual reasoning processes, or co-ordi-nating more happily, as it were, the right hand with the left, and also, as separately organized right-handed and left-handed profes-sions, through comparing and sifting the variety of our findings.

The context is not, however, one of pure rationality. The com-plex structure of academic life in which we are held requires much

Reprinted from "History and Sociology: New Opportunities for Co-operation," *American Journal of Sociology* 63, no. 1 (1957): 11–16. A paper prepared for a panel on "History and Sociology: What Can They Learn from Each Other?" at the session on "Sociological Study of Histori-cal Documents" at the annual meeting of the American Sociological As-sociation at Detroit, September 7, 1956.

else. Departmental solidarities build themselves around tradition, prestige, rivalry, personalities, and temperament. One may often marvel that rational reflection can proceed at all in this atmosphere of side shows and fireworks. Yet methodological discussion thrives, wherever it has encouragement, and is making headway. It is the second or auxiliary step, the promotion of empirical comparative study, that lags. How this step in turn may find encouragement is the theme of this paper, which seeks to locate the chief obstacles and to map a way around them.

Perhaps the most lethal obstacle is the proselytizing spirit. The terms in which our topic today has been cast, as to how we may learn from each other, leans a little dangerously in that direction. For the proposition that history and sociology may learn from each other is perennially attractive to those who look forward less to learning than to instructing and converting. On one side is a sincerely rooted feeling that whatever may once have been interesting about the dead inevitably dies with them, that written records can be of little use until a uniform system of record-keeping is instituted by social scientists, and that the tendency of historians to be preoccupied with individual experience and achievement, or even with the working of particular institutions at particular times, is unscientific, a waste of life. It follows that whoever still insists on digging into the past should at least work to establish laws of human development. On the other side there are some who feel that sociologists would be better occupied in reading history than in poking questionnaires through keyholes. Admittedly, expression of these feelings is seldom more than semiserious. Like the ponderous verses in which fifteenth-century professors of law and medicine would revile each other as thieves and butchers, they relieve the solemnities of academic routines. Yet behind them is a distrust that hinders co-operation.

To some extent distrust may be allayed by the fuller understanding of the present division of labor between us that methodology is gradually developing. For instance, that long-chewed bone, the issue of the intellectual superiority of a search for regularity, pattern, law, rather than for the particular shape of events and their sequence, is surely by now overripe for burial. The classic distortion of the contrast between science and history that identified them, respectively, with pure generality and pure particularity, and so with the giant growth of natural science, played to sociology's need, as a relative newcomer, for a family affiliation and prestige, is now coming to be modified by admission of the necessary interpenetration and interdependence, in all types of scientific and historical work, of both generalizing and descriptive activity. Economic historians, most of whom now have some theoretical training and have therefore bifocal points of view, have contributed helpful analyses,[1] but there is still no general appreciation of the diversity of methods that are employed by those working historians who first deploy fresh historical fact. The examples in so recent a treatise as Patrick Gardiner's,[2] supposedly to illustrate the role of generalization in historical writing, are drawn almost exclusively from broad moralizing treatments of well-known phases of political history; they bear no relation to the role of generalizing hypothesis in historical research. As one philosopher, Isaiah Berlin, who is also an intellectual historian, has lately remarked, "The 'logic' of various human studies has been insufficiently examined, and a convincing account of its varieties, with an adequate range of concrete examples drawn from actual practice, is much to be desired."[3]

Distrust arises also from the differences in outlook that correspond to the differing demands made on our professions. It is the age-old business of historians to create and maintain a sense of continuity within the larger units of social life, and to do so in a lively and dramatic fashion. They grow dull on pain of losing their market to novelists and journalists. All schools of Western history save the Marxist have met this demand by exalting the individual as actor, whether in heroic endeavor or in antisocial disturbance.

The public imposes on sociologists a contrary bias. They are paid to exalt the group, to work for the damping-down of all such individual vagaries, no matter how dramatic, as may be inconvenient to the group. Like medical columnists who expound rules for healthful living, they are looked to for advice on how to bring delinquent juveniles, drug addicts, the unhappily married, and criminals into conformity with current norms of adjustment. This practical concern with predictability, and with limited forms of social engineering, makes them feel at home with doctrines of social determinism.

There is here a potential clash between us, since non-Marxist historians cannot tolerate doctrines of determinism. They regard them as distasteful, unproved, and as symptoms of confusion. It must be realized that in doing so they project them on a far wider stage and take a far more rigid and thoroughgoing view of the matter than many sociologists do, who may feel no need to think further ahead than statistical projection leads. As to the wider stage, those who are accustomed to think primarily in terms of structure and to be uninterested in more than the broad trend of events may see no reason why changes in structure should not be determined or at least roughly predictable with increasing degrees of exactitude. For the historian, since there is interaction between event and structure, determinism would have to apply to both. Valid predictability could never be established for structure alone without reference to the course of events. It might appear to hold, yet reference to events would be bound to show that the explanation involved was in some respects incomplete or mistaken.

Controversy in this area has latterly been warming up, with Berlin and Bock exchanging charges of confusion and timidity.[4] The more heat that can be generated the better, provided only that some of it can be converted into research energy. For none of the key positions is well supported by empirical demonstration. Historians cannot reject the predictability of structural trends on logical grounds alone. Their skepticism is based in part on encounters in the course of research with numerous cases of unexpected innovation or with rapid changes in the form or function of institutions that could not have been predicted from a knowledge of their structure. Knowledge of this kind is haphazard; there has been no attempt, yet, to make it systematic.

Where, then, can we best look for common ground on which to test our differing views and doubts? At present there is no great overlap in the type of problems that we choose for research. Historians' knowledge of most of the matters to which the modern sociologist's interest in conformity and psychological adjustment directs him is slight and chaotic, and the majority of sociologists have shown only occasional interest in the national political structures to which historians have devoted so much labor.

One area that is promising, for the reason that we are both strong in it without claiming infallibility, is that concerning the fundamental problems of social stratification. Sociologists have a long lead in the relevant techniques of sampling and measurement and in the practice, essential here because of conflicts in the prevailing theories, of making at least one's major premises explicit. Comparability can thus be insured and controlled. In this connection the codification of basic elements of contemporary social theory by the Parsons school is of great initial service. A member of this school, Bernard Barber, is already breaking the path to which this paper points by co-ordinating a volume of studies of social stratification, being written by historians, set in different centuries. Work such as this, especially when it can be linked with new demographic research and with studies of the influence of different forms of family grouping and of law and custom relating to inheritance, can very substantially extend our knowledge of social systems.

Sociologists, still leading from their own areas of strength, could further offer theoretical analyses and model empirical studies of the more important of the problems of social control that they investigate in the contemporary scene. There would be no difficulty in finding social historians to probe situations illustrating comparable problems and in tracing historical changes in the policies by which they were handled. The results would find an interested audience among legal and political historians and historians of social philosophy. For the argument by which political historians, in particular, criticize sociological generalizations—that structural trends cannot be projected without reference to events—cuts both ways. Any full understanding of the course of events depends on a clear view of the structure of social relationships. In the field of medieval studies this has long been accepted as axiomatic.

There is no question that able sociologists are eager to promote such forms of comparative study. A start has been made. They can hardly, however, be expected to exert the long effort that will be required to produce results on any very impressive scale without moral support from their own profession. An audience of historians is not enough. Yet will the average sociologist join the audience? Will he be afraid, if he is seen reading a journal of "Comparative

Studies in Society and History," of being thought unscientific, anti-
quarian, a deviant in his profession, maladjusted? Positive and plausible reasons may be given for ignoring the new type of enterprise.
Knowledge of a single society, it will be urged, is sufficient for the
perception of regularity in human affairs and for a fair sampling of
their basic forms. Again, given the variety of the American scene, it
is only by long concentration on special problems that sociologists
can usefully advise policy-making agencies in the manner expected
of them.

Despite the truth of these assertions, sociologists cannot honestly say that they deal only with the contemporary scene and its special problems. In their capacity as university teachers they discourse
on society in general. The illustrations in their elementary texts and
introductory courses are culled freely in space and time. But whereas
there is scrupulous care for the accuracy of information taken from
research reports on contemporary matters, there is little or no concern to verify, by reference to works of up-to-date scholarship, the
accuracy of such information given as purports to relate to the past.
Statements abound that are pseudo-historical, that have as little contact with fact as a ballet dancer with earth.

We are here faced with a very obstinate tradition that tends to
be self-perpetuating. Students brought up on such a diet naturally
believe, out of loyalty and self-interest, that it is the best available.
To persuade them that historical material can ever rival, in depth of
suggestive detail, the content of a questionnaire or interview report
is next to impossible. Most are unable to look into historical data,
for their training has never required them to do so. At best they will
look into translated extracts from the writings of Max Weber but
probably without realizing that even Weber's powerful mind was
poorly informed as to oriental societies and that, in every field he
touched, a half-century of fresh research has supervened since he
thought out his classic generalizations.

To a lesser degree, a similar situation has ruled in American
anthropology. Here, however, antihistorical prejudice arose out of
the extreme difficulties of reconstructing the histories of preliterate
peoples. Now that some of these difficulties are being surmounted,
the prejudice is in full retreat. The new journal, *Ethno-History,* is
founded on realization that much misinterpretation has crept into

North American ethnology through neglect of historical interaction between Indian and white and is devoted to correcting the perspective.

If it may be shown that misinterpretations creep into structural studies through too summary dismissal of historical influences, perhaps a parallel appeal would find a hearing among American sociologists; the lengthening time perspective that they are inheriting as one academic generation succeeds another is preparing the way. It is implicit in a number of revisions of previously accepted theory; for example, in the revision of theories that too sharply differentiated urban and rural structures and attitudes. The new stress on the persistence in each of similar elements of popular culture will be congenial to historians.

A journal of comparative studies may therefore have a better chance of modifying attitudes of indifference to history if in addition to widening the sociological horizon in areas of strength, as suggested above, it probes weaknesses. The problems involved in taking adequate account of historical influences that may be at work in any situation chosen as the starting point of a piece of research are indeed a source of trouble to us all. Historians have no foolproof solution. Ideally, they aim at becoming familiar with all aspects of the culture of a period before singling out particular matters for investigation. This gives one hunches as to the points at which events, ideas, structures of relationship, are taking a genuinely new turn, modifying or breaking with regularities and directions set in the past. Hunches are tested by wide general reading and some check of the primary sources of the preceding period. But these are counsels of perfection that in practice are often bypassed as too laborious. Specialists in a period can develop enthusiasm for a priori judgments about its antecedents—judgments that will undergo intermittent flurries of revision with changing intellectual fashions. European historians of the sixteenth century, for example, now realize that they have too long been prone to interpret anything they observe as a new development without looking fully enough into its medieval antecedents. Communication between specialists in different periods, which should correct such tendencies, is hampered by the habit of presenting fresh findings in a manner that may be intelligible only to one's immediate fellows, that is, with a degree of allusiveness that is analogous to a private technical language. This baffles other types of specialist, repels the layman, and delays criticism of the general perspective or framework.

Another means of assessing what historical influences may be operative at a given starting point, a more summary means, has long been popular both among modern historians and in sociology. Devised by eighteenth- and nineteenth-century scholarship, it rested on a faith that the kind of society then developing in western Europe and America was the destined goal, or at least a necessary stage, perhaps desirable, perhaps undesirable, in human evolution. The more striking contrasts that were felt to prevail as between East and West, modern and medieval, European and American, were shaped, not into measured yardsticks of progress, but into a kind of litmus stick for ascertaining whether a given society or period was in a state of appreciable progress or relatively stagnant. If the former, all trends were assumed to be running toward individualism, increasing differentiation and complexity. If the latter, custom and tradition, interpreted as fixed irrational resistance to change, reinforced always by religion, would explain all.

We are all now handling such hypotheses with more caution, guarding against their reification in typology and model construction. But we have not yet exhaustively retested our stock of sociological and historical impressions for fallacies that cruder forms of the old hypotheses may have admitted. Comparative study could economically speed up this house-cleaning.

Comparative study can of course be no more than a tool in the service of hypothesis. Without fresh imagination we can do no more than dig ourselves into aimless labyrinthine researches. To be obliged to consider our material, however, in the light not only of its immediate context and of theory derived from this but of queries and hypothetical generalizations arising from someone else's consideration of an apparently similar problem in some different context is itself a stimulus to the imagination, and the experience need make no extra demands on that scarce and precious asset, our time. Indeed, our time could, as it were, be stretched further. There is no occasion to entangle ourselves in cumbersome co-operative projects in which everyone tries to out-talk everyone else in selling his own point of view, in which the stenographic record alone demands foundation financing. All that is essential is the linking of research already in progress through outline clarification of a series of representative problems that test interaction of event, idea, and structure. Outline clarification should proceed both on the plane of theory and in the empirical forms that the problems assume in different contexts. The more important relevant variables will then be progressively better understood as each problem is pushed into perspective through being considered in many different contexts.

The kinds of hypothesis that historians are best fitted to contribute to such work are those that probe intercultural contacts and historical continuities in search of common origins for recurrent attempted solutions of human quandaries. Some sociologists may prefer to branch off on other lines and to essay historical researches of their own for confirmation of their theses. They will find they need technical help. Historical research is a complex social enterprise in which one has to lean on technical aids, developed gradually through many generations of scholarship. Without these the most brilliant mind could make egregious blunders, as would any historian who essayed statistical calculations without adequate mathematics.

Perhaps, before long we will begin demanding that doctoral candidates both in history and in sociology each complete a minor thesis in the other's field. Differences that now sometimes bulk so large between us would then within a generation shrink to the dimensions of stray differences between individuals. We are unlikely to become so rational as to give up, altogether, our side shows and our fireworks.

NOTES

1. See in particular F. C. Lane's concluding chapter in F. C. Lane and J. Riemersma (eds.), *Enterprise and Secular Change* (Homewood, Ill.: Richard D. Irwin, 1953), and *The Social Sciences in Historical Study: A Report of the Committee on Historiography* (New York: Social Science Research Council, 1954). Cf. the view of Malinowski: "The hackneyed distinction between nomothetic and ideographic disciplines is a philosophical red herring which a simple consideration of what it means to observe,

to reconstruct or to state an historic fact ought to have annihilated long ago" (B. Malinowski, *A Scientific Theory of Culture and Other Essays* [Chapel Hill: University of North Carolina Press, 1944], p. 7).

2. *The Nature of Historical Explanation* (London: Geoffrey Cumberlege [Oxford University Press], 1952).

3. *Historical Inevitability* (London: Geoffrey Cumberlege [Oxford University Press], 1954), p. 5, n. 1.

4. *Ibid.;* cf. K. Bock, *The Acceptance of Histories* ("University of California Publications in Sociology and Social Institutions," Vol. III, No. 1 [Berkeley: University of California Press, 1956]).

What History and Sociology Can Learn from Each Other

A generation ago T. D. Eliot published some proposals for the fuller utilization of historical data in sociological induction. "All human behavior in groups," he wrote, "should furnish the inductive data of sociology," whereas reliance has hitherto been mainly on "contemporary social conditions, primitive races, early philosophies, and modern psychology."[1] This statement is as true today as it was in 1922, and it is perhaps the most important single fact to be taken into account in considering the present relations between history and sociology. It is not the object here to labor Eliot's point nor even to second with any great warmth his plan that sociologists should personally undertake the "socio-analysis" of vast masses of historical data. For the time being, the data of social psychology and of cultural anthropology are more congenial to most of those who enter sociology as a profession. A more agreeable way in which to broaden communication between history and sociology, as they are currently organized in the larger American universities, would seem to be through common interest in points of method and in comparative studies.

These suggestions are best viewed against a rough background sketch of some earlier *rapprochements* between history and sociology, and their outcome. Earlier in this century a number of historians looked to a sociological organization of their material for fresh starting points. In Europe, in its best-known phase, this movement

Reprinted from *Sociology and Social Research* 41, no. 6 (1957): 434–38.

was restricted to economic historians and to the historical sociology that they themselves, grappling with the larger problems of change whose explanation lay outside the competence of economic theory, created. The work of Max Weber, who succeeded at Heidelberg to the chair held by Knies, of the school of historical economists, grew out of this context. The impetus of the original movement came to this country in the person of Schumpeter. Among American historians its influence has been virtually limited to the entrepreneurial historians who have worked at the Research Center in Entrepreneurial History organized at Harvard by Arthur H. Cole. As may be seen from the Center's periodical, *Explorations in Entrepreneurial History*, it is a much attenuated influence, for the members of this group concentrate upon the business history and the economic sociology of industrial America and take little note of other phases of historical development. On American sociology, on the contrary, the influence of European forms of historical sociology has been immense. An incidental misfortune has been the circumstance that it has largely come to serve, in the training of social science students, as a substitute for history. Since historical research has meanwhile traveled far beyond the data on which the European schemes of historical sociology were originally based, the result has been, not to draw American sociologists and historians closer together intellectually, but rather to divide them.

Historical sociology was essentially a German product. French sociology, taking other forms, has had an independent entry into historical thought. Reviewing Maurice Halbwachs' *Les causes du suicide* in 1931, the historian Marc Bloch wrote of sociology, along with geography, as an influence that could potentially bring new life into the discipline of history.[2] In both this article and an earlier review of Halbwachs' *Les cadres sociaux de la mémoire*, Bloch showed profound appreciation of the work of Durkheim. His own first monograph, *Les rois thaumaturges*, tracing the history of belief in the healing powers of the French and English kings, his chapters in *La société féodale* on modes of thought and feeling and on the collective memory—indeed, all his writings show him continually fascinated by the social aspects of mental life. The same is true of his colleague Lucien Febvre. These two historians in 1929 founded the journal now known as the *Annales: économies—sociétés—civilisations;* and, although its chief content was historical, as editors they drew constant critical attention to new developments in sociology, both theoretical and empirical. Halbwachs, for example, reviewed American historical work for them and also wrote an article on the study of Chicago, entitled "Chicago, expérience ethnique."[3] A whole generation of French historians has come under the persuasive influence of Bloch and Febvre. These younger men do not look to any particular school of sociology for concepts or methods; they have simply learned to delineate social groups with care and clarity and to analyze all observable changes in social relationships.[4]

No sketch of the background of current relations between history and sociology can omit reference to that powerful personality Henri Pirenne, who created a new school of urban historiography. Primarily Belgian, it drew an international following. Deriving its primary impetus from Marxian sociology, in testing the hypothesis that urban culture in the medieval West grew up around the interests of the merchant classes, it has led to a long series of local studies of institutional development, class relationships, and community life. These are at the same time historical works and valid contributions to urban sociology.

As to the study of history in America, one cannot summarily chart the many diffuse currents of sociological thought that it harbors. Within American history proper, formal sociology has probably had less bearing on the situation than the natural interest in social analysis aroused by study of the rise of a new system of government and a new society. A generation ago there was a wave of enthusiasm for organizing this analysis along lines to be dictated by contemporary native sociological thought, but this enthusiasm, as voiced by H. E. Barnes (*The New History and the Social Sciences*), is now somewhat spent. Present-day historians are apt to be repelled by the ambiguities of the term *science* and are unmoved by its prestige.

What, then, do we wish to exchange? Restricting themselves to a single culture and to the short time span that they consider relevant to contemporary conditions, American sociologists by choice ignore the bulk of historical findings. Even within the present their interests are normally narrower than those of historians, who in dealing with the contemporary national scene treat foreign affairs, political, legal, and economic issues, as well as the rise and decline of

communities, corporations, families, ideologies, and the fortunes of
ethnic groups. The sharpening of problems for research in types of
phenomena with which sociologists have special experience, and difficulties that arise in the organization of the raw data pertaining to
these, would seem to offer the best ground for two-way discussion.

A word of caution is here in order. In formulating problems for
research the sociologist, if only as a matter of convention, is accustomed to relate them to general theory. The historian is bound by no
such custom. Unless there is a practical advantage to be gained by
making his theoretical premises explicit, he prefers to leave them
implicit. Much misunderstanding can arise from this difference in
conventions, as when the editors of a recent Social Science Council
Report concluded that historians stand in need not only of instruction in theory but of training also in elementary logic.[5] In reality,
when it serves to clarify an argument or exposition, a historian will
handle new elements of precise theory—economic, political, or legal
—explicitly enough. He may even, to the same end, cast his conclusions in the form of rules or laws that appear to govern cultural interchange.[6] In respect of basic sociological theory, however, he normally is reticent. This is not because its concepts are foreign to him,
but because they are familiar enough to be taken for granted. It is
the mark of the great historians who are held up to the student as
models that they grasp the society of which they write as a whole.
In such writing the sense of a systematic sociologist's definitions—
for example, "Society is best conceived of as a dynamic equilibrium
in which the various parts are continually interacting in such ways
as to maintain or change one another and perhaps the society as a
whole"[7] is so clear that explicit statement would be redundant.

In short, the historian offers considerable sales resistance to theoretical terminology, the more so as it departs from what he considers plain English. If the reasons behind it are not understood, this
attitude can be very frustrating to discussion. If treated with respect,
it can be a challenge. Let the sociologist prove to his colleagues, so
far as possible in plain English, that he is making real advances in
the perception, not only of broad axiomatic similarities in human
experience, but of significant differences. The test of the value of his
tools will come, not through general affirmations, but through com-

parison of his own special studies with historical research on allied matters.

Next to the perception of problems, on the agenda of discussion, would come questions of the observation, selection, and organization of factual evidence or data. Does firsthand observation, the overwhelming detail of the living scene, give an unqualified advantage, or are there compensating advantages in the severity of the criticism that the historian has to apply to his more limited sources? To him, every personal record is a psychological document, the shades of validity in its testimony to be checked by other kinds of evidence. Should the interview report, said now to be the key tool in the sociologist's kit, be similarly handled? Can the historian's techniques of criticism help the sociologist to counteract the bias of his interview work, which excludes those important classes of people who resent the interviewer's intrusion? In return, can the sociologist help the historian counteract the bias of his written sources, which too often reveal the lowest classes only in their economic relations or in their tangles with the law? How far is the sociologist's fuller observation of short-run change colored by his own effect upon the situation? Is any community quite the same after an interpersonal rating survey?

Finally, there are certain common interests in the handling of quantitative material. In many branches of history this is of small account; but in others—in economic history, in the dependence of sound social history on knowledge of population movement, inheritance, and social mobility, and sometimes in military history—it is a major concern. In periods prior to the nineteenth century the question is seldom one of refined statistical manipulation of perfect series, as is the case when a sociologist or demographer has access to modern census data, but is more often a complex problem of wringing significant hypotheses or approximate conclusions from imperfect data in broken series that are not strictly comparable. It seems probable that sociologists are often faced with similar difficulties, and that discussion of the expediency of adapting sampling techniques in such circumstances might well prove worth while.

The forms of discussion suggested here are unlikely to be fruitful if they are forced. The invitation to which these remarks are a response is perhaps a sign, however, that spontaneous interest in widening sociology's time-horizon is on the increase. T. D. Eliot's proposals of 1922 called for extending it by training seminars in historical material. The cumulative demands that technical training now makes on the student's time may often exclude this as a practical plan. The cumulative advance of historical research since Eliot wrote also raises difficulties unless historians are enlisted to conduct the seminars. We can all go astray in interpreting the literature of another discipline. A more challenging atmosphere of discussion would be created by bringing together fresh research contributions on similar problems as seen from our diverse points of view. A group at the University of Chicago is planning to create a new critical forum of the kind, in the near future, under some such title as *Comparative Studies in Society and History*.

NOTES

1. Thomas D. Eliot, "The Use of History for Research in Theoretical Sociology," *The American Journal of Sociology*, XXVII: 628 ff.

2. *Annales d'histoire économique et sociale*, III: 590.

3. *Ibid.*, IV: 11–49.

4. See the *French Bibliographical Digest: History*, Parts I and II. Published by the Cultural Division of the French Embassy, New York, 1956.

5. *The Social Sciences in Historical Study* (New York: The Social Science Research Council, 1954), especially p. 145.

6. Sir Hamilton Gibb, "The Influence of Islamic Culture on Mediaeval Europe," *Bulletin of the John Rylands Library*, 38: 82–98 (1955).

7. Bernard Barber, *Social Stratification: A Comparative Analysis of Structure and Process* (New York: Harcourt Brace and Company, 1957), p. 12.

Diachronic Methods in
Comparative Politics

The most challenging innovation that comparative politics has produced is the idea of extending its cross-cultural comparisons backwards in time. True, the idea is not wholly new—it occurred to Herodotus. But it found no firm place in Greek political science, because its implications for theory were not realized. For the same reason, the comparative study of societies through time has never had any secure footing in any of the American social sciences. Nor has the behavioral movement, of which comparative politics in this country is an offshoot, paid any particular attention to time-dimensions. On the contrary, its chief effect has been to heighten the fascination and widen the scope of that already wide problem-territory in which the gifted observer of a living scene commands so rich a universe. In consequence the behavioral sciences are overwhelmed by a torrent of findings which they are frantically trying to channel conceptually and to control by generalization. It is a tribute to the vigor and ingenuity of comparative politics that in its global extension of contemporary research it is trying to tie this, in a way that has never been systematically attempted before, to studies through time, and to direct both, together, to the testing of theory and to the generating of new theory.

A child of the age of jet-travel to international conferences, the idea has been rushed into action in large-scale projects with minimal

Reprinted from *The Methodology of Comparative Research,* ed. Robert T. Holt and John E. Turner (New York, 1970), pp. 345–58, 410–12.

waste of time in preliminary argument over the methods to be employed. Discussion has been diverted to choices among statistical techniques because these have been developing so rapidly, but seems now to be returning to the question of choice among methods.[1] This paper rejects as a red herring the notion that the choice is between quantitative and nonquantitative methods. Rather, methodological choice is seen as turning on one's degree of sensitivity to the uses of differences for the purpose of generalization, as well as of similarities.

The argument draws on earlier as well as recent experience with comparative methods. Assessment of the advantages of a method is in terms of its chances, in the light of experience, of overcoming three main difficulties that have hitherto hampered all efforts to apply comparative methods to human affairs. The essay concludes that comparative politics will in general stand a better chance of overcoming the more insidious of these difficulties if at least some of its studies cut much further back in time than is at present contemplated. Among some of the older social scientists a stock response to any such proposal is one of alarm. But the younger generation appears to be less fearful, and to have more curiosity. At the suggestion of students studying survey research methods at the University of Minnesota who read an earlier draft of this work, some illustrations have been added of kinds of historical material that survive in quantity yet have not been fully exploited, and of how an historian goes about comparative work.

THE MEANING OF DIACHRONIC ANALYSIS

The term *diachronic* is borrowed from anthropology. Synchronic comparison being there taken for granted (if only by way of the paradoxical fiction that the simpler societies have existed in a kind of timeless contemporaneity), any method that relies on successive synchronic comparisons within a chronological framework is called *diachronic*. This reliance is the one feature common to all of the methods of comparative politics to be reviewed here. It excludes only such survey research procedures as at the start necessarily have no precedent. However, to the extent that survey research procedures similar in nature are repeatedly applied in the same regions, they will become diachronic, as has happened to American sociological research on some parts of the home front.

The term could help comparative politics avoid clumsy circumlocutions. It is neat and neutral, free of the mixed associations that attach to the adjective *historical*. Unfamiliar to historians, most of whom would doubtless denounce it as jargon, it is no Trojan horse through which the techniques of purely narrative and descriptive historical writing could subvert the citadel of social science. It trails no ambiguous imagery: current talk of longitudinal and cross-sectional data unwarily evokes the image of a surgeon or of a planner confident that he is operating on a homogeneous body or on one to be made so. It puts one on guard against the vagueness of contrasting research as dealing either with the present or with the past. *The present* is a euphemism for the reach of people's active memories and of their hopes for the future, which in both directions is elastic. When the flow of events is fast and exciting, the reach of memory may shrink while hope runs farther into the future; in times of stagnation the reverse may occur. Research will be described here as "present-minded" if it is conducted within a time-perspective no longer than a life-span of some sixty years. Few diachronic studies that run up to the 1950s or 1960s have been systematically diachronic over a period even half this long, but whereas some have drawn extensively on knowledge of conditions prior to the twentieth century, others have done so only cursorily or not at all.

It is axiomatic that in order to generalize, diachronic methods, like any others, have to look first for similarities; the attention paid to individual differences has to be controlled by classification and by attempts at measurement, so that they will come up for analysis only as kinds and ranges of difference. A capacity to observe similarities and differences with equal care, while still selecting only those that will be relevant to generalization in terms of the concepts and hypotheses employed, is rare. Aesthetic sensibilities favoring similarity or difference seem to be among the many principles of prior selection at the stage of observation that escape conscious control. Again, the degree of flexibility that one can exercise in modifying received hypotheses, or in devising new ones, at the dictates of the evidence, depends probably on temperament as well as on training. In princi-

ple, all methods profess to embody some degree of impartiality at
the stage of observation and of flexibility at the stage of analysis, yet
their procedures may impose severe limitations on the latter, and
since the two stages are in practice never really separable, sensitivity to relevant differences may also be reduced. Comparative politics
offers a fascinating example of how in a new field encouraging experiment, methods continue to display the same range of variation
in these respects as has been customary.

The four methods so far adapted to diachronic use may be
ranked as follows, according to the degree of sensitivity to relevant
differences that is built into them: (1) the method of selecting closely
related groups of societies or political systems, with emphasis on the
study of concomitant variations; (2) the method of comparing two
or more societies exhibiting sharp contrasts as well as similarities;
(3) the method of working from polar typologies of traditionality
and modernity; (4) the method of interpretive model-building out of
quantitative aggregate data. The first two demand a high sensitivity
to cultural nuances and to changes in these through time, although
the first puts a higher premium on it. The second method can never
in any respect be as thorough as the first, and its value is indeed
mainly exploratory, in suggesting hypotheses rather than in firmly
testing them. The third imposes a rigid economy on sensitivity to
cultural nuances as likely at the start to be a mere distraction. The
fourth eliminates it altogether.

The last two are brave attempts to seize what is common in the
social and political transformations that accompany industrialization. Endeavoring to simplify without distorting, they implicitly incorporate the idea of direction derived from Western experience,
and work from models consisting of inventories of items selected as
measures or indicators of the extent and pace of change in that direction. Daniel Lerner, perhaps the outstanding protagonist of the
third method, defends basing these inventories on as few as four
processes which he regards as core characteristics of the take-off into
modernization: as a report of the UNESCO Paris conference of
April 1965 summarizes his views, "models should be kept simple and
abstract until it was quite clear that there was no parsimonious way
of accounting for well-established differences among empirical
cases."[2] In admitting the need, at some point, of elaborating the

models, this defense invites the question of what degree of care will be taken, along the way, to establish empirical differences. If data-gathering proceeds only by reference to very simple models, it could turn out, when these come to be elaborated, that much evidence of kinds of difference having a significant bearing on the conclusions has been ignored or thrown out as garbage. This garbage is retrievable only to the extent of the reliance on written records. To the extent of the reliance on oral informants, it will be irretrievable. The method in its diachronic aspect is therefore weak and will remain weak even if the process of elaboration of models leads it towards the greater rigor of the first method.

The fourth, the only wholly original method that has appeared, being tethered to the oddities of bureaucratic policy in the compilation of statistics, has little leeway to expand or vary its inventories. It is really an anti-method, filled with paradox. Instead of starting with a set of questions, it has to look around for questions that might be answered by the ranked correlations among aggregate data, the regional comparisons, and the indices of co-variancy that are its products. Of necessity most of these questions have a qualitative side to them; but the method itself has to stay austerely quantitative, trying to quantify the evolutionary idea that is implicit in its working model. It measures differences with maximum precision, but to the extent that its products are only a refined form of description and not self-explanatory, it is fair to say that it neglects differences that might qualify the similarities it presents, differences that escape official statistics and may be unquantifiable. This hardly matters if its role is mainly to help other methods cope with many problems that are in part quantitative. But its secure diachronic reach, because reliable statistics come only from the more advanced industrial nations, is very limited. Like a heavy truck flown to a planet where road-building has been sketchy, all it can do is career up and down one short highway, at present barely thirty years long. To explore this quantitative planet more thoroughly, jeeps are needed.

These last two methods embody only specific reasons for becoming diachronic. They aim at empirical generalization over a time-depth that is comfortably short, no longer than social science has often handled before. Their justification has certainly no bearing on the timeless propositions that guide the top-level ordering of general theory. The concepts of process with which they work—urbanization, industrialization, the spread of literacy, and so on—come from everyday talk rather than out of theoretical discussion. The concept of social mobilization is just academic shorthand, at a low level of abstraction, for topics of everyday discussion. The spread of these environmental changes is so entangled with new political phenomena that a political scientist can hardly retain authority as an expert on the world scene without some comparative study of them.

Yet experience with descriptive generalization about these processes of change, even if it has to huddle at first under the rather floppy umbrella of "modernization," and feels safe only by barricading off the farthest past by crude typology, leads on, simply through comparison of its conclusions, to higher generalization. The historical sociologists, who roam more freely, are helping to catalyze this. S. N. Eisenstadt has lately drawn together a number of signs that the concept of an institution, which has so often lent itself to static and mechanical uses, is being transformed under our eyes into the concept of institutionalization.[3] Reinhard Bendix takes a middle ground in advocating that a distinction be drawn between bureaucracy and bureaucratization.[4] If Eisenstadt reads the signs correctly, even theorists who have withdrawn from empirical research will have to take note of them.

These and other straws in the wind are still of no help to the student who wants to know if there is any general justification for diachronic methods.

The theoretical arguments for diachronic method appear in discussion of the first method listed earlier. They have been presented very concisely in a recent contribution to debate over the future of social and political anthropology, by Aidan Southall.[5] Southall takes it for granted that the health of a discipline is to be measured by the interplay between research and general theory, the latter being of little use as a guide unless it is responsive to correction or modification from the procedures of generalization from research. He attributes many of the weaknesses of structural-functional theory to the failure of research to provide the kinds of data and generalization which could correct ambiguities in the theory. This failure, he contends, has arisen from two errors of method. In the first place, the particular societies and political systems that have been confronted for comparison have been selected quite arbitrarily, because someone had happened to study them, or on the unproven assumption that they were genuinely representative of different types. With a few exceptions, such as Marshall Sahlins' work on Polynesia,[6] careful study and analysis of the range of differences among the several examples of any types have been neglected. The second error, especially noticeable in some of the early work on African political systems, has been to assume that they were static, or to handle sequences of change only casually. The primeval systems were seen as "set in amber."

Southall urges that comparative study concentrate on cognate societies, that is, on societies known to be similar in structure, traditions, and environment. As he insists, "The point is that *differences arising from similarities* are the most fruitful field from which to generalize."[7] The study should be diachronic in order to examine the variables at work both in conditions of stability and in conditions of stress, the temporal pattern or phasing of these being important. The period of time covered should be as long as possible in order that models, tried out on each society in turn, may be tested for explanatory power throughout a sequence of changes.

Southall's arguments echo and reinforce the reasoning behind the project now in progress for study of eleven of the small European democracies.[8] Much the same kinds of error have been made by political scientists in Europe as by social anthropologists in Africa. Generalization has been often from cases that were in obvious respects exceptional, and despite Europe's "past-mindedness," with indifference to gaps and anomalies in historical evidence used. Indeed, scholars in all our disciplines have displayed a truly bizarre individualism in their readiness to generalize from scattered cases or from pet examples arbitrarily described as typical. Such work can be correct only by accident or by brilliance of intuition. All types of theory, not only functional analysis, have suffered accordingly, and it is not the fault of the theorists.

The advantages of diachronic analysis, and the argument for running its more rigorous applications as far back in time as may be feasible, may be wrongly interpreted in either of two ways. It would be an error to greet the method as a means only to better control of variables in a greater quantity of situations from which analysis could then wash out the time element altogether. On the other hand, it would be even more foolish to suppose that what is intended is a futile attempt to present the exact length of time sequences involved in the interaction of variables as matter for generalization.

The bearing of rigorous diachronic method is on the tentative overtures that all existing theory, except the tightest of systems analysis, is ready to offer temporal relationships in the interplay of variables. For the most part these have been limited to intergenerational relationships. The use of these and other such overtures, and their extension through empirical generalization working with concepts of process, may result in stretching their temporal range. Far from being grounds for pessimism, the diagnosis of past errors in the bases of empirical generalization, now that we have methods for correcting them, is exhilarating.

CROSS-CULTURAL RESEARCH

One way in which diachronic method could be of use to comparative politics is through fresh analysis of sources of difficulty in cross-cultural work. As is well known, comparative methods were adopted in a number of the human sciences in the nineteenth century, under the stimulus of evolutionary thought, only to suffer a blight of discouragement in the 1890s.[9] Enthusiasm survived only in the young science of anthropology, where research soon outran the generalizing capacity derived originally from the idea of classifying and describing stages of evolution. In sociology, to the extent that it became cross-cultural, the reverse occurred. In political science there was a better balance, but here, as in history, comparative study long remained peripheral to the main professional interests. These four disciplines are the most closely related of those that have experimented with comparative methods: they have a common ancestry in ancient Greek thought, and all have both influenced and drawn on modern social philosophy. In short, they are cognate societies, and could be studied as such—with attention to internal intellectual and social structure, to the borrowing of ideas, and to what the public expected of them—by the rigorous method which Southall advocates. The study could start at least as far back as the mid-nineteenth century and run, picking up the professionalization of anthropology and sociology along the way, to the present. For better control of social variables, it could be conducted with the same research design in several different countries.

Such work would arrive at different conclusions according as the investigator inclined to one or other of two premises: (1) that interest in cross-cultural work self-evidently demonstrates the triumph of rationality over ethnocentrism; or (2) that irrationalities may still be disguised through rationalization. On the first premise, the obstacles to scientific fruition would be located quite simply in traditional imprecisions of method, in professional inertia, in lack of public support, in political circumstances that make for imbalances in the data obtainable. On the second premise, the range of difficulties is widened. The general impressions to which it gives rise may be summarized in sketches of different patterns of interplay between intellectual and social variables.

In one model, though the intellectual effort thrown into mastery of the natural environment may be very impressive,[10] intellect acquires more or less specialized roles in a society only in devising for it, and maintaining, a unique relation with supernatural powers.[11] Whether the religious specialists do their thinking in isolation or are influenced by knowledge of the religious thinking of other peoples is immaterial; in the model, the efficacy of myth or theology, and of ritual, for the solidarity of the group and for personal comfort, depends on avoidance of any involvement with the religious ideas and practices of other groups. The religious specialists can retain their function only as they discourage this by associating it with danger to the individual and by setting an example of incuriosity. But ethnocentrism towards contemporary groups is absolute only where it enforces spatial isolation, as in the case of religious sects withdrawing to a wilderness. It cannot rule out curiosity arising from intelligent interest in techniques and products, possibilities of trade, and modes of warfare. In a primitive setting, contacts with outsiders in friendly intercourse through chance or trade are a means of adding to the body of pragmatically useful knowledge.

In another direction, however, the dependence on religious specialists, and their control over curiosity, is absolute. Working from fear of death and of the dead, they merge the past into the relationships with the supernatural that are the basis of the group's solidarity. No motive for enquiry into past experience can then arise. Beyond the reach of the memory of the living, this perpetually is lost. The dead who are encountered in vision and dream speak in the terms dictated by myth. Since the latter will also shape whatever expectations of the future may exist, present-mindedness is watertight, literally encircled by myth.

It is easy, almost too easy, to explain all this by Durkheimian theory: consciousness is developed through myth within the containing bounds of ethnocentrism and present-mindedness, which are seemingly as necessary, as comforting to it, as the womb to the foetus. But one is then focusing on the aspect of consciousness that is most obviously social and value-charged, to the neglect of the logical powers that are being directed to mastery of the physical environment, are making the economic life of the group possible, and are improving it through invention and the borrowing of outsiders' techniques. This aspect of the myth-controlled society is harder to investigate because it lacks structured roles. Structure emerges in the role of the smith, but here a technical skill has taken on the mantle of awe, as though its value for the survival of the group could be given recognition only indirectly.

The erosion of myth by philosophy, in the educated Greek world of the fifth and fourth centuries B.C., failed to erode the old containing walls of ethnocentrism and present-mindedness. Like a religion just beginning to assert a claim to universalism but still rooted in localized experience, rationality fed on rough impressions of the latter, on intuitive reflection, and on a desire to replan society. It replaced the mythical relation with the past by typologies condensing recent Greek experience, with incurious side-glances at the barbarian world. This casual device for coping with the empirical past and present and with other cultures, and the habit of drawing moral generalizations supposedly applicable to all men and all ages out of one's philosophical hat, formed the tradition that Plato bequeathed to political science. As Averroës came close to admitting when he likened Plato's science to twelfth-century medicine because it had a practical branch and a theoretical branch, the two had little bearing on each other except normatively.[12] The possibility of carrying inventiveness further, of inventing the idea of a more equal partnership between intuition and observation, was impeded by the narrow base of the philosopher's role. As this was structured through the Academy, it leaned both in speculation and in political ambition towards open imitation of the role of the all-powerful myth-makers of old. Empirical curiosity had a freer rein in the Greek world than in a primitive society in conditions of cultural contact, but was still no better structured; it had no roles that could compete or be allied with that of the philosopher (save the allied role of physician). Ethnographic and even historical information about the barbarian world was acceptable but only on terms of pragmatic usefulness, political or economic. The labor that Herodotus devoted to inventing and implementing the idea of historical enquiry into a problem—the problem of moral justification of Athenian leadership—was by this criterion pointless.[13] The Academy's orientation towards the future, its satisfaction with controlling the past by typology, and its conviction that philosophy was the only road to moral truth preserved its present-mindedness intact.

Ultimately it became possible for the political scientist and the historian to borrow from each other and even to be united in one person, as in the case of Machiavelli, Montesquieu, and other persons of their times. Preconditions for this were some chastening of the claims of political science through being transplanted to a milieu dominated by a time-conscious religion, and public recognition of historical enquiry as having political and moral value. But the conditions of meaningful alliance appear to rest in some similar experience of error on both sides, in the discovery of hitherto unrecognized discontinuities which call for reinterpretation of the relationship of one's own time to the farther past. J. G. A. Pocock has explored this problem on a comparative basis, with special reference to a number of early modern European countries where diverse legal traditions had to be faced.[14] The consequence, where the problem was acute, was to give historians greater analytical ability, to force them to work out explanations, to acquire the power to compare one period with another instead of dwelling always on continuities. Political science, in turn, gained more comparative power than traditional typologies had provided. In Montesquieu's time, it began at last to respond to the age-old popular curiosity about Asia.[15]

Reformulation of the idea of progress, just when industrialization was gathering speed and stringing the nations out along a scale of measurement that had not obtruded before, rudely shoved everyone into problems of explanation. Resistance to explanations of past progress in terms that would allow of future narrowing of the gaps between the nations gave ethnocentrism, in its more blatant forms, a field day. Ethnocentrism was no less strong in the liberal views that looked for the improvement of backward nations through the spread of representative government, French education, or other products of Western history. It lurked in the assumption that Europe had already set the standards of progress.

Yet evolutionary thought, in stirring up ethnocentrism, at the same time made more of a fight against it possible. Comparative study became the arena of the fight. Two brief examples from English historical thought will illustrate the point. Thomas Arnold, who drew his sustenance from Vico and from more recent European philosophy of history, was hardly typical of early nineteenth-century English historians. Although he did not live long enough to carry out any comparative work, he was moving towards comparative study of the evolution of social structures, as the only means he could see, to make historical knowledge coherent. He generalized happily about "natural periods" in the history of nations.[16] But coming to the present (1840) he found himself wrestling with a bias towards the theory of inequalities in racial genius. This theory, one of the many ways of evading problems of explanation in history, could compliantly allow the genius of a nation that showed any unexpected advance to have been latent. But Arnold, hazarding the suggestion that the powers of the Slavonic nations "may be as yet only partially developed," added a geopolitical argument.[17]

One of the men Arnold influenced, E. A. Freeman, moved out of national history into the comparative study of past and contemporary political systems, including federalism. When the Oxford School of Modern History was founded in the middle of the century, he tried to get this activity built into its program, but failed because the idea ran against the policy of training specialists in ancient and modern history respectively.[18] In 1873 he proposed that his own generalizing interests be recognized as a new science to be called *Comparative Politics*. It was his hope that E. B. Tylor, with whom he was acquainted, would welcome this as a twin to his own newborn science, soon to become known as *anthropology*.[19] The hope was naive, because to Freeman the superiority of the "Aryan" races was a part of the divine order, daily fortifying his animus against Irishmen and Turks. But he was sufficiently shaken, on realizing that Tylor made "all man-folk one lot," to drop his scheme.[20]

The hardening of professional structures and standards in history at this time, around archival research, was a main factor in the lack of sympathy among historians for Freeman's proposals. A gentleman-scholar of the old style who would work only in his own library in the country, Freeman, when he finally became Regius Professor at Oxford, was out of touch with students. He had neither new facts nor new theory. But none of the professional structures proved capable of generating the dynamic theory that was needed. The elements were there, but it took Marx to fuse them; it was he who created the comparative politics of the nineteenth century.

There are similarities between all these situations and our own. But the changing conditions of life in the areas of cross-cultural research and the nature of professional training have made the differences more significant. Like the primitive trader on his rounds, the political researcher gets information of a practical character and avoids putting his nose in religious matters. If the conditions of life are changing, however, some of the facts will block out spheres of change in values. Again, the Greek philosophers' sense of superiority is well diffused among us, as regards the "non-West"; the stupidest freshman takes credit for Einstein. The sense of superiority in having been progressive is perhaps all we have in mind in speaking of a common Western ethnocentrism. But in so far as it used to rest on the notion that primeval African life, for example, or Chinese civilization, was static, it betrays ignorance of research in these fields.[21] Nor do we look for new extensions of industrialization to duplicate the early Western patterns, as Marx did.[22] We cannot hope entirely to eliminate ethnocentrism or present-mindedness, but we are learning to manage them better.

COMMON PROBLEMS OF HISTORY AND SOCIAL SCIENCE[23]

To guard against taking an ethnocentric view of "developing" nations, one is told repeatedly not to impose on them "the model of Western development." But what is this model? Historians are partly to blame for the vagueness of answers. Perhaps a first point of rapprochement between history and comparative politics should be to consider the kinds of error that have been common to work in history and in social science.

In the first place, the kinds of generalization that have been demanded of historians, and have consequently by feed-back dominated the interaction between historical and theoretical knowledge, have referred to long-run trends derived from conspicuous cases, to the neglect of tested generalization about possible reasons for nonconformity with these trends. Despite historians' love of exploring byways, they have left unexplored many that now seem important, such as the small European democracies, areas and sectors stagnating or regressing within a "developing" country, and many others. Cases of nonconformity to a trend, and patently divergent short-run trends, have alike been dismissed as unimportant or "erratic."

Historians have also often over-stretched the uses of typology to simplify their impression of the period just preceding the point of time at which they choose to dive into research. Ideally, they try to overhaul these impressions at intervals, in order to avoid taking all the movements they encounter as new. This problem is never wholly soluble, for the social environment regarded as a whole is always new, tradition is always being reconstituted, and tricks of perspective inevitably distort "transformations" earlier than the one being studied in detail. But there are certain recurrent areas of recognizable error—for example, those relating to problems of spatial and social mobility,[24] and the restructuring of social groups—in which historians are becoming more sophisticated. Discussion of their experience in such areas might be of help to social scientists adopting diachronic methods.

A third area of common danger is that of generalization about values. In abstract theory, in historical sociology, and in the ordering of research, values have been a wild card, with too little attention to opposition and conflict.[25]

One of the difficulties of communication via reading each other's work is that of differences in style of presentation. In playing down explicit statement of theory historians irritate social scientists by seeming to assume a deprecatory attitude to it: they seem to be saying, I arrived at my conclusions without any help from theory but simply from long and patient study of my empirical materials. What they are most aware of in each other's work is differences in point of view, a notion that includes a penumbra of presuppositions about the weighting of hypotheses which is not necessarily conveyed by the drill-ground parade of concepts that is mandatory in the opening paragraphs of a work in social science. Quantification is not an issue; as Carl Friedrich has remarked, " . . . how quality and quantity are combined depends on the nature of the problem."[26]

The use of cross-national or cross-regional comparison in historical work has been haphazard. Outside economic history there has really been little experience with the diachronic methods that have been discussed here. Marc Bloch's work on social structures has been a stimulus to further work on medieval aristocracies and peasantries, which by adding new techniques has radically revised some of his conclusions. Similarly, Pirenne's work has led on to much more systematic comparative studies of urbanization than are yet available for post-medieval Europe.[27] The trend towards comparative study, wherever it can lead to better formulation of a problem, is now strong. But even cooperative work has in many fields got no further than the preliminary stage of assembling parallel ranks of basic materials. At a later stage, it always turns out that fresh research in the primary sources is needed, all round.

Colossal labor has been devoted to organizing national archives in Europe, and in printing selections of their materials, and guides to them, but provincial archives and their acquisitions of private records have grown so continuously in this century that the demand now for guides to the total amount of historical material available, in order that selections may be made for processing in data banks, cannot be met very rapidly. Preliminary guides to the survival of the governmental records will obviously come first, and will themselves be an eye-opener into the long history of bureaucratization. Ecclesiastical archives are enormous, and private records relating to families, business firms, and associations flow continuously into provincial archives as their owners become aware that they are of value for research. Historians are accustomed to working slowly because they have to use literary sources, including newspapers, as well as explore archival materials. Where skilled content analysis can usefully save labor, they are open to its extension.

The techniques that historians have so far applied to bulky series of records are in many ways analogous to those of field research. Some of their sources are actually replies to governmental questionnaires—for example, Domesday Book—or judicial question-naires, in the records of courts employing inquisitorial procedures. It is also a useful technique of historical "reconstruction" to regard many other sources as though they were answers to questions from contemporaries, some of which would have been answered evasively in order to conceal the truth of the matter, some unreliably, and some honestly because at the time a check on the answer would have been possible or because no motive for concealment can be detected. Some historical sources give evidence that a live interview could not have elicited, for example, wills, of which there are vast series run-ning back in Europe to the thirteenth century, records of property transactions, of poor relief administration, and business accounts. Conventional rules that limit access to certain classes of recent rec-ords betray the fact that they may contain sensitive material.

Though the historian is inconsolably envious of the field re-searcher's opportunities to observe and question, he has the compen-sation of chronological depth. As survey research accumulates its own archives, it will be able to combine both advantages. Demo-graphic work offers the simplest examples of how they may be com-bined, because the age and sex structure of a community in a given year will reveal, when chronological patterning for that community is available, where that year stands in a repetitive cycle or in rela-tion to crises of unemployment or sickness.[28]

European historical work has long tended, as comparative poli-tics tends, to concentrate on central policy-making structures and on the mechanics of administration. It has gone also into the recruiting of officials and the personal composition of representative bodies, and into the more obvious aspects of venality, and is beginning to move into use of records of litigation and of criminal justice for evidence of the limits of tolerance of conflict and malaise. Montes-quieu generalized freely about the latter, but comparative material to set beside today's problems of political alienation in weak new states will take time to work up. But the fact that work on both fronts can proceed at the same time, if there are channels of com-munication, can be helpful to both.

A channel for communication of this kind now exists, in the form of an international quarterly conducted jointly by historians and social scientists, *Comparative Studies in Society and History,* and a brief report on its first seven years of operation is available.[29] The experiment continues to explore avenues of cooperation through bringing critical theoretical discussion to bear on fresh research in a variety of processes of change.

Some of this research is of the kind that will benefit from the large-scale processing of quantifiable and verbal data that new technology is making possible. But the nature both of the historical and contemporary materials and of the kinds of perceptiveness that are required for grasp of the new aspirations and new forms of action, which every age worth living in has engendered and our own so desperately needs, impose imbalances on much of the most important kinds of evidence, making it recalcitrant to the new technology. Like ethnocentrism and present-mindedness, imbalances in the evidence constitute difficulties, but they are also inescapable conditions of cross-cultural research. They can be wholly bypassed only at the cost of dullness and futility. Diachronic methods in free experimentation are a means of cross-checking on futilities before we go too far with them.

Harold Lasswell's picture of the ideal political science center of the future makes no mention of diachronic method. It invites the use of historical information, as though this could be produced by any pick-and-shovel man, in lumps for later processing. It assigns prehistorians, historians, and social anthropologists the task of providing "a map of the succession of human cultures."[30] This is a modest role. Like learned men of old invited to a princely court, the visitors would be allowed to answer such questions as the prince chose to put to them. Let us, in the map of the future of our professional culture, instead put a federal center.

NOTES

1. Stein Rokkan, "Trends and Possibilities in Comparative Social Science," *Social Sciences Information*, IV (December, 1965), offprinted as Publication no. 226 of the Chr. Michelsen Institute.

2. *Ibid.*, p. 17.

3. S. N. Eisenstadt, "The Study of Processes of Institutionalization, Institutional Change, and Comparative Institutions," in his *Essays on Comparative Institutions* (New York: Wiley & Sons, 1965), pp. 3–68.

4. Stein Rokkan, *op. cit.*, p. 11.

5. Aidan Southall, "A Critique of the Typology of States and Political Systems," in *Political Systems and the Distribution of Power*, A.S.A. Monographs 12 (1965), pp. 113–137.

6. Marshall D. Sahlins, *Social Stratification in Polynesia* (Seattle: University of Washington Press, 1958), and "Poor Man, Rich Man, Big-Man, Chief: Political Types in Melanesia and Polynesia," *Comparative Studies in Society and History*, vol. 5 (April, 1963), 285–304.

7. Southall, *op. cit.*, p. 131.

8. Rokkan, *op. cit.*, p. 12.

9. See Fritz Redlich, "Toward Comparative Historiography," *Kyklos*, 11 (1958), pp. 361–389, and Erich Hrothacker, *Logik und Systematik der Geisteswissenschaften* (Bonn, 1948), ch. 3.

10. See Claude Lévi-Strauss, *La Pensée Sauvage* (Paris: Plon, 1962), Ch. 1.

11. The reference is also to those especially responsive to myth, who would be among the "intellectuals" as defined in Edward Shils, "The Intellectuals and the Powers: Some Perspectives for Comparative Analysis," *Comparative Studies in Society and History*, vol. 1, no. 1 (1958), 5–22.

12. *Averroës' Commentary on Plato's Republic*, tr. and ed. by E. I. J. Rosenthal (Cambridge University Press, 1950), pp. 111–112.

13. For a recent assessment of Herodotus, see M. I. Finley (ed.), *The Greek Historians* (New York: Viking Press, 1959), pp. 1–7.

14. J. G. A. Pocock, "The Origins of Study of the Past: A Comparative Approach," in *Comparative Studies in Society and History*, vol. 4, no. 2 (1962), 209–246.

15. See Donald F. Lach, *Asia in the Making of the West*, Vol. I, Books I and II, *Century of Discovery* (University of Chicago Press), 1964.

16. Thomas Arnold, edition of *Thucydides*, Vol. I, 2nd ed. (Oxford, 1840), appendix I, pp. 503 ff.

17. Thomas Arnold, *Lectures in Modern History*, edited from the 2nd London edition by H. Reed (New York: Appleton, 1845), pp. 47–48.

18. W. R. W. Stephens, *The Life and Letters of Edward A. Freeman* (1895), I, 121–124.

19. Edward A. Freeman, *Comparative Politics* (New York, 1874), Ch. 1.

20. Stephens, *op. cit.*, II, 231 (letter to Tylor); two earlier letters to Tylor, *ibid.*, pp. 57, 77. Freeman, who in 1881 lectured in the United States, was uneasy in the presence of Negroes; he wrote to a friend, "This would be a grand land if only every Irishman would kill a negro and be hanged for it." *Ibid.*, p. 242.

21. Joseph Needham, *Time and Eastern Man* (London: Royal Anthropological Institute, 1965), p. 44; for a review of work now in progress on African history, see A. D. Low, "Studying the Transformation of Africa," *Comparative Studies in Society and History,* vol. 7, no. 1 (1964), 21–36.

22. For elaboration of this point, Reinhard Bendix, "Modernization and Inequality," *Comparative Studies in Society and History,* vol. 9, no. 3 (1967).

23. Bibliography relevant to this section is obtainable in mimeographed form as "Bibliography on problems and examples of comparative study in history," from the secretary of the Department of History, University of Michigan, Ann Arbor.

24. See S. N. Eisenstadt, *op. cit.,* pp. 275–304, for sociological comment.

25. For some examples, see Julian Pitt-Rivers, "Honour and Social Status," in J. G. Peristiany (ed.), *Honour and Shame: The Values of Mediterranean Society* (1966), pp. 19–78.

26. Carl J. Friedrich, "Some General Theoretical Reflections on the Problems of Political Data," at p. 58 in Richard L. Merritt and Stein Rokkan (eds.), *Comparing Nations: The Use of Quantitative Data in Cross-National Research,* 1966. For one political historian's reflections, William O. Aydelotte, "Quantification in History," *American Historical Review,* LXXI (April, 1966), 803–825.

27. Evidenced in Oscar Handlin and John Burchard (eds.), *The Historian and the City* (Cambridge: M.I.T. and Harvard University Press, 1963).

28. For historical evidence of this kind from Venice, Daniele Beltrane, *Storia della popolazione di Venezia dalla caduta della republica* (Padua, 1954).

29. Sylvia L. Thrupp, "A Working Alliance among Specialists: Comparative Studies in Society and History," *International Social Science Journal,* XVII (1965), 696–709. [See also pp. 332–45 of this volume.]

30. Harold D. Lasswell, *The Future of Political Science* (New York, Atherton Press, 1963), pp. 231–233.

Editorial from the First Issue
of Comparative Studies in Society and History

The process of Civilization depends on transcending Na-
tionality. Everything is tried by more courts, before a larger
audience. Comparative methods are applied. Influences
which are accidental yield to those which are rational.

LORD ACTON

University of Michigan MS. Add. 4908

This note of Lord Acton's expresses what many thinking men of his day felt. The idea of comparative study, borrowed from the natural sciences, especially from the much-admired science of anatomy, had brought new enthusiasm to bear on the study of man's life in society. Scholars, it was urged, should co-ordinate their aims in the faith that law, politics, economics, social organization and religion, and the thought that created and arose from all of these, would fall into a limited number of inter-related patterns. These in turn would reveal a broad common path of development through time.

As is well known, a skeptical reaction against these hopes had set in before the turn of the century. It was provoked partly by the carefree attitude towards their evidence that many writers had shown in the handling of comparison. Looking only for similarities in the institutions and the culture of different peoples and different ages they had too often, as even their most superficial critics had been able to show, neglected pertinent dissimilarities. In point of fact, the body of knowledge at their disposal had been insufficient for the testing of any ambitious generalizations. Ethnology had rested on

Reprinted from the first issue of *Comparative Studies in Society and History* 1, no. 1 (1958): 1–3.

travellers' tales, comparative religion on a few sacred texts, history was certain of little but the political development of the classical world and the European states, and the nature of the latters' economic policies. Considerably more was known of earthworms and other invertebrates than of the social life of human beings. Valid generalization could of necessity advance only slowly and tentatively, with the extension of research.

Today there is a revival of interest in the method of comparison, forced on us by the times. Without relinquishing the sense of nationality, we have acquired a sense of humanity. The notion of being ethnocentric has become a matter for reproach. Even scholarship is not free from reproach on this score, for, as many great names have pointed out, how can those who study only their own country tell what is truly unique about it?

For some people this position is bewildering. The advance of theory and knowledge makes professional life, even for the specialist in a restricted corner, increasingly arduous. How can he be master in several fields without losing his integrity as a craftsman? Will not comparative study turn him into a man who does not genuinely know anything? Confronted by a choice between possible error through insularity, and probable superficiality through spreading his operations, a sound scholar would prefer to stay in his corner.

Fortunately, this dilemma is a false one. Today's advocates of comparative study urge only that specialists in related fields compare notes on specific similar problems more frequently. While no one is against this, it is in most fields left to individual enterprise. Moreover, where it is a professional practice, as is the rigorous rule in anthropology, and as the existence of journals of comparative law, comparative religion and comparative literature attests, comparison relates usually to problems that are of immediate importance only in a single field.

What is advocated now is wider and more public exchange of information and ideas on matters that are of wider concern. For many believe that there is a definite set of problems common to the humanities, to history, and to the various social sciences. The belief is based upon the evident interaction that occurs in every society between cultural tradition, social organization, and new ideas, new aspirations, and new wants. In their character as specialists the art historians, the economists, the students of religion, and a score of other groups, mark out territory of their own that touches on such interaction. They multiply special problems in special languages. But no group has a monopoly of the recurrent problems of interaction, for example, of the problem of how political ideologies or religions spread, or of what may make certain elements of a cultural pattern for long periods resistant to change.

Problems of this order are common domain. They challenge co-operative attack through regular exchange of hypotheses and findings. This goes on, but haltingly. Unless new research is impressive enough to be published in book form, it may readily escape notice outside a single group of specialists. The reason for this neglect is not lack of awareness of the desirability of more interchange, but the fact that in presenting research articles to a specialist audience one may take it for granted that the broader questions at issue are understood. It is necessary to be explicit only in explaining new theoretical points or setting out new evidence. The outsider is baffled. He cannot see the wood for the trees, even though they may form part of the same wood, the same kind of general problem, with which he is himself engaged. In short, there is a real gap in our system of communications.

Comparative Studies in Society and History has been founded to bridge this gap, to serve as a forum for comparable work on recurrent types of problems of general interest. The plan has from the outset met with unexpectedly imaginative co-operation. At the time of writing, support comes from seventeen countries and as many different departments of learning.

Our contributors will select whatever approach to comparative study appears most appropriate to their purposes. Some may prefer the approach through the testing or application of theory, which has often been identified with "the comparative method." Where theory is precise, and there is a limited body of data of such a character that all of it can be rigorously checked from the point of view of each competing theory, this is undeniably the best plan. Its success in historical linguistics triumphantly proves the point. Very few of the recurrent cultural problems, however, present themselves under these conditions.

At the other extreme is the purely empirical approach. This has the disadvantage of allowing personal idiosyncrasy too much free play. Even economic historians, men trained to value objectivity through statistical measurement, will tend, in describing the same kind of institution, to count and measure different features of it. The results will then be of little or no use for comparative study. When descriptions lack formal measurement, lack of congruence between them is less readily detectible. Yet personal viewpoints in any complex scene differ inevitably. Two soldiers fighting side by side will not see the same battle.

It is probable that many contributors will prefer a third or mixed approach, drawing to some extent on theory as a means of control over empirical observation. But when they are breaking new ground, or when several writers are treating a similar problem, in different contexts, it will be of service to share working hypotheses. The editorial board will then act as a liaison force to aid in framing questions that may be circulated as a common guide. Such questions will never exclude free-ranging individual enquiry. Their aim will be simply to ensure the comparability of contributions.

Editorial bias is limited to two points. It will favor, although not exclusively, points of view that take as full account as possible of historical factors. This preference reflects the wishes not only of historians but also of anthropologists. Melville J. Herskovits has argued forcefully that his colleagues in that field will find the method of comparison more fruitful if they apply it not so much to areas delimited by geography as to "the analysis of cultures *lying within a given historic stream.*"[1] Again, in regard to theoretical models or concepts, or to new points concerning the logic of comparison, the editorial bias is to ask for their demonstration in action, in new discovery, rather than for their display in the abstract. . . .

NOTE

1. Melville J. Herskovits, "On Some Modes of Ethnographic Comparison," *Bijdragen tot de taal-, Land-, en Volkenkunde,* deel 112 (1956), 1–20. This article refers to a number of recent discussions of comparative method. An earlier discussion worth adding to the list is "The Body Politic," *The Collected Papers of Frederick William Maitland,* ed. H. A. L. Fisher (Cambridge University Press, 1911), III, pp. 285–303.

Comparative Studies in Society and History: A Working Alliance among Specialists

The experiment to be described here was designed to find out whether historians and social scientists have anything much to say to each other. What, if anything, would be gained by offering them a forum for joint discussion of significant new research? What kinds of subject matter, and what kinds of theoretical problem, would be of common interest? Would differences in specialist training give rise to misunderstandings?

The experiment began as one of the inter-departmental seminars that are of fairly frequent occurrence in American academic life. With widened support it was later converted into the international quarterly which for brevity's sake will be referred to here by its initials, as *CSSH*.[1] From the start this had subscribers in over fifty countries and in its seven years of operation has drawn writers from all of the main branches of social science and a variety of types and fields of history, in over twenty countries.

PREMISES: THE LIAISON ROLES OF COMPARATIVE STUDY

In a sense, the intention is simply to exploit the interest in comparison that is a part of all curiosity, although so direct an approach would of course be inane. The language of comparison is ambiguous. It is descriptive, expressing the infant's dawning recognition of sounds and smells as repetitive, or as like or unlike. It also covers measurement of like attributes on a scale. In ordinary prosaic con-

Reprinted from *International Social Science Journal* 17, no. 4 (1965): 644–54.

versation people will protest that two things are not "comparable," meaning only that they cannot be so measured, or cannot be added, or are complex. Poetic language uses comparison by contrast, which sharpens intuitive impressions. But comparative study analyses complexity, breaking it into sets of relationships, and noting recurrences and change in their components. Comparative methods will vary according as more or fewer components are perceived and as the relationships are viewed in different ways. These ways have sooner or later to be formulated in general terms.

Comparative study in consequence plays two opposite roles. One of these is divisive, the other is a liaison role played through co-operative experiment. It is divisive when its methods are guided by general terms or concepts that are the monopoly of a single theoretical tradition, and when it gears itself to new concepts that are for any reason uncongenial to a parent tradition. In the latter event the new comparative methods become the basis of yet another specialized tradition.

But in a society organized by occupation the separateness of intellectual traditions tends to be exaggerated, if only for the reason that men require a professional identification in which they can take personal pride. They are not thereby chained to standardized tools nor turned into separate species. Taxonomic discussion that carries any implication of this sort parodies the situation: a university is not a zoo. The specialist traditions among which the study of man and his works is parcelled out are flexible, permeable, and have access to a large pool not only of common knowledge and ideas, but as Abraham Kaplan has shown, of common methods.[2] It is because the techniques of comparative study lie in this public domain that they are able to play a liaison role. Even in the more theoretical sciences people continually try out new combinations of methods, and to test these by comparative study in differing contexts is an accepted mode of validation. When the approach is through some problem that persists through time and that no single science can do much to elucidate, theorists will as a last resort consult with historians. In the United States, the Social Science Research Council has helped to popularize this practice.

The *CSSH* venture had an opposite origin in that a small group of historians made the initial bid for co-operation. Their faith that other historians would back them up, not leave them alone in a den of theorists, rested largely on the growing influence of the work of Marc Bloch. Bloch's influence in directing historians towards comparative study has been reinforced since his death, not only by the great continuing vitality of the *Annales: Économies-Sociétés-Civilisations* and of the school of French historians of which it is the nucleus, but by new developments. One of these is the increased activity of Westerners in historical work on other continents; these people put new questions on the agenda for comparative study. Another development is the conference habit. At international historical conferences professional custom requires that there be general sessions for the airing of revisionist ideas and philosophical controversy. Latterly, the response has been equally lively and certainly more amicable, when a general session is given over to skillful pointing up of problems for comparative study in different nations. The response has moral overtones, for the record of intellectual nationalism weighs on the professional conscience. It has aesthetic overtones, for great comparative study wears the elegance to which all historical synthesis aspires. The response is also soberly critical. Yet, outside the circle of contributors to the *Annales,* historians do not widely practise transnational comparative study, and the *Annales* does not concentrate on this exclusively.

To use a hopeful cliché of historical writing, the time seemed "ripe" for turning from exhortation to hard work in alliance with theoretically-minded colleagues who have more experience with comparative methods. Social scientists have a quorum, which includes a psychologist, on the *CSSH* editorial committee and strong representation, especially in sociology and social anthropology but including political science and economics, on the advisory board. The editor is an historian, and there are advisory editors in a variety of historical fields. We have lost several invaluable advisers by death—Étienne Balazs, Melville J. Herskovits, and A. L. Kroeber—whose places have been taken by younger men.

CONTRIBUTORS' INTERESTS: SUBJECT-MATTER

About a third of the more than two hundred people who have written or are writing for *CSSH* are professional historians, and as many again are anthropologists or sociologists. Political scientists form the

largest group in the remaining third, which is rounded out by lawyers, economists, and psychologists, with some help from religious
and literary studies, philosophy, and linguistics. Their writing deals
for the most part with processes of cultural change, and more often
than not they take a longer-range view than is common among social
scientists. This is true whether their main interest is in people caught
in the pressures of "modernization," or in a pre-industrial society.
In either case they are chary of assuming that conditions prior to
the time on which they want to focus were frozen, even structurally,
or that they are irrelevant. Some of the best historical discourse—
judging it by professional standards—has come from social anthropologists, sociologists, political scientists, and from a philosopher;
conversely, some very shrewd sociological and political analysis has
come from historians.

What Marc Bloch's reviewing repeatedly remarked, a generation ago, is still however true, namely that many historians blur
those aspects of their research that are of more general significance
through plunging into the sources without drawing up any ordered
questionnaire beforehand. In comparative study, whether it is carried on by an individual or co-operatively, his advice on this point is
imperative. The *CSSH* editors therefore began by circulating a few
sample questionnaires to be revised by discussion among prospective
contributors. Within a year or two the need for this faded. The editors still play an unusually active role, through passing on suggestions and bringing about some degree of collaboration between people who may be working in widely separate fields yet puzzling over
similar general problems.

One of the series of essays written in response to suggestions
thrown out in the initial lead article by Edward Shils dealt with
groups of intellectuals. The comparative element was heightened
through the circumstance that the authors all chose to write on the
eastward movement of Western culture. One dealt with the rise of
an indigenous educated class in nineteenth-century Serbia, another
with the slow modernization of official styles of communication in
Turkey, three with nineteenth-century Russian intellectuals, and
four with a succession of crises faced by educated Chinese. There
was vigorous debate over the degree to which Russia, in contrast to
China, had by the turn of the last century become westernized. An

American and a Korean scholar co-operated in showing the different reasons that made for an eager reception of the ideas of Henry George by certain reformist circles in England and Japan, and by Sun Yat-sen. Edward Shils' sympathetic study, *The Intellectual between Tradition and Modernity: the Indian Situation,* was published as the first of a series of booklength supplements to the quarterly. Discussion of the subject has now moved to a novel psychiatric interpretation of the tensions felt by present-day Japanese students. Whereas the earlier essays all tried to convey the experience of individuals, but mainly compared social situations of conflict, this last group is debating how, taking the social situation to be a constant, one may compare the emotional reactions of individuals.

Contributors explore many angles of the functioning of States, using historical material both in comparison and for background. New structures that can be observed on the spot naturally lend themselves to techniques of study which cannot be used historically. Yet the new structures—even political parties, and especially the agencies that mediate between the central power and local districts —may still be in tension with older ones which because they had served broader functions do not die easily. The political observer of new States therefore sees far more when he can draw on the knowledge and methods of the anthropologist, the sociologist, and the historian. Again Edward Shils gave the lead through a two-part comparative study of "Political development in the new States," reprints of which were in such demand that it has been republished as a separate booklet. Two of the more interesting studies that followed bring history to the aid of first-hand observation in several parts of the Islamic world—Java, Pakistan, and the Middle East. They focus on the problem of finding "cultural brokers" capable of transmitting the reformist temper of leaders who are urban and secularist to a conservative village populace. In Africa, the backwardness of historical study of the African peoples makes it much harder for political observers to explore background connexions. D. A. Low contributed a constructively critical review article on recent attempts to remedy this, two of which, on the people of Buganda, also appeared in *CSSH.* Otherwise our Africanist writers tend to fall back on a functionalist approach which depends for its broader comparisons, as in David Apter's reflections on the role of opposition parties, on contrasts with Western experience and values. Two new studies will move into comparison of urban politics in East Africa and in the United States.

There is continuing discussion of judicial reform, both historically and as a contemporary policy problem, in Africa, Indonesia and India. This was opened by lawyers, whose technical knowledge is here essential. Studies are now shifting more to the actual behaviour of peasantry when customary law is interfered with, and to the role of different grades of the legal profession.

Many elements of these and other problems of political power echo back and forth through time. A part of S. N. Eisenstadt's broad-ranging study of the circumstances that enhance or impair the capacity of bureaucracies to carry out centralizing policies, appeared in our first issue. The origins of the modern State have been debated by medievalists with the help of a political scientist's interest in the viability of different types of field administration. The social attitudes and legal principles behind the welfare policies of modern States have been compared in the three cases of Great Britain, the U.S.A., and the U.S.S.R., with a scholarly flashback to medieval law and attitudes. Assembly voting has been analysed, by statistical methods which rather dwarfed comparison of the results, in nineteenth-century Britain and the Fourth French Republic.

Four types of scholar look at imperialism alternately through its effects on the conquerors and on the conquered. For example, one historian's comparisons of nineteenth-century British territories lead him to stress frontier turbulence as a factor continuously dragging the British into expansion. But why the turbulence? An anthropologist gives the answer by tracing the universal erosion of tribal sovereignty. Ending with his own observations of colonial policies at work in Australian New Guinea, his article is both history and anthropology, and a commentary, as well, on the contemporary world of foreign policy. Two anthropologists return to the effects of imperialism on the conquerors, through historical research on the life of British circles in nineteenth-century Benares and Guntur. The effects of different administrative policies are shown through the fate of the Aztec aristocracy under Spanish rule and the better fortunes of Javanese nobles under Dutch rule. The writers were an historian and a sociologist, the latter raising questions as to why imperial policies have differed. An Oxford classicist's recent "Reflections on British and Roman Imperialism" answer a good many of these questions.

Religion is a favourite subject, although usually treated in its relation to something else. Our first issue surveyed the whole gamut of positions that religion has occupied in relation to the State. One contributor has studied the relation of modern Buddhism to socialism, in Burma and Japan. Another compared its role in the Babi and Taiping movements. Joseph R. Levenson brought out other points of view in his "Confucian and Taiping 'Heaven': the political implications of clashing religious concepts." Our one contribution to date from the Socialist countries dealt with heretical movements in late medieval Europe. Movements inspired by the idea of restoring a lost Golden Age or of preparing for the advent of a Messiah appeared to interest so many contributors that a small conference was arranged on the subject. The conference explored ground that is common to field and historical studies, the points of departure being new work of both kinds prepared for the purpose, and general explanations advanced by Norman Cohn and George Shepperson. These papers were published, with a report of the discussion and some afterthoughts, as *Millennial Dreams in Action: Essays in Comparative Study*, the quarterly's second supplement.

Several other series of articles delve into aspects of pre-industrial worlds, both past and present, that have been obscured by too casually contrasting the "traditional" and the "modern." Simplifications of the past are essential—without them no one could find a starting-point for any research at all—and all of them are over-simplifications in having to sacrifice nuances of meaning. One can ask only that simplification be checked for positive error, lest this become enshrined in theory. Specialists in economic development are already revising too casual assumptions about the obstructive role of non-Protestant religions, and about the irrationality of the peasantry. By presenting fresh research and through review articles, *CSSH* writers are supporting this revisionist trend.

One such series arose from a re-interpretation, in the light of new work on ancient Palestine, of the earlier Biblical precepts on usury. Irfan Habib of the University of Alighari has produced abundant evidence of widespread money traffic in seventeenth-century India, arguing that Muslim religious tradition did not hinder the taking of interest and that Hindu religious tradition approved it. R. S. Sharma of Patna University has evidence from ancient and medieval India, in press, confirming the last point, and J. J. Spengler's work on Muslim economic thought lends confirmation, at least for the world that Ibn Khaldun knew, to the first point. Another series explores the role of Christian and Buddhist monasticism, the latter in ancient India and China and modern Mongolia, as an organizing stimulus in regional economic life. Jan Bazant, in a comparative study of early phases of industrialization in Mexico and Europe, makes incidental reference to the place of moral and aesthetic considerations in the planned foundation of Puebla as a city devoted to work. In review essays Folke Dovring absolves the peasantry of irrationality in their attitudes to innovation and shifts the charge of irrationality to the organizers of systems of bond labour; in any form, he argues, these have been self-defeating.

Two other series deal with phases of urbanization, and with social mobility in pre-industrial society. Ping-ti Ho's quantitative probing of the extent of this traditional China, now amplified in book publications, appeared initially in *CSSH*, and was followed by quantitative demonstration of exceedingly high mobility in pre-industrial Japanese cities. In press, as the quarterly's third supplement, is a strongly revisionist symposium, edited by James Silverberg, on *Caste and Social Mobility in India*.

A continuing series deals with the devices by which immigrants contrive to maintain a separate culture within the host society. Some of the papers on this subject are being republished in book form, as *Immigrants and Associations*, with a new theoretical introduction by L. A. Fallers.

These examples are enough to show the main lines of contributors' substantive interests. Other matters have been treated only occasionally, either because their comparative study has been well developed elsewhere, or because few people are able to handle them comparatively. When a very original idea is presented only through a single situation, it is often impossible to find any other examples through which tests of comparison could be applied. Many of the more ordinary subjects treated would be illuminated by parallel studies of art styles, ritual, of the circumstances favouring or hindering the communication of scientific thought, or of forms of personal relationship. There have been offers of all these, and a series on political cartooning in different nations is in preparation. The quarterly has to keep its substantive content varied. But the value of its exploratory comparative study lies in the discussion that the work of generalizing evokes.

CONTRIBUTORS' USE OF GENERALIZATION AND THEORY

Exploratory comparative study generates theoretical discussion. At every step it helps to make people more critically aware of generalizations which formerly they had taken for granted. Many contributors are able to turn directly from description or narration to theoretical reflection on the general problem at issue; theorists inject comment, and suspicions of dogmatism, ambiguity or naïveté give rise to debate. Independent theoretical essays examine ideas that have been influential in comparative study. Review articles consider groups of books whose relevance for comparative study altogether escapes notice when each is reviewed separately.

The drive, as in all vigorous theoretical discussion today, is towards raising new questions. Neither editors nor readers show any enthusiasm over descriptive studies merely fitted to types of structural-functional theory which have been successful in ordering certain areas of experience yet leave one still puzzling over why so many variant forms occur and how change gathers force. Perhaps all theory meets with this ingratitude: it inevitably leaves loose threads dangling, and if these relate to commonly perceived difficulties there is a clamour for new kinds of explanation. Contributors do however make use of familiar elements of theory in explaining situations which would otherwise appear odd or chaotic. The series on the forms of organization found among immigrant groups leans heavily on Weber and at some points on Simmel. The series on usury gains immeasurably from the concise comment in which Spengler digests relevant economic theory. By reading Ibn Khaldun from this same theoretical standpoint, Spengler was able not only to give that many-sided thinker a place in the history of economic thought, but to shed new light on the complexity of economic organization in late medieval Islam. These remarks carry no bias in favour of economic theory as the sole clue to better understanding of the systems of production and distribution found in pre-industrial societies. But placing the economist's explanation in polar opposition to explanations offered in terms of social relationships has become tedious. Two contributors—Marshall D. Sahlins, through comparison of village leadership and chieftainship roles in Melanesia and Polynesia, and Harold K. Schneider, through model construction based on East African material—bring much-needed new information and also new formulations of some of the problems involved.

Reflection on economic theory combined with historical study of bureaucracies, has gone into J. J. van Klaveren's theory of political corruption, which he applies to an African people. The African historical study it confronts is however open to interpretation through functional theory. Eisenstadt's studies are relevant here, and still other corroborative theory would be welcome.

But comparative study cannot rest on a simple division of labour between theorizing and description; the worker at the descriptive level has more to do than to choose between ready-made theories or even between suitable concepts. If all these are at hand his work is likely to be mechanical or a mere school exercise. The challenge of the more interesting problems often turns precisely on the fact that they are not yet precisely defined, that the ideas and concepts through which they are perceived are surrounded by ambiguity. Again, a concept that seems precise enough when applied in one context may take on a different coloration when applied to another. Comparative study is appealing not because it is easy but because it obliges one to wrestle with these difficulties. John W. Hall's discussion of Japanese feudalism shows how hard it is, even when the problem of feudalism is broken down into relationships of dependency, to pin down the constants in these. Yet he shows also that, even to the worker whose primary interest is in better understanding of one particular context, comparative study helps him to pin down the more slippery elements of a problem, and to grasp their relationships more clearly.

Our contributors doggedly prefer the more slippery problems to easier ones. They avoid the already well-demonstrated methods of comparative intellectual history conceived as the study of relationships among ideas at a high level of abstraction, preferring to see how far ideas may become altered as they pass from one culture to another. The problem crops up repeatedly in the series on intellec-

tuals. But the most imaginative attack on it came from Ali Al'Amin
Mazrui, now Professor of Political Science at Makerere University,
who set Edmund Burke down in the Congo to argue the issues of the
revolution there with tribal elders.

Comparative study makes people more sensitive to ambiguities
and perhaps hypersensitive to the dangers of ethnocentrism. In a
three-cornered debate over Donald Eugene Smith's book, *India as a
Secular State*, two reviewers raked over all his comparisons, explicit
and implicit, with the United States, and all of his interpretations of
a policy as "secularizing." One of these reviewers had the double
advantage of knowledge of American constitutional law and close
study of Indian policies on the untouchability issue. The second reviewer had himself contributed a study of secularization in Norway.
This had posed the issue as turning on whether religious specialists
form a distinct group, on what roles they play, and on the nature of
their contacts with the people at large. Smith then defended his book
through qualifications in it—reviewers tend always to overlook these
—and through appeal to Indian history. He did so constructively and
with evident enjoyment, for an author is rarely allowed to review his
own book. The debate does not resolve all of the difficulties inherent
in the idea of secularization, but through the play of paradox it
defines them.

Contributors have attacked the problem of differing concepts of
the rule of law, with verve and learning. It comes up in relation to
judicial reform in India, Indonesia and Africa, and also, on ground
more familiar to Westerners, in discussion of the origins of the modern State. Here the correlative to ethnocentrism is the tendency to
project modern formulations of the problem of sovereignty into one's
reading of past thinkers. Brian Tierney's suggestive essay on rule-of-
law thought since the thirteenth century is a model of how to avoid
any form of temporal ethnocentrism.

Standard methods of coping with the above difficulties are to set
up typologies, or to construct models. A sociologist contributed a
typology sorting out the ambiguities attached to the idea of nationalism. Two anthropologists have found it more fruitful to bypass the
idea altogether, and to look instead for the sources of personal identification with a nation or a culture. In Burma, exposed for centuries

to Indian influence on the one side and Chinese on the other, Edmund Leach is confident that the outcome has always been determined by regional ecology rather than by the boundaries of any of the numerous States that in the past have contended there for control, or even by linguistic frontiers. By using the methods of microstudy, Eric R. Wolf is able to explain why, in the same Alpine valley, the people of one community identify themselves with Germany and peasant tradition, and the people of another with Italy, urbanity, and an ideal of freedom that they associate with the United States. The explanation, worked out in terms of differences in social structure and in the patterning of community life, is expressed with great historical sensitivity.

None of the comparative work presented so far, either by individuals or in series of studies, has covered more than a dozen cases, and much of it has rested on only two or three. Comment does not carp at this failure to cover any total universe; critics rate studies according as they arrive by sound methods at an explanation, or a partial one, of an interesting problem; indeed, the mere clarification of the terms of a problem in such a way as to eliminate spurious explanations may receive a rating of acceptability. Whenever variables can be quantified, this has been done, but quantitative data have not provided the whole of any explanation; there has always been some crucial residue of the problem calling for explanation in other terms. When variables can be partially quantified, a writer may try to cover more cases. On the other hand, J. G. A. Pocock's approach to so unquantifiable a matter as "The origins of study of the past" is through as many as nine cases, some chosen to illustrate advances in self-conscious relation to the past, others to show stagnation. It is a model of comparativist reasoning. In series put together from the work of different individuals who happen to be interested in the same subject, the selection of cases has not been so well controlled. The same was true of the conference on movements of a millennial character: the selection of papers was out of balance because it proved impossible to get any that were good enough on urban or middle-class movements or on the more peaceable rural movements. The book nevertheless modified existing explanatory theory and mapped out new lines of inquiry.

THE GROUNDS FOR EVALUATION

If specialists ought not to fraternize, the enterprise that has been described is wholly pernicious, but if they should at least be allowed to
do as they please, it is reasonable to ask what this particular working
alliance has proved or learnt, what kinds of unfavourable criticism it
receives, and what is on its agenda for the future.

To prove that historians and social scientists can engage together in effective discussion of substantive and theoretical problems
was easy. Innumerable small groups knew this already. The mistake
to be avoided is emphasis on each other's differences; discussion of
these is perennial, but it usually invites frustration through evoking
stereotyped images and imperialist attitudes. It is as though diplo-
mats were foolish enough to open an international conference by
argument over their views of Lenin, or the problem of national sovereignty. Faced with matters of common interest, people put their
different abilities to work, co-operatively. The only breakdowns in
communication have occurred not through differences of discipline
but through inviting someone to comment comparatively on a single
case study that involved technical detail unfamiliar to him. These
mistakes were entirely the editor's fault and will not recur. But more
than this has been learnt. The methods of social scientists are much
more adaptable to the study of change over long periods than was
at first realized, and there is remarkable readiness, on the part of
social scientists concentrating on the present, to appreciate that the
variables they work with may be affected by historical factors.

The character of such unfavourable criticism as reaches the editor is helpful and a source of encouragement. There has been complaint that the standards set are too high: a welcome confutation of
other critics who had predicted that the quarterly was doomed to
superficiality. There is complaint that writers are allowed to intro-
duce too much detail. This helps to keep editorial pruning shears
sharp, and the standards of writing as high as is possible. Most of
the contributors write well, and some with wit. The only scholarly
tradition that we want to break is that of funereal solemnity. Many
scholars seem to regard the act of writing down their ideas as though
it were an act of interment, to be completed by a repellent title as
gloomy as a gravestone. In some historical circles there is a defensive

aloofness, in others a desire to pursue comparative history as a sovereign autonomous discipline. Both of these attitudes serve to bring into relief the real contribution of the quarterly—its stress on clearer formulation of problems. The contrary defensiveness of many social scientists obliges them to define the grounds of an a-historical attitude more clearly. This in itself is a step towards better understanding of what a sense of history involves—one of the subjects on the agenda for comparative study. Finally, the quarterly has been blamed for not starting out with a universalist theory. This proves— if proof were needed—that the working alliance on which it rests is not a dogmatic school. Though exploratory, it is alert to the limits of tolerance of theoretical naïveté as these have been lately defined by Max Gluckman.[3]

On the agenda, however, are progressive series of evaluations of the comparative methods that are being tried out both in the quarterly and elsewhere. All that this brief report could attempt was a survey of some of the lines of convergence. The continuing value of *CSSH* depends very much on international co-operation. It needs to extend its contacts with scholars in the Latin American world, in Japan, and still more widely. Only by so doing can it feed new material and ideas into methodological discussion both helpful to the study of change over long periods and relevant to contemporary problems. It needs also, both in the West and elsewhere, to reach into the more separate worlds of humanistic thought. Nothing human is alien to comparative study, and co-operation in it does not endanger the autonomy of separate traditions.

NOTES

1. *Comparative Studies in Society and History*, The Hague, Mouton and Company, 1958–1968; Cambridge University Press, 1969–.

2. Abraham Kaplan, *The Conduct of Inquiry*, San Francisco, Chandler Publishing Co., 1964.

3. Max Gluckman, ed., *Closed Systems and Open Minds*, Edinburgh and London, Oliver and Boyd, 1964.

Bibliographical Note

Born in England, Sylvia L. Thrupp was raised in British Columbia, taking her B.A. and M.A. degrees from the University of British Columbia. She received her doctorate from the University of London in 1931 and was a postdoctoral fellow at the London School of Economics from 1931 to 1933; her research then continued with a fellowship from the Social Science Research Council from 1933 to 1935. She taught at the University of British Columbia (1935–44), the University of Toronto (1944–45), and the University of Chicago (1945–61) and was a visiting professor at the universities of Iowa and Wisconsin before accepting a chair as Alice Freeman Palmer Professor of History at the University of Michigan in 1961. Her publications, listed in chronological order, include:

"The Grocers of London, A Study of Distributive Trade." In *Studies in English Trade in the Fifteenth Century*, edited by Eileen Power and M. M. Postan. London, 1933.

The Worshipful Company of Bakers. London, 1933.

"The Pedigree and Prospects of Local History." *British Columbia Historical Quarterly*. Vol. 4, no. 4, 1940.

"Social Control in the Medieval Town." *Journal of Economic History*. Vol. 1, supplement, December, 1941.

"Medieval Gilds Reconsidered." *Journal of Economic History*. Vol. 2, 1942.

"The Problem of Conservatism in Fifteenth-Century England." *Speculum*. Vol. 18, 1943.

The Merchant Class of Medieval London, 1300–1500. Chicago, 1948; Ann Arbor, 1962.

"Entrepreneurial History and the Middle Ages." *Bulletin of the Center for Entrepreneurial History*. Vol. 3, 1951.

347

Introduction to *An Essay of Drapery*, by William Scott. Kress Library of Business and Economics, Serial Publication, no. 9, Cambridge, Mass., 1953.

"What History and Sociology Can Learn from Each Other." *Sociology and Social Research*. Vol. 41, no. 6, 1957.

"A Survey of the Alien Population of England in 1440." *Speculum*. Vol. 32, 1957.

"The Role of Comparison in the Development of Economic History." *Journal of Economic History*. Vol. 17, 1957.

"History and Sociology: New Opportunities for Co-operation." *American Journal of Sociology*. Vol. 63, no. 1, 1957.

"Editorial." *Comparative Studies in Society and History*. Vol. 1, no. 1 (1958). Editorials and Reviews appear in subsequent issues.

"Hierarchy, Illusion and Social Mobility." *Comparative Studies in Society and History*. Vol. 2, no. 1, 1959.

Millennial Dreams in Action: Studies in Revolutionary Religious Movements. Editor. The Hague, 1962; New York, 1970.

"The Creativity of Cities." *Comparative Studies in Society and History*. Vol. 4, no. 1, 1961.

"Economy and Society in Medieval England." *Journal of British Studies*. Vol. 2, 1962.

"Gilds," *The Cambridge Economic History of Europe*. Vol. 3, chapter 5, 1963.

"The City as the Idea of Social Order." In *The Historian and the City*, edited by O. Handlin and J. Burchard. Cambridge, Mass., 1963.

"Tradition and Development: A Choice of Views." *Comparative Studies in Society and History*. Vol. 6, no. 1, 1963.

Change in Medieval Society: Europe North of the Alps, 1050–1500. Editor. New York, 1964.

"The Earliest Canterbury Freemen's Rolls, 1298–1363." (With Harold B. Johnson.) *Kent Records*. Vol. 18, 1964.

"Some Historians on Generalization." *Comparative Studies in Society and History*. Vol. 7, no. 1, 1964.

"Comparative Studies in Society and History: A Working Alliance among Specialists." *International Social Science Journal*. Vol. 17, no. 4, 1965.

"The Problem of Replacement-Rates in Late Medieval English Population." *Economic History Review*. 2d ser. vol. 18, no. 1, 1965.

"The Writing of West European History: A Bird's-Eye View of Trends between 1960 and 1964." *The Annals of the American Academy of Political and Social Science.* Vol. 359, May, 1965.

"Plague Effects in Medieval Europe." *Comparative Studies in Society and History.* Vol. 8, no. 4, 1966.

"Horizontal History in Search of Vertical Dimensions." (With Raymond Grew.) *Comparative Studies in Society and History.* Vol. 8, 1965–66.

Early Medieval Society. Editor. New York, 1967.

"Gilds." *International Encyclopedia of the Social Sciences.* 1968.

"Aliens in and around London in the Fifteenth Century." In *Studies in London History,* edited by A. Hollaender and W. Kellaway. London, 1969.

"Commentary." In *Anthropology and the Behavioral and Health Sciences,* edited by Otto von Mering and Leonard Kasdan. Pittsburgh, 1970.

"Diachronic Methods in Comparative Politics." In *The Methodology of Comparative Research,* edited by Robert T. Holt and John E. Turner. New York, 1970.

"The Dynamics of Medieval Society." *Proceedings of the XIII International Congress of Historical Science,* 1970. Vol. 1, Moscow, 1973, pp. 93–112.

"Medieval Industry 1000–1500." In *The Fontana Economic History of Europe,* edited by Carlo M. Cipolla. Vol. 1, chapter 6, 1972.

"Medieval Economic Achievement in Perspective." In *Essays on the Reconstruction of Medieval History,* edited by V. Mudroc and G. S. Couse. Montreal, 1974.

"Comparative Study in the Barnyard." *Journal of Economic History.* Vol. 35, 1975.

In Progress:

"Market Relationships." In *The Agrarian History of England and Wales,* edited by Joan Thirsk. Vol. II (1042–1350), Vol. III (1350–1500), Cambridge University Press; and further work on late medieval English rural society, on aliens in England, on medieval conceptions of other cultures, and on methods.

Index